MARK my WORD

MARK my WORD

Gospel Campaign in Akure, Nigeria. 850,000 people in a single meeting.

Revised Edition

A daily Devotional by

Reinhard Bonnke

365 daily devotionals from
Evangelist Reinhard Bonnke.

"Much more than a daily devotional,
this book will give you a passion for lost souls,
and motivate you to be a soul-winner."

"These are the 'power generators' of God:
the Cross of Calvary,
the Resurrection of Jesus Christ,
and the Holy Spirit Baptism."

Featuring: a brief daily motivational message …
a scripture verse for the day … where to find the Bible references …
a "Daily Power" phrase to carry you through the day … and more!

Mark my Word
English
Copyright © Full Flame GmbH 2001, 2003
ISBN 3-935057-84-9
Paperback Edition

Edition 2, Printing 1
10,000 copies

Hardback Edition ISBN 3-935057-18-0

All Scripture quotations are taken from the
New King James Version of the Holy Bible,
Copyright ©1982 by Thomas Nelson Inc., Nashville,
Tenessee, United States of America.

The daily Bible reading plan was compiled by
Robert Murray M'Cheyne (1813 - 1843)

Cover design by Isabelle Brasche
Typeset by David Lant
Edited by Jeanne Halsey, Evangeline van den Berg,
Paul Ras & Derek Weekes
Photographs by Peter van den Berg, Rob Birkbeck,
Roland Senkel and Tom Henschke

Published by:
Full Flame GmbH
Postfach 60 05 95
60335 Frankfurt am Main
Germany
www.fullflame.com

Visit the CfaN web site at www.cfan.org

Printed in Switzerland

Preface

A young man in his teens came to me one day, and said that the Bible is too old, and has no meaning anymore for the present modern day. I directed him to look at the sun in the bright morning sky. "Has the sun lost its power? Does it not shine and shed warmth upon the earth? Do we say that the sun is cold because it is old?"

2 Timothy 3:16-17 tells us that: "*All scripture is given by inspiration of God, and is profitable for doctrine, for reproof, for correction, for instruction in righteousness, that the man of God may be complete, thoroughly equipped for every good work.*" The Holy Bible affects human beings so strongly because all the Bible is God-breathed. It is more than a collection of moral principles; it is more than a good book; it is an inspired record, God's book. The prophets related what they saw and heard in human language, but their message came directly from God. Therefore, you can **Mark every Word** of your Bible and live by it!

I am, first and foremost, an evangelist, a soul-winner. God has given me a fire that burns in my heart, one that simply refuses to go out. Therefore, the way I view life is always filtered through that fire. If you want that same kind of fire to burn inside your bones, then you have got the right book! This is much more than a daily devotional that might give you some sort of a sweet lift to your morning – this book should daily ignite a passion for lost souls that will motivate you throughout your day and throughout your life!

My staff and I have deliberately designed this book to be a fast, intense, and penetrating daily study that will help you to keep your focus on the Lord Jesus Christ, and to remind you continually that, as Christians, our number one job is to reach the lost with the Good News! These are the "power generators" of God:

- The cross of Calvary
- The Resurrection of Jesus Christ
- Holy Spirit Baptism.

As often as possible – even while dealing with the practical issues of daily life – think about on these "power generators" and you will be infused with God's purpose for your life, and given encouragement to fulfill the ministry which he has given you.

Reinhard Bonnke

Introduction

God has given us his Word, the Bible, so that we can understand him better and grow strong in our faith. When you start reading it regularly, you will quickly discover that the Bible is a lifeline and a foolproof guidebook for you.

The Word of God silences the accuser and routs doubts! Many people think that they can base their faith on their feelings. The problem is that when their feelings plummet, their faith goes down with it! Your Christian faith is based on something far more solid than your feelings. It is based on what Jesus accomplished for us through his birth, life, death, and resurrection. John 1:14 declares it so clearly when it says, *"the Word became flesh and dwelt among us."*

It is through God's precious Word that:

- Your faith becomes strengthened and anchored.
- Your footsteps receive his light in the dark times of life.
- Your outlook becomes positive and upward when your spirit is tempted to look down and feel defeated.
- Your daily walk with the Lord becomes personal and relevant as you apply his precepts and principles to your life.

The Bible is a book you can completely rely on to tell you the truth about God - and about yourself. It does not contain the Word of God - it **is** the Word of God for you! As Jesus said, *"Heaven and earth will pass away, but my words will by no means pass away"* (Matthew 24:35).

God has given us two witnesses to reassure us of his love, acceptance, healing, forgiveness, and daily provision. These two witnesses are:

1. The Word of God (the Bible).
2. The Spirit of God.

As you read through this volume day by day - my sincere prayer for you can be found in the words that Paul the Apostle prayed for the Ephesians:

> *"I ask that the eyes of your understanding being enlightened; that you may know what is the hope of his calling, what are the riches of the glory of his inheritance in the saints, and what is the exceeding greatness of his power toward us who believe, according to the working of his mighty power"* (Ephesians 1:18-19).

Helpful Tips

Read each daily passage out aloud. Seeing as well as hearing the words will plant these truths deep in your heart and give you purpose, power, and motivation during your daily quiet time.

Make personal notes and highlight those sections, which speak to you, as you read through the daily passage. One of the tools that God can really use to lead and direct you through his Word, is by constantly bringing back to your mind specific passages that have spoken to you and that you have personally annotated. *"And you shall have the tassel* (personal note) *that you may look upon it and remember"* (Numbers 15:39.

Each day's reading has several key components:

- The daily commentary/teaching from Reinhard Bonnke's own writings.

- **Today's Scripture** - a relevant passage for each day.

- **Daily Power!** – a powerful statement of truth to strengthen you.

- **The Bible In A Year** reading plan. By faithfully following this, you will read through the Bible in a year as well as reading the New Testament and Psalms twice!

- **Mark My Word** cross-reference guide - for your further study. The biblical foundation for each day's passage can be read in greater detail, together with related passages.

God First

What better way to start a New Year than with a fresh commitment to put God first in your life! Prioritizing God sounds simple, but the pressures of our lives try very hard to push him out of the way ... and sometimes we find ourselves in that difficult place of suddenly stopping, reevaluating our lives, and realizing that we've somehow lost that all-important first love.

> "I beseech you therefore, brethren, by the mercies of God, that you present your bodies a living sacrifice, holy, acceptable to God, which is your reasonable service. And do not be conformed to this world, but be transformed by the renewing of your mind, that you may prove what is that good and acceptable and perfect will of God" (Romans 12:1-2).

Jesus demonstrated this sense of priority even as a young child – at the age of 12, he astounded his parents by stating: *"Did you not know that I must be about my Father's business?"* Later, in his ministry, he reiterated: *"I must work the works of him who sent me."* There was no question about it – Jesus' first priority was pleasing his Father. Of course, the first commandment is this: *"You shall have no other gods before me."* Right back in Moses' time, learning to put God first was a required priority. The second commandment reveals further how important he wants to be in our lives: *"You shall not make for yourself a carved image ... you shall not bow down to them nor serve them; for I, the Lord your God, am a jealous God."* Putting anything – careers, financial achievement, even relationships – ahead of God constitutes making an idol of it ... and our jealous God warns strictly against it.

Make a covenant right now: "Lord, I want to always put you first in my life, in everything I do. Enable me, by your Holy Spirit, to be consistent in this choice. Thank you!" When this prayer comes straight from your heart, then God's part of the equation is to respond to you with his strength and ability.

Today's Scripture
But seek first the kingdom of God and his righteousness, and all these things shall be added to you. (Matthew 6:33)

Daily Power!
Today I stand on God's promise that he will never leave me or forsake me. Therefore, I wholeheartedly put my trust in him!

Mark My Word
Exodus 20:1-17
Joshua 1:5, 8
Matthew 6:25-34
Luke 2:49
Revelation 2:1-7

The Bible In A Year

Morning
Genesis 1
Matthew 1

Evening
Ezra 1
Acts 1

2

Today's Scripture
My food is to do the will of him who sent me, and to finish his work.
(John 4:34)

Daily Power!
The Great Commission empowers me to be his evangelist. I am committed to fulfilling his will.

Mark My Word
Mark 16:15-20
John 4:34-38 8:32;
17:17
Ephesians 1:13
Colossians 1:3-5

The Bible In A Year

Morning
Genesis 2
Matthew 2

Evening
Ezra 2
Acts 2

Because evangelism is my reason for living, it is also my favorite topic. The evangelist is a man with a driving urgency, not a man with two minds. The gospel - and nothing else on earth - matters: not fame, money, earthly pleasures, nor life itself. Jesus had a total attraction for the wretched. It led him to the cross. He would bring his salvation and healing touch to broken lives, no matter what.

I believe in preaching a straightforward message - a gospel that speaks of sin, salvation, healing, and discipleship. I do this with the heartfelt conviction that it is preaching the Word of God that brings revival. Nothing more - nothing less.

> "God's Word is truth … you shall know the truth, and the truth will set you free … In him you also trusted, after you heard the word of truth, the gospel of your salvation … We give thanks to the God and Father of our Lord Jesus Christ, praying always for you, since we heard of your faith in Christ Jesus and of your love for all the saints, because of the hope which is laid up for you in heaven, of which you heard before in the word of the truth of the gospel."

There has never been revival without aggressive evangelism. The first time I witnessed thousands running forward to respond to the call of salvation, God opened my eyes, and I actually saw an invisible, mighty wave of Holy Spirit power arrive in the stadium (this was in Africa). A mass baptism in the Holy Spirit, accompanied by many mighty miracles, took place. I wept like a boy, and vowed to the Lord that, in obedience, I would move across all of Africa to bring the vision to pass. I reasoned that if God could do that to ten thousand people, he could do it to four hundred fifty million. I have a simple goal, which perfectly describes evangelism:

Heaven full - Hell empty!

God is with you and me, not because we have great faith, but because he has committed himself irrevocably. Faith is not just for the possible - that is not faith at all. The mightiest resource in the universe is the arm of God. The Lord of the harvest will send forth his laborers, which includes you and me.

Perfectly Certain

3

Another great way to start a New Year is to have assurance of salvation. When you are saved, you should know it. Otherwise, how can you be a witness for Christ? The Bible speaks clearly and positively … it does not stammer. When you read it, you become certain. Martin Luther once said, "The Holy Spirit is no skeptic." he writes no doubts. The promises of God are Yes and Amen, not No and Maybe. The gospel trumpet sounds no faltering note.

When an earthquake shook the Philippian jail and all who were in it, the jailor cried out, *"What must I do to be saved?"* Paul did not reply, "Well, what do you think? Do you have any ideas?" He made a firm statement of fact: *"Believe on the Lord Jesus Christ, and you will be saved, you and your household."* The gospel is God's message, not Christian opinion … and it is yours today!

What are the two greatest things God ever did? The Bible tells us that he created the heavens and the earth. Could anything possibly equal that - making our wonderful world, with its oceans, mountains and rivers, and filling the heavens with stars? In fact, God did do something else that was far more difficult. We call it the work of redemption. Creation cost God nothing - but that next task cost he everything.

At Creation, God blessed us with the energies of life. Then he blessed us with the gift of redemption, adding new life to ordinary life. Millions of people around the world enjoy it. They are jubilant. They exclaim and sing, "I am redeemed!" They cannot keep quiet about this wonderful gift that God has given them. Therefore, my friend, today I encourage you: rejoice in your salvation!

Today's Scripture
Believe on the Lord Jesus Christ, and you will be saved, you and your household.
(Acts 16:31)

Daily Power!
Reading God's Word is a constant source of assurance that I am saved, and I know it. his Word says it - God is not a man that he should lie.

Mark My Word
Numbers 23:19
Acts 16
1 Corinthians 1:17-20

The Bible In A Year

Morning
Genesis 3
Matthew 3

Evening
Ezra 3
Acts 3

Salvation Is Not Speculation

4

Today's Scripture
I know whom I have believed and am persuaded that he is able to keep what I have committed to him until that day. (2 Timothy 1:12)

Daily Power!
When I repent and believe, and come to the Lord and Savior Jesus Christ, he receives me and I am cleansed in his precious blood!

Mark My Word
Luke 19:10
John 6:37
Acts 2:38-39
2 Timothy 1:12

The Bible In A Year

Morning
Genesis 4
Matthew 4

Evening
Ezra 4
Acts 4

The genius who made the first electric dynamo, Michael Faraday, was not only a master of all the sciences, but also a Christian. In 1867 when he was dying, his friends asked him what his speculations about life after death were. "Speculations?" he asked in surprise. "Speculations?" I have none. I am resting on certainties!" Faraday's favorite Bible verse was: *"I know whom I have believed and am persuaded that he is able to keep what I have committed to him until that day."* He had no reservations about Biblical truth.

Some people argue that it is presumptuous to declare that we are saved, but that is false modesty in the light of so much scriptural evidence. When Christ confronts you with the question of your need, you should not respond, "I want to have my questions answered, and to give my view of salvation." Instead, you must repent and believe! Being saved is not a casual experience, something that you would hardly notice. When you repent and believe, and come to the Lord and Savior Jesus Christ, he receives you and you are cleansed in his precious blood!

> "Repent, and let every one of you be baptized in the name of Jesus Christ for the remission of sins; and you shall receive the gift of the Holy Spirit. For the promise is to you and to your children, and to all who are afar off, as many as the Lord our God will call" (Acts 2:38-39).

Take these two statements made by Jesus himself: *"All that the Father gives me will come to me, and the one who comes to me I will by no means cast out, for the Son of Man has come to seek and to save that which was lost,"* which means, that when you trust in Christ for his gift of salvation, he honors it.

Spiritual Need

People need the gospel, and their need creates a need in the heart of God. He needs to send us with the gospel! He knows that we must be born again, and he cannot just sit down on his throne, and do nothing about it. That would be completely contrary to all he has ever done.

> "Whoever calls on the name of the LORD shall be saved. How then shall they call on him in whom they have not believed? And how shall they believe in him of whom they have not heard? And how shall they hear without a preacher? And how shall they preach unless they are sent? … So then faith comes by hearing, and hearing by the word of God."

God knows our need, and is under compulsion to meet it. Likewise, if we, who are made in his image, know about the hungry of this world, we need to do something about it. Their need creates in us a need to help. If you and I have plenty, then we cannot merely stand by, and watch our neighbors die of starvation. The same is true of spiritual food. Our spiritual need lays a compulsion on the heart of God. Our attitude towards others should be the same.

What should we be doing to fulfill that need in God's heart? The same things that Jesus did, which were also a fulfillment of Isaiah's prophecy:

> "The Spirit of the Lord God is upon me, because the Lord has anointed me to **preach** good tidings to the poor; he has sent me to heal the brokenhearted, to **proclaim liberty** to the captives, and the opening of the prison to those who are bound; to proclaim the acceptable year of the Lord, and the day of vengeance of our God; to **comfort** all who mourn, to **console** those who mourn in Zion, to give them beauty for ashes, the oil of joy for mourning, the garment of praise for the spirit of heaviness; that they may be called trees of righteousness, the planting of the Lord, that he may be glorified" (emphasis added).

Today's Scripture
I must work the works of him who sent me while it is day; the night is coming when no one can work.
(John 9:4)

Daily Power!
My desire is to fulfill that compulsion which God has placed within my heart - to reach out to the unreached, to tell the untold, and to minister the gospel of Jesus Christ.

Mark My Word
Isaiah 55:1; 61:1-3
Luke 4:18
John 9:4
Romans 10:13-18

The Bible In A Year

Morning
Genesis 5
Matthew 5

Evening
Ezra 5
Acts 5

6

The World's Need

Today's Scripture
And I will establish my covenant between me and you and your descendants after you in their generations, for an everlasting covenant, to be God to you and your descendants after you.
(Genesis 17:7)

Daily Power!
Everything I need to know about life has already been written in God's Book of Life.

Mark My Word
Genesis 17:7
Judges 17:6; 18:1
19:1; 21:25

The Bible In A Year

Morning
Genesis 6
Matthew 6

Evening
Ezra 6
Acts 6

Imagine if Abraham or Moses suddenly arrived back from the past, or perhaps Mohammed or Buddha - what would that do for the world? Well, none of them will come, so it is idle to speculate. We are now in the third millennium, yet millions of people are still looking for a great global leader. They consult the stars, looking hopefully for a new age under a super-personality, who would bring accord between the races, peace among the nations, and the rich caring for the poor. Is it only sentimental fantasy?

The wish seems so common: "Oh, for a great cosmic king, an all-powerful leader to rule the rulers when they are unruly!" There is always a war somewhere, or injustice, or people being oppressed and slaughtered. The feeling that there should be a single mind guiding the nations in the ways of wisdom and prosperity is like an instinct for something that we have lost.

Age after age, we have seen great men rise to power, exerting their philosophical influence through political maneuvering and military strength ... only to fall again, leaving a legacy of bloodshed, economic ruin, corruption, and tyranny. Humanists think that they have the answers to mankind's needs, but they are overlooking the essential element of the "God-shaped space" which resides in the heart of man. Fill that space with alternatives - wealth, fame, pleasure, or power, and man is still left empty and unfulfilled.

All of life's great experiences are pinpointed in the Bible. It is not read for nothing. The Book of Judges describes a nation without a leader. After Israel settled in the Promised Land, there were two centuries of turmoil, anarchy, and civil war. The Book explains why: "*In those days, there was no king in Israel, and every man did what was right in his own eyes.*" This sounds so familiar, doesn't it? Today, we stand in peril of repeating the same mistakes made by the children of Israel those thousands of years ago. Let us always endeavor to promote Jesus Christ - the true King on the throne!

Only Jesus!

This Jesus! Nobody else had ever dared make such an amazing claim to provide *"living water"* - and fulfill it. He would ascend to glory where creation began, and change the order of things. Something not known before would surge from heaven to earth. He called it *"the promise of the Father."* That promise is for you today!

The Promise - From over eight thousand promises in God's Word, the designation *"the promise"* makes it stand singularly and significantly alone. Christ made it his own promise. The Father's gift to him is his gift to us, as John the Baptist said:

> "I did not know him, but he who sent me to baptize with water said to me, 'Upon whom you see the Spirit descending, and remaining on him, this is he who baptizes with the Holy Spirit.' And I have seen and testified that this is the Son of God."

There is a price we pay to receive that promise - but the price is well worth its cost … and it could never compare to the price, which Jesus paid for us - his life. *"Whoever desires to come after me, let him deny himself, and take up his cross, and follow me."* Later, when his own disciples asked him about sharing his glory, he responded, *"You do not know what you ask. Are you able to drink the cup that I am about to drink, and be baptized with the baptism that I am baptized with?"*

When we allow Jesus into our lives, he makes us new from the inside out; *"therefore, if anyone is in Christ, he is a new creation; old things have passed away; behold, all things have become new."* Today, allow that living water to infuse you with his love, joy, and strength, down into the deepest part of your heart.

Today's Scripture
You shall receive power when the Holy Spirit has come upon you; and you shall be witnesses to me in Jerusalem, and in all Judea and Samaria, and to the end of the earth.
(Acts 1:8)

Daily Power!
The Father's gift to Jesus is also a gift to me!

Mark My Word
Mark 8:34; 10:39
Luke 24:44-53
John 1:1-37
Acts 1:1-14
2 Corinthians 5:17

The Bible In A Year

Morning
Genesis 7
Matthew 7

Evening
Ezra 7
Acts 7

8

Jesus Never Changes

Today's Scripture:
Jesus went about all Galilee, teaching in their synagogues, preaching the gospel of the kingdom, and healing all kinds of sickness and all kinds of disease among the people.
(Matthew 4:23)

Daily Power!
I know that Jesus included my healing in his purpose on earth, so I accept his gift with thanksgiving.

Mark My Word
Matthew 4:23; 8:17
Mark 1:34; 4:1-9
John 5:17; 9:3-4
Acts 1:1-9; 10:38

The Bible In A Year

Morning
Genesis 8
Matthew 8

Evening
Ezra 8
Acts 8

Jesus healed multitudes - that was his mission. He came to heal as well as to save. He did not come from glory to earth only for those people who happened to be alive during that period in history. He did not come to bring relief merely to a few thousand people. That was only the beginning.

> "Then he healed many who were sick with various diseases, and cast out many demons; and he did not allow the demons to speak, because they knew him. And again He began to teach by the sea. And a great multitude was gathered to him, so that he got into a boat and sat in it on the sea; and the whole multitude was on the land facing the sea. Then he taught them many things by parables."

The Bible says that it was what "*Jesus **began** to do*." By his deeds, he showed us what he wanted to do, so that we can see what he was - and still is - like. He came to heal them so that he could heal you.

People living in the days of Jesus' earthly ministry possibly thought of Jesus more as a healer than anything else. He set out to heal. That was Jesus. He did not wait for the sick to come to him - he often went to them. The apostle Peter actually said that Jesus went around for that very purpose. Healing was a major part of his mission, and Jesus said God sent him to do those very works.

If a man spends eight years or more studying to become a doctor, when he has finished his studies, he will open a surgery to treat sick people. It would be ridiculous for a doctor not to practise after all his efforts to qualify. We read in Matthew: "*He himself took our infirmities and bore our sicknesses*." That is a quotation from the prophet Isaiah about the crucifixion. Christ bore your pains and your sins in his own body on the cross. If Jesus died for you, it is not too much to expect him to heal you.

The Faith Factor

The Bible was written for people with no real faith. Faith is not believing what we know is not true nor believing something for which there is no evidence. That is foolishness.

But if we have no faith, reading the Bible produces it. And if we have some faith, we get more the same way. There is no mystique about it. We are born believers, having faith every day in our doctors and bankers, in our spouses and bosses. Without this natural faith, we could not function. Faith is possible to everybody … including you!

Your brain is the "doubt-box." Of course people say, "Seeing is believing." But if you can prove it, faith is unnecessary! Not seeing is no reason for not believing. Nobody sees radiation, but we know its effects. Nobody sees God, but millions see his effect in their lives. Faith is a decision. Make that decision irrevocable today!

Faith, like wiring, carries power … but is not power. It links us to the Power Source - God in heaven. Many people seek power through thousands of theories and methods. Some Christian believers also seek the power of God by dubious processes, like extra-long prayer or touching sacred relics. But the mystic realms are not where the disciples found power. It is available on earth. Christ's death and resurrection made available all the divine power we could ever need. It is the simple faith of ordinary people that touches Christ, not mysterious spirituality. Christ said "*I am the way, the truth, and the life. No one comes to the Father except through me.*" He is the only mediator between God and man, and for that office, he paid the infinite price. Never underestimate the power of your faith.

Today's Scripture
Blessed are those who have not seen and yet have believed.
(John 20:29)

Daily Power!
Faith is possible to everybody … including me!

Mark My Word
John 14:6; 20:24-30;
1 Timothy 2:5

The Bible In A Year

Morning
Genesis 9, 10
Matthew 9

Evening
Ezra 9
Acts 9

The Faith Fuse

Faith has neither bulk nor weight, for it is something that you do. Jesus spoke of *"faith as a mustard seed,"* referring to something tiny, but with huge potential. Perhaps today, he might speak of faith as a fuse. Tiny as it is, it transmits the awesome power generated in power stations to our homes. Without it, every appliance is useless, unable to draw from that power.

Our faith - however small we think it may be - can accomplish great things.

> "Another parable he put forth to them, saying: 'The kingdom of heaven is like a mustard seed, which a man took and sowed in his field, which indeed is the least of all the seeds; but when it is grown it is greater than the herbs and becomes a tree, so that the birds of the air come and nest in its branches.'"

As believers, we know what we believe, and in whom we believe. Believing tests us. Taking God's Word at face value, accepting its divine authority, we plug into the very Source! Faith is the vital link. By it, the energies of heaven flow into the world ... and into your life. *"Believe on the Lord Jesus Christ, and you will be saved, you and your household."*

The greatness of God, the work of Christ, or the Word of God, without faith as small as a fuse wire is unavailable. The circuit is broken. Once connected, the fuse itself cannot help, but shows the effects of the power surging through it. It warms up! Faith makes us dynamic, exuberant, excited! Allow the fuse of faith to activate your life today.

> "What does it profit, my brethren, if someone says he has faith but does not have works? Can faith save him? ... Thus also faith by itself, if it does not have works, is dead. But someone will say, 'You have faith, and I have works.' Show me your faith without your works, and I will show you my faith by my works."

Today's Scripture
If you have faith as a mustard seed, you will say to this mountain, 'Move from here to there,' and it will move; and nothing will be impossible for you. (Matthew 17:20)

Daily Power!
Today I take God's Word at face value, accepting its divine authority, and connecting to the very source of life.

Mark My Word
Matthew 13:31-32; 17:14-21
Luke 17:5-10
Acts 16:31
James 2:14-19

The Bible In A Year

Morning
Genesis 11
Matthew 10

Evening
Ezra 10
Acts 10

The Hands Of Jesus

When Jesus walked on earth, and delivered people from the oppression of Satan, that old deceiver watched him. The blind saw, and cripples walked. Christ was destroying the works of the devil systematically. Satan ground his teeth with rage, and plotted to destroy the Lord Jesus Christ. He inspired evil men to crucify Christ. He gloated as they nailed down those wonderful hands of mercy. "Those hands will give me no more trouble," he thought. "It is all over!" What a mistake Satan made. The very blood he caused to be spilled now breaks the stranglehold of Satan upon men and women everywhere, especially for you and me!

> "In the midst of the seven lampstands One like the Son of Man, clothed with a garment down to the feet and girded about the chest with a golden band … He laid his right hand on me, saying to me, 'Do not be afraid; I am the First and the Last. I am he who lives, and was dead, and behold I am alive forevermore. Amen. And I have the keys of Hades and of death.'"

An atheist once challenged me on a television program, "I do not believe that there is any power in the blood of Jesus. The blood of Jesus has been around for two thousand years, and if there was any power in it - as you claim - the world would not be in such a sorry state."

I replied, "Sir, there is also plenty of soap around, and yet many people are still dirty. Soap does not make a person clean by just being around, not even if he works in a soap factory. If you want to know what soap can do - **you have to take it, and apply it personally**. Then you will see! That is how it is with the blood of Jesus. It is not enough to know about the blood, sing about it, or preach about it. I now challenge you, sir," I said, "apply the blood of Jesus to your sinful life, and you will join hundreds of millions of people all over the world who sing and say: 'There is power, power, wonder-working power, in the precious blood of the Lamb.'"

Today's Scripture
How much more shall the blood of Christ, who through the eternal Spirit offered himself without spot to God, cleanse your conscience from dead works to serve the living God? (Hebrews 9:14)

Daily Power!
The blood of Jesus has broken every stranglehold that Satan has tried to establish over my life.

Mark My Word
Hebrews 9:14
1 John 1:7
Revelation 1:9-20

The Bible In A Year

Morning
Genesis 12
Matthew 11

Evening
Nehemiah 1
Acts 11

12

Jesus Is Real

Today's Scripture
For the law of the Spirit of life in Christ Jesus has made me free from the law of sin and death. (Romans 8:2)

Daily Power!
I live my life in the fullness of Christ Jesus, and I am an overcomer through him.

Mark My Word
Mark 5:36
Romans 8:1-17
Galatians 4:1-7
James 2:19

The Bible In A Year

Morning
Genesis 13
Matthew 12

Evening
Nehemiah 2
Acts 12

If Jesus is real, why do we live as if he did not exist? If there is a Father in heaven, why do we behave as if we were orphans? If there is a Savior, why do we cringe in fear and misery? If there is a healer, why do we not we ask him for healing? If Christ is offering life in all its fullness, why do we scratch and peck around in the dust like chickens? Jesus says *"Do not be afraid; only believe."*

If things go wrong, they can also go right! If the devil can be effective, how much more can God! Faith is supposed to prove its worth in times of great need. For so many believers, that is precisely when it grinds to a halt. For them, faith only works in blessed Christian meetings. To put it figuratively, they wear their life preservers only so long as they are on the ship, and toss them off as soon as they fall into the sea. How ridiculous can you get? Let us embrace the living reality of Jesus Christ in our lives today.

Faith may follow a process like this:

1. **Believing something is true.**
   Believing that there is a God is not enough.
   The devil believes the same thing. But it is a start.
2. **Believing a person is genuine.**
   Many believe that Jesus was a good man.
   But he claimed to be much more - the Savior of the world!
3. **Believing in God's power.**
   Many believed in Christ's healing power.
   But they did not make him Lord and Savior.
4. **Believing as trust.**
   Trust makes faith personal.
   We trust people whom we feel will not fail us.
5. **Believing in Christ.**
   This is real faith. It is complete surrender to him.
   Allow him take over every area of your life.

God's Universal Health Scheme

Jesus Christ is the Great Physician, on call day and night. his surgery never closes, and you do not have to wait for an appointment. He specializes in all of the troubles that you may encounter, whether sickness of the soul, afflictions of the body, or the ills of society - and there are no fees. We all enjoy good health - when we have it. Unfortunately, so many people get up in the morning feeling run down. They start the day already exhausted, which was never God's idea. I trust that this is not you. The gospel of Jesus Christ is the "universal health scheme" for every nation on earth, and the Bible is its textbook. Somebody said that God meant our bodies to last a lifetime, with care.

Healing originated with God - it was not our idea. At the beginning of the Bible, when nobody had ever thought of such a thing, he healed people … and that was four thousand years ago. *"So Abraham prayed to God; and God healed Abimelech, his wife, and his female servants."* Nobody suggested healing to God, or begged him for it. He did it because it was his nature. He loved doing it.

If there is something that you do not like doing, you keep quiet about it. But if there is something that you do enjoy - perhaps a hobby, or a sport - you devote time to it, and usually talk about it as well. God did not keep quiet about healing - he could not. his heart was full of compassion. He not only talked about it, but did it as well.

The first page of the Bible says that *"God saw everything that he had made, and indeed it was very good."* The last page says that *"there shall be no more death, nor sorrow, nor crying."* There shall be no more pain. Things began very well, and they will end that way. Make that your choice today.

Today's Scripture
I am the LORD who heals you.
(Exodus 15:26)

Daily Power!
Jesus Christ is my Great Physician, on call day or night. I know that he hears me, and will answer when I call.

Mark My Word
Genesis 1:1-31; 20:17
Exodus 15:26
Revelation 21:1-7

The Bible In A Year

Morning
Genesis 14
Matthew 13

Evening
Nehemiah 3
Acts 13

Today's Scripture
I have come that they
may have life, and
that they may have it
more abundantly.
(John 10:10)

Daily Power!
God has made a
provision for my life of
fresh, lively, sparkling,
abundant, unending
waters of refreshment
and restoration.

Mark My Word
Exodus 17:1-7
Numbers 20:1-13
Luke 5:37-38
John 4:3-30; 10:9-11

The Bible In A Year

Morning
Genesis 15
Matthew 14

Evening
Nehemiah 4
Acts 14

Streams In The Desert

"If anyone thirsts, let him come to me and drink. He who believes in me, as the Scripture has said, out of his heart will flow rivers of living water."

Rivers of living water. Not bottles, but rivers - fresh, lively, sparkling, abundant, and unending. Some people live for what comes out of a bottle … but Jesus wants you to experience a fresh, vibrant 'river.' Television provides life's highlights for millions of people - just watching others live, or pretending to live; even for children, who have forgotten how to play.

Remember, people are always "going to live" but only after things change, after working for hours, when they have money, or when they get married, or retire, or go on holiday, or whatever. Jesus came to give you life now. No waiting - wherever you are, whatever you are doing. He makes life live.

New water, new wine:

"No one puts new wine into old wineskins; or else the new wine will burst the wineskins and be spilled, and the wineskins will be ruined. But new wine must be put into new wineskins, and both are preserved."

God wrote his plan for Israel in the wilderness, across a blackboard forty years wide. The Israelites did not have to drink stale, flat water from skins - the Lord opened bubbling streams from a rock. The Temple drink offering was a celebration in memory of that wilderness water. Jesus, however, gave it a new and glorious meaning, a symbol of the outpouring of the Holy Spirit. That symbol is a precious reminder for you today that God has made a provision in your life of fresh, lively, sparkling, abundant, unending waters of refreshment and restoration. Let that river flow in you today!

Finding God

We will only find God if we truly want him. As he says in the Bible:

> "I love those who love me, and those who seek me diligently will find me ... Surely you shall call a nation you do not know, and nations who do not know you shall run to you, because of the LORD your God, and the Holy One of Israel; for he has glorified you. Seek the LORD while he may be found, call upon he while he is near."

And he makes this cast-iron promise:

> "For I know the thoughts that I think toward you, says the LORD, thoughts of peace and not of evil, to give you a future and a hope. Then you will call upon me and go and pray to me, and I will listen to you. And you will seek me and find me, when you search for me with all your heart."

At the point of our deepest need, the Good News of Jesus Christ cuts in! Jesus saw his life as a rescue mission. He said that he had come *"to seek and to save that which was lost."* He also said that his death was no accident - because he had come to die, *"for the Son of Man did not come to be served, but to serve, and to give his life a ransom for many."*

Is peace our deepest need? No, although Christ has provided that also. *"Peace I leave with you, my peace I give to you; not as the world gives do I give to you. Let not your heart be troubled, neither let it be afraid."* The **Good News of Jesus Christ is our deepest need.** All the unrest, all the heartache and loneliness, all the pain and despair, all the sin and corruption, is replaced by the gospel. This is the plan that God had in mind for us all along - a rightful relationship with him, in which all of our needs are satisfied.

Make that your strongest desire today - that you are always in right relationship with Christ, because then you can change the world!

Today's Scripture
For I know the thoughts that I think toward you, says the LORD, thoughts of peace and not of evil, to give you a future and a hope. Then you will call upon me and go and pray to me, and I will listen to you. And you will seek me and find me, when you search for me with all your heart. (Jeremiah 29:11-13)

Daily Power!
My daily goal is to be in right relationship with Christ.

Mark My Word
Proverbs 8:17
Isaiah 55:5-6
Jeremiah 29:11-13
Mark 10:45
Luke 19:10
John 14:27

The Bible In A Year

Morning
Genesis 16
Matthew 15

Evening
Nehemiah 5
Acts 15

God's Identity

Today's Scripture
Therefore, since we have such hope, we use great boldness of speech.
(2 Corinthians 3:12)

Daily Power!
I believe that the essence of evangelism is showing what God is like - that means that every day of my life, I am representing him to the best of my ability, through his power and compassion.

Mark My Word
Genesis 28:10-22
Acts 4:13-31
2 Corinthians 3:12
1 Peter 2:9

The Bible In A Year

Morning
Genesis 17
Matthew 16

Evening
Nehemiah 6
Acts 16

It is a striking thing that God's identity is linked to man. He was first known through the life of Abraham, and was called *"the God of Abraham."* The world's ideas about God came first from seeing what sort of man Abraham was. his life portrayed his God, and served as a recommendation for him.

When Jacob first fled from home, and from the murderous threats of Esau, he referred to the Lord as the *"God of my father Abraham and God of my father Isaac."* That is how he identified God - by how their God had shaped their lives. This brought a sense of awe upon Jacob. He resolved that one day, their God would be his God. He did not feel that that could be a reality, until his own life reflected his God. If the name of Jacob was to be associated with his fathers' God, he wanted to maintain the reputation of that God.

Some people say, for example, "I believe in my mother's God" or "I believe in Paul's God" or "I believe in Jean's God." People talk about presenting the gospel in a nutshell - but the gospel can only be presented in a person. The gospel is more than a formula for getting to heaven when you die. The gospel offers life, not just a life belt. The essence of evangelism is to show what God is like.

> "But you are a chosen generation, a royal priesthood, a holy nation, his own special people, that you may proclaim the praises of him who called you out of darkness into his marvelous light."

Make this the cry of your heart today: "God, I want to be your **bold** evangelist, pointing the way to life in Christ Jesus."

Revival Is Work

If we want New Testament revival, we need to study the New Testament pattern to be sure of what to expect. If we take the book of Acts as the true ideal, then Acts also reveals the formula. It is absolutely clear; there was no other method than the preaching of the gospel. This is clearly stated in 1 Corinthians: *"it pleased God through the foolishness of the message preached to save those who believe."* They prayed, asking God to bless **their evangelism**, not for him to do the task which he had given to them.

People pray, "Do it again, Lord." But we should do again what the early church Christians did. When we do what they did, we shall get what they got. They preached, witnessed, and worked as if it all depended on them; and prayed as if it all depended on God. They depended on God, and God depended on them. Oh, that God can depend on you and me!

The early Christians were unceasing in their witness. *"Daily in the temple, and in every house, they did not cease teaching and preaching Jesus as the Christ."* Paul's witness in Ephesus caused the whole city to riot, and no wonder! He said *"I ... taught you publicly and from house to house, and remember that for three years I did not cease to warn everyone night and day with tears."* Even slaves found ways to preach Christ. Timothy is seen as a bishop today, but Paul told him to do the work of an evangelist, not just pray for revival.

Revival is a state of mind, not a time of year. Revival comes from people whose hearts are so hungry for God on a daily, personal basis that they transmit their passion for God to others - especially the unsaved, who wonder, "What makes that person so different? What does he (or she) have that I don't have ... and I need?" Make a revival mindset yours today!

Today's Scripture
Go into all the world and preach the gospel to every creature.
(Mark 16:15)

Daily Power!
I am committed to doing the work of evangelism, not just background preparation of prayer and financial support, but to put my own self into reaching the world for Christ.

Mark My Word
Mark 16:15
Acts 5:42, 20:20, 31
1 Corinthians 1:21

The Bible In A Year

Morning
Genesis 18
Matthew 17

Evening
Nehemiah 7
Acts 17

18

The Silent Planet

Today's Scripture
And Jesus, when he came out, saw a great multitude and was moved with compassion for them, because they were like sheep not having a shepherd. So he began to teach them many things. (Mark 6:34)

Daily Power!
The Word tells me that God invites me to meet him through prayer ... therefore, I commit to being one who prays.

Mark My Word
Genesis 1:26-28; 2: 8-10; 3:6-8
Psalm 14:2-3
Matthew 6:6
Mark 6:34

The Bible In A Year

Morning
Genesis 19
Matthew 18

Evening
Nehemiah 8
Acts 18

Why do we need prayer? In the beginning, Adam and Eve did not pray in the sense in which most of us understand prayer today. God and man seemed to enjoy almost family openness:

> "God created man in his own image ... male and female he created them. Then God blessed them, and God said to them, 'Be fruitful and multiply' ... The LORD God planted a garden eastward in Eden, and there he put the man whom he had formed ... the tree of life was also in the midst of the garden, and the tree of the knowledge of good and evil. So when the woman saw that the tree was good for food, that it was pleasant to the eyes, and a tree desirable to make one wise, she took of its fruit and ate. She also gave to her husband with her, and he ate ... and they heard the sound of the LORD God walking in the garden in the cool of the day, and Adam and his wife hid themselves from the presence of the LORD God among the trees of the garden."

Then the party broke up. Relations became strained and distant. C.S. Lewis described this world as "the silent planet" - silent toward heaven. Earth hung in space like a spiritual black hole, which gave no light. The Psalmist said:

> "The LORD looks down from heaven upon the children of men, to see if there are any who understand, who seek God. They have all turned aside, they have together become corrupt; There is none who does good, no, not one."

Why should we believe that the almighty Creator of the universe is even remotely interested in what is going on inside our hearts? Because the Bible emphatically says that *"when you pray, go into your room, and when you have shut your door, pray to your Father who is in the secret place; and your Father who sees in secret will reward you openly."* Prayer is a big subject in the Bible, because it is important to God. Today, renew your commitment to make prayer an important part of your life.

Blood Different From All Others

Our blood is ordinary, but the blood of Jesus is holy blood. There is power in the blood of Jesus, because no man who has ever lived has had blood like his. The blood of Jesus is holy simply because the Bible calls it precious, but there are also some other very interesting factors. Everybody inherits blood group factors at conception ... Jesus did not. Normally a blood test can prove whether or not a particular man is the father of a child. The blood of a child, and of his true father can be checked scientifically for some genetic connection.

With Jesus, there was a new situation - he had no earthly father. his blood could not be grouped because it was singular. It was independent of any genetic inheritance. The father of Jesus was ... the Father in heaven. The Bible is very careful to explain this.

God inspired Luke, the beloved physician, to tell us the facts, which he probably learned from Mary, the mother of Christ. She could speak without embarrassment to a doctor, so Luke gives us this report:

> "Then Mary said to the angel, 'How can this be, since I do not know a man?' And the angel answered and said to her, 'The Holy Spirit will come upon you, and the power of the Highest will overshadow you; therefore, also, that Holy One who is to be born will be called the Son of God.'"

What an awesome wonder is this blood! In him we have redemption through his blood, the forgiveness of sins, according to the riches of his grace. And again in whom we have redemption through his blood, the forgiveness of sins.

Today's Scripture
For as many as are led by the Spirit of God, these are sons of God.
(Romans 8:14)

Daily Power!
There is wonder working power in the precious blood of the Lamb!

Mark My Word
Luke 1:34-35
Romans 8:14
Ephesians 1:7
Colossians 1:14; 4:14

The Bible In A Year

Morning
Genesis 20
Matthew 19

Evening
Nehemiah 9
Acts 19

20

Divine Blood Type

Today's Scripture
But now in Christ
Jesus you who once
were far off have
been brought near by
the blood of Christ.
(Ephesians 2:13)

Daily Power!
The blood of Jesus
is the secret of my
heavenly adoption.

Mark My Word
Matthew 19:26
Luke 3:38
John 1:14
1 Corinthians 15:45
Hebrews 10:5

The Bible In A Year

Morning
Genesis 21
Matthew 20

Evening
Nehemiah 10
Acts 20

Mary and Joseph were engaged, but they had not yet come together as husband and wife. As a virgin, Mary conceived a child by a miracle of God. Therefore Christ did not have blood group factors from Joseph, or Joseph's ancestors. Jesus Christ was the only begotten of the Father. With regard to Mary's blood type, we know that a woman can bear a child, which has a blood group completely incompatible with her own. The mother's blood supports the unborn child through the placenta, which also prevents her blood entering the veins of her baby, unless some kind of damage causes a leak. The blood of Jesus was his own divine blood … and this is the secret of its power!

Only one other man ever had blood that was not genetically received - Adam, the first man. He is mentioned as being *"of God"* - that is, a special creation without any ancestor. The Bible calls Jesus *"the second Adam."* his body, like the first Adam's, was specially prepared as the Bible says. God caused Mary to bear a son without the normal biological necessities, for nothing is impossible for God.

> "Not with the blood of goats and calves, but with his own blood he entered the Most Holy Place once for all, having obtained eternal redemption. For if the blood of bulls and goats and the ashes of a heifer, sprinkling the unclean, sanctifies for the purifying of the flesh, how much more shall the blood of Christ, who through the eternal Spirit offered himself without spot to God, cleanse your conscience from dead works to serve the living God?" (Hebrews 9:12-14)

What is your spiritual "blood-type?" As a born-again child of God, you too can claim the redemptive blood type of a believer, an adopted heir of the Heavenly Father.

Proven Signs

Christians are calling for Christ's return … and we know that prayer will be answered any day. Why are we sure? The Bible tells us so!

Christ came the first time exactly as the Bible predicted … so he will surely come the second time as the Bible says. The Bible is the only Book that has ever predicted the future, and proved to be accurate. The Lord said *"I am ready to perform my word."*

Bible prophecy was fulfilled to the hilt by Christ's first advent. The Magi traveled many hundreds of miles, and found Jesus at Bethlehem, exactly where the Bible said he would be. The Bible prophets had foretold how he would be born, live, and die: his hands pierced, his clothes made a lottery, his grave *"with the wicked … and with the rich,"* and so on. One man, John the Baptist, knew about the Messiah from Scripture, and that he was about to appear. Before Jesus stepped into public life, John identified him: *"There comes One after me who is mightier than I, whose sandal strap I am not worthy to stoop down and loose. I indeed baptized you with water, but he will baptize you with the Holy Spirit."*

With all these unmistakable, proven signs of his first coming, we can watch the biblical signs for his second coming with perfect assurance that he will indeed fulfill his promise! And our part is to continue, gathering the harvest until he comes!

> "My food is to do the will of him who sent me, and to finish his work. Do you not say, 'There are still four months and then comes the harvest'? Behold, I say to you, lift up your eyes, and look at the fields, for they are already white for harvest! And he who reaps receives wages, and gathers fruit for eternal life, that both he who sows and he who reaps may rejoice together."

Today's Scripture

Thrust in Your sickle and reap, for the time has come for you to reap, for the harvest of the earth is ripe.
(Revelation 14:15)

Daily Power!

I am watching and waiting for Christ's return, completely confident that he will fulfill his promise.

Mark My Word

Isaiah 53:9
Jeremiah 1:12
John 4:34-36
Revelation 14:15

The Bible In A Year

Morning
Genesis 22
Matthew 21

Evening
Nehemiah 11
Acts 21

Miracle Territory

New Testament believers did not go around searching and probing to get a miracle. They lived on miracle territory! They were in the kingdom of God, and they perceived the miracle-working hand of God in every situation. Believers understood everyday Christianity to be miraculous - miracles through and through. That theme is common in the letters of the apostle Paul.

In the very first days of the church miracles abounded: miracles of salvation (imagine if your church suddenly had to accommodate three thousand new members in one day) … miracles of healing … miracles of fellowship (how inexplicable it must have appeared to onlookers to see slaves and masters embracing, and sharing all) … miracles of finances, and more. Just read the first five chapters of the Book of Acts to witness everyday miracles.

Miracles caught the attention of the authorities, and they frightened them, because they could not understand how they could be. *"What shall we do to these men? For, indeed, that a notable miracle has been done through them is evident to all who dwell in Jerusalem, and we cannot deny it."* But for all their displeasure, punishment, and denials, they could not stop the flow of the power of God - nor the boldness of the apostles.

Regrettably, what was normal then is not normal now. So much emphasis has been placed on finding new methods for miracles that it sounds as if it were all a profound secret. I want to remove the mystery, and get back to the simplicity that is in Christ. We shall look at a miracle, and then see something greater! Then let **you** and **me** see miracles in our own lives!

Today's Scripture
Jesus of Nazareth, a man attested by God to you by miracles, wonders, and signs which God did through him in your midst, as you yourselves also know. (Acts 2:22)

Daily Power!
As a believer, I accept that my every-day life is going to be filled with the miraculous - those signs that point others to Jesus Christ.

Mark My Word
Acts 2:22; 5:12-14; 6: 8; 8:13; 9:11; 15:12
2 Corinthians 11:3

The Bible In A Year

Morning
Genesis 23
Matthew 22

Evening
Nehemiah 12
Acts 22

Miracle Conditions

In Matthew 14, we read about a wonderful miracle, which helps us to understand how miracles happen. First, understand that the miracle conditions began while Peter was still in the boat. Suddenly, he became different. One minute, panicking, his hair standing on end, the next minute, daring to do what no mere man had ever done.

> "And when the disciples saw him walking on the sea, they were troubled, saying, 'It is a ghost!' And they cried out for fear. But immediately Jesus spoke to them, saying, 'be of good cheer! It is I; do not be afraid.' And Peter answered him and said, 'Lord, if it is you, command me to come to you on the water.'"

Peter found things different when he exercised faith. Some people simply accept things as they are, and do nothing at all about it. But we know that when Christ comes into a situation, then that situation can be changed.

> "So he said, 'Come.' And when Peter had come down out of the boat, he walked on the water to go to Jesus. But when he saw that the wind was boisterous, he was afraid, and beginning to sink he cried out, saying, 'Lord, save me!' And immediately Jesus stretched out his hand and caught him, and said to him, 'O you of little faith, why did you doubt?' And when they got into the boat, the wind ceased. Then those who were in the boat came and worshiped he, saying, 'Truly you are the Son of God.'"

If we look carefully at this story, we shall see something even greater than Peter's circumstances changing. The water was exactly the same. But **Peter had changed**. With his eyes fixed on Jesus, the sea billows still rolled, but Peter walked over them. Jesus saves us, our household, and the things around us. Miracles begin within you, and then affect your surroundings. The sea threatened Peter, opening its foaming mouth to swallow him, but Peter made it an open pathway when Jesus called him to come. Listen for that voice in your heart today. If you hear him calling you to do something, then step out of your boat in obedience, and move towards him. You can because the path has been cleared for your journey.

Today's Scripture
But Jesus looked at [them] and said to them, "With men this is impossible, but with God all things are possible." (Matthew 19:26)

Daily Power!
I choose to change, to line up with God and his Word, and see miracles happen in my life!

Mark My Word
Matthew 14:22-33; 19:26

The Bible In A Year

Morning
Genesis 24
Matthew 23

Evening
Nehemiah 13
Acts 23

24

Sickness Is Not God's Plan

Sickness in God's good world is like weeds growing among wheat. But make no mistake - God did not sow the weeds, *"an enemy has done this."* God sent Jesus, *"who went about doing good and healing all who were oppressed by the devil, for God was with him."* It was the Creator's protest against the sabotage of his work by the devil.

God planted cures in nature, which medical research keeps finding. Those cures are ours today. But the God who heals naturally also heals supernaturally. Scripture denies that sickness is God's will, and it credits healings to God. Today, his hand touches far more people than many realize. Throughout the world, many supernatural healings take place every year, proving that *"Jesus Christ is the same yesterday, today, and forever."*

When Jesus came, he offered to heal people. We read in John's gospel that he performed some of his miracles without being specifically asked. Without anybody suggesting it, he went to the Pool of Bethesda where there were hundreds of afflicted people. He approached one paralyzed man and asked him if he wished to be healed. The man did not even say "Yes," but Jesus healed him anyway. Later, he saw a blind man, and without even asking him what he wanted, Jesus restored his sight. That was Jesus yesterday … and that is Jesus today!

Jesus placed an importance on medicine. *"Those who are well have no need of a physician, but those who are sick."* He then promptly set about healing people! When you learn to work with God for your healing, whether he chooses to work through doctors, or through his own divine power, then you understand how much he loves you, and how he truly wants you to *"prosper in all things and be in health, just as your soul prospers."*

Today's Scripture
God anointed Jesus of Nazareth with the Holy Spirit and with power, who went about doing good and healing all who were oppressed by the devil, for God was with him.
(Acts 10:38)

Daily Power!
I resist the enemy, and his seeds of destruction. I accept God's plan for me to walk in physical health, even as my soul prospers!

Mark My Word
Matthew 13:24-30
Mark 2:17
John 5:1-47; 9:1-41
Acts 10:34-48
Hebrews 13:1-25
3 John 2

The Bible In A Year

Morning
Genesis 25
Matthew 24

Evening
Esther 1
Acts 24

Avoid Past Mistakes

A king in Israel was never God's plan for his people. He wanted his people to be ruled by his law in their hearts, and to be accountable only to him. He established judges and priests to help the people. They however, looked around; saw their neighboring nations with glittering kings and princes ... and preferred the outward show to the inward knowledge. Does that not sound familiar as our society today? We look to handsome, amusing leaders rather than those with quiet integrity. Modern statistics reveal that historically, the tallest of political candidates usually wins an election. Is that a valid criterion when good character and leadership qualities are really the issue?

Many years after entering the Promised Land, the Israelites had a king, and the nation became powerful and affluent. But rebellion, by the king's own treacherous son, drove him into exile. The son was killed, and the throne was vacant. Again came anarchy, and *"all the people were in a dispute throughout all the tribes of Israel."* But the lesson of the bitter past had been learned, and they knew the answer. *"Now therefore, why do you say nothing about bringing back the king?"*

Those episodes in the Scriptures pointed to yet another - Christ before Pontius Pilate. Pilate asked Jesus, *"Are you a king then?"* Jesus answered *"You say rightly that I am a king. For this cause I was born, and for this cause I have come into the world, that I should bear witness to the truth."* Pilate said to the Jews *"Behold your King!"* But they shouted *"Away with him, away with him! Crucify him ... we have no king but Caesar!"* In their blindness, they chose Caesar, a foreign oppressor, yet crucified Jesus, the Christ. Within their lifetime, Caesar destroyed Israel as a nation.

Is our world now in danger of yet another such oppressive leader arising to take over and dominate the economy, the government, and our very lives? The Bible tells us that the answer is yes! **Jesus Christ will return!**

Today's Scripture
Worthy is the Lamb who was slain to receive power and riches and wisdom, and strength and honor and glory and blessing.
(Revelation 5:12)

Daily Power!
I have only one king in my life - the Lord Jesus Christ - the only begotten Son of Almighty God.

Mark My Word
2 Samuel 13 to 19
Matthew 27:11-26
John 18:37; 19:14-15
Revelation 5:12

The Bible In A Year

Morning
Genesis 26
Matthew 25

Evening
Esther 2
Acts 25

26

"Even So, Come Lord Jesus!"

Today's Scripture
And the Spirit
and the Bride say,
"Come!" And let
him who hears say,
"Come!" And let him
who thirsts, come.
Whoever desires, let
him take the water of
life freely
(Revelation 22:17).

Daily Power!
Each day, as I follow
Jesus, I am changed
from glory to glory.

Mark My Word
Isaiah 53:5
Luke 1:17
Romans 2:32
2 Corinthians 5:17
Revelation 22:17

The Bible In A Year

Morning
Genesis 27
Matthew 26

Evening
Esther 3
Acts 26

The world has no king, only warring leaders. It was so in Israel - *"everyone did what was right in his own eyes."* Isaiah said *"All we like sheep have gone astray; we have turned, every one, to his own way."* We are all *"the sons of disobedience."* "But I haven't done those great sins!" self-righteous people protest. The Bible replies that *"those who practice such things are deserving of death, not only do the same, but also approve of those who practice them."* When we condone governments who encourage sin - passing laws to permit abortions … ousting public prayer because of a perverted understanding of the true meaning of the separation of church and State … dishonoring our elders by spending and wasting their savings … vilifying those who speak out against homosexuality … and so many other sociopolitical issues - we fall into the same trap that brought about the fall of the Roman Empire and many other great civilizations. **Compromise is the door to destruction.**

World religious leaders, like the secular authorities, only tell us how to help ourselves. We know what we should do - but doing it is another thing! We want strength, not advice. Religions are an added burden, laying down dogmas and rules. We want a Deliverer-King, a Savior. Jesus laid down his life - not rules. We cannot redeem ourselves, but Christ is the world's redeemer! A new age needs new people … and Christ creates *"new creatures!"* The Bible story shows that David took his throne again … and so will Jesus Christ. Christ declared that he would come back, and he will! Everything he ever said turned out to be true - it is impossible for this one promise not to be true also. For two thousand years, the tens of millions of the church of Christ have expected his return. The doctrine has taken many forms, but Scriptures teach the personal, visible presence of Christ on earth. This is the key hope of every Christian creed. The last prayer of the Bible is *"Amen! Come, Lord Jesus!"* Make that your prayer today.

The Golden Gift

Faith in Christ is different than any other kind of faith. It is not found in the Old Testament. In the New Testament, the word means believing into Christ, suggesting movement. Faith in Christ means moving close to him in trusting love. It is an embrace … and he extends his arms to you today.

This kind of loving embrace between man and his Maker comes only through Christ. Nobody in the Old Testament days could think of such a thing. God was Spirit - another kind of Being, too awesome to be approached except with fear and trembling.

> "The hour is coming, and now is, when the true worshipers will worship the Father in spirit and truth; for the Father is seeking such to worship him. God is Spirit, and those who worship him must worship in spirit and truth."

Yet one inspired book in the Old Testament Scriptures touches the heart of a new experience: the Song of Songs, a lyric of love that gathers up all its words of supreme love in one phrase *I am my beloved's and my beloved is mine*. This was an attitude towards God that nobody understood, until Christ came. Are you not glad that you can live and walk in a full understanding of how much he loves you?

Faced with his reality, ordinary people in the gospel suddenly knew that he was the Savior, a swift revelation followed by complete commitment.

> "However, when he, the Spirit of truth, has come, he will guide you into all truth; for he will not speak on his own authority, but whatever he hears he will speak; and he will tell you things to come. He will glorify me, for he will take of what is mine and declare it to you."

No longer was faith for the rare individual, as in the Old Testament. Somehow Calvary does what the awesome manifestations of Sinai could not do. Jesus is the great faith-creator. He himself said that "*no man comes to the Father except through me.*" He does not point to **a way** - he is **The Way!**

Today's Scripture
Jesus said to him, "I am the way, the truth, and the life. No one comes to the Father except through me." (John 14:6)

Daily Power!
By faith I live and walk in a full understanding of how much Christ loves me.

Mark My Word
Song of Solomon 2:4; 6:1-3
John 4:23-24; 14:1-21; 16:13-14

The Bible In A Year

Morning
Genesis 28
Matthew 27

Evening
Esther 4
Acts 27

A Present Tense Faith

Today's Scripture:
I am the Alpha
and the Omega,
the Beginning and
the End,' says the
Lord, 'who is and
who was and who
is to come, the
Almighty.'(Revelation
1:8)

Daily Power!
I have a present
tense God and he
has given me present
tense faith.

Mark My Word
Matthew 8:1-3
Hebrews 13:8
James 1:6-7
Revelation 1:4, 8

The Bible In A Year

Morning
Genesis 29
Matthew 28

Evening
Esther 5
Acts 28

A leper in the New Testament saw something about Christ that few others have seen:

> "When he had come down from the mountain, great multitudes followed him. And behold, a leper came and worshiped him, saying, 'Lord, if you are willing, you can make me clean.' Then Jesus put out his hand and touched him, saying, 'I am willing; be cleansed.' Immediately his leprosy was cleansed."

Meeting Jesus, this leper said *"if you will, you can make me clean."* Not "If you can, you will," but 'If you will, you can!' The Bible was not written to tell us what God can do - we know that he is Almighty - **the Bible tells us what God will do**.

It is easy to believe that God did things long ago ... but past tense faith is hollow unless it becomes a present-tense faith for today. John wrote of faith in three tenses: past, present, and future. He said *"Grace to you and peace from him who is and who was and who is to come ... and from Jesus Christ, the faithful witness."* What he will be, he is now and always has been!

"Jesus Christ is the same yesterday, today, and forever." Healing is a part of his nature. Therefore, to be consistent with himself, he will heal. The issue then becomes our faith - or lack of it (also known as doubt). *"Let him ask in faith, with no doubting, for he who doubts is like a wave of the sea driven and tossed by the wind. For let not that man suppose that he will receive anything from the Lord."* So do not let doubt interfere with what you know about the nature of God!

The God who created the universe did not go into retirement when the task was complete. What he did then shows us what he is now, and always will be - creative, active, and good. Creation was the first and greatest of all miracles. So what is the problem with God healing deaf ears or blind eyes? Yet too many have a "used-to-be" God, anchored in history.

We have a present-tense God, and he has given us a present-tense faith!

Aspects Of The Holy Spirit

There are many different expressions for the baptism of the Holy Spirit … being baptized in holy fire … endued with power … anointed with the oil of God … immersed in the Spirit … filled with the Spirit … walking, praying, living in the Spirit … our bodies being temples of the Holy Spirit … having another Comforter besides Christ himself. These are sketches, but color and details have to be added. The Bible is a picture gallery of the Holy Spirit in operation: it portrays signs, wonders, and miracles … men looking as if **they had been with Jesus** … the world turned upside down … people coming to know the Lord, enjoying a new experience. Not just religious enthusiasts, churchgoers - but a new breed with vibrant faith. Do you not enjoy having that vibrant faith percolating in you!

Paul says that *"even when we were dead in trespasses, (God) made us alive together with Christ (by grace you have been saved), and that we are strengthened with all might, according to his glorious power, for all patience and longsuffering with joy."* The Lord Jesus Christ promised that we would receive power. I compare baptism of the Holy Spirit to a household appliance that comes with a built-in electric cord. Unless you plug that cord into the source of power, the appliance does not function. All its potential is there - it may even carry a famous brand name - but it must be connected to the power for it to achieve its purpose. As recipients of God's free gift of salvation, we have been 'brand named' as his children … so now, let us come off the shelf of self-reliance, or the closet of timidity, and allow the Holy Spirit to energize us by his power.

As a born-again believer, you are special. You are a saint in his eyes, and the baptism in the Holy Spirit is for you. Jesus alone made it possible when he died, rose, and *"sat down at the right hand of the Majesty on high."* What a gift! Receive that gift today! You will never be the same again.

Today's Scripture

If you then, being evil, know how to give good gifts to your children, how much more will your heavenly Father give the Holy Spirit to those who ask him. (Luke 11:13)

Daily Power!

Today, I welcome and allow the Holy Spirit into my life to empower and strengthen me, and to lead me into all truth.

Mark My Word

Matthew 3:11
Luke 3:16; 11:13
John 14:16-17
Acts 1:8
Romans 8:26
1 Corinthians 6:19
Galatians 5:25
Ephesians 2:5; 5:18

The Bible In A Year

Morning
Genesis 30
Mark 1

Evening
Esther 6
Romans 1

30

God's Infinite blood

Today's Scripture
Let us hold fast the profession of our faith without wavering; for he is faithful that promised.
(Hebrews 10:23)

Daily Power!
Sin shall not have dominion over me, for I am not under law but under grace!

Mark My Word
Exodus 12:4
Matthew 14:33; 26:28
John 1:1, 14; 4:24
Romans 6:14
1 Corinthians 15:47
Hebrews 10:23
1 John 1:7; 2:2
Revelation 7:9, 14

The Bible In A Year

Morning
Genesis 31
Mark 2

Evening
Esther 7
Romans 2

There is a vast difference between the first Adam and the second Adam. *"The first man was of the earth, made of dust; the second Man is the Lord from heaven."* The blood of Jesus is holy. How can that be, seeing that God is Spirit? A spirit has no flesh and blood. The answer is simple. *"In the beginning was the Word, and the Word was with God, and the Word was God ... and the Word became flesh and dwelt among us."*

In the womb of Mary, Godhood and manhood became one. The blood of Jesus is the blood of *"the Son of God."* An individual's blood may legally be shed for another man - but the blood of Jesus Christ has no such limitation, because God's infinity is involved. The blood of *"the Son of God"* has grace to cover the sin of the whole world.

God demonstrated the enormous capacity of the blood when Israel left Egypt. The Israelites had to slay and eat the Passover lamb; but if a family was too small, they could share the lamb with another family. This is a lovely picture of Jesus - the Lamb of God too great for one household. He was the Lamb too great for merely the apostles at the Last Supper. John later wrote that *"He himself is the propitiation for our sins, and not for ours only but also for the whole world,"* and then later in visions, he saw *"a great multitude that no one could count, from every nation ... they have washed their robes and made them white in the blood of the Lamb."*

How we thank God that *"if we walk in the light as he is in the light, we have fellowship with one another, and the blood of Jesus Christ his Son cleanses us from all sin."* With the remission of sin comes the New Covenant of grace. *"For this is my blood of the new covenant, which is shed for many for the remission of sins."*

Knowing God

Above all else, know the Lord. How easy it is to ask the wrong person for the things we need! We do not usually ask a plumber for medicine, nor a doctor to repair a water pipe. Know who God is!

> "(God) grant you, according to the riches of his glory, to be strengthened with might through his Spirit in the inner man, that Christ may dwell in your hearts through faith; that you, being rooted and grounded in love, may be able to comprehend with all the saints what is the width and length and depth and height - to know the love of Christ which passes knowledge; that you may be filled with all the fullness of God."

Do not address a vague somebody somewhere up there in the stratosphere, with no idea of who he is, or how he might react. Do not be like the liberal preacher who thought of God as "a kind of oblong blur," or like the Athenians with an altar "*to the unknown god.*" Some people even talk of "seeking the unknown." That kind of mystical nonsense is like begging from any passerby, hoping to meet a billionaire. It is far better to know the billionaire personally! To recognize God's true identity always encourages more intelligent and more effective praying. God is our Father.

What kind of reaction can we expect if we treat God as an "oblong blur"? The Almighty has made almighty efforts to tell us about himself, even to sending his own Son, Jesus Christ. To ignore what he says involves a deliberate and dangerous resolution to remain in ignorance - exactly what we might expect when the devil influences us. To brush aside the greatest spiritual knowledge ever revealed is suicidal! Even God himself can do nothing more for us then. People question, "Why, if God is all-powerful, does he not do this or that?" But God is not only all-powerful, but He is also all wise, holy, and just. Furthermore, he has his own prior plans, which are not likely to be changed by one of our impulses. You do not ask a surgeon performing an operation to make you a cup of tea. We must at least flow in the direction of the divine stream. Jump into the reality of Christ alive in you today!

Today's Scripture
God said to Moses, "I AM WHO I AM." And he said, "Thus you shall say to the children of Israel, 'I AM has sent me to you.'"
(Exodus 3:13-14)

Daily Power!
My heavenly Father is all-wise, all-knowing, all-powerful, all-loving, holy, just, and compassionate, and he has blessed me with every spiritual blessing in the heavenly places in Christ.

Mark My Word
Exodus 3:13-14
Acts 17:22-23
Ephesians 1:3; 3: 14-21

The Bible In A Year

Morning
Genesis 32
Mark 3

Evening
Esther 8
Romans 3

It is a crime to bend God's exclamation mark
into a question mark.

The church that is not saving the lost is lost itself!

These are the power generators of God:
The cross of Calvary!
The resurrection of Jesus Christ!
The Holy Spirit Baptism!

The Principles Of Power

If Christianity is to progress, we must follow the divine way. Christ knew that the world would expand. There are now sixty times more people alive than when he was here. He expected that all the world would hear his quiet words spoken so long ago in an obscure Roman province, not by normal propaganda methods, but by his power. Because the world hovers between spiritual life and death, utmost consideration must be given to anything that can secure the destinies of precious people.

Just as in the wilderness, Jesus was tempted to misuse divine powers when he had been filled with the Holy Spirit ... so others are likely to be tempted in the same way. The temptation springs from pride, which corrupts our sincere motives for the power gifts, and produces flamboyant behavior and egotistical display. Jesus was tempted by Satan to throw himself off the pinnacle of the Temple. One thing to be taken to heart is that the supernatural is not always sensational. We may attract personal admiration by our gifts, but our job is to set people's eyes on Jesus. When Paul and Barnabas were offered worship at Lystra, they were horrified, running among the people to assert that they were not divinities.

> "And as Moses lifted up the serpent in the wilderness, even so must the Son of Man be lifted up, that whoever believes in him should not perish but have eternal life."

> "When you lift up the Son of Man, then you will know that I am he."

Jesus said that this generation seeks a sign. Sensation always has a market. We can exploit a situation and use the gifts of God for our own advantage. Simon Magus wanted the Holy Spirit in order to bolster his prestige. Uzza died for his presumption in putting his hand upon the ark of testimony. If anyone says, "I would like the gift of healing" or some other gift, the proper response is, "Why?" Motive is vital. Be certain your motives are Christ-centered.

Today's Scripture
And as Moses lifted up the serpent in the wilderness, even so must the Son of Man be lifted up, that whoever believes in him should not perish but have eternal life. (John 3:14-15)

Daily Power!
The supernatural is not always sensational ... Our job is to set people's eyes on Jesus.

Mark My Word
1 Chronicles 13:10
Matthew 4:1-11; 12:39
John 3:14-15; 8:28
Acts 8:9, 19; 14:8-18

The Bible In A Year

Morning
Genesis 33
Mark 4

Evening
Esther 9, 10
Romans 4

2

The Divine Imperative

Today's Scripture
For whoever calls on the name of the LORD shall be saved. How then shall they call on him in whom they have not believed? And how shall they believe in him of whom they have not heard? And how shall they hear without a preacher? And how shall they preach unless they are sent?
(Romans 10:13-15)

Daily Power!
One thing I can claim every day of my life – Jesus Christ is my healer!

Mark My Word
John 3:7, 16
Romans 5:8; 10:13-15
James 1:18

The Bible In A Year

Morning
Genesis 34
Mark 5

Evening
Job 1
Romans 5

God does what he is. He is Love therefore he must love. He is a Savior therefore he must save. He has revealed himself to be a Healer therefore he must heal.

In the gospel of John, this comes out in the imperatives of Jesus. When Jesus said that *"you must be born again,"* he meant that he himself must do it for us. We cannot rebirth ourselves. Only God can bring such a thing about. The apostle James declared that *"He chose to give us birth through the word of truth."* Rebirth comes by the Word of truth – the gospel. If the world is to be saved, then people must hear the gospel. If they are to hear the gospel, then somebody must preach it. That is a command for you and for me to fulfill.

Redemption is like creation – nobody thought of it but God. Redemption never crossed anyone's mind, not even that of the wisest person who ever lived. There are many religions in the world, but not one of them offers redemption. People believe in many different gods, but not one of them is a redeemer. There are many holy books, yet only one of them brings us the Good News of Redemption – the Bible.

Some religions promote attaining peace … others promise wealth and favor … some encourage self-improvement – but they are all empty promises, as they do not address the ultimate question: "What happens after death?" Only God answered that, through his Son: *"For God so loved the world that he gave his only begotten Son, that whoever believes in him should not perish but have everlasting life."*

Jesus Christ is the redeemer who gives eternal life. Our responsibility is to spread that good news of the redeemer to the lost world.

Light Reflectors

'The Christian's main business is evangelism' – that means it is our business. It is important that evangelism remains important. It is important for the countries evangelized, and for the countries evangelizing.

When Paul was in Troas, he preached all night. A young man called Eutychus fell out of a window, and Paul restored him to life. We read that *"there were many lamps in the upper room where they were gathered together."* Well, there are many lamps among us … I trust. The virgins in the parable of the Bridegroom all had lamps (the same Greek word, lampas), but half of the lamps had gone out. That does not mean that the lamps were burning slightly. It means that half of them were not even lit!

> "Then the kingdom of heaven shall be likened to ten virgins who took their lamps and went out to meet the bridegroom. Now five of them were wise, and five were foolish. Those who were foolish took their lamps and took no oil with them, but the wise took oil in their vessels with their lamps. … At midnight a cry was heard: 'Behold, the bridegroom is coming; go out to meet him!' Then all those virgins arose and trimmed their lamps. … The bridegroom came, and those who were ready went in with him to the wedding; and the door was shut. Afterward the other virgins came also, saying, 'Lord, Lord, open to us!' But he answered and said, 'Assuredly, I say to you, I do not know you.'"

We cannot be half-alight! We either shine, or we are patches of shadow. I wonder if fifty-fifty is a general average among Christians? Half the virgins were asleep and unprepared. So was Eutychus – and look what happened to him! People who go to sleep on the job, whose lamps have gone out because they had no oil – people like this are bound to fail! Perhaps that is why we read; *"Awake, you who sleep, arise from the dead, and Christ will give you light."* Today is a good day to make sure your life is awake, and prepared for whatever God has for you!

Today's Scripture
If then your whole body is full of light, having no part dark, the whole body will be full of light, as when the bright shining of a lamp gives you light. (Luke 11:36)

Daily Power!
Father, I pray that my lamp may be completely filled with your Spirit, and that I may be your light shining in my world today.

Mark My Word
Matthew 25:1-13
Luke 11:36
Acts 20:7-12
Ephesians 5:1-21

The Bible In A Year

Morning
Genesis 35, 36
Mark 6

Evening
Job 2
Romans 6

4

Unlocked Doors

Today's Scripture
Because I live, you
will live also. At that
day you will know that
I am in my Father, and
you in me,
and I in you.
(John 14:19-20)

Daily Power!
The gospel of Jesus
Christ must be
preached.

Mark My Word
John 14:19-20
Matthew 18:18
Revelation 1:18

The Bible In A Year

Morning
Genesis 37
Mark 7

Evening
Job 3
Romans 7

The most famous escape artist of all was Harry Houdini, a show business star. Police would lock him up in a cell and, as they walked away, he would follow them. He was free within seconds. Except once! Half an hour went by and Houdini still was fuming over the lock. Then a policeman came and simply pushed the door open. The door had never been locked! Houdini was fooled, trying to unlock a door that was not locked.

Likewise, Christ has gone right through the castle of Giant Despair. He has the keys *"of Hades and of death,"* and he has opened the gates. So why are millions sweating, trying every trick to get out of their evil habits and bondages? They join new cults or old heathen religions, hear new theories, or go to psychiatrists. But why? Jesus sets men free. He does it all the time.

I remember a man who told me that he too was a spiritual counselor. However he did not believe that Jesus Christ is the Son of God, nor that the Bible is the Word of God. I wondered, therefore, how this so-called counselor helped anybody. "Do they come to you, and then go away with broken hearts?" I asked. "Oh no," he assured me, "I just calm them down." I looked him in the eye and said, "Mister, a man on a sinking ship needs more than a tranquilizer. Don't calm him down. He is going down already. When Jesus comes to a man in a shipwreck, he does not throw him a tranquilizer and say, "Perish in peace." He reaches down his nail-scarred hand, grips him, lifts him, and says to him, *"because I live, you will live also."* This is the gospel of Jesus Christ that must be preached. Jesus is the Savior of our world. This message is life, peace, and health for spirit, soul, and body. Speak it boldly today!

Terrible Truth

In a hospital, a doctor is meeting with one of her patients. She has some bad news to tell him. He only has a few weeks to live. The Bible has similar news to tell us. It has both good news and bad news for us – starting with the bad news.

The problem of suffering and evil does not stop on our TV screens. It is easy to point the finger at the stories we see on the news and say, "That's the problem with the world today!" Instead, the problem is much closer to home – the problem is actually in our own hearts.

The Bible is not just honest about human suffering and evil in the world – it forces us to be honest about ourselves too. Jesus pinpointed this when he said: *"But those things, which proceed out of the mouth, come from the heart, and they defile a man. For out of the heart proceed evil thoughts, murders, adulteries, fornications, thefts, false witness, blasphemies."* Jesus used a simple, rather old-fashioned word to describe what has gone wrong with us – the word **sin**.

Originally, archers used the word **sin** to describe what had gone wrong when their arrows had not hit the bulls-eye. "To sin" means to miss the mark of what God intended us to be. One part of the Bible says this: *"All have sinned and fall short of the glory of God."* This makes sense. We have all done things that we feel ashamed of. We have all hurt other people … and ourselves.

But the Bible goes even further. It says that sin is a negative bias, a force that constantly spoils our best aim. It is not just that we occasionally do wrong things, but that there is a deep problem inside. It is like a cancer that makes us go wrong. The question is how can sin – the cancer – be cured? The answer comes from God's own Word. The cure is only possible through the shed blood of Jesus Christ. Thus a songwriter of old wrote, "What can wash away my sin? Nothing but the blood of Jesus!" Walk in the fullness of that cleansing flow today!

Today's Scripture
For all have sinned and fall short of the glory of God. (Romans 3:23)

Daily Power!
The sin of my heart has already been addressed by the cleansing blood of Jesus. I have free access to that blood whenever I repent of my sins.

Mark My Word
Mark 7:20-22
Romans 3:22-24

The Bible In A Year

Morning
Genesis 38
Mark 8

Evening
Job 4
Romans 8

6

Today's Scripture
But let him ask
in faith, with no
doubting, for he who
doubts is like a wave
of the sea driven and
tossed by the wind.
(James 1:6)

Daily Power!
It is my desire to
know God more
and more each day.
Therefore I will seek
him in his Word,
the Bible, where his
nature and character
are clearly written.

Mark My Word
Isaiah 45:3-5
Ephesians 3:20-21
James 1:4-7, 17

The Bible In A Year

Morning
Genesis 39
Mark 9

Evening
Job 5
Romans 9

Know God, his ways, his counsel, his character! All his attributes are laid open in his Word. Read it! This is the secret of so many Christians' wonderful faith and confidence – their path to God guided by Scripture.

"Now to him who is able to do exceedingly abundantly above all that we ask or think, according to the power that works in us, to him be glory in the church by Christ Jesus to all generations, forever and ever. Amen."

Learn to know God – he already knows you.

"I will give you the treasures of darkness and hidden riches of secret places that you may know that I, the LORD, who call you by your name, am the God of Israel … I have even called you by your name; I have named you, though you have not known me. I am the LORD, and there is no other; there is no God besides me."

The Epistle of James, which is largely about prayer, speaks of God's goodness as always shining like the sun: *"Every good gift and every perfect gift is from above, and comes down from the Father of lights, with whom there is no variation or shadow of turning."* We know that James was picturing a sundial, which registers the sun's movement by its shadow. When there is no shadow, it is noon, because the sun is at the zenith, and casts no shadow. God never casts a shadow because he is always at the zenith. He never varies, changes, or declines. For everybody, he is always the same prayer-answering God.

Some people have learned to pray the Bible – that is, they read the richness of the Word, and make it their personal prayer. For instance, I might pray this way: "I shall let patience have its perfect work in me, that I may be perfect and complete, lacking nothing. And if I lack wisdom, I shall ask of God, who gives to all liberally and without reproach, and it shall be given to me." Combining your prayers with God's Word is one of the most powerful and effective weapons that you can ever utilize!

The Heart-Interest Of God

Alfred, Lord Tennyson, only told half the truth when he wrote: "More things are wrought by prayer than this world dreams of." The other half is this: more things are not handled in prayer than this world dreams of. We live dangerously, leaving many important matters out of our prayers. Unanswered prayers are usually the ones that were never prayed. *"Until now you have asked nothing in my name. Ask, and you will receive, that your joy may be full."* Interceding for the salvation of the nations, however, receives immediate attention. *"Now this is the confidence that we have in him, that if we ask anything according to his will, he hears us. And if we know that he hears us, whatever we ask, we know that we have the petitions that we have asked of him."* It touches the heart-interest of God.

> "God be merciful to us and bless us, and cause Your face to shine upon us that Your way may be known on earth, Your salvation among all nations. Let the peoples praise you, O God; Let all the peoples praise you. Oh, let the nations be glad and sing for joy! For you shall judge the people righteously, and govern the nations on earth."

Right now, my friend, pray this prayer of repentance and renewing of conviction:

> "My Heavenly Father, I yearn to feel Your heart, to see what Your eyes see, to have greater compassion for the lost and dying of my world today. Forgive me when I've been careless or thoughtless, and neglected my daily intercession for the lost. Renew in me Your very fire of salvation – that gift which I've received and treasure – and rekindle in me a passion for souls that drives me to my knees. I know this is Your heart … now make it mine. In the name of my Lord and Savior, Jesus Christ. Amen."

I know that the Holy Spirit has heard your heart-felt prayer today, and I know that he will answer speedily. More than ever before … become an intercessor today!

Today's Scripture
It is Christ who died, and furthermore is also risen, who is even at the right hand of God, who also makes intercession for us.
(Romans 8:34)

Daily Power!
Interceding for the salvation of the nations touches the heart-interest of God. That is where I choose to put my heart also.

Mark My Word
Psalm 67:1-7
John 16:24
Romans 8
1 John 5:14

The Bible In A Year

Morning
Genesis 40
Mark 10

Evening
Job 6
Romans 10

We Need A Deliverer

Today's Scripture
And Jesus came and spoke to them, saying, 'All authority has been given to me in heaven and on earth. Go therefore and make disciples of all the nations, baptizing them in the name of the Father and of the Son and of the Holy Spirit, teaching them to observe all things that I have commanded you; and lo, I am with you always, even to the end of the age.'
(Matthew 28:18-20)

Daily Power!
Jesus Christ is my Deliverer.

Mark My Word
Matthew 23:37-38;
28:18-20
Romans 1:20-32

The Bible In A Year

Morning
Genesis 41
Mark 11

Evening
Job 7
Romans 11

Israel rejected their greatest son, their true king … and, by and large, the world does the same. The world today is leaderless, shepherdless, and without a king. Where are we, and where can the world turn to for true authority? As individuals, we find that unless God rules our lives, the devil will. The Bible simply states the obvious when it declares that the whole world is led by the devil. We need a Deliverer!

Christ left his imprint, but it is like a King-in-exile. The world wants to manage its own affairs. To them, he is the "absentee Lord." People only want people to help them.

> "For since the creation of the world his invisible attributes are clearly seen, being understood by the things that are made, even his eternal power and Godhead; so that they are without excuse, because, although they knew God, they did not glorify him as God, nor were thankful, but became futile in their thoughts, and their foolish hearts were darkened. Professing to be wise, they became fools, and changed the glory of the incorruptible God into an image made like corruptible man."

When Jesus made his official entry into the capital city of Jerusalem, he wept, saying, *"How often I have longed to gather your children together as a hen gathers her chicks under her wings, but you were not willing. Look, your house is left desolate to you."* Christ's great apostle Paul described things similarly: *"And even as they did not like to retain God in their knowledge, God gave them over to a debased mind, to do those things, which are not fitting."* Let us choose our Deliverer wisely!

Jesus The King

What will Jesus do when he comes again? We can judge that by his first coming – it altered the destiny of nations. his second coming will do all that, and more. He is the Prince of Peace. The first time, he lived in obscurity, never wrote a book, and died seemingly as a victim of political intrigue – but nobody has affected the world like he has. his next appearance will not be as a humble babe in a manger. He declared that his return would be *"in power and great glory."* It will shake and reshape the world.

> "And I heard a loud voice from heaven saying, 'Behold, the tabernacle of God is with men, and he will dwell with them, and they shall be his people. God himself will be with them and be their God. And God will wipe away every tear from their eyes; there shall be no more death, nor sorrow, nor crying. There shall be no more pain, for the former things have passed away. Then he who sat on the throne said, 'Behold, I make all things new.'"

Knowing Jesus Christ as our King makes our lives very, very different. Being a follower of his does not mean that we suddenly become super-people, raised far above the ranks of ordinary men. Rather, being his followers means that we become *"fishers of men, deny ourselves, and take up our cross to follow him."*

Whatever shape the world takes – the rise and fall of empires, *"wars and rumors of wars,"* technology and sociological progress – you and I have this great assurance: Our King, the Lord Jesus Christ, not only lives in our hearts today, but his kingdom is an everlasting kingdom! That is a tremendous truth, is it not?

> He has on his robe and on his thigh a name is written:
> KING OF KINGS AND LORD OF LORDS.

Today's Scripture
And he who does not take his cross and follow after me is not worthy of me. He who finds his life will lose it, and he who loses his life for my sake will find it.
(Matthew 10:38-39)

Daily Power!
I am a child of the kingdom, because I follow in the footsteps of my King, the Lord Jesus Christ.

Mark My Word
Zechariah 9:9
Matthew 4:19; 10:38-39; 16:24; 21:5
Luke 21:27
Revelation 21:1-8

The Bible In A Year

Morning
Genesis 42
Mark 12

Evening
Job 8
Romans 12

10

Today's Scripture
Jesus said to her, 'Did
I not say to you that
if you would believe
you would see the
glory of God?
(John 11:40)

Daily Power!
Because I believe, I
know that I will see
the glory of God!

Mark My Word
John 11:17-44
Romans 12:2
2 Corinthians 4:3-4
Philippians 3:13-14
James 2:23

The Bible In A Year

Morning
Genesis 43
Mark 13

Evening
Job 9
Romans 13

Breakthrough Faith

Unbelief sees today's miracles as suspect. People say that Bible miracles were real, but today's are spurious, or that today's tongues cannot be the same as at Pentecost: God answered prayer then, but now it is coincidence. How did Jesus reply to this pessimism? *"If you would believe you would see the glory of God."* Rationalization is one of the biggest excuses: "Well, he was not really sick in first place" or "The medication had done its work, it was just a matter of time before the results showed up" or "She is in remission." The Bible clearly tells us that all people are 'spiritually blind' until their eyes are opened by the truth of God's Word, often at that miracle-moment called salvation.

"But even if our gospel is veiled, it is veiled to those who are perishing, whose minds the god of this age has blinded, who do not believe, lest the light of the gospel of the glory of Christ, who is the image of God, should shine on them. For it is the God who commanded light to shine out of darkness, who has shone in our hearts to give the light of the knowledge of the glory of God in the face of Jesus Christ."

People often pray, "Use me, O Lord" ... and then do nothing! You cannot wait to feel faith. Faith is not a feeling. You simply do what should be done when you know that you cannot succeed unless God helps you. The whole Bible is written to break down unbelief, and build up our trust in God.

"Do not be conformed to this world, but be transformed by the renewing of your mind ... Abraham believed God, and it was accounted to him for righteousness. And he was called the friend of God ... forgetting those things which are behind and reaching forward to those things which are ahead, I press toward the goal for the prize of the upward call of God in Christ Jesus."

We talk of big believers with great faith – but some event inspired and encouraged them. They took their opportunity, changed their attitude, and believed. **Faith is a leap into the light, not into the dark.** Jesus never commended people – he commended their faith. Be a Believer!

Down-To-Earth Faith

God has done something about the evil and suffering in our world. Over two thousand years ago, he sent his Son into one of the world's worst trouble spots – Palestine. He grew up to become a carpenter, living in a country occupied by foreign troops.

Surrounded by violence, poverty, and disease, Jesus spent his life bringing the love of God to ordinary people. He healed the sick. He taught people to love those who hated them. He showed people how much God loved them. He turned the minus of their lives into a glorious plus. *"God anointed Jesus of Nazareth with the Holy Spirit and with power, who went about doing good and healing all who were oppressed by the devil, for God was with him ."*

But Jesus also made some powerful enemies. In the end, the politicians fixed it for him. He was arrested, beaten up, and handed over to the occupation troops. They took him to the local killing ground, and put him to death. If there had been TV then, it might have made the evening news. *"And we are witnesses of all things which he did both in the land of the Jews and in Jerusalem, whom they killed by hanging on a tree."*

Some people say that the Christian faith is out of touch with reality. But the life and death of Jesus show that this simply cannot be true. A real Jesus was pinned with real nails to a real piece of wood, and shed real blood. The cross was a terrifying, bloody execution. It was as down-to-earth as you can get. *"Him God raised up on the third day, and showed him openly … and he commanded us to preach to the people, and to testify that it is he who was ordained by God to be judge of the living and the dead."*

Christianity does not turn a blind eye to human suffering. Like the bulletins we see on the news, the crucifixion of Jesus shows us that something has gone terribly wrong with the human race. But unlike those bulletins, the crucifixion also shows us that there is a solution. It tells us that God has done something to change it all! That is his promise to you and to me today.

Today's Scripture
All authority has been given to me in heaven and on earth. Go therefore and make disciples of all the nations, baptizing them in the name of the Father and of the Son and of the Holy Spirit, teaching them to observe all things that I have commanded you; and lo, I am with you always, even to the end of the age. (Matthew 28:18-20)

Daily Power!
A real Jesus was pinned with real nails to a real piece of wood, and shed real blood. He did this all for me!

Mark My Word
Matthew 27 and 28
Acts 10:38-42

The Bible In A Year

Morning
Genesis 44
Mark 14

Evening
Job 10
Romans 14

12

The Secret Of Revival

Today's Scripture
Now, Lord, look on their threats, and grant to Your servants that with all boldness they may speak Your word, by stretching out Your hand to heal, and that signs and wonders may be done through the name of Your holy Servant Jesus.
(Acts 4:29-30)

Daily Power!
O God let your revival come through me.

Mark My Word
Psalm 68:18; 119:50
Habakkuk 3:2
Mark 4:14
John 5:24
Acts 4:29-30
Ephesians 4:7
1 John 3:14

The Bible In A Year

Morning
Genesis 45
Mark 15

Evening
Job 11
Romans 15

The Early church was alive and lively, always in action. That is what passing *"from death to life"* meant for them. They lived in revival times! The secret of true revival is in the Word. *"Your Word has given me life."* People often try to learn what revival is by studying past revivals, special seasons in past centuries. We have chosen to call these events revivals. Then we look at them to see what a revival is. This is a circular process. It is far safer to examine the New Testament.

There is a saying that every revival springs from prayer. Obviously this is assumed, for Christians pray, and therefore they must have prayed before any revival. In actual fact, there is no evidence of anyone praying for revival in the New Testament. The famous prayer, *"O Lord, revive Your work"* was an Old Testament prayer. Nevertheless, God answered, and revived his work. The answer to that prayer was Jesus and Pentecost. When Peter preached in that first Pentecostal meeting, he saw something that had never been seen on earth before. Something happened on that day that neither Elijah, nor Isaiah, nor Jeremiah ever saw – three thousand people repenting, and being saved. Only the revived can pray revival prayers – the dead pray dead prayers. Revival comes through the revived. Are you one of the revived?

To each one is given grace, a free gift … and when that has been done, the Lord plants each one in the church. God gives only the gifted to the church. We are nothing until he does a work in us. But everyone is a gift because everyone has a gift. The parable of the Sower says that *"the sower sows the Word."* He plants in you what he wants planted in the world.

A Witness To The Light

To dispel the darkness, it is no use arguing with it – just switch on the light! Polemic is no substitute for truth and the Holy Spirit. No amount of darkness can put out the light of a single candle.

I noticed an interesting thing in John's gospel. Jesus said that John was the burning and shining lamp. Earlier in John, we read: *"And the light shines in the darkness, and the darkness did not comprehend it. There was a man sent from God, whose name was John. This man came for a witness, to bear witness of the Light, that all through him might believe."*

It struck me that if the light was already shining, why was John needed? When the sun rises, we all know about it, and do not need anybody to testify that it is daylight. The answer is *"He was not that Light, but was sent to bear witness of that Light."* Is a witness necessary? Does that mean that God needs you and me? Yes!

What is God's command to us about being lights to the world? First, he exhorts us to be available light.

> "You are the light of the world. A city that is set on a hill cannot be hidden. Nor do they light a lamp and put it under a basket, but on a lampstand, and it gives light to all who are in the house. Let your light so shine before men, that they may see your good works and glorify your Father in heaven."

Then he encourages us to be sure that our light is good.

> "The lamp of the body is the eye. If therefore your eye is good, your whole body will be full of light. But if your eye is bad, your whole body will be full of darkness. If therefore the light that is in you is darkness, how great is that darkness!"

Let your good light shine today!

Today's Scripture
For it is the God who commanded light to shine out of darkness, who has shone in our hearts to give the light of the knowledge of the glory of God in the face of Jesus Christ (2 Corinthians 4:6).

Daily Power!
I am a single candle burning in the darkness – a light that no man can put out because it is God's light shining through me!

Mark My Word
2 Samuel 22:29
Matthew 5:14-15; 6: 22-23
John 1:1-14; 5:35
2 Corinthians 4:6

The Bible In A Year

Morning
Genesis 46
Mark 16

Evening
Job 12
Romans 16

Light Versus Darkness

What is a witness to light? If you look into the sky on a clear night, the moon is shining. Men have been to the moon, and they know it has no light of its own. Also, space around the moon is in pitch-blackness. We all know, of course, that the moon only reflects the light that comes from the sun. If the sunlight passes through space to reach the moon, why is all the sky dark around the moon?

The answer is, as the famous fictional detective Sherlock Holmes, would say, "Elementary, my dear Watson!" Light is invisible. You only know light is there at all when it strikes an object.

Space is completely empty. There is nothing there to catch the light from the sun, until it reaches the moon. Actually, space is full of light but it looks dark. This universe is full of God. He is *"the Father of lights"*, and all light comes from him. But millions walk in profound darkness. How can that be? How can people walk in spiritual darkness when the whole universe is steeped in the light of God?

> "The lamp of the body is the eye. If therefore your eye is good, your whole body will be full of light. But if your eye is bad, your whole body will be full of darkness. If therefore the light that is in you is darkness, how great is that darkness!"

Jesus commanded us: *"Let your light so shine before men, that they may see your good works and glorify your Father in heaven."* Later, Paul the apostle reminded us: *"But we all, with unveiled face, beholding as in a mirror the glory of the Lord, are being transformed into the same image from glory to glory, just as by the Spirit of the Lord."* Let us choose to be reflectors of God's light in a world of darkness.

Today's Scripture
Then Jesus spoke to them again, saying, I am the light of the world. He who follows me shall not walk in darkness, but have the light of life. (John 8:12)

Daily Power!
Without Christ in my life, I have no light. But because he infuses me with his light, not only do I reflect his light, but I can be a source of light and life in the darkened world around me.

Guide Study
Matthew 5:16; 6: 22-23
John 5:19; 8:12
James 1:17

The Bible In A Year

Morning
Genesis 47
Luke 1:1-38

Evening
Job 13
1 Corinthians 1

Who Is The Holy Spirit?

As much as we may wish for it, the Lord does not send publicity by heavenly mail to tell us who he is! The works performed by his Holy Spirit are seen on earth. The Holy Spirit is a Person – he is God in action. Creation came as *"the Spirit of God was hovering over the face of the waters."*

When God chose his servants, the power of the Holy Spirit rested upon them. *"See, the Lord has called by name Bezalel … and he has filled him with the Spirit of God … and he has put in his heart the ability to teach. And again "The Lord raised up a deliverer for the children of Israel … the Spirit of the Lord came upon Othniel, and he judged Israel."*

After these judges, the prophet Samuel guided an entire nation for a lifetime. How? *"Holy men of God spoke as they were moved by the Holy Spirit."* The prophet Micah testified, *"but truly I am full of power by the Spirit of the Lord."*

These are portraits of the Holy Spirit. This is that Spirit whom Christ promised, the Spirit of wisdom and knowledge, creative, empowering, healing – the Spirit of strength, confidence, and virtue. Our heavenly Father sends the Holy Spirit to be with us. He is the One who never leaves us. *"And I will pray the Father, and he will give you another Helper, that he may abide with you forever – the Spirit of truth, whom the world cannot receive, because it neither sees him nor knows him; but you know him, for he dwells with you and will be in you. I will not leave you orphans; I will come to you."*

God's power is not a kind of super-charge for people already gifted with great personality and drive, but is for those who need it, the weak, and the unknown. It is great to have that dynamic working in your life!

Today's Scripture

He gives power to the weak, and to those who have no might he increases strength.
(Isaiah 40:29)

Daily Power!

I am a disciple of the Lord Jesus Christ, filled with joy and with the Holy Spirit.

Mark My Word

Genesis 1:2
Exodus 35:31-32, 34
Judges 3:9-10
Isaiah 40:29
Micah 3:8
John 14:16-18
2 Peter 1:21

The Bible In A Year

Morning

Genesis 48
Luke 1:39-80

Evening

Job 14
1 Corinthians 2

16

Christ's Secret Weapon

Today's Scripture
Now when they saw the boldness of Peter and John, and perceived that they were uneducated and untrained men, they marveled. And they realized that they had been with Jesus. (Acts 4:13)

Daily Power!
Not by might nor by power, but by my Spirit, says the Lord of hosts.

Mark My Word
Zechariah 4:6
Acts 2:14-21; 4:1-31; 17:1-34
1 Corinthians 4:1-21

The Bible In A Year

Morning
Genesis 49
Luke 2

Evening
Job 15
1 Corinthians 3

The world two thousand years ago was a wild place. It was a place of bloodshed, uncontrolled passions, and fanatical hatreds. Its chief pleasures were immorality, idolatry, indulgence, and – worst of all – cruelty. The crowds considered it a wonderful day's outing to listen to the shrieks of tortured and dying people. The disciples had to take the gospel to that world ... and the gospel centered on the cruelty suffered by Jesus. It was also a place of much learning. The influences of the great Greek thinkers were strong, and new ideas were eagerly sought. The disciples offered no radical new ideas ... only the story of a crucified Messiah. Peter, James, John, Simon, and Thomas were unsophisticated and untutored – they even spoke with a Galilean accent! They were the very opposite of city elegance. What hopes had Christianity, left in the hands of a few rough-handed, unscholarly fishermen, who were jealous of one another and full of doubts? So, thinking of these men and their world, the gospel looked doomed to fail from the start. Twelve local men, who had never traveled beyond Israel before, were to go into the whole of the Roman Empire to conquer its conquering armies, to shake the emperor on his throne, and to convert the wild tribes on its borders.

> "But Peter, standing up with the eleven, raised his voice and said to them, 'Men of Judea and all who dwell in Jerusalem, let this be known to you, and heed my words. For these are not drunk, as you suppose, but this is what was spoken by the prophet Joel: And it shall come to pass in the last days, says God, that I will pour out my Spirit on all flesh ... and it shall come to pass that whoever calls on the name of the Lord shall be saved.'"

No doubt Jesus did anticipate those twelve becoming a world force, but he trusted twelve men – sons of toil, some of them almost peasants – to provide the vital first link between himself and the mighty church to come. Christ's secret was the empowerment by the Holy Spirit on the day of Pentecost. Well, what are you afraid of? You are already empowered by the Holy Spirit!

Unusual Miracle Conditions

In the miracle story from Matthew 14, it was Christ himself who put the disciples where they were. He made the disciples get into the boat, and go on ahead of him to the other side.

> "Immediately Jesus made his disciples get into the boat and go before him to the other side, while he sent the multitudes away. And when he had sent the multitudes away, he went up on the mountain by himself to pray. Now when evening came, he was alone there. But the boat was now in the middle of the sea, tossed by the waves, for the wind was contrary."

The boat was buffeted by the waves because the wind was against it. So troubles may arise when we are (or even because we are) doing God's explicit will; but we must give God time and let him work all things together for good. That is true for you and me.

Jesus, in fact, was in charge. He had seen them struggling out on the Sea of Galilee while he was up on the hillside. Do not worry: the Lord has good eyesight! God does not guarantee us permanently calm seas or prosperous voyages. Even Paul was shipwrecked three times. The disciples were fighting the elements in one of those lumbering boats of their day, for the very reason that that was where God wanted them! Many people feel disillusioned about this very thing. They do what is right yet suffer for it. But we need not worry. The trouble that comes when God puts us where he wants us is a miracle in the making! The stormy winds of Galilee were the first component of a wonder for Peter and his companions.

Why do we think miracles should only occur in optimal conditions, such as a vibrant Christian church service? We usually need a miracle when we are in the direst of problems! Never limit God as to when he can touch your life with his miracle power!

Today's Scripture
Therefore, having been justified by faith, we have peace with God through our Lord Jesus Christ, through whom also we have access by faith into this grace in which we stand, and rejoice in hope of the glory of God.
(Romans 5:1,2)

Daily Power!
Jesus is in charge of my life, and he is with me always.

Mark My Word
Matthew 14:22-36
Mark 6:45-52
Romans 5:1-4

The Bible In A Year

Morning
Genesis 50
Luke 3

Evening
Job 16, 17
1 Corinthians 4

We All Need Miracles

Today's Scripture
And we know that all
things work together
for good to those who
love God, to those
who are the called
according to his
purpose.
(Romans 8:28)

Daily Power!
I know that troubles
may arise, even when
I am doing God's will,
but I rely on him to
work things together
for his glory and my
good.

Mark My Word
Job 5:7
Psalm 91:14-16
Mark 6:47-48
Romans 8:28

The Bible In A Year

Morning
Exodus 1
Luke 4

Evening
Job 18
1 Corinthians 5

Difficulties do not always indicate we are doing God's will. Sometimes they show us we are doing our own will. We land ourselves with problems. For that matter, "*Man is born to trouble, as the sparks fly upward.*" This is natural in our fallen world. Also, there is a devil.

Whether a situation is our fault or not, we all need a miracle at one time or other. Difficulties arise for all of us, perhaps in health, occupation, marriage, family, or some other area of our lives. Some people find their sins and failures rattling around behind them, like the skeletons getting out of the closet! Like the disciples in their boat, we can sit amid waves of worry, conjuring up haunting specters. The sudden appearance of Jesus was also part of the disciples' fears! They needed a miracle, and nothing less would do!

God wants his children to live within the guidelines of his Book, and then we would never need miracles to help us out of our problems. But, because our human nature is so sin-ridden, our own stubborn pride is so prevalent, and our enemy is doing his utmost to sabotage us, our need for supernatural intervention is strong. And because Christ came to redeem us, which includes access to his divine power, we have a right to miracles!

> "Because he has set his love upon me, therefore I will deliver him; I will set him on high, because he has known my name. He shall call upon me, and I will answer him; I will be with him in trouble; I will deliver him and honor him. With long life I will satisfy him, and show him my salvation."

Thank God that he did not intend us to live our lives without miracles. his original plan was that, even after you have done your best, you would still be dependent upon him to meet your needs.

Longing For God

From the beginning of human existence, there has been a natural longing for God to manifest himself in unshadowed reality. The universal cry is for God to convince the world that he is God.

> "Why do the nations rage, and the people plot a vain thing? The kings of the earth set themselves, and the rulers take counsel together ... He who sits in the heavens shall laugh; The Lord shall hold them in derision. Then he shall speak to them in his wrath, and distress them in his deep displeasure ... Now therefore, be wise, O kings; be instructed, you judges of the earth. Serve the LORD with fear, and rejoice with trembling. Kiss the Son, lest he be angry, and you perish in the way, when his wrath is kindled but a little. Blessed are all those who put their trust in him."

Even the ungodly demand hard evidence of God, and scoff, "He is not apparent." The wicked man says to himself *"God has forgotten; he hides his face; he will never see."* A similar situation troubled the Psalmist himself, who asked, *"Why do you stand afar off, O LORD? Why do you hide in times of trouble?"* Indeed, the wish for God to prove himself is implicit in many Psalms, and the frequent plea is: *"Let God arise, let his enemies be scattered!"*

The ways in which it was hoped that God might reveal himself were closely linked to the culture and outlook at the time. Israel, a small, beleaguered nation, visualized God as a mighty warrior coming to champion their cause. Even in Christian times, thoughts of how God might awe the world have varied considerably. So too have ideas about what Christians should do to bring it about.

Renewal has come to the church at various times throughout the Christian era, but it has taken different forms, some of which have appeared strange. It has been said that the history of America is the history of religious revivals. However, God was not simply inactive for seventeen hundred years, until the Evangelicals came along. Jesus said, *"I will build my church,"* and despite everything that has taken place since he made that statement, he has steadily continued to do just that. Be Christ's church today!

Today's Scripture
The fool has said in his heart, "There is no God." Oh, that the salvation of Israel would come out of Zion! When the Lord brings back the captivity of his people. (Psalm 14:1, 7)

Daily Power!
I am a part of God's church-building, kingdom-populating army.
Our motto is: heaven full – hell empty!

Mark My Word
Psalm 2:1-12; 10:1-18; 14:1-7; 68:1
Matthew 16:18

The Bible In A Year

Morning
Exodus 2
Luke 5

Evening
Job 19
1 Corinthians 6

The King And His Kingdom

Today's Scripture
Humble yourselves in
the sight of the Lord,
and he will lift you up.
(James 4:10)

Daily Power!
Humility and the fear
of the Lord are the
true riches of life.

Mark My Word
Proverbs 22:4
Mark 10:31
Acts 17:16
James 4:1-10

The Bible In A Year

Morning
Exodus 3
Luke 6

Evening
Job 20
1 Corinthians 7

We hear about radical politicians, but there has never been one yet who reversed the ways of the world with its materialism and godlessness. Yet when Paul and Silas went to Thessalonica, the unbelieving Jews said, *"These who have turned the world upside down have come here too."* Unbelief had damaged their eyesight. But for their distorted vision, they would have seen that the world was already upside down, long before the arrival of Paul and Silas. But that is why they had come – to put it the right way up!

> "Where do wars and fights come from among you? Do they not come from your desires for pleasure that war in your members? Do you not know that friendship with the world is enmity with God? Whoever therefore wants to be a friend of the world makes himself an enemy of God."

We are so used to the world despite the fact that friendship with the world is enmity with God. The world's standards are the opposite of everything God wants. Money is priority number one. People with money are at the top, the privileged elite. The rest may grovel in the dust. Big business crushes ordinary people. Achieve greatness by standing on everybody else's shoulders, and you will be honored and envied. The trials of ordinary people do not touch the world's greats.

But the kingdom of God reverses these world principles and priorities. Jesus said *"Many who are first will be last, and the last first."* The Lord puts the people last whom the world puts first. First in the kingdom of Christ are the poor in spirit, not those who are laughing all the way to the bank with fat profits. Then come those who mourn, not those with a permanent (probably fake) grin on their faces. Next on the list of blessed are the meek, not those who walk all over others to get to the front. The humble shall upstage the proud. Blessed are those who hunger and thirst for righteousness, not those who change their politics to win votes. Blessed are the merciful, not the vengeful, or the retaliators. Blessed are the pure in heart, not the devious. Then follow the peacemakers, not the war makers; and the persecuted, not the compromisers. Let your life be an instrument to usher in the kingdom of God.

Using Your Parachute

Two skydivers jump from a plane at 15,000 feet. Both are wearing parachutes. One of them folds his arms, ignores the ripcord, and says to himself' "I am perfectly safe because of my parachute." He is still saying these words as he hits the ground at over a hundred miles per hour, smashing into a million pieces. The other skydiver knows that he will be safe only if he does something. He pulls the ripcord and lands safely.

You and I may know about the Christian faith. You and I may respect Jesus, and agree that what he did on the cross is the answer to our deepest needs. But until you and I actually ask for his help, and commit our lives to him, it is like falling with a closed parachute. We need to take urgent action. We need to pull the ripcord while there is still time!

The ripcord is this: *"Believe on the Lord Jesus, and you will be saved."* There is nothing else you or I can do. We cannot save ourselves. We can only throw ourselves on what Jesus achieved for us on the cross. He has done everything that we need. *"Nor is there salvation in any other, for there is no other name under heaven given among men by which we must be saved."*

How do we know this is true? We can stake our lives on the promises given to us in the Bible, and proved in real life by hundreds of millions of Christians:

> "The Lord upholds all those who fall. Now to (Jesus) who is able to keep you from stumbling, and to present you faultless before the presence of his glory with exceeding joy, he is also able to save to the uttermost those who come to God through him, since he always lives to make intercession for them."

Although your life may sometimes feel like it is spinning out of control, you can draw on the assurance that the Holy Spirit is never farther away than your next prayer.

Today's Scripture
Now to him who is able to keep you from stumbling, and to present you faultless before the presence of his glory with exceeding joy, to God our Savior, who alone is wise, be glory and majesty, dominion and power, both now and forever. Amen. (Jude 24-25)

Daily Power!
I, the LORD your God, will hold your right hand, saying to you, "Fear not, I will help you."

Mark My Word
Psalm 145:14
Isaiah 41.13
Acts 4:12; 16:31
Hebrews 7:25
Jude 24-25

The Bible In A Year

Morning
Exodus 4
Luke 7

Evening
Job 21
1 Corinthians 8

22

Riches Of Assurance

Many people want assurance of salvation to register in their feelings. This is a common mistake, which often has a disastrous outcome. God never said that emotions would be the test of salvation. Assurance is not dependent on psyche, but on his eternal Word. Although the human soul is a masterpiece of creation, it was made to fluctuate with experience, registering ups and downs, being glad, or being sad, according to the state of the mind, even after salvation. Saved people do not have ever-smiling faces, like plastic masks. They have entered God's original plan for their lives, and have no need to consult their emotions to determine whether they are saved or not.

Salvation is embedded in the rock of the eternal Word. Jesus said: *"Heaven and earth will pass away, but my words will by no means pass away."* This is the *"cleft of the rock"* to which we must flee whenever Satan attacks us with doubts. We are saved because the Word of God says that we are saved. Whatever I feel, my conviction remains unshakable.

The first Christians were not uncertain. Scripture says that they were to *"abound in hope,"* having *"abundance of joy"* and *"abundance of grace."* To abound means to have enough with some to spare; a surplus, like the twelve baskets of food left over after Jesus fed the five thousand. Assurance of salvation is not over-confidence, but a deep, settled peace, which fills the soul at those moments when the devil whispers his doubts.

Paul described Christians in Colosse as having *"all riches of the full assurance."* Riches of assurance! That word "riches" in the original Greek is "ploutos" the root of the word "plutocrat," which means somebody who reigns by his wealth. I do not mind being a spiritual plutocrat, being wealthy in confidence in God. The letter to the Hebrews speaks of *"full assurance"* and in Thessalonica they had *"much assurance,"* literally, much fullness. That is the true fullness, being rich in faith towards God.

The Power Comes With The Task

We need God-power and God needs manpower. The usual ratio is ninety nine percent God-power to one percent manpower. When Joshua stood on the borders of a whole land to be conquered, God said, "*I will be with you.*" When the task is assigned the means to complete it are also given. The ability, the wisdom, and the power of God are made freely available.

We can only do what we have power to do. If God asks us to do more than is in our power, he makes up for the deficiency! We do what we can, and God does what we cannot. Whatever we do on this planet is limited by the power available. In past centuries, power was only physical strength, muscle power. They built the pyramids, dug the great canals of Suez and Panama, and cut roads through the mountains – all by brawn. The Seven Wonders of the ancient world are examples of brawn power. Now we have a thousand modern wonders brought into being by new power sources, not brute strength. Nothing is impossible when the right kind of power is operating. Jesus said *"You shall receive power when the Holy Spirit has come upon you; and you shall be witnesses to me … to the end of the earth."* The church has too often trusted scholarship, erudition, genius, logic, and philosophy. But Paul said *"God has chosen the foolish things."* If we are to evangelize the world by cerebral methods, we will never do it. That has been tried for centuries. But real church growth has been brought about by the simple message of the gospel touching people from all walks of life.

God promises that you will never be given too much to bear, and that you will not be asked to do more than you are capable of doing with his help. Not only in your speech – *"praying … that utterance may be given to me, that I may open my mouth boldly to make known the mystery of the gospel"* – but also in your actions. Therefore, be a doer today in every way that he leads you!

Today's Scripture
We are fools for Christ's sake, but you are wise in Christ! We are weak, but you are strong! You are distinguished, but we are dishonored.
(1 Corinthians 4:10)

Daily Power!
O Lord, open my lips, and my mouth shall show forth Your praise.

Mark My Word
Joshua 1:5
Psalm 51:15
Acts 1:8
1 Corinthians 1:27
Ephesians 6:18-20

The Bible In A Year

Morning
Exodus 6
Luke 9

Evening
Job 23
1 Corinthians 10

24

The Promise Of Power

Today's Scripture
Rejoice because your
names are written in
heaven.
(Luke 10:21)

Daily Power!
Thank you for giving
me the gift of Your
Holy Spirit as my
continual source of
power!

Mark My Word
Matthew 10:1, 5-8, 40
Luke 9:2; 10:2-3,
18-19

The Bible In A Year

Morning
Exodus 7
Luke 10

Evening
Job 24
1 Corinthians 11

In Matthew 10 and Luke 9, we have the first limited commissioning of the twelve disciples for a pilot mission, which took place while Jesus was still on earth. It was a miniature project to exemplify the full-scale operation that was to follow after the empowering of Pentecost, and it explains to us what the power of Pentecost was going to be.

"And when he had called his twelve disciples to him, he gave them power over unclean spirits, to cast them out, and to heal all kinds of sickness and all kinds of disease … These twelve Jesus sent out and commanded them, saying: 'Do not go into the way of the Gentiles, and do not enter a city of the Samaritans. But go rather to the lost sheep of the house of Israel. And as you go, preach, saying, 'The kingdom of heaven is at hand.' Heal the sick, cleanse the lepers, raise the dead, cast out demons. Freely you have received, freely give … He who receives you receives me, and he who receives me receives him who sent me.'"

Luke chapter 9 gives a similar account of this first commissioning. *"He sent them to preach the kingdom of God, and to heal the sick."* Luke chapter 10 recounts the commissioning of seventy-two others: *"Then he said to them, 'The harvest truly is great, but the laborers are few; therefore pray the Lord of the harvest to send out laborers into his harvest. Go your way; behold, I send you out as lambs among wolves.'"* Then the Word reports: *"Then the seventy returned with joy, saying, 'Lord, even the demons are subject to us in your name.' And he said to them … 'Behold, I give you the authority to trample on serpents and scorpions, and over all the power of the enemy, and nothing shall by any means hurt you. Nevertheless do not rejoice in this, that the spirits are subject to you, but rather rejoice because your names are written in heaven.'"*

So long as Jesus was there with them, they had power … but when he left, they had another Helper and power source: the Holy Spirit. He is your same power source today!

The Acts Of The King

If Christ Jesus did no more than continue doing what he did when he first appeared on earth, what a happier world it would be! One man who personally knew Jesus said that *"He went about doing good, and healing all who were oppressed of the devil, for God was with him."* This meant that Jesus did things nobody else ever did. To multitudes, his very presence brought certainty of forgiveness and healing. He lifted the fallen, delivered the devil-possessed, and championed the oppressed. his graciousness and understanding overwhelmed people. his words created astonishment.

Crowds thronged him, and wanted to put him on the throne. Instead, he let his enemies put him on the cross. He came as a Savior, not as a Caesar. He was the redeemer, not a rebel leader. He lived the most extraordinary life, an inspiration to other good lives. His enemies took it as the end when he expired on the cross. It was, in fact, the beginning! They were dealing with somebody, the likes of whom nobody had ever encountered before. He conquered death; rose from the tomb robed in immortality, ascended to God, and left the promise that every eye would see him again.

At the onset of his ministry, he told everyone what he was going to do:

> "And he was handed the book of the prophet Isaiah. And when he had opened the book, he found the place where it was written: "The Spirit of the LORD is upon me, because he has anointed me to preach the gospel to the poor; he has sent me to heal the brokenhearted, to proclaim liberty to the captives and recovery of sight to the blind, to set at liberty those who are oppressed; to proclaim the acceptable year of the LORD." ... And he began to say to them, "Today this Scripture is fulfilled in your hearing." So all bore witness to him, and marveled at the gracious words, which proceeded out of his mouth."

He fulfilled every prophecy, every promise. When later he promised that he would return for his own, he will fulfill that promise too. This is our King Jesus!

Today's Scripture
Jesus went about all Galilee, teaching in their synagogues, preaching the gospel of the kingdom, and healing all kinds of sickness and all kinds of disease among the people. Then his fame went throughout all Syria; and they brought to him all sick people ... and he healed them.
(Matthew 4:23-24)

Daily Power!
Because Christ Jesus lives in me, I can do the same things, which he did!

Mark My Word
Isaiah 61:1-2
Matthew 4:23-24
Luke 4:17-22
Acts 10:34-48

The Bible In A Year

Morning
Exodus 8
Luke 11

Evening
Job 25, 26
1 Corinthians 12

26

Today's Scripture
Jesus Christ is the same, yesterday, today and forever.
(Hebrews 13:8)

Daily Power!
I rejoice in my Lord and Savior Jesus Christ. He is as alive today as he was in Bible days, and he is the Lord who heals me.

Mark My Word
Exodus 15:26
Malachi 3:6; 4:2
Hebrews 13:8

The Bible In A Year

Morning
Exodus 9
Luke 12

Evening
Job 27
1 Corinthians 13

We read, *"Jesus Christ the same yesterday, today and forever."* Jesus is alive, just as ready to heal now as he ever was. He is not like the moon, which has phases, sometimes showing a darkened portion. He is *"the Sun of Righteousness … with healing in his wings."* What Jesus was, he is, and will be, *"for I am the Lord, I do not change."*

Miracles are part and parcel of the gospel of Jesus Christ, not something added on as an afterthought. He said that he had come *"to preach the gospel to the poor."* He did, and he was very popular among the poor people of his day (and largely unpopular with the wealthy, ruling class). He said that he had come *"to proclaim liberty to the captives."* He did, releasing bonds of sickness and even death. He said that he had come *"to give sight to the blind."* He did, many times, both in physical healings, and in opening spiritual eyes to God's truths. He said that he had come *"to set at liberty those who are oppressed."* He did that also, delivering demon-possessed people.

All the things that he said he would do, from miracle healings to life-changing teaching, he did. From start to finish, Christianity is supernatural, beginning as resurrection life and power. Healings demonstrate the essential truths of Christianity, and show us Jesus as he really is. If we look back, we see that what Jesus was then, he is now.

If we look forward, we see that he will be what he was. He is not becoming great – he **is** great! He is now at the height of his greatness. He always was, and always will be, the healer and the Savior. Jesus Christ is our great redeemer!

The Banner Of God

Roman soldiers used ensigns for signaling in battle, occasionally perfuming them with oils, and decorating them with flowers. Jews considered these ensigns to be spiritually offensive. Nowadays, we do not regard ceremonial objects with the same appreciation or revulsion as did the Romans or Jews of centuries gone by, but we can learn a lot by understanding how people revered banners in Bible times: "*You have given a banner to those who fear you, that it may be displayed because of the truth.*"

During the exile of the Hebrews in Egypt, they had no banner. They were unknown, unorganized, and without distinction. As slaves, they had no identification, no flags, and no rights. When the tribes finally escaped, they were as refugees, united only in huddled fear – a mixed rabble. Only Moses and Aaron kept them together, and even then, some of them probably suspected them of being religious fanatics. The tribal families clung to each other for mutual support. The first few days were critical. Then murderous bands of Amalekite plunderers began to harass their flanks, picking off stragglers and stripping them of their meager belongings. Joshua had to muster what men and arms he could. It was a pitiful show, since they did not have so much as a rag raised on a pole to rally them. However, Moses had his own bare hands to raise to the God of heaven … and the Amalekites were routed. "*And Moses built an altar and called its name, The-LORD-Is-My-Banner; for he said, 'Because the LORD has sworn: the LORD will have war with Amalek from generation to generation.'*"

God gave Israel a name and nationhood, but no national symbol. Moses surveyed Joshua's Israelite force – primitive but victorious, undistinguished by a single fluttering pennant or token, an army without pageantry – and said, "Yahweh Nissi – the Lord is my banner." He replaced heraldry by reality. Later, Israelite tribes each adopted its own standard. When Joshua welded together Israel's first real army on Canaan's soil, a formidable figure confronted him, whom Joshua attempted to challenge. The response was, "*as Commander of the army of the LORD I have now come.*" That heavenly Commander-in-Chief needed no ensign and never lost a battle! And he is your Chief today!

Today's Scripture
Then all this assembly shall know that the LORD does not save with sword and spear; for the battle is the LORD'S, and he will give you into our hands.
(1 Samuel 17:47)

Daily Power!
His banner over me is love.

Mark My Word
Exodus 17:15-16;
Joshua 5:14;
Psalm 60:4

The Bible In A Year

Morning
Exodus 10
Luke 13

Evening
Job 28
1 Corinthians 14

28

The True Banner

Today's Scripture
And I, if I am lifted up
from the earth, will
draw all peoples
to myself.
(John 12:32)

Daily Power!
The cross of Jesus
Christ is my enduring
symbol of hope,
salvation, and
healing.

Mark My Word
Numbers 21:8-9;
Isaiah 62:10-11;
John 3:14-15; 12:32;
Galatians 3:1

The Bible In A Year

Morning
Exodus 11 to 12:21
Luke 14

Evening
Job 29
1 Corinthians 15

If ever Israel can be said to have displayed a national symbol, it is in the events described in Numbers 21: *"Then the LORD said to Moses, 'Make a fiery serpent, and set it on a pole; and it shall be that everyone who is bitten, when he looks at it, shall live.' So Moses made a bronze serpent, and put it on a pole."* It was a strange standard indeed. But in that lost wilderness, God's own true banner was first displayed. Today, it is the greatest symbol in the world – the cross. The link is made clear in the New Testament: *"And as Moses lifted up the serpent in the wilderness, even so must the Son of Man be lifted up."* Isaiah said, *"Lift up a banner for the peoples!"* … *"Say to the daughter of Zion, 'Surely your salvation is coming.'"*

> "So Moses made a bronze serpent, and put it on a pole; and so it was, if a serpent had bitten anyone, when he looked at the bronze serpent, he lived … And as Moses lifted up the serpent in the wilderness, even so must the Son of man be lifted up; that whosoever believes in him should not perish, but have eternal life."

Paul seems to have been thinking in such terms when he wrote, *"Before whose eyes Jesus Christ was clearly portrayed among you as crucified."* He uses a word based on the Greek: "grapho" – "to write" or "to inscribe." It has been translated "to placard." The cross of Christ is the sign writing of Almighty God on the billboards of history. Our banner is no mere arbitrary artistic design, but the Lord himself, visible to all, riveted to that wooden "pole," exhibiting forever his unrestrained love, the living banner of a dying Savior. We set him forth, the crucified One and through him we conquer. Today, go and conquer for Christ!

To Each Generation

Christ's Great Commission is not a scrap of paper, blown to our feet from centuries ago. It is Jesus, standing in the midst of his church forever, saying, *"Go ... lo, I am with you."* Suppose Jesus said that to you personally – would you take more notice of it? Just imagine you had a vision of the Lord in your church, like John experienced on Patmos ... or Jesus spoke to everybody, saying, *"Go into all the world and preach the gospel to every creature ... and these sings will follow those who believe"* – what would you do? Would you continue living with a business-as-usual attitude? Or would you press on more urgently to witness for Christ?

If anyone wonders whether the Great Commission is relevant today, they may as well ask if plowing and harvesting are relevant ... or if getting out of bed is! Relevant is not the word. The task is urgent. It is supposed to be our existence! The name Christian developed because it easily identified believers – they were the people who always talked about Christ. The Christian's business is not busyness, but witness. Witnessing is the commerce of the people of the kingdom of God.

The written commands of Christ in Scripture are just as immediate as if he had spoken to us personally in a vision. The Great Commission is our authorization, and our work in this task is not optional. The Lord does not ask, "Would you mind helping me? I would like to invite you." He says: *"You did not choose me, but I chose you and appointed you that you should go and bear fruit, and that your fruit should remain."* Jesus was not talking about the call to salvation, but rather of the call to service. We do not serve at our discretion. The Great Commission is like a draft call-up, not a suggestion for our consideration. We are not to go for the sake of going, but for the sake of being sent by Jesus. In fact, Christ's command is much more than that – Jesus turns us into witnesses. He changes our nature by his Spirit within us. He did not say, "Go witness." He said, **"Be witnesses!"** It was a creative word. He chose you and then made you a light bearer.

Today's Scripture
If then your whole body is full of light, having no part dark, the whole body will be full of light, as when the bright shining of a lamp gives you light. (Luke 11:36)

Daily Power!
The Great Commission is not a suggestion for our consideration; it is our authorization for action.

Mark My Word
Matthew 28:16-20;
Mark 16:15-17;
Luke 11:36;
John 15:16

The Bible In A Year

Meditate on the following:

Romans 1:16 For I am not ashamed of the gospel of Christ: for it is the power of God to salvation for everyone who believes.

You must be plugged in
before you can be switched on!

Jesus does not choose us because of what we are;
but because of what he makes of us.

Why does God use one minister more than another?
When you have two stoves,
one hot and the other cold –
which one will you use to make a cup of tea?

Sin In The 21st Century

When looking for a cure for sin, we need to understand the disease. How does sin work in our world?

> "Therefore, just as through one man sin entered the world, and death through sin, and thus death spread to all men, because all sinned … Nevertheless death reigned from Adam to Moses, even over those who had not sinned according to the likeness of the transgression of Adam, who is a type of he who was to come. For if by the one man's offense many died, much more the grace of God and the gift by the grace of the one Man, Jesus Christ, abounded to many."

Towards the end of the 19th century, humanists believed that mankind had finally come of age. They said we were too mature to make war, and that scientific progress would guarantee a wonderful, peaceful future for the human race. At heart, human beings were essentially good. We had evolved into higher beings – emerging from the jungle by an evolutionary law that guarantees "the survival of the fittest."

However, this sort of optimism and faith in human progress has suffered a number of severe setbacks. In 1867, the Swedish chemist, Alfred Nobel, invented a new high explosive that he named "dynamite." He was convinced that dynamite had made war too horrible ever to happen again – but he quickly discovered that there was no shortage of buyers for his new explosive. He went on to make a vast fortune from his invention. At the end of his life, he left the profits to fund the five Nobel Prizes. These include the Nobel Peace Prize – paid for by the sale of high explosives! Just as the Bible says, *"And the way of peace they have not known."*

Man with all his ingenuity, cannot **make** peace, cannot **find** peace, cannot **know** peace … apart from that *"perfect peace"* which only comes from God through Christ Jesus: *"You will keep him in perfect peace whose mind is stayed on you because he trusts in you."* Let the peace of Christ envelope you today.

Today's Scripture
Peace I leave with you, My peace I give to you; not as the world gives do I give to you. Let not your heart be troubled, neither let it be afraid. (John 14:27)

Daily Power!
My heart rejoices in these words: And the Word became flesh and dwelt among us, and we beheld his glory, the glory as of the only begotten of the Father, full of grace and truth. (John 1:14)

Mark My Word
Isaiah 26:3
John 1:14-17; 14:27;
Romans 3:17; 5:12-14

The Bible In A Year

Morning
Exodus 12:22
Luke 15

Evening
Job 30
1 Corinthians 16

2

World-Wide Sin

Today's Scripture
Wash me and I shall
be whiter than snow.
(Psalm 51:7)

Daily Power!
Exchanging my sinful
nature for the purity
of Jesus Christ is the
best decision I will
ever make.

Mark My Word
Psalm 51:1-19
Isaiah 19:1-4
Matthew 24:6-7

The Bible In A Year

Morning
Exodus 13
Luke 16

Evening
Job 31
2 Corinthians 1

The First World War shattered the optimism of many people about human progress, but some tried to cling on by calling it "the war to end all wars." However, the 20th century went on to become the most murderous in history. Adolf Hitler even used the "law of the survival of the fittest" as a justification for the Holocaust – slaughtering those he considered unfit to survive.

> "I will set Egyptians against Egyptians, everyone will fight against his brother, and everyone against his neighbor, city against city, kingdom against kingdom. The spirit of Egypt will fail in its midst, I will destroy their counsel."

The genocides and wars caused by people such as Hitler, Stalin and Pol Pot have killed off any optimism about human goodness or the future of the human race. And as optimism has shrivelled up, it has left our culture with nothing to believe in.

> "And you will hear of wars and rumors of wars … For nation will rise against nation, and kingdom against kingdom. And there will be famines, pestilences, and earthquakes in various places."

This is just a glimpse of how sin has done its devastating work in the world during the 20th century. But how does it affect us at the personal level? We must not only consider world-wide sin. We must look into our own individual hearts, to see where sin has eroded basic human goodness. We must root out sin, be washed clean and fresh, and have something good to contribute to our world!

Turning your life over to Jesus Christ – exchanging your sinful nature for his purity – is the best decision you can ever make. Now walk in the fullness of that decision today!

The World Depends On Us

People cannot see the light of invisible things until somebody else catches it and reflects it. The sun's rays would not be seen on earth until they radiate the molecules of the atmosphere, the dust and moisture. The sun fills millions of miles with light … but there is no trace of it until it is reflected. The moon sails in invisible sunlight, and passes on enough light for us to find our way.

The apostle Paul talked about *"the King eternal, immortal, invisible."* The light of God is constant, brilliant. It is never intermittent. But who sees it? People walk in darkness. The stark fact is that the only light they will ever see is reflected light. Just as John was *"a burning and shining lamp,"* a witness to the Light – so are believers. We are commanded to *"walk in the Light,"* for if we don't, there will be no light. The world depends upon light reflectors – that is you and me! If our gospel is hidden, it is hidden to those who are lost.

The Psalmist knew what it meant to "walk in the Light": *"For you have delivered my soul from death. Have you not kept my feet from falling, that I may walk before God in the light of the living?"* Jesus encouraged his disciples to persevere in "walking in the light": *"A little while longer the light is with you. Walk while you have the light, lest darkness overtake you; he who walks in darkness does not know where he is going. While you have the light, believe in the light, that you may become sons of light."* Walking in the light is **active** – waiting on God is passive. To wait on God for his light to shine on us is an Old Testament concept. The last ones who "waited" were the one hundred and twenty in the Upper Room. Now God waits on us. Green means "Go"! When the light turns green, you do not need a permit from the "Secretarial Department of Traffic and Transportation" – you just "Go"! Remember this command: *"But be doers of the Word, and not hearers only, deceiving yourselves."*

Today's Scripture

The Lord is not slack concerning his promise, as some count slackness, but is longsuffering toward us, not willing that any should perish but that all should come to repentance. (2 Peter 3:9)

Daily Power!

Lord, make me like John the Baptist – to be a constant, burning lamp, a shining witness to those who walk in darkness.

Mark My Word

Psalm 56:13
John 12:35-36
2 Corinthians 4:3-6
1 Timothy 1:7
James 1:22
2 Peter 3:9
1 John 1:7

The Bible In A Year

Morning

Exodus 14
Luke 17

Evening

Job 32
2 Corinthians 2

4

Ceaseless Light

Today's Scripture
In him was life, and the life was the light of men.
(John 1:4)

Daily Power!
I choose to have an open face to the world, so that people may see the glory of God in me.

Mark My Word
Exodus 34:35
Malachi 4:2
John 1:1-4
2 Corinthians 3:13
James 1:17

The Bible In A Year

Morning
Exodus 15
Luke 18

Evening
Job 33
2 Corinthians 3

In Exodus and 2 Corinthians, we learned that the face of Moses shone with the glory of God, but he veiled his face. The reason that he veiled it was not humility (humble as he was) – it was because the glory would fade, and he knew it would be a bad thing if the superstitious people of Israel saw the glory disappearing. They would draw wrong conclusions from the diminishing effect. So he veiled his face altogether so that they would not know whether his face was shining or not whenever God gave him audience.

> "But whenever Moses went in before the Lord to speak with him, he would take the veil off until he came out; and he would come out and speak to the children of Israel whatever he had been commanded. And whenever the children of Israel saw the face of Moses, that the skin of Moses' face shone, then Moses would put the veil on his face again, until he went in to speak with him ... unlike Moses, who put a veil over his face so that the children of Israel could not look steadily at the end of what was passing away."

Paul's point is that the light of God – his glory – in the Christian age does not fade. It is permanent. We can have an open face to the world, so that people may see the glory of God in us.

James makes a similar statement: *"Every good gift and perfect gift is from above, and comes down from the Father of lights, with whom there is no variation or shadow of turning."* The sun causes a shadow as it turns, and the shadow moves. You see that on a sundial, and that is how we know the time. When there is no shadow, the sun is directly overhead at its zenith. In fact, God never casts a shadow at all, because he is always at the zenith. And he never shifts from that perfect position. The light of God is ceaseless, not temporary, and always fully on. *"But to you who fear my name the Sun of Righteousness shall arise with healing in his wings."*

The Power Of The Blood

There is power and redemption for everyone in the blood of Jesus Christ. A Buddhist told me that she could not understand how that could be. "Maybe," she said, "one man could die for a hundred, or at most, for a thousand … but never for all mankind."

Not only Buddhists, but people of many religions find the teaching of forgiveness through the blood of Jesus revolutionary. People generally expect to pay for their sins, either now or in some other existence. The Christian revelation is the glorious fact that Jesus has paid it all. Our doubts are traitors when they prevent us from proving the power of Christ's cleansing blood.

> "I have been crucified with Christ; it is no longer I who live, but Christ lives in me; and the life which I now live in the flesh I live by faith in the Son of God, who loved me and gave himself for me. I do not set aside the grace of God; for if righteousness comes through the law, then Christ died in vain."

True forgiveness is as substantial as the cross on which Christ bought it. None of us can understand forgiveness unless we are taught by experience. If the joy of it could be communicated, some would consider it too wonderful to be true. You can be assured, however, that divine forgiveness is not a fairy tale or wishful thinking. It rests on a rock-solid foundation, on the historic fact of Jesus Christ's redemptive sacrifice. He suffered *the just for the unjust, that he might bring us to God."* The cross was no fiction. Real blood fell on real ground. And this real blood brings real cleansing to real sinners – and for you and me! – and does much more besides.

Today's Scripture
But God demonstrates his own love toward us, in that while we were still sinners, Christ died for us.
(Romans 5:8)

Daily Power!
Because there is power and redemption for everyone in the blood of Jesus Christ... there is power and redemption for me in the blood of Jesus Christ!

Mark My Word
Acts 13:38
Romans 5:9
Galatians 2:20-21
1 Peter 3:18

The Bible In A Year

Morning
Exodus 16
Luke 19

Evening
Job 34
2 Corinthians 4

6

Ringing Confidence

Today's Scripture
Now by this we
know that we know
him, if we keep his
commandments.
(1 John 2:3)

Daily Power!
My Heavenly
inheritance has been
guaranteed by the
Holy Spirit of God.

Mark My Word
Matthew 11:25
Acts 2:36; 15:8; 17:31
Ephesians 1:13-14;
4:30
1 John 2:3; 5:20

The Bible In A Year

Morning
Exodus 17
Luke 21

Evening
Job 35
2 Corinthians 5

The whole New Testament rings with confidence. Peter spoke positively when preaching in Jerusalem: *"Let all the house of Israel know assuredly, that God has made that same Jesus … both Lord and Christ."* He later brought the news about the conversion of the Gentiles and said that *"God … acknowledged them by giving them the Holy Spirit."* The Ephesians received the "earnest" (guarantee) of their spiritual inheritance and were "sealed" with the Holy Spirit. What a contrast to nervous indecision!

The Corinthians were told: *"Now we have received, not the spirit of the world, but the Spirit who is from God, that we might know the things that have been freely given to us by God."*

Any doctrine which leaves you guessing about your soul's salvation is completely out of harmony with the New Testament. Paul told the skeptics of Athens: (God) *"has appointed a day on which he will judge the world in righteousness by the Man who he has ordained. He has given assurance of this to all by raising (Jesus) from the dead."* You do not have to guard your salvation as if it would disappear if you were careless. The Lord preserves your soul! The only one who wants you to doubt your salvation is Satan himself, who stands to lose you from his evil grip!

If you want even more proof, read the epistles of John. In one short letter, he uses two Greek verbs normally translated "know" forty-two times, like this:

> "Now by this we **know** that we **know** him, if we keep his commandments … By this we **know** that we are in him … And we **know** that the Son of God has come and has given us an understanding, that we may **know** him who is true; and we are in him who is true, in his Son Jesus Christ. This is the true God and eternal life."

This does not make Christians "know-it-alls." Salvation does not depend on your intelligence or analysis of abstract theological concepts. In fact, Jesus rejoices because he can say to his Father in heaven: *"I thank you, Father, Lord of heaven and earth, that you have hidden these things from the wise and prudent and have revealed them to babes."* God has revealed these things to you!

The Forerunner

7

The crowds had more than once wanted Jesus to be King and conquer the much-hated Roman armies of occupation in the land of the Jews, but he refused. his servants did not fight to make him an earthly Lord. He had a new way! Nailed and helpless, Jesus conquered the Roman commander in charge of the squad of soldiers assigned to carry out executions. Within three hundred years, Rome itself had been conquered – not by the booted feet of military forces – but by the bleeding feet of Jesus hanging on the cross. The last pagan emperor, Julian, tried to restore the old worship of the gods, but the tides, released by Christ's death, were too powerful; Julian cried out in agony, "Oh Galilean, you have conquered!" The cross stands fast, an *anchor of the soul.*" This figure of speech is found in Hebrews: *"This hope we have as an anchor of the soul, both sure and steadfast, and which enters the presence behind the veil, where the forerunner has entered for us, even Jesus, having become high priest forever, in the order of Melchizedek."*

There is a seagoing picture from those ancient days. A ship comes into harbor, but cannot draw too near the shore in the darkness. So a sailor – called the "forerunner" – gets into a boat with an anchor and a line connecting ship and anchor. As he rows, the line linking anchor and ship is played out. Eventually, the forerunner's boat reaches the shore, and the sailor secures the anchor on land. In the morning, the ship needs no sails. The crew of the ship begins to wind in the anchor cable. However, it is not the anchor which moves but the ship. Slowly the vessel is winched towards the shore.

Your "forerunner" is Jesus, who has entered through the veil and made fast your anchor. Your salvation is secure like the anchor ashore which the crew cannot see. Christ is no longer visible to you … He is "ashore" in glory, and *"you are attached, by faith, to glory by him."* Day by day, the cable is shortening and pulling you nearer and nearer to your forerunner. Eventually you will reach Heaven's shore … and what will you see? Your forerunner waiting to greet you, because where he is, there you may also be. Faith links you already and will bring you to him at last. That faith is your assurance.

Today's Scripture
This hope we have as an anchor of the soul, both sure and steadfast, and which enters the presence behind the veil. (Hebrews 6:19)

Daily Power!
To "see and believe" means to see Jesus tasting death for every man … and for me.

Mark My Word
John 14:3
Hebrews 6:19-20

The Bible In A Year

Morning
Exodus 18
Luke 22

Evening
Job 36
2 Corinthians 6

8

Strategic Weaponry

Today's Scripture
And when you pray, do not use vain repetitions as the heathen do. For they think they will be heard for their many words. Therefore do not be like them. For your Father knows the things you have need of before you ask him.
(Matthew 6:7-8)

Daily Power!
When I pray then I exceed my human limitations.

Mark My Word
Matthew 6:1-15;
Ephesians 6:10-13, 18

The Bible In A Year

Morning
Exodus 19
Luke 22

Evening
Job 37
2 Corinthians 7

Christians have a world to reclaim and regain for God. The enemy has brought about vast destruction, death and wickedness. Prayer opens up God's Armory with its superior weapons. If we think we do not need to pray, we do not know what we are up against! If we think we can manage on our own achievements, we simply make ourselves the devil's laughing stock. **Prayerless means defenseless.** Cleverness and science are a feather duster against a tank. The limitless greatness of the cross is needed against the cosmic evil.

Prayer and intercession cast out the entrenched enemy, violate his borders, and retake lost territory. The devil hates this kind of prayer. Praying here is not "meditative, retiring breathing." It is heaven's militancy! It is not a muttered litany, but a high "C" soul-shriek! Prayer is an aggressive multi-purpose weapon put in our hands by God to overcome every kind of satanic resistance. The man who prays exceeds human limits. Believers are authorized to go to the counter of Heaven's Supply Store for superhuman resources.

God is strong, and he wants you strong. So take everything the Master has set out for you, well-made weapons of the best materials. And put them to use so you will be able to stand up to everything the devil throws your way. This is no afternoon athletic contest that we will walk away from and forget about in a couple of hours. This is for keeps, a life-or-death fight to the finish against the devil and all his angels. Pray long and hard.

The mental image here is a far cry from the old man with meekly folded hands – it is much more like seeing the **warrior** who is well-armed and ready for combat! Picture yourself that way today … well-armed, equipped and ready to do battle in the name of the Lord!

The New And Living Way

The coming of Christ was the beginning of the end for the devil. The spiritual advance goes on today. The armies of God form a new race of men and women – a holy nation, born-again, presenting the Word of God with faith and power.

> "Therefore take up the whole armor of God, that you may be able to withstand in the evil day, and having done all, to stand. Stand therefore, having girded your waist with truth, having put on the breastplate of righteousness, and having shod your feet with the preparation of the gospel of peace; above all, taking the shield of faith with which you will be able to quench all the fiery darts of the wicked one. And take the helmet of salvation, and the sword of the Spirit, which is the word of God; praying always with all prayer and supplication in the Spirit, being watchful to this end with all perseverance and supplication for all the saints."

We have new access to God, a new method of operation and new authority *"by a new and living way"* through Christ Jesus! Victory is assured! *"The creation itself also will be delivered from the bondage of corruption into the glorious liberty of the children of God … For we were saved in this hope."* Why live as if we were not on speaking terms with the Lord? He dwells with us. We are not mere neighbors, living with a brick wall between us. The Lord has broken down the middle wall. We have been *"brought near by the blood of Christ."* The Christian life means "life with God," with everything centered on him, God-oriented. The Holy Spirit gives us "utterance" to get through to God.

Christ's model prayer ends with: *"For Yours is the kingdom and the power and the glory forever."* God's is the power – ours is the prayer. Prayer is necessary, not just "nice" – it is a vital part of the equation. Ezekiel the prophet pictures the currents of the Spirit as waters to swim in. The Lord provides the waters, but you do the swimming. Without prayer, you are not "in the swim" at all! So go ahead and jump in today … the water is flowing … and the answers from heaven are on the way!

Today's Scripture
And they overcame him by the blood of the Lamb, and by the word of their testimony, and they did not love their lives to the death.
(Revelation 12:11)

Daily Power!
I am a member of the army of God, part of a new race of men and women – a holy nation, born-again, presenting the Word of God with faith and power.

Mark My Word
Ezekiel 47
Matthew 6:13
Acts 2:4
Romans 8:21-25
Ephesians 2:13; 6:13-18 Hebrews 10:10

The Bible In A Year

Morning
Exodus 20
Luke 23

Evening
Job 38
2 Corinthians 8

10

The Climax Of Time

Today's Scripture
Then they will see the Son of Man coming in a cloud with power and great glory. Now when these things begin to happen, look up and lift up your heads, because your Redemption draws near.
(Luke 21:27-28)

Daily Power!
I await your second coming with great joy Lord Jesus!

Mark My Word
Matthew 6:7-15
Luke 21:27-28
Acts 1:11
1 Thessalonians 1:10

The Bible In A Year

Morning
Exodus 21
Luke 24

Evening
Job 39
2 Corinthians 9

Christ's return is the climax of all time. Historians have said they find no pattern in the events of the past ... but there is. The true way to see history is through the Bible. It points to a unifying plan that will bring everything together and make sense of it all. Christ is returning!

The very moment Jesus left the earth, God sent angelic messengers urgently to reassure and impress upon his followers that he had not gone for good. *"This same Jesus, who was taken up from you into heaven, will so come in like manner as you saw him go into heaven."*

That promise chimes like a peal of bells throughout scriptures, and has rung in the Christian church for twenty centuries. The apostle Paul stated that while we serve God in this life, we are *"to wait for God's Son from heaven, whom he raised from the dead."*

Starting at the beginning of the New Testament, we find that the first three books – the Gospels of Matthew, Mark and Luke – point to Christ's coming and his kingdom. It is emphasized in stories and plain teaching, including whole chapters – Matthew 24 through 26, Luke 21, Mark 13. Christ taught us to pray about it in his famous Sermon on the Mount: *"Your kingdom come, your will be done on earth as it is in heaven."* The fifth Christian book, Acts, telling us how Christianity spread, includes sermons by apostles in which they preached the truth of Christ's return.

All this is more than just dry facts from an old book. These are **true signs** that not only did he come the first time as the Book said he would ... but **Christ will come again, just as he said!** What a tremendous promise that is for you and me!

Bought Back

The Bible speaks of our being *"redeemed with the precious blood of Christ,"* which means that we were "bought back" by Jesus. By following Satan and sin, man sold himself to the devil and had to be redeemed. When Jesus paid for our redemption with his precious blood, does that mean that the blood was paid to Satan? No, definitely not!

The price for our salvation was paid into the Court of God's Justice, as Hebrews 9 indicates:

> "And according to the law almost all things are purified with blood, and without shedding of blood there is no remission. Therefore it was necessary that the copies of the things in the heavens should be purified with these, but the heavenly things themselves with better sacrifices than these. For Christ has not entered the holy places made with hands, which are copies of the true, but into heaven itself, now to appear in the presence of God for us; not that he should offer himself often, as the high priest enters the Most Holy Place every year with blood of another — he then would have had to suffer often since the foundation of the world; but now, once at the end of the ages, he has appeared to put away sin by the sacrifice of himself. And as it is appointed for men to die once, but after this the judgment, so Christ was offered once to bear the sins of many. To those who eagerly wait for him he will appear a second time, apart from sin, for salvation."

The Lord paid the full price. The divine currency for our salvation was not in his pocket, but flowed in his veins! There was no question of negotiation, discount, rebate, or bargaining! Jesus gave the last drop of his heart's blood for us. Therefore our salvation cannot be challenged by anyone on earth, in heaven or under the earth, not in time nor in eternity! Because of the blood of Jesus, **you are irrevocably saved!** Praise him for that today!

Today's Scripture
And as it is appointed for men to die once, but after this the judgment; so Christ was offered once to bear the sins of many. To those who eagerly wait for him, he will appear a second time, apart from sin, for salvation. (Hebrews 9:27-28)

Daily Power!
He paid a debt he did not owe, I owed a debt I could not pay.

Mark My Word
Hebrews 9:16-28
1 Peter 1:18-19

The Bible In A Year

Morning
Exodus 22
John 1

Evening
Job 40
2 Corinthians 10

The Mark Of The Blood

Today's Scripture
But now in Christ
Jesus you who once
were far off have
been brought near by
the blood of Christ.
(Ephesians 2:13)

Daily Power!
I bear the blood-
mark of Jesus Christ
with both pride and
humility.

Mark My Word
Leviticus 8:23
Ephesians 2:13

The Bible In A Year

Morning
Exodus 23
John 2

Evening
Job 41
2 Corinthians 11

I can explain one of the most thrilling, often overlooked truths about the blood of Jesus. It marks those who trust in Jesus Christ, and distinguishes them from everybody else. The first mark is **internal**, the sign of inner cleansing. When a sinner calls on the name of the Lord to be saved, and takes Jesus Christ personally as his Savior, the blood of Jesus does a deep and thorough work. We are clean in soul and mind, conscious, subconscious or unconscious. Every evil image is thrown down. No more nightmares about hell and judgment, but divine visions and dreams. It is wonderful to dream about Jesus! Our past has gone and God remembers it no more. There is no need to keep digging it up and asking again for forgiveness. God never recalls it. This, however, does not mean that we are already "spiritually perfected Christians." As we feed on the Word of God, we will be led by the Holy Spirit from dimension to dimension.

The next mark is **external.** I can explain it through the Bible – it was foreshadowed in the Old Testament and fulfilled in the New Testament. In the Old Testament we read:

> "Moses slaughtered the ram and took some of its blood and put it on the lobe of Aaron's right ear, on the thumb of his right hand and on the big toe of his right foot."

This is the New Testament fulfillment: after Jesus has cleansed us inwardly from all our sins by his blood, an outward mark is impressed upon us. Just as there was one drop of blood upon the right ear, on the thumb and on the big toe, so the born-again believer is blood-marked. Of course, this is not a sign on our physical body, but one which both heaven and hell can discern. When God's people walk through the streets, the demons can spot them. I imagine one evil spirit calling to another, "Can you see over there? That one has the blood-mark of Jesus on his ear, toe and thumb. He belongs to Jesus Christ! Don't try to touch him – it's too dangerous. Dare to touch him and you will have a legion of angels to contend with!" You are marked by the blood of Jesus Christ!

Typical Revival

The 18th century saw the birth of what has been called "evangelical Christianity," although evangelical truths have always been woven into the tapestry of Christian faith. Evangelicalism arrived on the religious scene with extraordinary marks, and for nearly two centuries, powerful emotional and physical occurrences – such as prostration, anguish of soul, and outcries – were part of the responses that accompanied the new evangelism. Special times such as these are identified as "revival."

Today, revivals are being idealized. They are considered to be God, and the Christian faith, at their peak. A revival atmosphere, in the classic sense, is sought as the sign of a God-blessed church. Some preachers minister as "revivalists" – itinerants fostering revival-type reactions, warmth and fire, in churches. A revival, such as is recorded in the work of Wesley, is taken as the answer to the ancient cry of the soul for God to come forth from the "hiding places of his power." Israel cried out for God to display his reality by destroying their enemies … but now Christians cry out for God to draw them to himself. The motivation is different – but "revival" is the desired response.

Did you know the word "revival" does not appear in the Bible? There are numerous references to people who are "revived" from illness or death, or when a nation's broken spirit was "revived" by new trust in God … but the term "revival" is a man-made expression. Perhaps we put too much emphasis on our constructions, and not enough trust in God and his mercy?

The accounts of the times of Wesley, Whitefield, Edwards, Evans, and others fill many people with longing. Stories of these times are told repeatedly today, and prayer has increased for a true manifestation of divine power. However, despite intercession, the decades of the 20th century have seemed increasingly different from the revival times of the 19th century – in Western countries, at least. The reason why "revival tarries" is usually held to be the deficient lives of Christians. What an indictment! We want to be God's instruments of bringing revival to this world!

Today's Scripture
I indeed baptize you with water unto repentance, but he who is coming after me is mightier than I, Whose sandals I am not worthy to carry. He will baptize you with the Holy Spirit and fire.
(Matthew 3:11)

Daily Power!
O Lord, send Your revival, and start the work in me.

Mark My Word
Matthew 3:1-17

The Bible In A Year

Morning
Exodus 24
John 3

Evening
Job 42
2 Corinthians 12

14

All Prayer

Today's Scripture
Pray without ceasing.
(1 Thessalonians 5:17)

Daily Power!
I am charged by
Jesus Christ himself
always to pray and
never to lose heart.

Mark My Word
Luke 11:1-4; 18:1
Acts 12:5
Romans 1:9
Ephesians 6:18
1 Thessalonians 2:13;
5:17
2 Timothy 1:3

The Bible In A Year

Morning
Exodus 25
John 4

Evening
Proverbs 1
2 Corinthians 13

Turn over each page of the New Testament and mark every prayer reference ... then you will see how prayer is emphasized. In the first gospel alone, there are forty-one references, and two hundred and thirty throughout the New Testament, some of them extensive, with ten different words for prayer. We read about *"praying always with all prayer and supplication in the Spirit."* Different methods and moods – all available for man to use against the devil.

> "Now it came to pass, as he was praying in a certain place, when he ceased, that one of his disciples said to him, 'Lord, teach us to pray, as John also taught his disciples.' So he said to them: 'When you pray, say: Our Father in heaven, Hallowed be Your name. Your kingdom come. Your will be done On earth as it is in heaven. Give us day by day our daily bread. And forgive us our sins, For we also forgive everyone who is indebted to us. And do not lead us into temptation, But deliver us from the evil one.'"

Some texts use one special word – like a hammer to drive the nail in deeply – the adverb "without ceasing" (in Greek: ektenes, adialeiptos), which comes only six times in Scripture and only about prayer, as if this were the one thing never to let up:

> "Prayer was made without ceasing of the church unto God for him ... Without ceasing I make mention of you always in my prayers ... We give thanks to God always for you all, making mention of you in our prayers, remembering without ceasing your work of faith ... We also thank God without ceasing ... Pray without ceasing."

Jesus himself taught that *"men always ought to pray and not lose heart."* That becomes his charge to you today! Pray ... and do not lose heart!

Equipped With Power

Jesus never sent his disciples out without equipping them with **power**:

> "And Jesus came and spoke to them, saying, 'All authority (power) has been given to me in heaven and on earth. Go therefore and make disciples of all the nations, baptizing them in the name of the Father and of the Son and of the Holy Spirit, teaching them to observe all things that I have commanded you; and lo, I am with you always, even to the end of the age. Amen.'"

> "And he said to them: 'Go into all the world and preach the gospel to every creature. He who believes and is baptized will be saved; but he who does not believe will be condemned. And these signs will follow those who believe: in my name they will cast out demons; they will speak with new tongues; they will take up serpents, and if they drink anything deadly, it will by no means hurt them; they will lay hands on the sick, and they will recover.'"

The "signs" were **power signs**. We are commissioned to only one kind of ministry: **a power-sign gospel!**

> "Jesus came and stood in the midst of them, and said to them, 'Peace be with you.' When he had said this, he showed them his hands and his side. Then the disciples were glad when they saw the Lord. So Jesus said to them again, 'Peace to you! As the Father has sent me, I also send you.' And when he had said this, he breathed on them, and said to them, 'Receive the Holy Spirit.'"

The Father sent his Son in the power of the Holy Spirit … and Christ never anticipated that we would go to the nations with anything less! A power ministry is not merely a "possibility" – it is the **only one** Jesus envisioned! It is normal experience for those who go in Christ's name … by definition. It is our ministry, together, today!

Today's Scripture
'Peace to you! As the Father has sent me, I also send you.' And when he had said this, he breathed on them, and said to them, 'Receive the Holy Spirit.' (John 20:21-22)

Daily Power!
The precious Holy Spirit is as near as my next breath – and I know he is breathing on me.

Mark My Word
Matthew 28:18-20
Mark 16:15-18
John 20:21-23

The Bible In A Year

Morning
Exodus 26
John 5

Evening
Proverbs 2
Galatians 1

16

Pentecost Gave Us Keys

Today's Scripture
And I will give you the keys of the kingdom of heaven, and whatever you bind on earth will be bound in heaven, and whatever you loose on earth will be loosed in heaven.
(Matthew 16:19)

Daily Power!
Thank You, Father, for your Holy Spirit's power at work in my life today!

Mark My Word
Matthew 16:19

The Bible In A Year

Morning
Exodus 27
John 6

Evening
Proverbs 3
Galatians 2

The Christian age is the power age. In the Old Testament, we read of the God of wonders performing marvels at the Red Sea, and under Elijah and Elisha. But not much more stands out in the thirty-nine books of the Old Testament … except that on occasions, the power of the Holy Spirit fell upon a few individuals and the prophets. Then Jesus gave Peter the keys of the kingdom of heaven! Those keys are not jangling from Peter's belt at his post beside the Pearly Gates – the keys are the gospel of Christ crucified and the Holy Spirit. He opened the kingdom … and today we have the same keys. Peter saw what nobody on earth had ever seen before: three thousand people in one day turning in repentance and being born again by the Holy Spirit. Then the apostles went out and put the power of those keys to the test. The dead were raised; the deaf, blind and crippled restored to full health; multitudes turned to Christ, and a new thing arose in the world: the church of Jesus Christ.

Pentecost is the giving of the Holy Spirit to the world in manifest form. It is God at work in the physical and material world. We only know of one form of the Spirit, and that is in manifestation. There is no "resting" Spirit, no Spirit in quiescence. The essence of Pentecost is the moving of the Spirit – the mighty wind from heaven and the flaming tongues of fire. The Holy Spirit is only known at work. There is no Spirit without movement, any more than there is a wind without movement. A wind that does not blow is not a wind at all. Wind is never quiet, or just an atmosphere. The Holy Spirit is a gale, and nobody can stand still in a force-eight gale and talk politely about the atmosphere! Where the Spirit is there is action, the miraculous – God in operation!

Any talk of "miracles as belonging to the past" denies the very purpose and nature of the gospel, as well as the character of the Holy Spirit. The Spirit is sent to work in this world. Deny the miraculous, the power of the Holy Spirit – and you deny what Christianity is supposed to be: God's power in action in the present age of living men and women. That is what makes this age the Christian age. Perhaps we ought to call this the Holy Spirit age! Let us live in this age to the full!

God's Own Banner And Bow

When Noah saw the earth desolated by the Flood, he must have been traumatized. Afterwards, whenever the skies grew dark overhead, he would need reassurance. God said, *"I have set my rainbow in the clouds, and it will be the sign of the covenant between me and the earth."* The rainbow is the flag of God, the seven-colored royal standard. No icon, no regimental colors and no imperial symbol could match that!

> "O Lord my God, in you I put my trust … my defense is of God, who saves the upright in heart. God is a just Judge, and God is angry with the wicked every day. If he does not turn back, he will sharpen his sword, he bends his bow and makes it ready; he also prepares for himself instruments of death, he makes his arrows into fiery shafts … I will praise the Lord according to his righteousness, and will sing praise to the name of the Lord Most High."

The word "bow" in Genesis 9:13 (where it is translated "rainbow") is the same Hebrew word as for a bow which is used to shoot arrows – a weapon of war … but what a weapon, spanning the whole horizon! What mighty arrows it must shoot when God goes into battle against the devil! *"The LORD shall go forth like a mighty man; he shall stir up his zeal like a man of war. He shall cry out, yes, shout aloud; he shall prevail against his enemies."*

The rainbow is not a mere phenomenon of natural beauty, but a divine reminder of God's archery. The divine graphics span the whole Bible, for when we reach the book of Revelation, we read. *"A rainbow … encircled the throne … From the throne came flashes of lightning."* God's mighty arrows. No wind can blow a rainbow away and no devil can switch it off. The battle truly belongs to the Lord. You may suffer life's storms, when ominous blackness fills your skies, but that arching splendor of prismatic color in the rain cloud, seen with your mortal eyes, is the objective standard of God to reassure you. It is a sign of God's love bent to the world and to you. Receive his love today!

Today's Scripture
For the weapons of our warfare are not carnal but mighty in God for pulling down strongholds.
(2 Corinthians 10:4)

Daily Power!
The rainbow is far more than a trick of light and water – it truly is God's promise.

Mark My Word
Genesis 8:13
Psalm 7:1-17
Isaiah 42:13
Revelation 4:3-5

The Bible In A Year

Morning
Exodus 28
John 7

Evening
Proverbs 4
Galatians 3

18

Today's Scripture
The Spirit himself bears witness with our spirit that we are children of God. (Romans 8:16)

Daily Power!
What a privilege it is to call my wonderful Heavenly Father, "Daddy!"

Mark My Word
Matthew 22:29
Romans 8:16
Galatians 4:4-7
2 Peter 1:4

The Bible In A Year

Morning
Exodus 29
John 8

Evening
Proverbs 5
Galatians 4

After you have believed what the Word of God says about the certainty of your salvation through Jesus Christ – and **only after** – the Holy Spirit becomes active in your life: *"The Spirit himself bears witness with our spirit that we are children of God."* Note that the Bible uses the word "spirit" twice, once with a capital letter – denoting God's Spirit – and once with a small letter – denoting the human spirit. God's Spirit witnesses to your human spirit that you **are** a child of God. You received a divine nature, and your new heart tells you God is your Father. Then you have a close relationship with him and cry, *"Abba, Father!"* This settles the matter completely, because then even your feelings will adjust to the testimony of the Holy Spirit within you.

> "But when the fullness of the time had come, God sent forth his Son, born of a woman, born under the law, to redeem those who were under the law, that we might receive the adoption as sons. And because you are sons, God has sent forth the Spirit of his Son into your hearts, crying out, "Abba, Father!" Therefore you are no longer a slave but a son, and if a son, then an heir of God through Christ."

The key is that after repentance and faith, you **believe** the Word of God, otherwise you can never even start being sure of your salvation. It says that God calls you his child – so you can be certain that he is your Father … and all other believers are your brothers and sisters. This puts the whole Family of God together, without distinction or discrimination by race, or wisdom, or age, or education, on earth or in heaven. glory be to God!

If people try to show off their learning by posing weighty problems, supposedly to display their "intellectual honesty," Jesus simply says they *"are mistaken, not knowing the Scriptures nor the power of God."* Logic cannot possibly embrace the dimension of eternal salvation which comes from the mind and heart of God. You cannot put God in a test tube. Let the Word of God be your Guide today.

Scripture Dynamite

What did Jesus preach? Jesus talked about himself. On the Emmaus road, walking with Cleopas and a friend, he explained to them, going throughout the Scriptures, the *"things concerning himself"* – all his teaching goes back to himself. For example, after he had left Nazareth and begun his wonderful ministry, the gospel of Luke tells us that Jesus returned one day and went into the synagogue. For twenty years he had attended that very synagogue faithfully every week. The custom was to allow men who were known to read the Scriptures, and perhaps comment on them afterward. Naturally, when Jesus was present at the synagogue again, he was invited to do this. The gospel message was found in the Old Testament – in fact, the Old Testament is full of the gospel! Luke tells us that Jesus read from Isaiah 61:

> "The Spirit of the Lord is upon me, because he has anointed me to preach the gospel to the poor, he has sent me to heal the broken-hearted, to proclaim liberty to the captives and recovery of sight to the blind, to set at liberty those who are oppressed, to proclaim the acceptable year of the Lord."

No doubt, many in the synagogue knew that passage by heart, for those words had been read for eight hundred years. The scroll of the Scriptures was handed back. The synagogue leader took it with great reverence, kissed it, and put it away, to be forgotten until the next week. But suddenly, that scroll seemed to become a stick of dynamite: the Word on the lips of Jesus produced effects all right – it awakened the drowsy congregation! He showed them that the Word was about himself. There are seven distinct statements in that verse and they all apply to him, as well as to the present. *"Today,"* he dared to announce, *"this Scripture is fulfilled in your hearing."* Thus he declared himself to be the Anointed One – the Christ, the One to perform all those promised exploits. Proclaim liberty! Do not preach for effect, for pulpit display, or to charm, excite, or scare folk. Do not preach to calm people down. You can preach for all kinds of effects, but Jesus simply announced liberty. He proclaimed, that day in the synagogue, that the Jubilee had begun. He showed them what a true Jubilee would be: deliverance! It would be a Jubilee – not merely for Israel – but for the whole world. A Jubilee for you … and for those to whom you speak the gospel!

Today's Scripture
And he began to say to them, "Today this Scripture is fulfilled in your hearing." So all bore witness to him, and marveled at the gracious words which proceeded out of his mouth.
(Luke 4:21-22)

Daily Power!
The gospel of Jesus Christ on our lips will produce spiritual dynamite.

Mark My Word
Isaiah 61:1-2
Luke 4:18-22
Luke 24:13-28

The Bible In A Year

Morning
Exodus 30
John 9

Evening
Proverbs 6
Galatians 5

Yesterday, Today, Forever

Today's Scripture
The Spirit of the Lord is upon me, because he has anointed me to preach the gospel to the poor; he has sent me to heal the broken-hearted, to proclaim liberty to the captives and recovery of sight to the blind, to set at liberty those who are oppressed, to proclaim the acceptable year of the Lord.
(Luke 4:18-19)

Daily Power!
I yield myself to be the tool that God uses to show his compassion to all people.

Mark My Word
1 Kings 17:1-24
2 Kings 4:1-44
Luke 7:11-17

The Bible In A Year

Morning
Exodus 31
John 10

Evening
Proverbs 7
Galatians 6

Here is an example of Christ's consistency from Luke's gospel, when Jesus raised a young man from the dead in the village of Nain.

> "And when he came near the gate of the city, a dead man was being carried out, the only son of his mother; and she was a widow … When the Lord saw her, he had compassion on her and said to her, 'Do not weep.' Then he came and touched the open coffin, and those who carried him stood still. And he said, 'Young man, I say to you, arise.' So he who was dead sat up and began to speak. And he presented him to his mother."

We read that Jesus had compassion on the weeping mother. In the same region, the great prophets Elijah and Elisha had both also raised mothers' sons from the dead. That was eight hundred years before.

Now notice this: in each case, the Bible says that Elijah and Elisha gave the sons back to their mothers … and **Jesus did exactly the same.** He raised the young man from death and gave him back to his mother.

Two millennia have not made any difference to his power or compassion! Generation after generation have experienced Christ's healing touch. We recognize his fingerprints, his typical way of working. He is like the noonday sun and never switches off. His powerful sunlight kills the virus of evil.

Two millennia have passed since he left earth and ascended to the Father … but that makes no difference to his power or compassion in your life today or in mine! Our healing is based in his resurrection power! *He is alive.*

Allergic To God?

Sin causes a catastrophic breakdown in relationships. We can see this breakdown all around us: violence in the streets … child abuse … hatred between people of different races and nationalities … corruption … marriages that are wounded and killed by one or both partners. One Hollywood actress said, "I have found that divorce lawyers – not diamonds – are a girl's best friend."

The final casualty in this chain of breakdown is our relationship with God. Cut off from God, we feel the pain of separation from him. For many people, life has no meaning or purpose. This is not how God planned it. He created us to live in a relationship of love with him. But instead, we have run away and hidden from God, as if we were allergic to him:

> "Then the eyes of both of them were opened, and they knew that they were naked; and they sewed fig leaves together and made themselves coverings. And they heard the sound of the Lord God walking in the Garden in the cool of the day, and Adam and his wife hid themselves from the presence of the Lord God among the trees of the Garden."

Jesus put it like this: *"Light has come into the world, but men loved darkness instead of light."* Lost in the darkness, far from home, what hope is there for us? It is important to review these questions to see where God has brought us **from** – the hopeless, filthy depths of sin – and so we are better equipped to offer his light of hope and salvation to the world still lost in the darkness today.

> "In him was life, and the life was the light of men. And the light shines in the darkness and the darkness did not comprehend it."

Let the light of Christ Jesus fill your heart – and shine from you today!

Today's Scripture
Even the righteousness of God, through faith in Jesus Christ, to all and on all who believe.
(Romans 3:22)

Daily Power!
I am thankful to God that I am not what I used to be.

Mark My Word
Genesis 3:7-8
John 1:4; 3:19
Romans 3:22.

The Bible In A Year

Morning
Exodus 32
John 11

Evening
Proverbs 8
Ephesians 1

22

How To Rout Doubt

Today's Scripture
Most assuredly, I say to you, he who hears my Word and believes in him who sent me has everlasting life, and shall not come into judgment, but has passed from death into life.
(John 5:24)

Daily Power!
I walk by faith, not by feelings.

Mark My Word
John 5:24; 8:44
1 Corinthians 2:3
2 Corinthians 1:8; 4:9

The Bible In A Year

Morning
Exodus 33
John 12

Evening
Proverbs 9
Ephesians 2

Paul's feelings in Corinth were of weakness and trembling, and even fear for his mortal life. Nevertheless he **knew** that God was with him. He was often *"cast down,"* he said, and *"despaired even of life,"* but it left his assurance of hope absolutely unaffected. Do you know that the devil can bring on lying feelings? If he does not succeed in confusing you with lying words, he resorts to depressing your emotions. However, remember the Bible's warning that Satan is the father of lies – he is a master at the game. Some people feel saved one day and not the next, but the day after that it seems as if their salvation has come back. All feelings! If you do not believe Satan's lying words, do not believe the lying feelings he gives you either.

What should you do? The answer is: Go to the Word of God. Find a Scripture like John 5:24 … and read it over and over again!

The Word is your birth certificate. God says you are his child, you have eternal life, and that Word is never wrong. You will not be lost. You just believe it, and believe it you must!

A little boy had received Jesus as his Savior at Sunday School. his teacher had hammered John 5:24 into him, and he had underlined it in his New Testament. That night he got into bed, read his Bible, prayed, and switched off the light. Then the devil came bringing doubts, suggesting that he was not saved. The boy quickly switched on the light and read John 5:24 again. He was happy that the Bible had not changed! It still said he **possessed** eternal life. Once more he switched off the light, and again doubt came back. This time, he said, it was as if it came from under his bed. Once more he switched on the light, and turning again to John 5:24, held his New Testament under the bed and said, "Look, devil, if you don't believe me, then read it for yourself: *I have passed from death to life*. I am a child of God!" In simple, child-like faith – accept that promise as yours today!

The Imperatives Of Jesus

When Jesus said: *"You **must** be born again,"* it meant that he also had to say almost immediately: *"The Son of Man **must** be lifted up."* He used the same word, **must**. Our need becomes his need to meet our need.

Jesus lived under a constant sense of the imperative will of God. He **must** save because we need to be saved. He said: *"I have other sheep"* – sheep that **must** be saved - *"them also I **must** bring."*

> "If a man has a hundred sheep, and one of them goes astray, does he not leave the ninety-nine and go to the mountains to seek the one that is straying? And if he should find it, assuredly, I say to you, he rejoices more over that sheep than over the ninety-nine that did not go astray. Even so it is not the will of your Father who is in heaven that one of these little ones should perish."

This revelation of God becomes our basis for both faith and evangelism. The God of the Bible – our Lord Jesus Christ, the changeless One – will never let us down. You and I go at his bidding with our hands in his … and we introduce him to a weary world.

Jesus infected the apostle Peter with this urgent need to reach the lost:

> "The Lord is not slack concerning his promise, as some count slackness, but is longsuffering toward us, not willing that any should perish but that all should come to repentance."

Let me remind you that the initiative is not with us – it is with God. Behind everything is the moving Spirit of God. That being the case, we are either relevant, or irrelevant to what God is doing. Oh, let us strive always to be relevant to what God is doing in the world today!

Today's Scripture
And as Moses lifted up the serpent in the wilderness, even so must the Son of Man be lifted up, that whoever believes in him should not perish but have eternal life. (John 3:14-15)

Daily Power!
My Heavenly Father desires a true relationship with me, therefore he sent his very best that I might enter into that relationship with a pure heart.

Mark My Word
Matthew 18:12-14
John 3:1-21; 10:7-18
2 Peter 3:9

The Bible In A Year

Morning
Exodus 34
John 13

Evening
Proverbs 10
Ephesians 3

24

Our Highest And Noblest Task

Today's Scripture
To open their eyes,
in order to turn them
from darkness to light,
and from the power
of Satan to God, that
they may receive
forgiveness of sins
and an inheritance
among those who
are sanctified by faith
in me.
(Acts 26:18)

Daily Power!
I am dedicated to
preaching the gospel
of Jesus Christ, and
thus building his
eternal kingdom. This
is a higher and nobler
task than any other.

Mark My Word
Psalm 119:46
Matthew 10:18-20
Acts 26:1-32

The Bible In A Year

Morning
Exodus 35
John 14

Evening
Proverbs 11
Ephesians 4

Paul the apostle, persecuted for his Lord, was one day brought up from a foul-smelling dungeon under the king's palace, with his wrists sore because of the iron manacles, and appeared in court. He lifted his hands, fetters clinking, and preached Christ to the proud and noble assembly in their splendor of purple and gold. They were destined to be remembered – but only because Paul stood before them that day. Their prisoner – a little Roman Jew from Tarsus – immortalized **them**.

Claudias Lysias, the centurion … Governor Felix … Ananias, the high priest … Tertullus the orator … Drusilla, wife of Felix … Procius Festus … King Agrippa and Queen Bernice – it sounds like the role-call of some high-society soiree. These names probably would not have survived into history but for Luke writing about them in telling of the trials of Paul and the acts of the Early church. While Paul spoke, he was changing the future of Europe and the whole world. Smelling of the prison, Paul's great heart was breaking in compassion for them – kings, companions, courtiers, and all. He concluded his defense by saying: *"I would to God that not only you, but also all who hear me today, might become both almost and altogether such as I am, except for these chains."*

Today, we are called to address the great and mighty of our world. We reach the small and obscure because they are always more open to hear the loving truths of the gospel. But we must also purpose to reach those in authority: *"I will speak of Your testimonies also before kings and will not be ashamed."* Boldness and obedience are keys to such witness:

> "You will be brought before governors and kings for my sake, as a testimony to them and to the Gentiles. But when they deliver you up, do not worry about how or what you should speak. For it will be given to you in that hour what you should speak; for it is not you who speak, but the Spirit of your Father who speaks in you."

This is the lot of God's servants even today. Preaching the gospel of Jesus Christ – and thus building his eternal kingdom – is a higher and nobler task than any other. I invite you to join me in this splendid mission of the King of kings and the Lord of lords!

John's Problem

John the Baptist had a similar problem to that of the prophets Jonah and Elijah: he preached the fire of judgment, saying:

> "You brood of vipers! who warned you to flee from the coming wrath? ... The ax is already at the root of the trees, and every tree that does not produce good fruit will be cut down and thrown into the fire ... his winnowing fork is in his hand to clear his threshing floor and to gather the wheat into his barn, but he will burn up the chaff with unquenchable fire."

That is so much like the preaching of the fiery Elijah that it sounds ironic when Luke adds, *"With many other words John exhorted the people and preached the Good News to them"*! "Hell fire" equals "Good News"?

John later saw Jesus at work and saw no flaming judgments fall. He sent to ask Jesus if he had identified the wrong man as Messiah. Jesus sent back the messengers to describe the mercies of God among the afflicted and dying, and to deliver a message: *"Blessed is the man who does not fall away on account of me."*

How do you and I judge the man who rapes and murders children? Deserving of judgment ... or of mercy? How do we act towards the prostitute who lures men into depravity and deadly diseases? Eligible for hell-fire to cleanse away her sin ... or a helping hand extended to redeem? If it were up to us – human beings – we would have wiped out our entire species years ago! But God continually loves us human beings, and he pours out his compassion and mercy upon us generation after generation. It is he who inspires the heart of the evangelist to shine the Good News into a dark and filthy world – and that is yours and mine!

Today's Scripture
Jesus answered and said to them, "Go and tell John the things you have seen and heard: that the blind see, the lame walk, the lepers are cleansed, the deaf hear, the dead are raised, the poor have the gospel preached to them. And blessed is he who is not offended because of me."
(Luke 7:22-23)

Daily Power!
I want my life to be an example of that merciful compassion which Christ exhibited so freely throughout his life, even to his death.

Mark My Word
Luke 3:7-18; 7:22-23

The Bible In A Year

Morning
Exodus 36
John 15

Evening
Proverbs 12
Ephesians 5

26

Today's Scripture
I press toward the goal for the prize of the upward call of God in Christ Jesus. (Philippians 3:14)

Daily Power!
Dear Lord, this is my prayer: give me opportunity today to share my faith for Your glory.

Mark My Word
Luke 17:5
Romans 1:17; 10:17
Philippians 3:14

The Bible In A Year

Morning
Exodus 37
John 16

Evening
Proverbs 13
Ephesians 6

If we have no real faith, reading the Bible produces it. If we have some faith, we get more the same way. We do not acquire faith first and bring it to Scripture. Scripture encourages faith: *"Faith comes by hearing the Word of God."* Many who do not believe, do not read the Bible. They are sick and leave the medicine with the bottle tightly corked. People without faith should be "warned" that if they open the Bible, they are likely to finish up as believers!

The Bible brings us to the cross. People do not start moving mountains until they have been to Mount Calvary. They could not even move a molehill – or a mole. Real faith does not start at the university – but we will certainly have less if we go there without any! If we have not been to where Christ saves, not even a Doctor of Theology will do. The starting pistol is fired from the "green hill far away outside the city wall." From there, we tread on and on towards the mark of the high calling of God in Christ. Walking in doubt is like being caught in a thick fog. We need radar … and faith provides it in this world of uncertainty: *"The righteousness of God is revealed from faith to faith; as it is written, 'The just shall live by faith.'"* Believe God! It is life's greatest adventure.

> "And the apostles said to the Lord, 'Increase our faith.'
> So the Lord said, 'If you have faith as a mustard seed, you
> can say to this mulberry tree: Be pulled up by the roots
> and be planted in the sea, and it would obey you.'"

I want to offer knowledge and experience across the area of faith as widely as I can. Whether people are far along the road, or just beginning, or have not even started … I want to come alongside them and share treasures with them that I have collected over a lifetime. And as you grow in your walk with the Lord I want you to go and do the same. Your faith is too precious to hide … **share** it as often as you can … and **show** it by the way you live today and every day.

The Secretary Of The Trinity

I once heard someone say that the Holy Spirit is the "Secretary of the Trinity." When I thought about it, I had to agree. A secretary's work is to communicate the decisions of the board to the people concerned. And now, after you have received Jesus as your Savior, the Holy Spirit immediately swings into action. A "registered letter" arrives, as it were, at the door of your heart with something like the following message:

Dear ……………………………….. (put your own name here),

I have been advised by the Father and the Son to inform you that your sins are forgiven and blotted out: *"Having wiped out the handwriting of requirements that was against us, which was contrary to us. And he has taken it out of the way, having nailed it to the cross."* (Colossians 2:14)

Furthermore, I have been instructed to let you know that your name has been written in the Lamb's Book of Life in heaven: *"Rejoice because your names are written in heaven."* (Luke 10:20)

I am to exhort you to be faithful unto death: *"Do not fear any of those things which you are about to suffer. Indeed, the devil is about to throw some of you into prison, that you may be tested, and you will have tribulation … Be faithful until death, and I will give you the crown of life."* (Revelation 2:10)

An incorruptible crown and inheritance is waiting for you in heaven: *"Blessed be the God and Father of our Lord Jesus Christ, who according to his abundant mercy has begotten us again to a living hope through the resurrection of Jesus Christ from the dead, to an inheritance incorruptible and undefiled and that does not fade away, reserved in heaven for you, who are kept by the power of God through faith for salvation ready to be revealed in the last time."* (1 Peter 1:3-5)

Finally, I am to urge you to *"be strong in the Lord and in the power of his might."* (Ephesians 6:10)

Yours most faithfully and ever-abidingly (see John 14:16),
on behalf of the Trinity,
The Holy Spirit.

Today's Scripture

The Spirit himself bears witness with our spirit that we are children of God. (Romans 8:16)

Daily Power!

My "love letter" from God is engraved upon my heart.

Mark My Word

Luke 10:20
John 14:16
Ephesians 6:10
Colossians 2:4
1 Peter 1:3-5
Revelation 2:10

The Bible In A Year

Morning
Exodus 38
John 17

Evening
Proverbs 14
Philippians 1

28

Understanding The Holy Spirit

Today's Scripture
Come near to me,
hear this: I have not
spoken in secret from
the beginning; from
the time that it was, I
was there. And now
the Lord God and his
Spirit have sent me.
Thus says the Lord,
your redeemer, the
Holy One of Israel;
I am the Lord your
God, who teaches
you to profit, who
leads you by the way
you should go.
(Isaiah 48:16-17)

Daily Power!
Holy Spirit, teach me
Your truths.

Mark my Work
Isaiah 48:16-17
2 Peter 1:3

The Bible In A Year

Morning
Exodus 39
John 18

Evening
Proverbs 15
Philippians 2

Multitudes have been baptized in the Holy Spirit during our gospel campaigns, and we regularly witness mighty manifestations of the power and love of God. I want to explain the understanding that I have gained from these events. My final authority has been Scripture. Certainly, experience has helped me grasp the things of the Spirit, but as Peter wrote, God *"has given to us all things that pertain to life and godliness."* Scripture validates experience.

In sharing my understanding of the things of the Spirit, I try to show that my conclusions are arrived at through the Word, illuminated by what I have seen. There are many alternative views. Variations are sure to exist, unless a standard authority is accepted and agreed upon to judge all such teachings. Experience itself varies, but the scriptures do not. There is a natural appetite to hear about the things that God has done, and a tendency to draw primarily from experience – the Word is often regarded only as a backup, if used at all. This "anecdote theology" is not new. There are theories of revival, for example, which have been claimed as being based purely on studies of what has happened in the past. I was concerned about this approach … and I determined that my starting point **must** be the Word. That is where I stand. Our pneumatology (the things of the Spirit) had to be subject to the judgment of what the Word says. This was wholesome discipline.

Experience must be challenged by scripture – experience must not challenge scripture nor adapt scripture to what "happens to happen." Nevertheless, you will see that I illustrate my teaching with the things that God has been doing in our evangelistic campaigns. Among Christians who pray for and support the nation-shaking work of Christ for all Nations, there are many viewpoints on doctrines, including that of the Holy Spirit. I pray that this contribution to the understanding of the work of the Holy Spirit ministers to you.

Our Mission Is Compassion

Elijah was the scourge of Baal, of Jezebel, and of her pathetic husband, King Ahab. Jesus did not come as a scourge – he bared his own back to the scourge, not ours. He showed to us the ultimate reality behind the universe: a heart beating with infinite longing and concern over every one of his creatures. In fact, the more sunken in the pit the people were, the more he bled for them. That kind of love is the true spirit of evangelism.

You and I know people are going to hell, and if we care about them, we should warn them. But we should warn them as if they were our own children walking on the brink of an active volcano. Hatred should be not present in our preaching. Our mission is compassion. Because hell opens its mouth to devour sinners, we should feel the greater anxiety for their souls. We cannot gloat in satisfaction and shout for joy over sinners in Hell. Warnings are one thing – threats another.

> "How shall we escape if we neglect so great a salvation, which at the first began to be spoken by the Lord, and was confirmed to us by those who heard him; God also bearing witness both with signs and wonders, with various miracles, and gifts of the Holy Spirit, according to his own will."

Jonah found it difficult to preach. He enjoyed preaching wrath, but knew that God did not enjoy being angry. God is longsuffering (eternally patient): *"The Lord is longsuffering and abundant in mercy, forgiving iniquity and transgression."*

> "For God is my witness, how greatly I long for you all with the compassion of Jesus Christ. And this I pray, that your love may abound still more and more in knowledge and all discernment, that you may approve the things that are excellent, that you may be sincere and without offense till the day of Christ."

With the compassion of Jesus Christ as our motivation, you and I should joyfully present the gospel to the world!

Today's Scripture
But he was wounded for our transgressions, he was bruised for our iniquities; the chastisement for our peace was upon him, and by his stripes we are healed.
(Isaiah 53:5)

Daily Power!
I am filled with the fruit of the Spirit: love, joy, peace, longsuffering, kindness, goodness, faithfulness, gentleness, self-control.

Mark My Word
Numbers 14:18
1 Kings 16:1-34;
18:1-46; 19:1-21; 21:
1-29 2 Kings 9;
Isaiah 53:5
Jonah 3:1-10
Galatians 5:22
Philippians 1:8-10
Hebrews 2:3-4

The Bible In A Year

Morning
Exodus 40
John 19

Evening
Proverbs 16
Philippians 3

MARCH

30

Today's Scripture
For we do not wrestle against flesh and blood, but against principalities, against powers, against the rulers of the darkness of this age, against spiritual *hosts* of wickedness in the heavenly places. (Ephesians 6:12)

Daily Power!
When it feels like I am living my life "behind enemy lines," I remember that Christ Jesus came to rescue me from the power of the enemy.

Mark My Word
Genesis 1:28
Matthew 4:8-10
John 12:31; 14:30;
16:11 Romans 1:21
Ephesians 2:2
Colossians 1:21
1 John 5:19.

The Bible In A Year

Morning
Leviticus 1
John 20

Evening
Proverbs 17
Philippians 4

Under Attack!

Think of what happens to a country at war – in some cases, it is totally cut off from the outside world. No more commerce or trade, no more mail or telephone conversations. Much the same thing happened when the human race surrendered to sin and the devil. We were cut off from the outside world – from God, from the world of the Spirit. Demonic forces occupied this world and dominated our attitudes. Divine power lines were severed and a permanent spiritual blackout occurred.

Originally, God put man in charge to manage this world – *"Then God blessed them, and said, 'Be fruitful and multiply; fill the earth and subdue it; have dominion over the fish of the sea, over the birds of the air, and over every living thing that moves on the earth'"* – but we were a pushover to sin and the devil swayed people. The Bible makes this clear:

> "The whole world lies under the sway of the wicked one ... Our foolish hearts were darkened ... The prince of the power of the air... now works in the sons of disobedience ... alienated and enemies in your mind by wicked works."

Three times Jesus called the devil *"the ruler of this world."* When the devil offered the kingdoms of this world to Christ, Jesus did not contest the devil's ability to do so:

> "Again, the devil took him up on an exceedingly high mountain, and showed him all the kingdoms of the world and their glory. And he said to him, 'All these things I will give you if you will fall down and worship me.' Then Jesus said to him, 'Away with you, Satan! For it is written: you shall worship the Lord your God, and him only you shall serve.'"

Therefore, since he has cut off our rightful communication with God, it is up to us to learn how to re-establish those lines and not let them be severed again! Make your connection to God today ... keep it strong all day long!

"Classic Revival"

A late example of a "classic revival" took place in 1949 on the islands of Harris and Lewis in the Hebrides. With the dawning of the third millennium, the longing for a repeat of the times of classic or traditional revival grips millions. The glorious and exciting vista of the anticipated revival fills the wide screen of the whole world, and is no longer limited to a particular church or local renewal. The need for revival on that kind of international scale is urgent enough.

Prayer is made, so that the divine fire which burned in Welsh villages or similar communities will encircle the globe, remembering that, *"with God, all things are possible."* It would change everything. No more struggle and constant effort, discouragement and ongoing sacrifice, constant witnessing and endless prayer … but brilliant gospel success.

I believe a lack of revival in our world today begins with individuals recognizing that we have, perhaps, become like the church of Ephesus:

> "I know your works, your labor, your patience, and that you cannot bear those who are evil. And you have tested those who say they are apostles and are not, and have found them liars; and you have persevered and have patience, and have labored for my Name's sake and have not become weary. Nevertheless, I have this against you, that **you have left your first love.** Remember therefore from where you have fallen, repent and do the first works."

Remember that great joy you experienced when first you received Jesus as **your** Savior? Are we so selfish that we cannot desire to freely share that joy with others who have never heard? Is revival to refresh the saved – or to reach the lost, to rescue those who are dead in their sins? Let us strive to seek to be God's agents of revival!

Today's Scripture

And it shall come to pass afterward that I will pour out my Spirit on all flesh; your sons and your daughters shall prophesy, your old men shall dream dreams, your young men shall see visions. And also on my menservants and on my maidservants I will pour out my Spirit in those days.
(Joel 2:28-29)

Daily Power!

I will return to my first love – Jesus!

Mark My Word

Joel 2:28-32
Revelation 2:1-7

The Bible In A Year

Morning
Leviticus 2 and 3
John 21

Evening
Proverbs 18
Colossians 1

Our brain is the doubt box.

A fuse that works will feel the power first.

Don't confuse, don't refuse, but check your fuse!

God's Counter-Attack

Just as in wartime, countries have secret agents and the means of maintaining contact with them, so the Lord has his men and women and keeps in contact with them. Amos the prophet said, *"Surely the Lord does nothing, unless he reveals his secret to his servants, the prophets"* – men like Enoch, Noah, Abraham, Moses, Elijah, Daniel, Isaiah. The whole nation of Israel was to have been God's ally against the occupying enemy from hell … but they failed to perceive his plan and comply with it.

The Lord revealed one great secret to his servants, the prophets – namely, that there was to be an invasion of Fortress earth from the outside. And it took place – Christ came to the shores of Satan's usurped dominion, proclaiming the kingdom of God and displaying its power: *"If I cast out demons with the finger of God, surely the kingdom of God has come upon you."*

> "What then shall we say to these things? If God is for us, who can be against us? … who shall separate us from the love of Christ? Shall tribulation, or distress, or persecution, or famine, or nakedness, or peril, or sword? As it is written, 'For your sake we are killed all day long; we are accounted as sheep for the slaughter.' Yet in all these things we are more than conquerors through him who loved us. For I am persuaded that neither death nor life, nor angels nor principalities nor powers, nor things present nor things to come, nor height nor depth, nor any other created thing, shall be able to separate us from the love of God which is in Christ Jesus our Lord."

That means that you **can** come out from beneath Satan's ruthless grip and walk unencumbered with God! So stand up and walk in that liberty … today!

Today's Scripture

You are of God, little children, and have overcome them, because he who is in you is greater than he who is in the world. (I John 4:4)

Daily Power!

I have enlisted in God's army, and I am ready to fight the enemy!

Mark My Word

Amos 3:7
Luke 11:20
Romans 8:31-39
1 John 4:4

The Bible In A Year

Morning

Leviticus 4
Psalm 1 and 2

Evening

Proverbs 19
Colossians 2

2

How To Become A True Intercessor

Today's Scripture
You are my friends if you do whatever I command you. No longer do I call you servants, for a servant does not know what his master is doing; but I have called you friends, for all things that I heard from my Father I have made known to you.
(John 15:14-15)

Daily Power!
As I am learning more and more about God and his character. I desire to become his friend – one to whom he listens and with whom he wants to cooperate.

Mark My Word
Genesis 18:1-33
2 Chronicles 20:7
Isaiah 41:8-10
John 15:14-15
James 2:23

The Bible In A Year

Morning
Leviticus 5
Psalms 3 and 4

Evening
Proverbs 20
Colossians 3

A true intercessor must have some standing with both parties – God and the lost. We know people but we must also know God! Abraham was a good example of someone who knew God. The cities of Sodom and Gomorrah had become morally perverted. God proposed to remove them, but said, *Shall I hide from Abraham what I am doing?* When Abraham learned that these two cities were listed for destruction, he took up their case with God ... and went a long way along the road to saving them. He was qualified – because he knew God and the cities. He was called *"the friend of God."* Why? *"Abraham believed God, and it was accounted to him for righteousness. And he was called the friend of God."*

True believers are the King's friends at Court, his confidantes, people to whom he listens and with whom he wants to cooperate.

> "But you are my servant, Jacob, whom I have chosen, the descendants of Abraham my friend ... I have taken you from the ends of the earth ... and said, 'You are my servant, I have chosen you and have not cast you away; fear not, for I am with you, be not dismayed, for I am your God. I will strengthen you, I will help you, I will uphold you with my righteous right hand.'"

These people whom he honors are to be his intercessors. That is what Scripture means by "a friend." Jesus said, *"I no longer call you servants ... Instead, I have called you friends, for everything that I learned from my Father I have made known to you."* A friend-intercessor will have the mind of the Lord, who does not tell us things for mere interest, but for us to pray about it. A "word of knowledge" is not necessarily for public consumption, but often for private prayer. Pray today – and ignite a fresh fire and inner desire to do God's will in every way!

God's Property

We human beings look after our property and protect it. You can be absolutely sure that God also looks after his property. We cost God too much for him to neglect and lose us. We were *"bought at a price,"* even the precious blood of Jesus. When Jesus takes over, he saves and keeps us. As long as we follow him, he will not allow repossession of his property by unclean spirits: *"He who dwells in the shelter of the Most High will rest in the shadow of the almighty."* *"They overcame him by the blood of the Lamb and by the word of their testimony; they did not love their lives so much as to shrink from death."* This is the glorious and perfect protection which the Lord gives his children, free of charge.

> "No weapon formed against you shall prosper, and every tongue which rises against you in judgment you shall condemn. This is the heritage of the servants of the Lord, and their righteousness is from me, says the LORD. No curse can be fastened on you, and no witchcraft can harm you. Like a flitting sparrow, like a flying swallow, so a curse without cause shall not alight."

We serve a mighty God ... not a struggling God who sometimes might lose battles. He cannot be blackmailed, nor forced to compromise with the devil. He could never go into partnership and share his right-of-possession of you with any evil spirit. Follow Jesus and you are wholly the Lord's. Reinhard Bonnke lives with this assurance – I am marked by the blood of Jesus, and nobody can pluck me from his hand. Satan cannot kidnap my soul. It is hidden with Christ in God, which is a safe in a strongroom, and bears the seal-mark of the blood. You too are marked by the blood of Jesus.

Today's Scripture
For you were bought at a price; therefore glorify God in your body and in your spirit, which are God's.
(1 Corinthians 6:20)

Daily Power!
What a joy to be able to shout: "I am God's property!"

Mark My Word
Psalm 91:1
Proverbs 26:2
Isaiah 54:17
1 Corinthians 6: 20
Colossians 3:3
Revelation 12:11

The Bible In A Year

Morning
Leviticus 6
Psalms 5 and 6

Evening
Proverbs 21
Colossians 4

4

Family Is A Divine Purpose

Today's Scripture
For in him we live and move and have our being.
(Acts 17:28)

Daily Power!
I am a child of God.

Mark My Word
Psalm 68:6
Luke 17:21
Acts 17:28

The Bible In A Year

Morning
Leviticus 7
Psalms 7 and 8

Evening
Proverbs 22
1 Thessalonians 1

In Acts 16, Paul told the Philippian jailer: *"Believe on the Lord Jesus and you will be saved, and your household."* his household? There would be more under his roof than today's statistical family with 2.3 children. There would be his wife, adult sons and their wives, daughters, servants, slaves, and possibly grandparents. Could his faith save their souls? We may as well ask if a father's cup of coffee could satisfy his family! The household could be saved, but each one must believe on the Lord Jesus. Nobody can be saved secondhand through his father or mother. God has no grandchildren. But this phrase, *"you and your household,"* did mean something. It was no throwaway line. Behind it lay Paul's understanding of the purposes of God spelled out in the scriptures. He knew that in scripture, "family" has a divine purpose. It is mentioned over three hundred times in scripture, and is what the whole world is all about. Paul had much to say about "the household" in his letters.

Family is God's idea. He created the family. *"He sets the solitary in families."* That is his blessing. He never intended separation, isolation and individualism. Modern individualism is not a product of Bible teaching, but came from philosophical thought. We might say that the roots of family life are in the very nature of God as Father, Son and Holy Spirit. The family reflects God more than an individual life.

The perfection of God's glory needs the whole *"household of God."* God made families because unity is necessary for all Creation. Thus prayer for our family has the ear of God. We were made for interdependence with one another. *"We are our brother's keepers."* We came from him, and that can never change. Everything is forever united in him as normal. *"In him we live and move and have our being."* Jesus prayed, *"That they may be one, just as We are one,"* because there had been a rupture of unity which Christ came to rectify and restore. That unity for which Christ prayed would not be artificial or imposed. It would bring back real unity for you and me, as intended.

The Objective Of Our Work

The nine men who wrote the Christian Scriptures of the New Testament all spoke of Christ's return, and to them it was clear that it was that hope which gave meaning to their faith and an objective for their work. The main writer, Paul, went into much detail: how Christ would appear … what he would do … what the state of the world would be. He wrote more than three pages of his great letter to the church in Corinth, chapter 15, and made the return of Jesus the keystone of the future. Here are some of his words:

> "Christ died for our sins according to the Scriptures. He rose again the third day according to the Scriptures. As in Adam, all die, even so in Christ, all shall be made alive, but each one in his own order. Christ the firstfruits; afterward those who are Christ's at his coming."

When he was preaching to the intellectuals in Athens – then the greatest city of learning on earth – he said, *"God has appointed a day on which he will judge the world in righteousness, by the Man whom he has ordained. He has given assurance of this to all, by raising him from the dead."*

John was closer to Christ than anybody, and he rested his hope on Christ's return. He wrote: *"Beloved, now we are children of God; and it has not yet been revealed what we shall be, but we know that when him is revealed, we shall be like him, for we shall see he as he is."*

Furthermore, John wrote the Book of Revelation – or "the Apocalypse" – with twenty-one chapters of prophecy concerned with Christ's return as Lord of lords. It ends with the words of Jesus: *"He that testifies these things says, 'Surely I come quickly.'"*

This is God's promise to you and to me!

Today's Scripture
But now Christ is risen from the dead, and has become the firstfruits of those who have fallen asleep. For since by man came death, by man also came the resurrection of the dead. For as in Adam, all die, even so in Christ, all shall be made alive.
(1 Corinthians 15:20-22)

Daily Power!
Soon I shall be like him, for I shall see him as he is.

Mark My Word
Acts 17:31
1 Corinthians 15:1-58
John 3:1-3
Revelation 22:20

The Bible In A Year

Morning
Leviticus 8
Psalm 9

Evening
Proverbs 23
1 Thessalonians 2

6

Searching In Darkness

Some people see no hope in any direction. Tragically, they give up and sink into despair. Others try to escape from it all. As one person observed, "People can't stand too much reality – that's why we have soap operas!"

Longing for real life, some people get tangled in a web of destruction – often in the most common and obvious snares, such as drugs or drink. These addictions have never solved one single problem ... but have created millions. Those who cannot live **without** drugs and drink also cannot live **with** them. They produce only a chemical dream, a mirage in a waterless desert: "*Now the ones that fell among thorns are those who, when they have heard, go out and are choked with cares, riches, and pleasures of life, and bring no fruit to maturity.*"

Others become addicted to the pursuit of success. Their diaries get fuller, their bank accounts fatter, their cars faster – but they never catch up with happiness. Like mountaineers, millions of people display enormous courage, determination and ingenuity to get to the top ... but they find only emptiness when they get there:

> "And I will say to my soul, 'Soul, you have many goods laid up for many years; take your ease; eat, drink, and be merry.' But God said to him, 'Fool! This night your soul will be required of you; then whose will those things be which you have provided?'"

Meanwhile, in today's "religious supermarket," many people are hypnotized by "do-it-yourself salvation." The shelves are crowded with New Age products: pyramid power ... hypnotherapy ... transcendental meditation ... white magic – all of them are a sham, and some of them are lethal. They offer nothing that can reach the heart of the human problem: "*Those by the wayside are the ones who hear; then the devil comes and takes away the Word out of their hearts, lest they should believe and be saved.*"

You need more than a cheap solution or a quick fix – **you need peace with God.** You need him to forgive you, to bring you home, and to restore you in the relationship that he has always wanted to have with you.

Faith Is A Venture

One morning, Jesus walked along the shingled edge of Lake Galilee and beckoned to fishermen. He said, "*Follow me!*" At that moment, everything began for them. Before it had only been fish, and then it became people, action, and changing world history, with ever-increasing faith and effects. Jesus did not call them – nor you, nor me – to switch off smiles and wear sackcloth, to turn ordinary people into stick-in-the-mud people. He was not so conventional himself! The disciples caught his bubbling spirit, which challenged the stuffy establishment. He showed them new things – especially faith and love – and by them, they conquered the world.

God is the Deliverer, the Emancipator, and the Savior. He is God only to the free. **Faith is a venture that turns Life into an adventure.** Doubts get us nowhere. They are mooring ropes. Believing God means that we cast off, like ships designed for riding the high seas and going somewhere. Faith inspires – doubt paralyzes. Faith says, "*I can do all things through Christ who strengthens me.*" Unbelief does nothing. Faith in God is exciting – unbelief is depressing.

"*If you abide in my Word, you are my disciples indeed. And you shall know the truth, and the truth shall make you free.*" We become what we were born to be only when we are "born-again" by faith in Christ Jesus. "*Therefore if the Son makes you free, you will be free indeed.*" The world's greatest book on freedom is the Bible. The very idea of freedom came from the Bible, not from Greece or Rome. Read it! Remember, God made the first free nation ever seen on earth – Israel – and he wants to put a sense of liberty in our very souls. God opposes tyranny. The gospel makes us the freeborn sons of God.

> "For this reason we also, since the day we heard it, do not cease to pray for you, and to ask that you may be filled with the knowledge of his will in all wisdom and spiritual understanding; that you may walk worthy of the Lord, fully pleasing him, being fruitful in every good work and increasing in the knowledge of God."

Go – and walk in your godly freedom today ... in Jesus' name!

Today's Scripture
Therefore if the Son makes you free, you shall be free indeed. (John 8:36)

Daily Power!
Today I walk in the freedom given me by Christ Jesus my Lord.

Mark My Word
Matthew 4:19
John 8:36
Philippians 4:13
Colossians 1:9-10

The Bible In A Year

Morning
Leviticus 10
Psalms 11 and 12

Evening
Proverbs 25
1 Thessalonians 4

8

Motivation

Today's Scripture
You became
followers of us and
of the Lord, having
received the word
in much affliction,
with joy of the Holy
Spirit, so that you
became examples to
all in Macedonia and
Achaia who believe.
For from you the
word of the Lord has
sounded forth, not
only in Macedonia
and Achaia, but also
in every place. Your
faith toward God has
gone out, so that we
do not need to say
anything.
(1 Thessalonians 1:6-8)

Daily Power!
I have faith. I am filled
with the Spirit, and I
burn for God!

Mark My Word
1 Thessalonians 1:8

The Bible In A Year

Morning
Leviticus 11 and 12
Psalms 13 and 14

Evening
Proverbs 26
1 Thessalonians 5

The world cannot see what motivates Christians to shine brightly in a darkened place. In ignorance, they only see Christians as "religious enthusiasts." Unbelievers are like sheep who cannot understand why human beings listen to music. Jesus told us that the Holy Spirit is not given to the world. That makes unbelievers basically different, almost alien, as if they were from Mars.

However, one candle is lit from another candle. The fire – the light of God – is transmitted. That is why we are here. Paul the apostle spent only a few days introducing the gospel to the people of Thessalonica, but a little later in a letter to them, Paul congratulated their enthusiasm, saying, "Your faith in God has become known everywhere." Faith lights the lamps that show the way.

We begin, perhaps, with no faith – a minus. But at the cross, the flame of faith leaps into our hearts, bringing the Holy Spirit, salvation and forgiveness. At that place, Christ's infinite work is accomplished, and faith makes it ours. We believe and receive. The Holy Spirit translates all that Jesus did for us into our personal experience. We are the lights of the world. The world likes to think religion is dying, but in vast areas of the world, the death rattle is heard in the throat of secularism. As Christ is to Resurrection, godlessness is to death. They are both synonyms. People are not finding satisfaction in what mere governments can do, and are turning to the things of the Holy Spirit. That is the situation. Have faith – be filled with the Spirit – and burn for God! Let the seven-branched lamp standard be ablaze!

If you believe, and I believe,
and we together strive;
the Holy Spirit will come down,
and nations will revive.

Daily Bread

Prayer is an important topic in the Word of God. The apostle Paul often uses a word meaning "keep at it, persevere, be a stayer, show stamina, stick at it, keep awake!" Translate these texts like that yourself:

> "Continue earnestly in prayer, being vigilant in it … Continuing steadfastly in prayer … We will give ourselves continually to prayer … praying always with all prayer and supplication in the Spirit."

The way Jesus speaks of prayer is not quite like some might suppose. He said, "*Ask, and it will be given to you. Seek and you will find. Knock, and it will be opened to you.*" These words are in the Greek present indicative: "be asking, be seeking, be knocking." But elsewhere he used a different tense (aorist) indicating a single, completed action: "*Give us this day our daily bread.*" Ask once, but ask every day. "*Give us this day*" – ask for each day's need daily. That is how God likes it. We do not have faith for everything for a whole year – that would be arrogant! We come to him as children over and over, asking for the Bread of Life – the Holy Spirit – daily, not once forever. We always receive every day!

The concept of "daily bread" was first seen with the newly-liberated Israelites in the wilderness:

> "Then the Lord said to Moses, 'Behold, I will rain bread from heaven for you. And the people shall go out and gather a certain quota every day, that I may test them, whether they will walk in my law or not.'"

From that day to this, God has been **testing us** to see if we have faith in him on a **daily** basis. And so it is with prayer – we must be faithful on a daily basis to participate in prayer with God.

Today's Scripture
Praying always with all prayer and supplication in the Spirit, being watchful to this end with all perseverance and supplication for all the saints.
(Ephesians 6:18)

Daily Power!
It is my privilege as a child of God to come to him every day, with the open-hearted expectation of a child, knowing that my Father loves me!

Mark My Word
Exodus 16:1-5
Matthew 6:11; 7:7
Acts 6:4
Romans 12:12
Ephesians 6:18
Colossians 4:2

The Bible In A Year

Morning
Leviticus 13
Psalms 15 and 16

Evening
Proverbs 27
2 Thessalonians 1

10

God Hears Prayer

Today's Scripture
Now this is the
confidence that we
have in him, that
if we ask anything
according to his will,
he hears us. And
if we know that he
hears us, whatever
we ask, we know that
we have the petitions
that we have asked
of him.
(1 John 5:14-15).

Daily Power!
I have confidence that
each time I call on
my Heavenly Father,
he is always at home
– he always hears me
when I pray.

Mark My Word
Psalm 86:7; 91:15
Isaiah 58:9; 65:24
Jeremiah 33:3
Matthew 6:8; 7:8-11;
10:40
1 John 5:14-15.

The Bible In A Year

Morning
Leviticus 14
Psalm 17

Evening
Proverbs 28
2 Thessalonians 2

Scripture consistently declares that prayer will **always** be heard:

> "Your Father knows the things you have need of before you ask him … Everyone who asks receives, and he who seeks finds, and to him who knocks it will be opened … This is the confidence that we have in him, that if we ask anything according to his will, he hears us. And if we know that he hears us, whatever we ask, we know that we have the petitions that we have asked of him."

Have you ever tried someone's telephone number again and again, without getting through to that person? After awhile you wonder, "Did I write that number down correctly?" But our Heavenly Father has our number – right down to the very number of hairs on our heads: "*But the very hairs of your head are all numbered*" – and he cares intimately about you!

> "Or what man is there among you who, if his son asks for bread, will give him a stone? Or if he asks for a fish, will he give him a serpent? If you then, being evil, know how to give good gifts to your children, how much more will your Father who is in heaven give good gifts to those who ask him!"

When you call on God – you will **never** get a busy signal or a phone that just rings with no answer:

> "Give ear, O Lord, to my prayer; and attend to the voice of my supplications. In the day of my trouble I will call upon you, for you will answer me … He shall call upon me, and I will answer him; I will be with him in trouble, I will deliver him and honor him … Then you shall call, and the Lord will answer; you shall cry, and he will say, 'Here I am' … Call to me, and I will answer you, and show you great and mighty things, which you do not know."

I believe that it was even God who originated the idea of "call waiting": "*It shall come to pass that before they call, I will answer; and while they are still speaking, I will hear.*"

The Spirit Yearns

The important principle of faith is: Christ Jesus is alive in me. Many wait for the Spirit to move, but he must move in the direction they want. The moving of the Spirit is not just in our feelings. There is a strange and neglected verse in James: "*The Spirit who dwells in us yearns jealously.*" The Holy Spirit within us conflicts with fleshly desire, urging us into service for him.

Let us look at Ephesians: "*For by grace you have been saved through faith – and that not of yourselves, it is the gift of God.*" Faith is a mutual act between God and me. There are two spirits in opposition: the spirit of the devil, and the Spirit of God. They both pressurize us. First, we read of "*the spirit who is now at work in those who are disobedient,*" then we read that when we are saved: "*We are … created in Christ Jesus to do good works.*" When we do his will, do his good works, it is by his grace. We cannot pride ourselves on it. The glory is all the Lord's.

Perhaps you have noticed that Jesus never commended **people**, but he commended their **faith**. If we have small faith, do not worry … everybody starts there – or with no faith at all! Even the apostles were called, "*little faiths.*" If you are dissatisfied with yourself, God made you that way. "*The Spirit who dwells in us yearns jealously.*" He plans to strengthen us.

If you consider yourself to be a poor believer, there can be a breakthrough. The whole Bible is written to break down unbelief and build up your fortifications of trust in God. It is to bring you the peace of perfect rest in God.

Today's Scripture

For by grace you have been saved through faith, and that not of yourselves; it is the gift of God. (Ephesians 2:8).

Daily Power!

The main objective of God's Word is to bring me into the peace of perfect rest in God.

Mark My Word

Ephesians 2:2, 8, 10; James 4:5.

The Bible In A Year

Morning
Leviticus 15
Psalm 18

Evening
Proverbs 29
2 Thessalonians 3

12

Today's Scripture
For he who speaks in a tongue does not speak to men but to God; for no one understands him; however, in the spirit he speaks mysteries. (1 Corinthians 14:2).

Daily Power!
The baptism of the Holy Spirit is essential for successful Christian life.

Mark My Word
Acts 2:1-4
2 Corinthians 14:2

The Bible In A Year

Morning
Leviticus 16
Psalm 19

Evening
Proverbs 30
1 Timothy 1

Power!

Power! That is the essence of the gospel. A powerless gospel preacher is like an unwashed soap salesman. Singing "There is power in the precious blood of the Lamb" … and then having to fast and pray for a month to get power does not add up. At the beginning of my Christian life, I had an experience of the Holy Spirit coming into my life which I believe was as great as that of any disciple on the day of Pentecost. It seemed to me that the God who fills heaven and earth crowded into my soul.

> "When the day of Pentecost had fully come, they were all with one accord in one place. And suddenly there came a sound from heaven, as of a rushing mighty wind, and it filled the whole house where they were sitting. Then there appeared to them divided tongues, as of fire, and one sat upon each of them. And they were all filled with the Holy Spirit and began to speak with other tongues, as the Spirit gave them utterance."

Peter managed to stand up and preach, but the physical effects of my baptism in the Spirit would certainly have been too much for me to stand and preach immediately, as tremendous as my empowering was for later service. I will tell you how it happened to me … but I ought to say that nobody should think that God ever gives the Spirit in exactly the same way to everyone.

It happened like this: I was a boy of eleven in Germany when my father told me about special prayer meetings for the baptism in the Holy Spirit. Ever eager for the things of God, I begged him to take me along. A missionary from Finland was visiting the church, and he explained the truth of the baptism in the Holy Spirit. We had just knelt down when the power of God began to pour into and over me. Joy unspeakable filled my heart, and I began to speak in other languages, as the Spirit gave me utterance. It was like a Heavenly fountain opening up within me – it is still flowing today! It was one of the most precious events in my life – and one I trust you too have experienced.

Apply The Blood

In the entire Bible, no blood except the blood of Jesus is called precious. Millions of animals had been slaughtered to atone for sin, but their blood was not precious. The Old Testament sacrifices of Israel were simply poured away at the sides of the altars – powerless.

Suppose you have a table with a big stain on its surface. When visitors come, you cover the stain with a tablecloth so that nobody will notice it. The stain is covered, but not removed. This is the meaning of the Old Testament word atonement – "covered." The rivers of blood of millions of sacrificial animals were not able to "take away" sin, but only to cover it for a while. That is the reason why John the Baptist was so excited when he saw Jesus come to the River Jordan, and cried: "*Behold! The Lamb of God who takes away the sin of the world!*"

Jesus' blood works "under the tablecloth" and behind every one of our facades. It tackles the root sins and problems of all people who put their faith in Jesus Christ. The blood of the Lamb of God alone has value and power to save. his sacrifice was, and is, sufficient for you and me – for all men, women, boys, and girls, no matter how old they are. The apostle Peter is the one who called the blood of Jesus "precious" – "*but with the precious blood of Christ, as of a lamb without blemish and without spot*" – because he personally witnessed the crucifixion and death of his best friend. With his own eyes he saw his Master's blood pour out of his body. Peter **knew** the true value of the precious blood of Jesus – and that is what you and I must learn to value and honor today.

Today's Scripture
In him we have redemption through his blood, the forgiveness of sins, according to the riches of his grace. (Ephesians 1:7).

Daily Power!
I know that I was not redeemed with corruptible things, but with the precious blood of Christ.

Mark My Word
John 1:29
Ephesians 1:7
1 Peter 1:19.

The Bible In A Year

Morning
Leviticus 17
Psalms 20 and 21

Evening
Proverbs 31
1 Timothy 2

14

God's Unchanging Heart

Today's Scripture
God is not a man that he should lie, nor a son of man that he should repent. Has he said, and will he not do? Or has he spoken, and will he not make it good? (Numbers 23:19).

Daily Power!
Look into the Word of God and see his consistent character and heart.

Mark My Word
Genesis 20:1-18
Numbers 23:19
Isaiah 55:6-12

The Bible In A Year

Morning
Leviticus 18
Psalm 22

Evening
Ecclesiastes 1
1 Timothy 3

God works by prompting prayer. When God wants to do a certain thing, he inspires prayer that he may do it – he only works that way. In Genesis 20, we read about the first healing recorded in Scripture. It was the prayer of Abraham that brought forgiveness and healing to the whole household of the Philistine chief, Abimelech. However, this was not Abraham's idea – it was the Lord's! He told Abimelech to ask Abraham to pray for him to be healed. He inspired Abraham to pray, and inspired Abimelech to expect Abraham's prayer to be answered. It was all of God. And by healing a heathen family, God had committed himself – he could never again be any different.

The Lord had revealed what he was, and he could not go back on it. God shows himself by his deeds, and his deeds do not stand in contrast to his nature. He never repeats himself, for he has an infinite store of new approaches and plans. He has shown that healing is what he wants to do.

God's reliability and trustworthiness are undoubted, and what he says to the just, he also says to the sinner:

> "Seek the Lord while he may be found. Call upon him while he is near. Let the wicked forsake his way, and the unrighteous man his thoughts; let him return to the Lord, and he will have mercy on him; and to our God, for he will abundantly pardon … So shall my Word be that goes forth from my mouth; it shall not return to me void, but it shall accomplish what I please, and it shall prosper in the thing for which I sent it."

His deeds demonstrate his unchanging heart. The same love, the same will he always had, ensure his deeds cannot violate his character.

Samson And Christ

15

If we need anybody back in our world today, it is Jesus Christ! Nations could relax, peace and security would be realized. This is the wonderful thing about Christ – he is "the Coming One."

The Book of Judges refers to Israel without a king. It told us that God raised up deliverers. One deliverer was Samson … and there was a strange reaction to his prowess. Israel's leaders, in cowardly fear of their oppressors, tried to betray Samson, and he fell into the hands of enemies. They blinded him and set him to hard labor in prison. The final scene saw Samson crush the leadership of the enemy, sacrificing his own life. He was not afraid. his supreme effort smashed their power.

It is an allegory. The world's deliverer – Jesus Christ – like Samson, was betrayed and bound. Then, by his death, Christ brought deliverance. He broke the power of evil on the cross, once and for all time.

Samson had earlier been bound hand and foot, but when his enemies came upon him, he rose and broke free. Similarly, Christ was immobilized with nails through his feet, and finally shut up in the silence of the tomb. But Christ the Deliverer broke free, and rose triumphantly back to God who sent him!

Today, you and I can identify with Christ Jesus, our Deliverer!

Today's Scripture
For it pleased the Father that in him all the fullness should dwell, and by him to reconcile all things to himself, by he, whether things on earth or things in heaven, having made peace through the blood of his cross. (Colossians 1:19-20).

Daily Power!
My redeemer, my Deliverer, Christ Jesus, lives in me today!

Mark My Word
Judges 13 to 15:20
Colossians 1:19-20

The Bible In A Year

Morning
Leviticus 19
Psalms 23 and 24

Evening
Ecclesiastes 2
1 Timothy 4

16

"Kiss The Son"

Today's Scripture
Your kingdom come,
your will be done,
on earth as it is in
heaven.
(Matthew 6:10)

Daily Power!
I will obey the Lord
and do business till
he comes.

Mark My Word
Psalm 2:12
Proverbs 11:30
Isaiah 9:6
Matthew 6:10
Mark 16:15
Luke 19:13; 24:46-48
Acts 2:14-39
Revelation 22:20

The Bible In A Year

Morning
Leviticus 20
Psalm 25

Evening
Ecclesiastes 3
1 Timothy 5

The apostle Peter said, "*Therefore let all the house of Israel know assuredly that God has made this Jesus, whom you crucified, both Lord and Christ.*" Jesus Christ took that office when he ascended to heaven. In order to carry out the work, he must return. It can only be accomplished on earth. That was always God's purpose.

Jesus was born to die. The disciples feared, and probably hated, the religious leaders and the Romans who put Jesus to death, but they quickly learned that even his death was part of his plan:

> "Thus it was necessary for the Christ to suffer and to rise from the dead the third day, and that repentance and remission of sins should be preached in his name to all nations, beginning at Jerusalem. And you are witnesses of these things."

From that understanding, they learned to extend forgiveness and reconciliation, even with those who persecuted them. This they could do because they respected and honored the Kingship of Christ Jesus, and took up his assignment to them: "*Go into all the world and preach the gospel to every creature.*"

The everlasting King is poised on the threshold – "*the government will be upon his shoulder.*" He will take over global responsibilities. No power on earth or in hell can prevent it! Psalm 2 warns the nations: "*Kiss the Son, lest he be angry and you perish from the way when his wrath is kindled but a little.*" Blessed are all those who put their trust in him. When he comes, the whole world in every corner will know. He will remove from his kingdom everything that offends. his coming is as sure as the dawn.

How do you and I know Christ is returning? Christians everywhere are praying, "*Even so, come Lord Jesus.*" "*Thy kingdom come!*" … and those prayers will be answered any day now! And while we are waiting upon his return, we obey his command: "*Do business till I come!*" We do not just sit around waiting for him to return, but continue doing the work of the kingdom – winning souls! "*He who wins souls is wise.*" Today, that should be your occupation and mine!

History In Advance

This is the time of ripening for the final harvest. Both wheat and tares fill the field. Satan can see that his opportunities are slipping away – it is now or never for him. So the greatest display of wickedness, lawlessness and degradation is ahead. But believers have more to think about than mere survival. There are likely to be persecutions, and no doubt blood will flow. Our thoughts, however, are on triumph and conquest for Jesus. The build-up of enemy forces is being more than matched by an ever-increasing measure of the Holy Spirit: "*When the enemy comes in, like a flood, the Spirit of the Lord will lift up a standard against him.*"

The greatest outpouring, the greatest anointing of God's power ever known, is coming upon us. Past revivals will seem as nothing when Pentecost breaks upon the entire church. We already get glimpses of it – the battle of the anointed against the anti-anointed. We now know what it means in Revelation chapter 12: "*And they overcame him by the blood of the Lamb, and by the word of their testimony, and they did not love their lives to the death.*" That showdown is fully described:

> "So the great dragon was cast out, that serpent of old, called the devil and Satan, who deceives the whole world; he was cast to the earth, and his angels were cast out with him. Then I heard a loud voice saying in heaven, 'Now salvation, and strength, and the kingdom of our God, and the power of his Christ have come, for the accuser of our brethren, who accused them before our God day and night, has been cast down.'"

Bible prophecies like these are history written in advance! When the devil is out to trouble the world, God will trouble the devil. God will do what he said he would, even to the dot on the last "i." Hallelujah! We rejoice! We know! The future is settled beforehand, and the last hour is determined, with its very glorious conclusion. And this is the period we are now entering!

Today's Scripture
And they overcame him by the blood of the Lamb and by the word of their testimony, and they did not love their lives to the death.
(Revelation 12:11)

Daily Power!
What God has said will come to pass.

Mark My Word
Isaiah 59:19
Revelation 12:9-11

The Bible In A Year

Morning
Leviticus 21
Psalms 26 and 27

Evening
Ecclesiastes 4
1 Timothy 6

18

Made And Saved For God's Glory

Today's Scripture
And God raised us up with Christ and seated us with him in heavenly places that in the ages to come he might show the exceeding riches of his grace in his kindness toward us in Christ Jesus.
(Ephesians 2:6, 7)

Daily Power!
Jesus suffered to bring many sons to glory – that includes me!

Mark My Word
Titus 2:13
John 13:31, 32

The Bible In A Year

Morning
Leviticus 22
Psalms 28 and 29

Evening
Ecclesiastes 5
2 Timothy 1

It is astounding to think that the God who created the whole world also created each one of us. What is more, he did not make us for ourselves, just so that we could be happy creatures, but for himself, for his own glory. If we live for the glory of God we live in harmony with the purpose for which God made us. That means peace. To live for money, self-gratification or some purpose other than God is to live a life of stress, fighting nature and colliding with the stream of God's will. If we seek his glory, we move along with all things to the destined greatness of eternal glory.

And we are saved, not just for our own benefit, but also for the glory of God. Why? *"… that in the ages to come he might show the exceeding riches of his grace in his kindness toward us in Christ Jesus."* That is why Jesus suffered so much for us, paid such a price – to bring his Father glory.

When Jesus comes again, he will fill the whole earth with his glory. That is **the** hope. We are looking for *"the glorious appearing of our great God and Savior, Christ Jesus."*

God is working out his own glory and we need never worry that Christianity will fail or that faith will disappear. God is the architect of his purposes. Nothing we puny humans can do will in the end prevent the whole universe honoring him and seeing his glory. We shall be in his glory, part of it, sharing in the joy and light and life and wonder. That is really something to look forward to!

The "Impossible" Jesus

People talk of Christianity but forget that at the heart of it is this greatest hope: Christ's Second Advent. We cannot pick and choose the bits we like and still call it Christianity. We know that he is coming back because he was raised from the dead. He rose, so he will come. Paul said so when he was preaching in Athens to intellectuals! It was the kind of absolute logic they liked. Peter also said that God, in *"his abundant mercy has begotten us again to a living hope through the resurrection of Jesus Christ from the dead … for salvation ready to be revealed in the last time."*

Jesus made many tremendous promises, which he kept. He promised to rise from the dead – nobody could, or would accept it. It was impossible, and they did not think that he meant it. But he did; and he walked out of the tomb. **Jesus deals in impossibilities.** *"You are the God who does wonders."* He came out of the grave. Therefore, coming from glory is no problem.

> "For Christ has not entered the holy places made with hands, which are copies of the true, but into heaven itself, now to appear in the presence of God for us; not that he should offer himself often, as the high priest enters the Most Holy Place every year with blood of another – he then would have had to suffer often since the foundation of the world; but now, once at the end of the ages, he has appeared to put away sin by the sacrifice of himself. And as it is appointed for men to die once, but after this the judgment, so Christ was offered once to bear the sins of many. To those who eagerly wait for him he will appear a second time, apart from sin, for salvation."

Christ died and came back from the grave, and now he lives! Fantastic? Yes, but not fantasy. It is where history is going. If not, then history is going nowhere at all. With great joy, you and I hold onto that tremendous promise: Jesus Christ will come again for us!

Today's Scripture
Blessed be the God and Father of our Lord Jesus Christ, who according to his abundant mercy has begotten us again to a living hope through the resurrection of Jesus Christ from the dead.
(1 Peter 1:3)

Daily Power!
I now have a living hope through the resurrection of Jesus Christ from the dead.

Mark My Word
Hebrews 9:24-28
1 Peter 1:3, 5.

The Bible In A Year

Morning
Leviticus 23
Psalm 30

Evening
Ecclesiastes 6
2 Timothy 2

20

Our God-Given Rights

Today's Scripture
For unto us a Child is born, unto us a Son is given; and the government will be upon his shoulder. And his name will be called Wonderful, Counselor, Mighty God, Everlasting Father, Prince of Peace. Of the increase of his government and peace there will be no end.
(Isaiah 9:6-7)

Daily Power!
Jesus died my death that I might live.

Mark My Word
Isaiah 9:6-7
Luke 22:27
John 3:16; 4:42;
14:2-3
2 Corinthians 9:15
Revelation 1:7

The Bible In A Year

Morning
Leviticus 24
Psalm 31

Evening
Ecclesiastes 7
2 Timothy 3

We know Christ is coming back because he belongs here. He is "*the Man Christ Jesus.*" He was born here ... ate here and grew here ... breathed here and lived here ... was tempted just as we are – but never sinned. He was falsely accused here ... tried and convicted here ... beaten and reviled here ... and he shed his blood here. He rose again in a renewed and immortal body, yet which bore the marks of his death on the cross. The Son of Man is tied to this world of men, forever, incorruptible, the Resurrection and the Life!

He has two homes – earth and heaven ... with us, and with the Father. He went to God because he came from God ... He will come back here because he came from here.

> "In my Father's house are many mansions; if it were not so, I would have told you. I go to prepare a place for you. And if I go and prepare a place for you, I will come again and receive you to myself; that where I am, there you may be also."

He belongs to God and belongs to us. As he loved the Father, and went to him ... because he loves us, he will come to us. When the new heaven and earth come, he will belong to both.

Our greatest right is our claim on Jesus Christ: "*God so loved the world that he gave his only Son*" ... "*his indescribable gift.*" We own him like God owns him, earth as much as heaven. "*Unto us, a Child is born, and unto us, a Son is given.*" He put himself under obligation to us by his incredible grace. One of our God-given rights is to see him here on earth. That is our inviolable privilege: "*Every eye shall see him.*"

Intercession Brings Results

After a crusade meeting, a lady came to me and told me how she had been molested by evil spirits for many years, and despaired of her life. I was moved, and the Lord told me to fast and pray for her. Next day, I was praying for her with all of my heart, when at noon, I suddenly experienced a breakthrough. The glory of the Lord filled my soul, and the Holy Spirit said to me, "It is done."

That evening, I met the lady again. Before I could say anything, she reported with shining eyes, "God has done the miracle! Today at noon, I experienced a mighty deliverance in my home." What God does on a small scale, he will also do on the largest.

Moses was perhaps the greatest intercessor (before Christ). After he led the Israelites out of Egypt – a feat wrought miraculously by the mighty hand of God – the children of Israel dared to complain about their newfound freedom in the wilderness: "We don't have enough food … We don't have enough water … We are vulnerable out here … We want to go back to Egypt!"

God threatened to destroy them and their ingratitude, yet again and again, Moses prevailed with God not only to spare them, but to provide for them generously and miraculously. Intercession is not made because someone deserves God's mercy, but because he is kind and loving and generous.

What needs are there in your own life that you need intercessory prayer for? There is no embarrassment in asking a fellow-believer to pray with you – that is a privilege for both of you – which is bound to bless the two of you!

Today's Scripture
Now this is the confidence that we have in him, that if we ask anything according to his will, he hears us. And if we know that he hears us, whatever we ask, we know that we have the petitions that we have asked of him.
(1 John 5:14-15)

Daily Power!
It is the privilege of believers to pray for one another.

Mark My Word
John 16:22-24
1 John 5:14-15

The Bible In A Year

Morning
Leviticus 25
Psalm 32

Evening
Ecclesiastes 8
2 Timothy 4

22

Moved By Feelings Of Concern

Today's Scripture
I am the Good Shepherd; and I know my sheep ... I lay down my life for the sheep. Therefore my Father loves me, because I lay down my life that I may take it again. No one takes it from me, but I lay it down of myself. I have power to lay it down, and I have power to take it again. (John 10:14-18)

Daily Power!
Father, take me out of my "comfort zone" and put me in a place where Your heart of compassion beats in my own, giving me greater concern for the lost.

Mark My Word
Exodus 32
John 10:14-18; 15:13

The Bible In A Year

Morning
Leviticus 26
Psalm 33

Evening
Ecclesiastes 9
Titus 1

The story in Exodus 32 is a strange episode, but shows us the heart of a true intercessor. Israel had escaped from Egypt after a fantastic display of omnipotence that made God seem physically near. Above them towered Mount Sinai, with the cloud of God's glory concealing Moses, who had ascended to speak with God. The people thought that he had deserted them. Their simple minds were soaked in the superstitions of Egypt and its gods, so they made a golden calf to lead them back to Egypt.

The Lord said that he would put an end to them because of this appalling lapse, and begin a new nation through Moses. Moses' pity overcame his anger, and he pleaded for the nation that God called *"a stiff-necked people."* Moses countered by calling them *"Your people,"* adding, *"Oh, these people have committed a great sin ... Yet now, if you will forgive their sin – but if not, I pray, blot me out of your book."* Here, words failed him, such was the force of his compassionate outburst. he offered to die as an atonement for Israel's sin.

His offer was turned down because only the Son of God could atone for sin. This was true intercession.

Moses had not been pushed into it. He had brought this rabble of tribes to nationhood like a woman bringing a child into the world. They broke his heart, but he still defended them from the inevitable disaster of their own folly. *"Greater love has no one than this, than to lay down his life for his friends."* Are you exasperated by an unsaved friend or relative? **Pray for them!** They do not need a piece of your mind – they need the prayers of your heart.

Believers Who Did Not See Miracles

The idea that God disappeared is an old fear of unbelief. Israel participated in the Exodus, saw his glory, and knew it was all true. But within months, they became mistrustful. They wanted something to see. So they made a golden calf, to lead them back into slavery! Unbelief always leads to slavery. Faith means freedom.

However, they all lost their passports and visas of faith in God, and never crossed the border into the Promised Land – with two exceptions: Caleb and Joshua, who held onto their faith and entered in. Unbelief is that old. It is neither clever nor modern. Eve doubted. From that moment for her and us, it is a satanic nonsense and foolishness that never did anybody any good. If we are to deal with God, how on earth can it be but by trusting him? What trust is he likely to have with those who give him the cold shoulder, or pretend that he does not even exist? He owes us nothing, and if that is the way we want it, that is the way he will let it be: "*And even as they did not like to retain God in their knowledge, God gave them over to a debased mind, to do those things which are not fitting.*"

After the death of Joshua, very few ever saw a miracle until Christ came, except under Elijah and Elisha. In fact, very little happened that was supernatural. Yet men and women displayed amazing faith. Jesus spoke of them and said, "*Blessed are those who have not seen and yet have believed.*" They read the Scriptures, and believed that the God of the Exodus could not fail them and would work on their behalf. He did! David, for example, never saw a miracle, and had only the sketchiest experience of the supernatural – yet he went ahead in that total expectation of divine help. Today, three thousand years later, his faith is still a model for us. Stand firm in your faith today!

Today's Scripture
If you abide in my Word, you are my disciples indeed. And you shall know the truth, and the truth shall make you free. (John 8:31-32)

Daily Power!
The just shall live by faith.

Mark My Word
Exodus 32:1-35
John 20:29
Romans 1:17, 28

The Bible In A Year

Morning
Leviticus 27
Psalm 34

Evening
Ecclesiastes 10
Titus 2

24

Today's Scripture
That which is born of the flesh is flesh, and that which is born of the Spirit is spirit.
(John 3:6)

Daily Power!
The world may wobble around me, but I am centered on Christ Jesus.

Mark My Word
Genesis 3:3-4
Proverbs 14:33-34
John 3:1-21
Romans 12:2

The Bible In A Year

Morning
Numbers 1
Psalm 35

Evening
Ecclesiastes 11
Titus 3

God is our center, not this world. People say that we Christians are eccentric. An eccentric object wobbles around a point that is off-center, but that is what the Bible calls "the world"! It is not believers – evangelists, witnesses, Christians – who are eccentric, but the world! The world wobbles as it revolves around itself, but the believer is centered on God.

When people in the church talk about making the gospel relevant, they usually mean that we need to show that the gospel has something in common with the world of industry, entertainment or commerce. They have it backward! The question is whether the world is willing to relate to the message of the cross. Too bad for the world if it is not, for it **will** be judged at the cross. If the world is not relevant to the gospel, then the world is drifting - it has no anchor. *"And do not be conformed to this world, but be transformed by the renewing of your mind, that you may prove what is that good and acceptable and perfect will of God."*

The mistaken belief that "church and state should be separate" is not a new idea. The enemy has been trying to put people ahead of God in importance since the beginning of time: *"Then the serpent said to the woman, 'you will not surely die. For God knows that in the day you eat of it, your eyes will be opened, and you will be like God, knowing good and evil."* But God's Word proclaims, *"Wisdom rests in the heart of him who has understanding, but what is in the heart of fools is made known. Righteousness exalts a nation."*

Another thing that I hear people say is, "Evangelists answer questions the world is not asking." Thank God for that! We are **giving answers**, ready for when the world decides to ask the right questions. Because it is asking all the wrong questions, any answers would be equally wrong. Purpose in your heart to be ready with God's answers to every situation in life.

God Made Families

God wants families saved. The unity in the heart of Creation makes prayer for a family work. The Old Testament tells of God's family-work: he chose Israel from the days of Abraham and Sarah, and the tribes of Jacob.

They did not make themselves notable. They tended to blend into the neighboring heathen nations, where their identity would be lost. But their indifference showed God's great determination for the family to flourish! Despite themselves, he made Israel distinguished in racial character. After four thousand years, Israel is the most distinct single family on earth. No other race suffered such attempts at genocide, because no other race was so personal to God. The Nazi star upon their clothing was, in fact, a testimony by their enemies of their unbreakable family relationship. Captivity, loss of homeland, Jewish dispersion; nothing destroyed it, because Israel is God's sign to the world concerning his family design and purpose!

Isaiah pointed this out:

> "But now, thus says the Lord, who created you, O Jacob, and he who formed you, O Israel: 'Fear not, for I have redeemed you; I have called you by your name; you are Mine. For I am the Lord your God, the Holy One of Israel, your Savior; I gave Egypt for your ransom, Ethiopia and Seba in your place. Since you are precious in my sight, you have been honored, and I have loved you … Fear not, for I am with you; I will bring your descendants from the east and gather you from the west … Bring my sons from afar and my daughters from the ends of the earth – everyone who is called by my name, whom I have created for my glory; I have formed him, yes, I have made him.'"

Like a family named after the father, Israel bore God's name, **Isra-El**. "El" is basic Hebrew for the Deity. Today, wear your true name – "Christian" – with pride!

Today's Scripture
Fear not, for I have redeemed you, I have called you by your name, you are Mine. When you pass through the waters, I will be with you, and through the rivers, they shall not overflow you. When you walk through the fire, you shall not be burned, nor shall the flame scorch you; For I am the Lord your God.
(Isaiah 43:1-3)

Daily Power!
I am Christ's, and Abraham's seed; therefore I am an heir according to the promise.
(Galatians 3:29 paraphrased)

Mark My Word
Isaiah 43:1-28
Galatians 3:29

The Bible In A Year

Morning
Numbers 2
Psalm 36

Evening
Ecclesiastes 12
Philemon 1

26

Where can I go from Your Spirit? Or where can I flee from Your presence? If I ascend into heaven, you are there; If I make my bed in hell, behold, you are there. If I take the wings of the morning, and dwell in the uttermost parts of the sea, even there Your hand shall lead me, and Your right hand shall hold me. (Psalm 139:7-10)

Daily Power!
He himself has said, "I will never leave you nor forsake you."

Mark My Word
Hebrew 13:5
Psalm 139:7-10
Ezekiel 16:1-14
Hebrews 13:5

The Bible In A Year

Morning
Numbers 3
Psalm 37

Evening
Song 1
Hebrews 1

Concentrated Care

"As for your nativity, on the day you were born your navel cord was not cut, nor were you washed in water to cleanse you; you were not rubbed with salt nor wrapped in swaddling cloths. No eye pitied you, to do any of these things for you, to have compassion on you; but you were thrown out into the open field, when you yourself were loathed on the day you were born. And when I passed by you and saw you struggling in your own blood, I said to you in your blood, 'Live!' Yes, I said to you in your blood, 'Live!' I made you thrive like a plant in the field; and you grew, matured, and became very beautiful."

Ezekiel 16 likens the concentrated care of God for Israel to finding a newborn child cast out, which he saved, nursed, and nourished to become a beautiful woman. This parable typified God's intentions with the whole of humanity. When he brought the world and its inhabitants into existence, he did not walk away and leave us to our own devices, not even when we deliberately broke away. The Creator-creature bond can never be annulled. No matter how far we draw away, our existence is dependent on him. *"If I make my bed in hell, behold, you are there."* The link between Creator and his creatures may be stretched as slender as a spider's thread, but cannot be broken. He is always aware of us.

How often do we think that we are alone in this world, and it is always an uphill struggle to try to find where God must be hiding. Yet know this: the concentrated care that God lavishes on you, whether or not you recognize his hand active in your life, he gives because he **wants to**, not because you deserve it.

His love for you is without limit, and his gift of salvation – where your estrangement from him is erased and you are drawn close to his heart – is given freely.

Jesus – God And Man

We know that Jesus is coming back because he is one of us – just like you and me! We read in Hebrews 2: "*Inasmuch then as the children have partaken of flesh and blood, he himself likewise shared in the same, that through death he might destroy him who had the power of death, that is, the devil.*" He belongs to the family of man, and he will not desert his family, nor stay away forever.

Jesus Christ was fully human, conceived by God, but born of a woman. It was his intention to live a full life, and to readily identify with us. If his sole purpose was to be a sacrifice for our sins, he could have been crucified as an infant. But he chose to endure all the heartaches and hardships that we do, because of his great compassion for us. "*For we do not have a high priest who cannot sympathize with our weaknesses, but was in all points tempted as we are, yet without sin.*" Jesus was the Son of Man **and** the Son of God.

But "*there is one God and one mediator between God and men, the Man Christ Jesus.*" A mediator has links to both parties. He is the only mediator – like Jacob's ladder – set up between heaven and earth. Jesus binds heaven and earth, God and man, together in himself. His presence on earth will be the most natural thing of all. This is the great hope to which we cling!

Today's Scripture
But we see Jesus, who was made a little lower than the angels, for the suffering of death crowned with glory and honor, that he, by the grace of God, might taste death for everyone.
(Hebrews 2:9)

Daily Power!
I have a mediator between almighty God and myself - the Lord Jesus Christ.

Mark My Word
1 Timothy 2:5
Hebrews 2:5-14; 4:15

The Bible In A Year

Morning
Numbers 4
Psalm 38

Evening
Song 2
Hebrews 2

28

Jesus In The Real World

Today's Scripture
God demonstrates his own love toward us, in that while we were still sinners, Christ died for us. (Romans 5:8)

Daily Power!
Christ himself bore my sins in his own body on the tree, that I, having died to sins, might live for righteousness (1 Peter 2:24 paraphrased)

Mark My Word
Matthew 1:23; 27: 27-56
Romans 5:8
2 Corinthians 5:21

The Bible In A Year

Morning
Numbers 5
Psalm 39

Evening
Song 3
Hebrews 3

Who was Jesus? The Bible tells us that he was "*Emmanuel - God with us.*" Jesus showed us God getting involved in the real world. He got his hands dirty! He got his hands nailed to a cross! And he did it so that we could be set free from the power and devastation of sin.

When Roman prisoners were marched out to be crucified, they carried the crossbeam on their shoulders. With their arms tied to the beam, they walked, bent double, to the place of execution. That is how Jesus walked through Jerusalem to the execution hill called Calvary.

> "Then the soldiers of the governor took Jesus into the Praetorium and gathered the whole garrison around him. And they stripped him and put a scarlet robe on him. When they had twisted a crown of thorns, they put it on his head, and a reed in his right hand. And they bowed the knee before him and mocked him, saying, 'Hail, King of the Jews!' Then they spat on him, and took the reed and struck him on the head. And when they had mocked him, they took the robe off him, put his own clothes on him, and led him away to be crucified."

It was as if he was carrying a. banner – a giant sign – proclaiming an awful truth in a language that the whole world could understand and never forget. The crossbeam carried by Jesus speaks of our human minus or negative – the failure and sin that lies in the heart of us all.

The cross shows us God's incredible response to human suffering. God himself entered into our suffering, and took our sin on himself. Jesus, although he was completely innocent and without sin, was made to be "sin for us." As one of the first Christians put it: "*While we were still sinners, Christ died for us.*"

On that hill, Jesus put the crossbeam of our sin and wickedness across the upright. He changed our human **minus** into God's **plus**. Jesus released the power of God's mercy, forgiveness and healing to anyone who would come to him and simply ask for it. That means me!

Saints In Lights

Look at them! What a blaze of glory glitters down the endless stream of redeemed humanity! Here is one of the first. Mary, once torn apart inwardly by seven demons, sat in love near his empty tomb, as his everlasting worshipper: *"Now when he rose early on the first day of the week, he appeared first to Mary Magdalene, out of whom he had cast seven demons."*

Here is Peter – Jesus had to work hard on him, but now he is resplendent in divine light: *"Blessed be the God and Father of our Lord Jesus Christ, who according to his abundant mercy has begotten us again to a living hope through the resurrection of Jesus Christ from the dead."*

And here is Paul, who persecuted him: *"But the Lord said to him, 'Go, for he is a chosen vessel of mine to bear my name before Gentiles, kings and the children of Israel.'"* The thief who mocked him; Zacchaeus, into whose house and life the Lord Jesus came. The trail of light passes down the long centuries. Those who love Jesus: martyrs, apostles, saints, people who praised God while their fingers burned like tapers, evangelists, pastors, missionaries, humble workers, the faithful, you and me.

He saved a poor sinner like me! One day we shall be there with the saints in light, drawn from all tribes, all bathed in his glory. Former adulterers, homosexuals, thieves, liars, perverts, witches, murderers, addicts, Satanists, the covetous, the idolaters, the unclean; sophisticated and unsophisticated side by side, learned and simple hand in hand – all washed in the blood of Jesus! Such is the population of the kingdom of God! This is the glory of the King: rejoice today, that your name is written in the Lamb's Book of Life!

Today's Scripture
O God, You are my God; early will I seek you; my soul thirsts for you, my flesh longs for You in a dry and thirsty land where there is no water. So I have looked for you in the sanctuary, to see Your power and Your glory. (Psalm 63:1-2)

Daily Power!
My name is written in the Lamb's book of life. I will rejoice and give thanks!

Mark My Word
Psalm 63:1-11
Mark 16:9
Luke 19:1-10
Acts 9:15
1 Peter 1:3.

The Bible In A Year

Morning
Numbers 6
Psalms 40 and 41

Evening
Song 4
Hebrews 4

30

Christ's Great Commission

It was impossible to act on the Great Commission before the Day of Pentecost. Jesus had told his disciples to wait. **Then** things started to happen! The evangelism that took place on that one day produced the church. But, what is the church? Are we clear about its nature and its purpose? The church is an extension of the compassion of the Lord Jesus, of his comfort, his healing, his goodness. "*Jesus of Nazareth … went about doing good and healing all who were oppressed by the devil, for God was with him.*" That is the church and that is what we should be doing!

The church is his body, we are told. God has no arms but ours with which to embrace this pitiable world. Love is his supreme characteristic. I feel that we are only his body to the degree that we show evidence of his compassion. A loveless church is no church. The love of God personified in Jesus needs to be in the church. "*Let this mind be in you which was also in Christ Jesus.*"

The church continues the day of Pentecost, when it burst into view with speaking in tongues, with prophecy and fire! If the church is not like that – no fire, no tongues, no prophecies, no evangelism, no bold preaching of Christ and the Resurrection, no triumphant certainty and promise – how can we identify it as the same church?

Without the power and manifestation of the Spirit, we are left with human wisdom and energies. Relied upon alone, they leave the church an empty shell. You do not need to belong to that "church," but to the living church of Christ!

The gospel is not an alternative,
it is God's ultimatum.

The Bible is the constitution of the kingdom of God.

Unity is not uniformity.

God's Living Stones

The five "gifts" listed in Ephesians – apostles, prophets, evangelists, pastors, and teachers – are given to meet the aim of building up the body of Christ. The purpose is made clear in Paul's first letter to the Corinthians: "*...the manifestation of the Spirit is given to each one for the profit of all.*"

He names again three of the same gifts – apostles, prophets and teachers – but in place of evangelists and pastors, he refers to those who work miracles, have the gifts of healing, speak with tongues, and interpret. He continues saying that the church is built up (edified) by prophecy and tongues. All these gifts are given to believers for the benefit of their fellow-believers, to build up the unity of the church. There are no dead stones, only living stones, equipped to serve.

The whole theme of Ephesians is not what we are, but what **He is.** It is Christ with whom we should be concerned, not church offices. God at work in us and through us, by him and for him. He is "*the fullness of him who fills all in all.*" He does not evangelize, but expects us to do so by his endowment. When we are his, then we are his voice, his hands and his feet. He is the fullness filling us, filling the church, and making it what it is. Behind everything is the gift of his grace. What a treasure we have within us – and completely equipped to fulfill his assignment!

Later in Ephesians, Paul listed the equipment needed to be effective soldiers in God's army ... and then he tells us that even soldiers receive promotions: "*For which I am an **ambassador** in chains, that in it I may speak boldly, as I ought to speak.*"

To walk with God's own authority, to speak boldly the **truth** to the world in Christ's name, and with his love is your divine responsibility! Walk in that authority.

Today's Scripture
Coming to him as to a living stone, rejected indeed by men, but chosen by God and precious, you also, as living stones, are being built up a spiritual house, a holy priesthood, to offer up spiritual sacrifices acceptable to God through Jesus Christ. (1 Peter 2:4-5)

Daily Power!
Thank You, Father, that you have established me as one of Your living stones in the kingdom!

Mark My Word
1 Corinthians 12:1-31; 14:1-39
Ephesians 1:23; 4:11
6:1-24

The Bible In A Year

Morning
Numbers 8
Psalm 44

Evening
Song 6
Hebrews 6

2

Today's Scripture
Speak, Lord, for your
servant hears.
(1 Samuel 3:9)

Daily Power!
I am eternally grateful,
Father, that you have
chosen me to be your
beloved child.

Mark My Word
1 Samuel 3:1-21
Luke 6:12-17

The Bible In A Year

Morning
Numbers 9
Psalm 45

Evening
Song 7
Hebrews 7

Hardly Supermen

The twelve disciples were anything but supermen. How did Jesus choose his apostles? In the gospel of Luke, we read:

> "Now it came to pass in those days that he went out to the mountain to pray, and continued all night in prayer to God. And when it was day, he called his disciples to himself; and from them he chose twelve whom he also named apostles: Simon, whom he also named Peter, and Andrew his brother; James and John; Philip and Bartholomew; Matthew and Thomas; James the son of Alphaeus, and Simon called the Zealot; Judas the son of James, and Judas Iscariot who also became a traitor. And he came down with them and stood on a level place with a crowd of his disciples and a great multitude of people from all Judea and Jerusalem, and from the seacoast of Tyre and Sidon, who came to hear him and be healed of their diseases."

Jesus prayed "*all night*" before he selected his disciples. Usually it is thought that through the night, God dropped the name of each apostle one by one into the mind of the Lord – "You should pick Bartholomew, Matthew, Thaddeus …" – and that the Lord made a list of divinely nominated and approved characters. Perhaps he took one hour over each one of them to establish that he had got it right. He prayed all night means – so experts propose – twelve hours, one hour for each apostle!

Now I dare to ask: was that really what He did – to ask for the guidance to choose men of just the right calibers and potential, men whose greatness God could see beforehand? Or was Jesus, in fact, wrestling with the temptation to choose the brilliant, the influential, the mighty? I can imagine that it could be so. It could have been twelve hours of prayer struggling between the way of the world (to plan success by appointing gifted men) … and God's way. If that is the case, do you think God would have chosen **you** or **me**? Let us believe, together, that each of us has his divine calling engraved in our hearts … and let us treasure and thank he for that calling today.

Jonah – The Reluctant Evangelist

When you read through the Bible, beginning at Genesis, you will find nothing said about evangelism until you get to the little book of Jonah – a book that stands out from the rest of the Bible. It is almost the evangelist's vade mecum – a personal handbook for daily use.

Though most people are acquainted with Jonah, many (including some Christians) do not believe the story presented in this book. They think that there is "something fishy" about the story of Jonah! However, Jesus and his contemporaries regarded it as history, not as a fable, or even a parable. And whoever wrote down the story of Jonah knew how to write. This small book deserves our close attention.

> "This is an evil generation. It seeks a sign, and no sign will be given to it except the sign of Jonah the prophet. For as Jonah became a sign to the Ninevites, so also the Son of Man will be to this generation … The men of Nineveh will rise up in the judgment of this generation and condemn it, for they repented at the preaching of Jonah, and indeed a greater than Jonah is here."

The prophet Jonah lived about eight hundred years before Christ. He heard the call of God to go to Nineveh, the last capital city of the Assyrian Empire. It stood on the River Tigris, six hundred miles as the crow flies due east from where Jonah lived. Instead of going to Nineveh, however, Jonah bought passage on a ship to Tarshish – that is, going west – in the other direction. He was desperate to get away from his obligation … Nineveh was the **last place** he wanted to go!

Have you ever been in that place – where God asked you to do something for him, to go somewhere for him … and you just did not want to do it? I know I have! Yet, I have found that every time I stepped out in faith to obey him, his mercy was always there to lead and guide me: "*In you, O Lord, I put my trust … For you are my Rock and my Fortress; therefore, for your name's sake, lead me and guide me.*" If God is asking you to step out in faith to do something today … just say "Yes" and let him lead you and guide you … today!

Today's Scripture
Salvation is
of the Lord.
(Jonah 2:9)

Daily Power!
Lord, strengthen me,
so that where you
lead I will follow.

Mark My Word
Psalm 31:1-3
Jonah 1 to 4
Matthew 12:38-42

The Bible In A Year

Morning
Numbers 10
Psalms 46 and 47

Evening
Song 8
Hebrews 8

4

Going Down

Today's Scripture
Jesus said to him, "If you can believe, all things are possible to him who believes." (Mark 9:23)

Daily Power!
My constant assurance is that with God, all things are possible!

Mark My Word
Jonah 1 to 4
Matthew 19:16-26
Mark 9:14-29

The Bible In A Year

Morning
Numbers 11
Psalm 48

Evening
Isaiah 1
Hebrews 9

When we read about Jonah, note the way that his flight is described. Jonah chapter one says he went **down** to Joppa ... then he went **down** into the ship ... and then went **down** into the ship's hold. Then when a storm came, the sailors threw Jonah **down** into the sea, and a great fish swallowed him up, and he went **down** into the belly of the big fish. He then prayed, saying to the Lord, "*You cast me into the deep ... I went down to the moorings of the mountains.*" After the fish had vomited Jonah onto dry land, the Lord spoke a second time, and the text says, "*Jonah arose.*" Going to preach when God sends us is elevating – we arise!

Let us have a little sympathy for Jonah: Nineveh really did have a fearsome reputation! One or two of their kings were decidedly brutal, some of the worst to ever walk the earth. They took pleasure in atrocities and cruelties so monstrous that they shock us even today. Jonah certainly did not relish the thought of a confrontation with men like that. How could a foreigner hope to preach against them and come out alive?

Of course, he did eventually go ... and Nineveh fully repented of its wicked ways. Jonah's preaching was effective. Yet Jonah wanted to see the judgment of God fall on Nineveh ... and who could blame him? He had warned the city that God was about to destroy it. Their wickedness had reached the ears of God, and judgment was what they deserved. But the city repented, and God withheld his judgment (at least for a period of time – less than two hundred years later, Nineveh was totally destroyed).

Sometimes you and I feel like God is calling us to impossible tasks – but take heart: God is the God of the impossible!

Seven Rules Of Prayer

(1) **Ask in faith in God.** We cannot ask too much, and blow a fuse by overloading the demand on divine help. **Ask!** That is Christ's **command**, so you cannot be outside the will of God by asking ... but you can tie his hands if you do not ask.

(2) **Do not come apologetically.** Ask anyway, and let God decide how to act. We have made it such a mark of high piety to ask only for what God wants that it contradicts what Jesus said: "*And whatever you ask in my name, that I will do.*" God allows mature believers free choice over large areas of their lives – and blesses what they decide.

(3) **Forgive as God forgives you:** "*And whenever you stand praying, if you have anything against anyone, forgive him, that your Father in heaven may also forgive you your trespasses.*"

4) **Do not pray** "*to be heard of men,*" but with sincerity. Remember: God is full of grace.

5) **Pray in the name of Jesus.** Since we are in Christ, one with him, when we pray in the name of Jesus, we are speaking with Christ's merits imputed to us. Use common sense.

(6) **Cherish the Word of God.** Notice the balance of this sentence: "*If ... my words remain in you, ask whatever you wish, and it will be given you.*" The Psalmist wrote: "*If I had cherished sin in my heart, the Lord would not have listened.*" Treasure the Word of Christ; do not cherish iniquity.

(7) **Deal with obstacles to answered prayer.** James warns why many times we may not be heard: "*He who doubts ... should not suppose that he will receive anything from the Lord ... You ask and do not receive, because you ask amiss, that you may spend it on your pleasures.*" Wisdom in prayer is essential.

Apply these guides to your prayer life and see for yourself how prayer really does change things!

Today's Scripture

But love your enemies, do good, and lend, hoping for nothing in return; and your reward will be great, and you will be sons of the Most High. For he is kind to the unthankful and evil world.
(Luke 6:35)

Daily Power!

In obedience to Christ's command – "Ask!" – I will spend time today in prayer.

Mark My Word

Psalm 66:18
Matthew 5:23-24; 21:22
Mark 11:25
Luke 6:35-37; 18:10-14
John 14:13; 15:7; 16:23
James 1:6-7; 4:3

The Bible In A Year

Morning

Numbers 12 and 13
Psalm 49

Evening

Isaiah 2
Hebrews 10

6

Perfect Wisdom

Today's Scripture
I am God, and there is none like me, declaring the end from the beginning, and from ancient times things that are not yet done, saying, "My counsel shall stand, and I will do all my pleasure." (Isaiah 46:9-10)

Daily Power!
Whenever I pray, God weighs my requests against his plan-without-time, and then answers accordingly.

Mark My Word
2 Kings 20:1-21;
21:1-26;
Isaiah 38:1-22;
46:9-10
Jeremiah 17:10
Matthew 1:1-17
Luke 22:32

The Bible In A Year

Morning
Numbers 14
Psalm 50

Evening
Isaiah 3 and 4
Hebrews 11

Jesus prayed: "*Not my will, but yours be done.*" We are not all-wise and do not make perfect petitions. If we had unlimited power, we would soon make a mess of things. God, however, will not be persuaded to do what is folly – not even to please somebody. his answers are wiser than our prayers, even his "**No!**"

It used to be taught that when King Hezekiah prayed for longer life and God granted it, that this was actually **against** God's will – "*Thus says the Lord, the God of David your father, 'I have heard your prayer I have seen your tears, surely I will heal you … surely I will add to your days fifteen years.*" This was taught, because it was during those fifteen years that Manasseh, Hezekiah's wicked son, was born. Later, for over fifty years, Manasseh led the nation into wickedness. But, if Hezekiah had died without a son, then David's line would have come to a premature end. Therefore, it was in God's will to grant the extra fifteen years.

In Christ's "family tree," there are princes and criminals, prostitutes and warriors, kings and idolaters – and so there are in every family tree. From generation to generation, God is constantly seeking those who will turn their hearts toward him: Noah found his favor in the midst of sin … Abraham turned away from the false gods of Ur … Rahab the harlot helped save the people of Israel … Ruth left the idols of Moab and married Boaz, to become grandparents of David the king … and so on. Only God knows:

> "The heart is deceitful above all things, and desperately
> wicked; who can know it? I, the Lord, search the heart,
> I test the mind, even to give every man according to his
> ways, according to the fruit of his doings."

God does nothing against his will – even his "long-term" will – because he knows the end from the beginning, and never makes a mistake. Therefore … you can pray on with confidence … for your prayers are not in vain!

Prepare Your Family

The minds of children – indeed all of us – need protection, for which we have a full set of spiritual armor: "*Put on the whole armor of God that you may be able to stand against the wiles of the devil.*"

That is why every father in Israel was commanded to teach the children around their table the words of the covenant of God: "*These words which I command you today shall be in your heart. You shall teach them diligently to your children, and shall talk of them when you sit in your house, when you walk by the way, when you lie down, and when you rise up.*"

The need is underlined in the Bible by the tragic fact that not every godly man had godly children, which usually ended in tragedy. The high priest Eli and the prophet Samuel both had sons who broke their fathers' hearts: "*Now the sons of Eli were corrupt; they did not know the Lord ... Therefore the sin of the young men was very great before the Lord, for men abhorred the offering of the Lord ... Now it came to pass when Samuel was old that he made his sons judges over Israel ... But his sons did not walk in his ways; they turned aside after dishonest gain, took bribes and perverted justice.*" When our children do not follow godly ways, they can bring whole nations to ruin.

God had appointed priests and judges to rule his people Israel, but when Samuel's sons became godless, the people began to clamor for a different way of government – which ultimately took Israel back into the wilderness of godlessness. Training our children to walk in godly ways, and then helping them maintain that walk into their adult years, is more important than doing it just for our own satisfaction. It works closely with God's ultimate plan: that our families will be shining examples of godly living in a world filled with darkness and anarchy.

Today's Scripture
Train up a child in the way he should go, and when he is old he will not depart from it. (Proverbs 22:6)

Daily Power!
Lord, you have the words of eternal life, help me to live by them and show the world that they are true.

Mark My Word
1 Samuel 2:12, 17; 8: 1-3 Proverbs 22:6
John 6:68
Ephesians 6:10-17

The Bible In A Year

Morning
Numbers 15
Psalm 51

Evening
Isaiah 5
Hebrews 12

8

First Generation

Today's Scripture
Let us eat and be merry, for this my son was dead and is alive again; he was lost and is found.
(Luke 15:23-24)

Daily Power!
My life is an example to others, for good or evil!

Mark My Word
Deuteronomy 30:19
Luke 15:11-32
Romans 6:23; 10: 9-10

The Bible In A Year

Morning
Numbers 16
Psalms 52, 53 and 54

Evening
Isaiah 6
Hebrews 13

God has no grandchildren. We teach our children to know God, to understand his Word, and to walk in righteousness. We believe that our well-taught children will turn to God, and we also believe in the promise that our households will be saved through our witness. But there is no automatic guarantee that our children will follow after God – parents cannot choose to **make** their children righteous. As godly parents, we must train our children; pray fervently for their salvation, and that of our loved ones; but whatever decisions they make are up to them! That is free will: "*I have set before you life and death, blessing and cursing; therefore choose life, that both you and your descendants may live.*"

God cares so much for his children that he constantly seeks them, wooing them with love. But even the best-raised children can be stubborn and rebellious, wandering away from their godly heritage. The perfect example is the parable of the Prodigal Son:

> "A certain man had two sons, and the younger said, 'Father give me the portion of goods that falls to me.' So he divided to them his livelihood. And not many days after, the younger son gathered all together, journeyed to a far country, and there wasted his possessions with prodigal living … But when he came to himself, he said, 'I will arise and go to my father, and will say to him: Father, I have sinned against heaven and before you … Make me like one of your servants.' And he arose and came to his father. But when he was still a great way off, his father saw him and had compassion, and ran and fell on his face and kissed him … 'For this my son was dead and is alive again; he was lost and is found.'"

I do not know of any Christian parents of wayward children who would not respond with joyful tears when their loved ones returned to God! As Christian parents, our responsibility is to set a good, consistent example for our children, and then believe that the attractions of sin will be shown for their actual evil nature, and that our children will return voluntarily to a personal relationship with God. God has chosen children – all of them are "first generation."

The Cross: The Logo Of God's Love

The story of Jesus does not end with the crucifixion. If it did, the cross would be a symbol of crushing defeat and despair. The Good News is that Jesus not only destroyed the power of sin on the cross, He also destroyed the power of death. On the third day, God raised him back to life, triumphant over darkness, death and Satan:

> "And behold, there was a great earthquake, for an angel of the Lord descended from heaven, and came and rolled back the stone from the door, and sat on it … and the guards shook for fear of him, and became like dead men. But the angel answered and said to the women, 'Do not be afraid, for I know that you seek Jesus who was crucified. He is not here, for he is risen, as he said. Come, see the place where the Lord lay.'"

Jesus, the carpenter of Nazareth, turned the wood of the cross into the Door to Life. That is the deep heart of the Good News: **The cross has the power to transform us.** Minus is turned to plus, negative to positive. On the cross, darkness changes to light, death to life, hate to love, chains to freedom, fear to faith, despair to joy, brokenness to wholeness… and hell to heaven!

Jesus is still alive! He is here today, to reverse every curse and to cancel Satan's evil work. Sinners are forgiven. The sick are made well. Broken relationships are restored. Against the power of Jesus on the cross, the forces of evil will finally be defeated! This is why the cross is the symbol or logo of the Christian faith. It belongs to Jesus alone. No founder or leader of another religion would dare to use this logo because it stands for something that they themselves have never done!

None of them has been crucified for the sins of the world. None of them has been raised from the dead. None of them can give us the help we so desperately need. Only Jesus is able to save us. As he said: "*I am the way, the truth, and the life; no one comes to the Father except through me.*" Embrace the cross of Jesus Christ – not as a symbol of death – but as God's transforming promise to turn negative into positive.

Today's Scripture

In my Father's House are many mansions; if it were not so, I would have told you. I go to prepare a place for you. And if I go and prepare a place for you, I will come again and receive you to myself, that where I am, there you may be also.
(John 14:2-4)

Daily Power!

The message of the cross is foolishness to those who are perishing, but to us who are being saved it is the power of God.

Mark My Word

Matthew 28:1-20
John 14:1-6
1 Corinthians 1:18

The Bible In A Year

Morning

Numbers 17 and 18
Psalm 55

Evening

Isaiah 7
James 1

10

The God who loves us so completely is also the One who holds ultimate power in the universe. He is the One who created all things simply by calling them into being. The Bible also tells us that Jesus, as God's Son, is the brightness of God's glory.

Hanging on the cross, Jesus appeared to be anything but powerful. Laughed at by the crowds, tortured by the soldiers, deserted by his friends, slowly bleeding to death – Jesus seemed helpless. Yet it was at the cross that the Power of God was released!

> "With him they also crucified two robbers … and those who passed by blasphemed him, wagging their heads and saying: 'Aha! You who destroy the temple and build it in three days, Save Yourself and come down from the cross.' Likewise, the chief priests also, mocking among themselves with the scribes, said: 'He saved others, himself he cannot save. Let the Christ, the King of Israel, descend now from the cross, that we may see and believe.' Even those who were crucified with him reviled him."

One way to picture it is through nuclear power. In every atom, positive and negative forces are held together in balance. But, when the atom is split, positive splits from negative and power is released, either for destruction or for benefit. Something like this happened on the cross. Hanging there, Jesus experienced in himself two opposing forces: the negative of our sins, and the positive of God's Love. Jesus was the holy, perfect Son of God, and yet on the cross, he was made "*sin for us.*" There he became the cosmic center where all evil and goodness meet.

Finally, Jesus overcame evil, which split away, setting loose new powers of righteousness and resurrection. Evil, death, guilt and fear are conquered, while the saving power of God's love is released for everyone who asks. Within three days, this new power swung into action, when Christ gloriously rose from the dead. Jesus Christ is alive today: is that not great news! Go out and share the Good News with someone you love today!

Today's Scripture
For he made him who knew no sin to be sin for us, that we might become the righteousness of God in him.
(2 Corinthians 5:21)

Daily Power!
That I may know him and the power of his resurrection, and the fellowship of his sufferings.

Mark My Word
Mark 15: 27-32
2 Corinthians 5:21
Philippians 3:10
Hebrews 1:3

The Bible In A Year

Morning
Numbers 19
Psalms 56 and 57

Evening
Isaiah 8 to 9:7
James 2

The Tingling Impulse

I was just a young boy when I received the baptism of the Holy Spirit, but soon after that initial experience, I was in a service which my father was leading in North Germany. During the prayers I began to be impressed to do something that I knew my father would not like, even though it was nothing wrong. Inexplicably, I could not stop thinking about a woman on the opposite side of the church. This feeling grew stronger, not just in my head: it seemed to be all over me. I tingled with this feeling more and more, like steadily increasing voltage. I tried to push it out, but the tingling current became stronger. "I shall have to do it!" I spoke to myself. "But what will she say … and what will Father do?" So I crouched down behind the seats, and step-by-step, moved across to her. Then I whispered: "I want to pray for you."

She looked at me and answered: "All right, pray for me!" I put my hand on this grown woman – and something happened: the current in my body seemed to jolt right out into her.

At that point, Father could not help but notice. He asked: "Reinhard, what are you doing?"

The lady responded for me: "Reinhard put his hand on me, and I felt the power of the Lord go through me … and look! I am well! I am healed!" At that time, I did not know the spiritual principles behind this healing; if we are obedient, there is enough power from God. I still had to learn that lesson, and many like it.

Many times one hears about the awe-inspiring visitations and revelations of others. They are exciting, but they often leave people feeling downcast because they themselves have had nothing like it. They think that they must be inferior to these God-used people. I want you to know the truth about the Holy Spirit; he is for all Christian workers, not only for those who happen to have had some rare and fantastic moments. Many will be like new people when they discover these truths – I trust this is true for you, too.

Today's Scripture
You shall receive power when the Holy Spirit has come upon you.
(Acts 1:8)

Daily Power!
And (add your name), full of faith and power, did great wonders and signs among the people.

Mark My Word
Acts 1:1-8; 2:1-47; 6:8

The Bible In A Year

Morning
Numbers 21
Psalms 58 and 59

Evening
Isaiah 9:8 to 10:4
James 3

When The Spirit Comes

Today's Scripture
For it is the God who commanded light to shine out of darkness, who has shone in our hearts to give the light of the knowledge of the glory of God in the face of Jesus Christ.
(2 Corinthians 4:6)

Daily Power!

Christianity is the Holy Spirit in action, making the Word of God happen.

Mark My Word
John 14:6
Acts 1:5, 8
2 Corinthians 4:6

The Bible In A Year

Morning
Numbers 21
Psalms 60 and 61

Evening
Isaiah 10:5
James 4

There is a promise that we are so familiar with that we may have lost sight of its tremendous wonder. It is one of the most impossible and fantastic expectations that any person could ever entertain: "*You shall be baptized with the Holy Spirit … you shall receive power when the Holy Spirit has come upon you.*" Could this really happen in the 20th century? It did for me. I cannot think of anything more wonderful for humans than that. It means being filled with God. It is not giddy happiness without substance. The Holy Spirit is not a tranquilizer. Rather, his presence is heart-moving. God sends his power into the tough situations of life. He is the original Life-Force meant for us all. Over the years, fresh enlightenment has burst upon me. It is all so wonderful! God wants me to share it with the whole world in my preaching.

Christianity is divine power in action! Christian truth is alive. The breath of God animates the gospel, or it would remain a dead body of truth instead of living truth. Jesus said: "*I am the Way, the Truth, and the Life.*"

Christianity is the Holy Spirit in action, making the Word of God happen. The gospel is what it claims to be. When a champion athlete stands on the track, we do not need to argue in order to prove that he is world-class. Just fire the starting pistol!

The gospel of Christ is alive, so I go into a stadium and let the gospel do its own thing. Everybody can see that it is alive. It is the work of the Holy Spirit. Believe me when I tell you that what I have witnessed the power of the gospel do in a stadium filled with thousands, that same power will do in a single heart that is filled with a desire to receive all that God has for it!

Demystifying Faith

There are some odd ideas about faith. Faith is not believing what you know is not true nor believing something for which there is no evidence. That is foolish. The Bible is a book about faith ... and the elementary fact is that faith is built-in. We are born believers. If you think you have no faith – try not believing in anything or anybody, your spouse, doctor, bank, boss, or banker. There are no guarantees. We put our lives into the hands of surgeons; we trust drivers of trains, cars, and planes; we eat food prepared by total strangers: all without thinking of faith. But that's what it is.

Faith is a kind of immune system filtering out fears that otherwise would paralyze all activity. When it fails, we develop phobias and compulsions. Jesus said not to have phobia but faith. Stop using this faculty of faith, and you would never get out of bed in the morning or step outside. In this world, a million troubles are coiled to strike like a cobra.

But we carry on, usually quite regardless and confident. The Bible says: "*God has dealt to each one a measure of faith.*" Christ said: "*Only believe,*" because we can.

Getting married is one of the best illustrations of faith I know. Did any bride or bridegroom ever imagine the other was perfect? Yet they commit themselves to each other for life, for better or worse. One bride refused to repeat the words "I take thee for better for worse," retorting: "I only take him for worse. I know he'll never be better." She still went ahead, confident ... but not optimistic!

There is no mystique about faith. Perhaps little children are the biggest believers. Many a time I have lifted a child in my arms, but not one ever screamed for fear of falling. Jesus himself carried a child as an illustrated sermon. He said that the child carried a passport to the kingdom of God. Faith does not come by murdering common sense. It is not a peculiar psychology developed with great effort by bizarre "saints" in isolated caves, living on bread and water. It is natural. Doubt is peculiar – irrational, in fact. It is the only thing that ever surprised Jesus.

Today's Scripture
God has dealt to each one a measure of faith. (Romans 12:3)

Daily Power!
Faith is natural, doubt is irrational.

Mark My Word
Mark 5:36
Luke 8:50
Romans 12:3.

The Bible In A Year

Morning
Numbers 22
Psalms 62 and 63

Evening
Isaiah 11 and 12
James 5

14

Today's Scripture
The path of the just is like the shining sun, that shines ever brighter unto the perfect day.
(Proverbs 4:18)

Daily Power!
Faith is a perfectly ordinary thing that makes us outstanding in the eyes of God.

Mark My Word
Proverbs 4:18
Hebrews 11:1-40

The Bible In A Year

Morning
Numbers 23
Psalms 64 and 65

Evening
Isaiah 13
1 Peter 1

People often confuse faith and virtue. Virtue is developed. People talk about "big believers," as if believing came in sizes like suit jackets. But we can have faith even when we know we are not very good. Sinners can have faith – otherwise they could never be saved! Nobody is good … but Christ taught us that *all* can believe. He commended some people for their faith – but they were foreigners, quite ignorant of doctrine. The Bible does the same. In Hebrews chapter 11, it has a "Roll of Honor," listing heroes and heroines of great faith. They are remembered not for valor or kindness, but for their complete reliance upon God. Faith is a perfectly ordinary thing that makes us outstanding in the eyes of God. Scripture states: "*Without faith it is impossible to please him.*" By faith, it is possible to please God … and faith is possible to everybody.

We are what we believe. We had better watch what we believe. We make that decision, and it, in turn, makes us. Some believe in UFOs: or that the earth is alive, or in voices from the dead. There are a million things to believe … but God is supreme. We are focused on believing in God. There are those who believe in believing. Surveys show that practically everybody believes in a god: some sort of god, somewhere. The question is: what sort?

Believing tests us. The kind of god we believe in forms the window into our soul – believing in Christ, or Karl Marx, for example. Following a faith that only demands a few prayers – what does that say about us? Minimum-effort religions can be quite popular – small demands, big following – cheap faith for people who have sold their inheritance for a "bowl of stew."

Jesus Christ asks everything: *"Give me your heart."* A broad religion is an easy road but gets narrower and leads to nowhere. Hold fast to this truth: your faith in Christ is a narrow road that gets wider and goes some where.

Miracles And Skepticism

Miracles today are always suspect. "Tongues couldn't be the same tongues as on the Day of Pentecost" … "Angels were real then, but they are hallucinations now" … "Bible miracles were real miracles but not today's" … "There was real revival two hundred years ago, but the quality is missing today." Critics think that people do not even pray like they used to do, and all the greatest men and women of God lived yesterday: "There were giants in the earth in those days, but Christians now are all pygmies." As Jesus said: "*O you of little faith … how long shall I be with you?*"

When Jesus went to the grave of Lazarus and began to show what he was about to do, telling them to remove the stone blocking the mouth of the tomb, Martha was shocked, protesting: "*Lord, by this time there is a stench, for he has been dead four days.*" his reply still comes ringing in all our ears, rattling against our impervious pessimism like welcoming rain on the hard wilderness:

> "If you would believe, you would see the glory of God!"

Only doubt and you will not move a molehill, never mind a mountain. That day, the God of the past performed the greatest wonder ever seen: Lazarus walked out of the grave.

The God of Moses and Elijah is not behind you, but ahead of you! You cannot update him. He has brought in the kingdom age, the dispensation of the Holy Spirit. his message to you and me is loud and clear … "*all things are possible to him who believes!*"

Today's Scripture
Jesus said:
"If you can believe, all things are possible to him who believes."
(Mark 9:23)

Daily Power!
When I believe, then all things are possible.

Mark My Word
Matthew 6:30; 17:17
Mark 9:23
John 11:39-40

The Bible In A Year

Morning
Numbers 24
Psalms 66 and 67

Evening
Isaiah 14
1 Peter 2

16

Revival Is Here!

Today's Scripture
If my people who
are called by my
name will humble
themselves, and pray
and seek my face,
and turn from their
wicked ways,
then I will hear from
heaven, and will
forgive their sin and
heal their land.
(2 Chronicles 7:14)

Daily Power!
Lord, help me to
humble myself, to
pray and seek your
face and to turn from
my wicked ways.

Mark My Word
2 Chronicles 7:14
Acts 7:56

The Bible In A Year

Morning
Numbers 25
Psalm 68

Evening
Isaiah 15
1 Peter 3

People have been brought up in Charismatic churches, but are still praying week in and week out, year in and year out: "Lord, send the old-time power." Send it? He already has! That is what Pentecost means – **the Holy Spirit has come.** The Lord rent the Heavens – Jesus came and tore them open again like the veil of the Temple when he soared back to God. When Stephen, the first Christian martyr, had a vision moments before they stoned him, he said: "*Look! I see the heavens opened and the Son of Man standing at the right hand of God!*" Praise God: the veil is torn … and no devil in hell has a needle and thread big enough to stitch it up again!

An often-quoted passage of Scripture comes to mind: "*If my people who are called by My name will humble themselves, and pray and seek My face, and turn from their wicked ways, then I will hear from heaven, and will forgive their sin and heal their land.*" The sequence is important; it gives us **directions** to revival. First, we who call ourselves Christian must **humble ourselves.** This means that we must recognize that without God, we can do nothing. Second, we must **pray and seek his face.** This means that we do not yell at God to "send a revival," but simply worship and adore him, seeing him for who he is, not what he does.

The third point – **turn from their wicked ways** – is perhaps the most difficult of all. It goes to where our priorities should lie: in making him first in our lives. Then we read, "*I will hear from heaven*"; which means that there has been a conversation between us and God. Finally, God answers: "*I will forgive their sin and heal their land*" – which is his outpouring on both the long-time Christian and the brand-new seeker. Revival should never be bottled up inside the walls of our churches.

Take it to the people who need it!

Geared To God

Relevance is a matter of position and focus. You and I are only relevant when we relate to what the Holy Spirit is doing. We are often told our ministry has to be geared to the times. This is nonsense! We are geared to God. The machinery of heaven is turning, wheels within wheels.

> "And I will give you the keys of the kingdom of heaven, and whatever you bind on earth will be bound in heaven, and whatever you loose on earth will be loosed in heaven."

It is the machinery of heaven – not of industry – that must be our concern. To be geared to the world means turning our gospel into another form of materialism – just another way to rake in money and goods. What makes us relevant is not whether our message fits the situation – "*Do not be conformed to this world,*" the Bible tells us – but whether the situation corresponds to the truth of Christ. In fact, the world is of no importance if it does not relate to God.

This self-important, sin-filled world is destined to pass away, to be replaced by God's perfect order: "*Now I saw a new heaven and a new earth, for the first heaven and the first earth had passed away … There shall be no more pain, for the former things have passed away.*"

You and I need to get our priorities right. We either get into the mainstream of revelation – the love of God for a wasted world – or we drift into a backwater filled with debris of theological controversy and church politics. Our priority must be the same as that of the Spirit.

Why is the Holy Spirit here? The Holy Spirit is given to make us witnesses … and his own work is to highlight the work of Christ and activate it in human lives. If you want to move in the Spirit, you need to get into that kind of activity because that is what he is doing!

Today's Scripture
I beseech you therefore, brethren, by the mercies of God, that you present your bodies a living sacrifice, holy, acceptable to God, which is your reasonable service. (Romans 12:1)

Daily Power!
I am in Christ and I will focus on the leading of the Holy Spirit.

Mark My Word
Ezekiel 10:6
John 16:9-11
Acts 1:8
Romans 12:1-2
Revelation 21:1-7

The Bible In A Year

Morning
Numbers 26
Psalm 69

Evening
Isaiah 16
1 Peter 4

18

Faith Pins Hope

Today's Scripture
Has not God made
foolish the wisdom
of this world? For
since, in the wisdom
of God, the world
through wisdom did
not know God, it
pleased God through
the foolishness of the
message preached
to save those
who believe.
(2 Corinthians 1:20-21)

Daily Power!
I confess with my
mouth the Lord Jesus
and I believe in my
heart that God has
raised him from the
dead. I am saved!

Mark My Word
Psalm 46:1
John 20:29
Romans 10:9
1 Corinthians 1:21
Hebrews 11:6
James 2:19

The Bible In A Year

Morning
Numbers 27
Psalms 70 and 71

Evening
Isaiah 17 and 18
1 Peter 5

Believing is not just brain cells in motion – there should be a response. Do we **do** what we believe? If we believe in seed, we plant it. A man who owns an aeroplane, but will not risk flying is a contrary character. It will get him exactly nowhere. We may as well believe in Mickey Mouse as Almighty God if we do not expect him to do anything. In his short epistle, James – the half-brother of Jesus, an upright and forthright character – made some hard-hitting remarks: "*You believe that there is one God? You do well. Even the demons believe, and tremble!*" He talked about them as lovers of money, impatient with God, and said that faith that does not work is not faith. God is not a figure of theory or past history but "*a very present help.*"

People say: "I'll believe it when I see it." No, they won't – they can't. You can only believe, or have faith, in what you do **not** see. What you see is fact, and is not up for believing. If you can prove it, faith does not come into it. Nobody believes two plus two equals four – they know so! But **God wants faith!** "*Without faith it is impossible to please God … Blessed are those who have not seen and yet have believed.*" That is the way to get God's blessing – not by being so clever that you believe nothing unless you can run your tape measure round it.

This was Paul's point when writing to the Corinthians. He was familiar with the great thinkers of Greece. They had discovered the certainties of mathematics. Reason worked for figures, so they imagined it would work for everything else – the meaning of Life, God, and the whole business of Life. They set thinkers off on a red herring trail that lasts to this day! Paul knew what had happened, and told the learned thinkers of Corinth: "*… the world through wisdom did not know God.*" Faith is a **personal** relationship, not a mathematical relationship between numbers. You may know what God did, but you have to trust him for tomorrow. There can be no guarantees.

The Eye To The Unseen

Faith is akin to love; it is a heart matter. We do not decide to fall in love after weighing all the pros and cons. Couples get married on trust, not on scientific evidence or conclusive logic. Faith is the eye to see the unseen. Physical optics are not the instruments to perceive God. He is a Spirit. Mortal eyes are too weak to discern *"the invisible God … the King eternal, immortal, invisible."* We have to deal with him as he is. *"He who comes to God must believe that he is, and that he is a rewarder of those who diligently seek him."*

But there is a better way of seeing. Eyes can play tricks. Plato, the greatest of the Greek philosophers, said that nothing is ever actually how it looks to us. But Moses *"endured as seeing him who is invisible."* If we only believed what we **saw**, what would a blind man believe? Radio waves fill your room, but who would know without a receiver? God is invisible Spirit, and it is as useless to argue and expect God to be what he is not, as it is to expect the moon to be made of green cheese. *"Blessed are those who have not seen and yet have believed"* – they are on the track of truth!

Wanting a God that they can see has led people into vast mistakes. People have made God in their own image, which the God of the Bible certainly is not! It led to idolatry, erecting images and icons. Today, some treat the living earth as God. They have a pretty big god … but the God of the whole earth is rather bigger. That is where the gospel steps into the picture – this God did become **visible**. He *"became flesh and dwelt among us and we beheld his glory as of the only begotten of the Father."* That verse comes from John's gospel, which is all about seeing. In the first chapter alone, there are eighteen references to seeing. John wrote about knowing as seeing. He wrote a letter beginning: *"That … which we have heard, which we have seen with our eyes … the Word of Life."* John saw in Christ the Word of Life. **Let others see that Word in your life today!**

Today's Scripture
That which we have seen and heard we declare to you, that you also may have fellowship with us, and truly our fellowship is with the Father and with his Son Jesus Christ. (1 John 1:3)

Daily Power!
Lord, I believe that you are the Christ, the Son of the living God.

Mark My Word
John 1:14; 11:27; 20:29 Colossians 1:15 1 Timothy 1:17 Hebrews 11:27 1 John 1:1, 3

The Bible In A Year

Morning
Numbers 28
Psalm 72

Evening
Isaiah 19 and 20
2 Peter 1

20

Transforming Power

Today's Scripture
Nor is there salvation in any other, for there is no other name under heaven given among men by which we must be saved. (Acts 4:12)

Daily Power!
Father, in Christ you have blessed me with every spiritual blessing. Let me bless one other today, in his name.

Mark My Word
John 14:6
Acts 4:10-12
Ephesians 1:3-14

The Bible In A Year

Morning
Numbers 29
Psalm 73

Evening
Isaiah 21
2 Peter 2

Since the Resurrection of Jesus, a wave of spiritual power has swept forward, bringing God's new life to everything it touches. The power of God's forgiveness, which sets us free; the power that enables us to forgive those who have hurt us; the power to resist what we know is wrong; the power of God's Spirit, who brings us the new life of Jesus; the power of God's love, which fills us with love for him and for others.

> "Blessed be the God and Father of our Lord Jesus Christ, who has blessed us with every spiritual blessing in the heavenly places in Christ … In him we have redemption through his blood, the forgiveness of sins, according to the riches of his grace … In him also we have obtained an inheritance."

"Every spiritual blessing" – now what sort of spiritual blessing would you like to have active in your life? Whatever it is, just remember that God's blessings are given to us to bless us, certainly, but also to make us a blessing to others!

How can we know this power for ourselves? How can we discover this love of God which is able to transform our lives? Only one man who has dared to answer: "*I am the Way, the Truth, and the Life. No one comes to the Father, except through me.*" **Jesus is the only way** by which our sins can be forgiven, and our right relationship with God the Father re-established. his death on the cross was the final sacrifice needed. Nothing else is required. his resurrection is the absolute proof that he is the Son of God. his Holy Spirit is our means of tapping into God's transforming power. Live in the fullness of that power today!

The Voice Of Love

I have often wondered how Jesus sounded when he spoke. Once, Jesus pronounced seven woes against certain cities. But I wonder what the tone of his voice was. I imagine Jesus spoke those judgments with a voice of sorrow. What love filled his voice, what tears filled his eyes, even when he went to Jerusalem to be rejected! His heart would show in his tone of voice. What kind of tone did those privileged people hear?

The gospel of Luke records that they *"marveled at the gracious words which proceeded out of his mouth."* The Temple police were sent to arrest Jesus – they came back spellbound and disarmed. How did Jesus sound when he cried: *"Father, forgive them for they do not know what they do?"*

D.L. Moody once spoke in London, England to an invited audience of a thousand or so "rationalists." The meeting was fiercely hostile, but Moody literally sobbed, with tears running down his beard, as he pleaded with them to turn to Christ. Suddenly, the meeting broke and hundreds turned to Christ. Those people were never the same again.

I do not mean that the gospel should be turned into sob-stuff, a tear-jerker. The voice of Jesus did far more than stir people's emotions – their reaction was not tears, but joy. He told his disciples that he spoke to give them peace and joy. In fact, there was no pathos in the words or teaching of Jesus, nothing that people today would call "syrupy-sweet sentimentalism." The gospel sound should be triumphant, certain, with a note of gladness!

This is, of course, a long way from – and in stark contrast to – the warning voice of Jonah in doomed Nineveh. But grace and truth came to light through Jesus Christ. There is no bell that rings as loudly as love. You and I should always speak with Christ-like words of love.

Today's Scripture
These things I have spoken to you, that my joy may remain in you, and that your joy may be full.
(John 15:11)

Daily Power!
Lord I desire to speak evil of no one, but to be peaceable, gentle, showing all humility to all men, in the love of Christ.

Mark My Word
Jonah 3:1-5
Matthew 23:37
Luke 4:22; 15:11; 23:34
John 7:46; 14:27; 15:11
Titus 3:2
Revelation 2:1-29; 3:1-22

The Bible In A Year

Morning
Numbers 30
Psalm 74

Evening
Isaiah 22
2 Peter 3

22

How Sin Happened

Today's Scripture
For the wages of sin
is death, but the gift
of God is eternal life
in Christ Jesus
our Lord.
(Romans 6:23)

Daily Power!
I have made my
choice to accept the
gift of salvation.

Mark My Word
Genesis 3:1-24
Romans 6:23

The Bible In A Year

Morning
Numbers 31
Psalms 75 and 76

Evening
Isaiah 23
1 John 1

When God first put Adam and Eve in the Garden of Eden, they did not know sin. When Satan tempted Eve, and she succumbed, she learned about *"the knowledge of good and evil..."* which opened the door to sin. Sin is doing evil in God's sight or separation from God. But the opportunity to do good is also there. Adam and Eve were cursed in the Garden because of sin – that is when death, pain and sickness entered into the picture – and God himself said:

> "'Behold, the man has become like one of us, to know good and evil. And now, lest he put out his hand and take also of the tree of life, and eat and live forever' – therefore the Lord God sent him out of the Garden of Eden."

Because man now existed in a state of sin, he could not live forever that way. Imagine, an awful eternity steeped entirely in sin! It was God's decision to spare man an endless separation from himself, but he also knew that there would be a terrible price to pay to mend that gulf – the life of his only begotten Son.

Every man is created in God's image, and within every man there exists a place that was fashioned only for God. So many spend their entire lives trying to fit other things into that God-shaped space. There is only One who will fit there: our Lord and Savior Jesus Christ. *"For the wages of sin is death, but the gift of God is eternal life in Christ Jesus our Lord."* To accept or reject the gift of salvation – that cannot be decided by loving parents, nor legislated by churches, governments or societies – it must be individually chosen and acted upon.

> "If you confess with your mouth the Lord Jesus and believe in your heart that God has raised him from the dead, you will be saved. For with the heart one believes unto righteousness, and with the mouth confession is made unto salvation."

You can exhibit "on the outside" what appears to be godly living – but it is what you believe **deep inside** your heart that makes all the difference.

Godly Families

Not every godly man in the Bible had godly children – the high priest Eli and the prophet Samuel were vivid examples of this. But perhaps the most significant example of this sad truth was found in the life of Israel's greatest historical personality – King David. One of his sons, Absalom, murdered his brother, Amnon, for a treacherous act of rape and incest against his sister, Tamar. From this evil episode sprang another. Pampered Absalom tried to take the throne from David, resulting in the loss of his own life in the civil war that he began. On his deathbed, King David learned that yet another son had been killed in an attempt to mount the throne illegally. Tragedy followed tragedy ... yet David was a man after God's own heart!

When news was brought to David that Absalom had been killed, he was beside himself, weeping, crying aloud: "*O my son Absalom – my son, my son Absalom – if only I had died in your place! O Absalom, my son, my son!*" David saw himself in his son. He himself had been treacherous, murdered a faithful and good man, and stolen his beautiful and beloved wife. He wrote a Psalm of public repentance – but he had set an unrighteous example which Absalom followed. The pathos of David echoes to this day. "*If only I had died in your place*" – for it was with himself that the blame lay. David's complex character proved powerful in his family's attitudes. They needed greater exposure to the Law, the Words of God, as he commanded.

If we pray with our families, it is not enough. The means and method of God is to share the **Word of God**. It speaks louder than testimony. God is on our side when we set out to create godly families, and families of families. We are helping create a family of God through whom all the earth can be blessed. This is his focus and way. Let us make every effort to rebuild our broken down family altars today!

Today's Scripture
Teach me your way, O Lord, I will walk in your truth; Unite my heart to fear your name. (Psalm 86:11)

Daily Power!
My family will follow my example more than my words. Therefore, I will strive to live by your Word.

Mark My Word
2 Samuel 18:33
Psalm 86:1-17.

The Bible In A Year

Morning
Numbers 32
Psalm 77

Evening
Isaiah 24
1 John 2

From Zero To Ten

Today's Scripture
I eagerly expect and hope that I will in no way be ashamed but still have sufficient courage so that now as always Christ will be exalted in my body, whether by life or death.
(Philippians 1:20 NIV)

Daily Power!
To my lowly zero, Jesus has added his glorious one – and now we are a "perfect ten"!

Mark My Word
I Corinthians 1:28
Philippians 1:8

The Bible In A Year

Morning
Numbers 33
Psalm 78:1-37

Evening
Isaiah 25
1 John 3

Throughout the Old Testament, the divine method which God chose to select the leaders of his people was to choose nobodies, rejects: "*The base things of the world and the things which are despised God has chosen, and the things which are not, to bring to nothing the things that are.*" Jesus prayed … and came back to pick the most unlikely apostles – almost anybody! He bumped into young men without any qualities at all – other than very human character traits: impetuous Peter … his quieter brother Andrew … James and John, the hot-headed sons of Zebedee … rational Thomas … sociable Philip … and thieving Judas.

When God chooses, it is not important what we are – it is what he makes of us that counts. He chose an unlikely bunch of local men. One or two of them were picked only because they were relatives – James and John were the sons of Salome, who is believed to be the sister of Mary the mother of Jesus. They had always known him. Jesus took a stroll along the beach where local fishermen happened to be, and called them. It looked as though he picked the first young fellows he bumped into that morning.

When people are not successful in Germany, those who constantly fail in their efforts in daily life, we call them "zeros." But these are the ones God is especially interested in! When Jesus calls a "zero" and the "zero" responds – he or she will soon find out that the Lord is the number one … and a zero next to a one equals **ten**! In other words: **Jesus gives value to every zero as long as he is the number one!** The worthless become highly valuable. This is the way that God builds his kingdom. So it was with the first disciples … and so it is today. I claim this as my own testimony too … and so should you! Make sure that Jesus Christ is number one in your life today!

Witnesses, Not Lawyers

It has become an established practice that preachers should present the case for the defense of Jesus Christ. It has also been said that preachers are like lawyers in court. Ministers are supposed to be like barristers talking to congregations as if to a jury, arguing to get a verdict in the favor of Jesus. That approach looks so right, plausible and sensible. But is it? No, not at all! That is our human approach, trying to convey the gospel message with the wisdom of words.

Jesus needs no defending. The time has gone when Jesus was dragged to the bar of Rome to be judged by Pilate. Today, Pilate stands at the bar of history and Jesus is his Judge. We are not lawyers, but **witnesses**! Normally, a witness only describes what he or she has seen. Sometimes, however, a witness is a piece of evidence: perhaps a man has been cruelly attacked and injured. He appears in court to display himself, the damage and the injury. his injuries speak for themselves. He himself is a piece of evidence.

We believers are not lawyers, pleading in defense of Jesus. We are witnesses. Witnesses do not argue, plead, or make speeches. They simply speak the truth, stating what they know. When Peter preached on the day of Pentecost, he said that the one hundred and nineteen standing with him were all witnesses of the resurrection. In fact, not one of them had seen Christ's actual resurrection – yet that resurrection had **transformed** them. They were themselves alive with resurrection life, filled with the fire of God. They were the evidence that Jesus was alive! If Jesus had still been dead, they would not have been as the crowd then saw them. They would have been as they were before – cringing, slinking into the safety of a locked room for fear. Now, they were fearless, and it was the turn of the crowd to be afraid, to be filled with fear and awe.

Be certain that you have that resurrection evidence alive in you today!

Today's Scripture
And they were all filled with the Holy Spirit and began to speak with other tongues, as the Spirit gave them utterance. (Acts 2:4)

Daily Power!
Lord, make me bold to speak daily from my heart what you have done for me.

Mark My Word
Acts 2:1-32

The Bible In A Year

Morning
Numbers 34
Psalm 78:38

Evening
Isaiah 26
1 John 4

26

Two Gifts

Daily Power!
The Holy Spirit is God and he is my Helper!

Mark My Word
Genesis 1:2
Exodus 3:14
John 14:12, 16-17

The Bible In A Year

Morning
Numbers 35
Psalm 79

Evening
Isaiah 27
1 John 5

The Father gave us two gifts, both personal and equal. First, he gave us his Son … and then he gave us his Spirit. Jesus ranked the Spirit alongside himself, describing him as *"another Helper."* He said it was better for the Spirit to come than for he himself to remain with us in the flesh. The Holy Spirit's commission is to continue Christ's work of ministry on earth. Jesus healed the sick, for example, and the Holy Spirit follows the pattern of Christ.

> "Most assuredly I say to you, he who believes in me, the works that I do he will do also; and greater works than these he will do, because I go to my Father … And I will pray the Father, and he will give you another Helper, that he may abide with you forever – the Spirit of truth, whom the world cannot receive, because it neither sees him nor knows him; but you know he for he dwells with you and will be in you."

How do we know who the Spirit is? The Holy Spirit is the third Person of the Trinity – God in action. Whenever there are supernatural operations, they are by the Spirit. All divine manifestations, such as the gifts, are always by the Spirit. When God moved on the world in the beginning, it was by his Spirit. The Father's will is spoken by the Word, and performed by the Spirit. He executes the will of the Godhead.

The only Spirit that Jesus promised us is the miracle Spirit, the Holy Spirit. There is no non-miracle Holy Spirit. To claim to possess the Holy Spirit and deny the very work that has always distinguished him can only grieve him. It is he who began with the supreme physical wonder of creating the world. He does not change his nature. What he was, He is and always will be – God operating in the earthly sphere. *"I AM WHO I AM."* The Holy Spirit who made the world supernaturally should have no difficulty in continuing supernaturally. And that Holy Spirit is **your Helper** today!

When Jesus Comes

God said, "*It is not good for man to be alone.*" So Jesus came to be the inimitable companion of humankind. his coming was like the light of dawn on the first day of creation. Men come and go but Jesus stays forever. A myriad stars appear in the heavens but sunrise eclipses them all.

Life without other people, loved ones and friends, is incomplete. Possessions and pleasures are never properly enjoyed without company. But even the best of companions is only a reflection of God's own friendship. "*You have made known to me the path of life; you will fill me with joy in your presence.*" Jesus came to earth as a gift, a friend to all: "*The large crowd heard him gladly.*"

Jesus' coming has never been forgotten, but his exit from this world is even more deeply etched on the world's memory than his entry. The last view of him on this earth was with his arms stretched wide on the cross as if to enfold us in his embrace. God had said to Israel, "*All day long I have held out my hands to a disobedient and obstinate people*" (Romans 10:21, referring to Isaiah 65:2) and Christ Jesus was the living picture of that, even while dying.

> **His death is a fact about the human race. It marked humankind,the single most notable event in history. His cross is the world's number-one man-made object!**

All this is the stuff of the gospels: the immortal succumbing to mortality, the Son of God dying as the Son of Man, and a secret triumph running through it all to a sequel of resurrection hope. Hallelujah!

Today's Scripture
I have come that they may have life and have it to the full.
(John 10:10b)

Daily Power!
Jesus Christ has made the path of true life known to me.

Mark My Word
Genesis 2:18
Psalm 16:11
Mark 12:37

The Bible In A Year

Morning
Numbers 36
Psalm 80

Evening
Isaiah 28
2 John 1

Becoming A Child Of God

Today's Scripture
Do not enter the path of the wicked, and do not walk in the way of evil. Avoid it, do not travel on it; turn away from it and pass on.
(Proverbs 4:14-15)

Daily Power!
I repent and I believe in the gospel.
Christ in me the hope of glory.

Mark My Word
Proverbs 4:14-15
Mark 1:15
Romans 10:13

The Bible In A Year

Morning
Deuteronomy 1
Psalms 81 and 82

Evening
Isaiah 29
3 John 1

If you are ready to come to the cross for the help that you need, there are two steps which you need to take now. These steps are called "repent" and "believe." As Jesus said: *"Repent and believe in the gospel."* What do these two steps mean?

Repent: It simply means "change your mind." Picture it like this: you are making a journey, and you have taken a wrong turn. You are driving further and further away from where you want to go. You need to stop, turn around completely, and start traveling in the right direction.

This will mean taking time to examine how you live. You will need to ask God's forgiveness for all that is wrong in your life – and ask him to save you and set you free. Repentance means that you turn away from your sin, and toward God. If you change your position, then Jesus will change your situation.

Believe: Faith is an act – not a feeling. Only you can decide to believe. Only you, as an individual, can pull that "faith ripcord of belief." If you do that now, the Lord will not delay by "investigating" your worthiness, or your past. No matter who you are, or where you are, as soon as you repent and believe, the parachute opens – with a bang! – and you are safe in his hands.

Jesus has never failed yet, and he will not fail you either. Here and now, the rip-cord is in your hands by the promise of God. The Bible is clear about it: *"Whoever calls on the name of the Lord shall be saved."* One believing call, in simple language which you would use in calling a friend for help, addressed to Jesus Christ for forgiveness and salvation, is the way the parachute of salvation opens. God himself will intervene for you. He promised it. Pull the rip-cord quickly, wherever you are!

The New Way

The first Christians crossed the Bible landscape in an aura of prayer. They revelled in prayer, and with good reason. Their kind of praying was a new thing – using the authority of the name of Jesus! The New Testament speaks of *"fellowship with the Father"* but Israel did not pray "Our Father." They had such a lofty concept of God that he seemed unapproachable, the Sovereign Lord of Hosts, mighty in battle, or, at best, "a present help in trouble." Only an elite band enjoyed God's company and intimate prayer life with him.

Most knew God only second-hand, via a priest or prophet. In a sense, people called on the Lord in their own name: *"Lord, remember David!"* the Psalmist wrote, hoping for a personal favor. We can **try** to get God's attention on our own merits, but we will always fall short: *"But we are all like an unclean thing, and all our righteousnesses are like filthy rags … For all have sinned and fall short of the glory of God."* Because we are sin-infested, God cannot even **look** at us, unless our sins are covered by the cleansing blood of the Lamb of God.

> "Most assuredly I say to you, he who believes in me, the works that I do he will do also; and greater works than these he will do, because I go to my Father. And whatever you ask in my name, that I will do, that the Father may be glorified in the Son. If you ask anything in my name, I will do it."

And that brings us right back to where we started: we pray in the name of Jesus, the One who enables us to approach the holy throne of God. That is your right and mine: **to speak, to pray, and to act in the name of Jesus!**

Today's Scripture
Let us therefore come boldly to the throne of Grace, that we may obtain mercy and find grace to help in time of need.
(Hebrews 4:16)

Daily Power!
My relationship with my heavenly Father is determined by my relationship with his Son Jesus Christ, for it is he who gives me the use of his name because of his sacrifice on Calvary.

Mark My Word
Psalm 46:1; 132:1
Isaiah 64:6
John 14:12-14
Romans 3:10-23
Hebrews 4:16

The Bible In A Year

Morning
Deuteronomy 2
Psalms 83 and 84

Evening
Isaiah 30
Jude 1

30

Today's Scripture
Therefore, since we are receiving a kingdom which cannot be shaken, let us have grace, by which we may serve God acceptably with reverence and godly fear.
(Hebrews 12:28)

Daily Power!
Rejoice with me, for I have found my sheep which was lost!

Mark My Word
Genesis 12:2-3
Matthew 25:31-46
Luke 15:6
Hebrews 11:8-10;
12:28

The Bible In A Year

Morning
Deuteronomy 3
Psalm 85

Evening
Isaiah 31
Revelation 1

When we first read about Abraham, he was in the city of Ur of the Chaldees, with his father, Terah. Like all cities, it had an official god, and families had a shrine for their own household god, as in India today with its millions of gods. However, a *"Most High God"* was acknowledged – and Abraham heard his voice. It was a sovereign act. It came from God's side, not Abraham's – God breaking through.

God has shown concern for the world. When nobody sought him, he sought them. Abraham was not seeking God – probably nobody was. He made Abraham aware of who he was, and then gave him simple instructions to leave Ur. He was not told where to go, but he set off. The Bible stresses that Abraham lived in tents, away from houses and streets. Why? To get paganism, city manners and customs flushed out of his system. Abraham had been born and bred in an idolatrous civilization. God was to purge him of everything except what he showed him. He showed him a destiny beyond his own interests and in the future of nations. God said: *"I will make you a great nation and I will bless you ... and in you all the families of the earth shall be blessed."*

In Abraham's time, people everywhere lived for themselves, usually by fighting everybody else around. One day the nations will be judged. Christ painted a picture of a vast drama on the stage of the whole universe: the Judgment of the Nations. They have to give account of themselves. God's eyes of concern run through the whole earth. Why do we have faith? To bless ourselves? To become wealthy and be prosperous? If we have such faith, God gave it. But he enriches us in order to enrich others, to "pass it on." Abraham lived on that level. Let God's purpose be yours.

God At Work

Some people who talk about "moving in the Spirit" seem to think and act as if **they** are the ones moving the Spirit. This is not biblical: "*Who has directed the Spirit of the Lord, or as his counselor has taught him?*"

Jesus was often criticized by authorities and religious leaders because he did not confine his ministry to the elite, but rather, spent much of his time with sinners – prostitutes, criminals, moneylenders, beggars, the sick, the outcast. They just did not understand the compassion that moved him:

> "What man is there among you who has one sheep, and if it falls into a pit on the Sabbath, will not lay hold of it and lift it out? Of how much more value then is a man than a sheep? Therefore it is lawful to do good on the Sabbath."

God is not moving secretly. He has not suddenly shot off in some new and unexpected direction, only spotted by a few members of some spiritual elite. We still find God at work among people who are down: the sinful, the hopeless, the derelicts. "Following Jesus" – is a far better expression than "moving in the Spirit." Follow him, and you will go where he goes, "*doing good and healing all who are oppressed by the devil.*" Praise be to God!

Jesus himself said: "I don't do anything unless I've seen my Father do it … I don't say anything unless I've heard my Father say it … I simply imitate my Father" (paraphrased). Having that Christ-like attitude – that is the Spirit of God moving in our hearts, and he utilizing our responsiveness to him. This is the best equipment we can have to walk in this world and do the works of him who sends us. Make a choice to equip yourself today with all of your spiritual weapons, so you are ready to go into battle!

Today's Scripture
When Jesus heard that, he said to them: "Those who are well have no need of a physician, but those who are sick. But go and learn what this means, 'I desire mercy and not sacrifice. For I did not come to call the righteous but sinners to repentance.'"
(Matthew 9:12-13)

Daily Power!
If anyone desires to come after me, let him deny himself, and take up his cross, and follow me.
Matthew 16:24

Mark My Word
Isaiah 40:13
Matthew 9:12-13;
12:11-12
John 5:19-23; 9:4
Acts 10:38

The Bible In A Year

Morning
Deuteronomy 4
Psalms 86 and 87

Evening
Isaiah 32
Revelation 2

God says:
Do not plan with that which is in your pocket,
but with that which is in my pocket.

God says:
For every deadline I will throw you a lifeline.

The church is not a pleasure boat, but a lifeboat.
From the captain to the cook,
all hands on deck for saving souls!

Reason For Believing?

Not seeing is no reason for not believing. Nobody sees radiation – we simply wait for its warming and lighting effects. Nobody sees air (unless it is badly polluted) – we simply breathe it in and out. Nobody sees God – but millions find his effect in their lives every day! Things happen that can only be from him. Even one prayer answered - one healing - one miracle - one deliverance from addiction – is evidence of him. Two thousand years ago, this report was given: *"How God anointed Jesus of Nazareth with the Holy Spirit and with power, who went about doing good and healing all who were oppressed by the devil, for God was with him."* Peter testified to unmistakable evidence of God!

But it was not just one prayer answered, or one miracle manifested ... and all this taking place was not only two thousand years ago. **Today,** millions are healed, millions delivered, millions of prayers answered, millions have experiences which can only be attributed to Jesus Christ risen from the dead. *"Jesus Christ is the same yesterday, today and forever."* When I step on a platform in Africa, or India, or anywhere else, often – without any touch of mine – the blind begin to see, the deaf to hear, the dumb to speak, the cripples to walk, and those driven to madness by clinging spirits of evil are released. It is not psychology, for babies are healed, even in the womb. The greatest effect is deliverance from sin and guilt, and the transformation of people's attitudes and personalities – **Jesus saves!**

Why should we care what Jesus did two thousand years ago, unless it was written to give us inspiration and hope for what he can and does do today? He taught with wisdom and insight that caught the attention of would-be intellectuals and philosophers, and turned their hearts toward God. He ministered healing with compassion and authority, not to people who deserved to be healed, but simply because he cared so much for them that he desired to relieve their suffering. He sacrificed his very own life, not because they demanded his death, but because he was being obedient to his Father. There was no hypocrisy in Jesus two thousand years ago, and there is nothing but truth in him today.

Today's Scripture
Jesus Christ is the same yesterday, today, and forever.
(Hebrews 13:8)

Daily Power!
I do not see God, but I know his presence in my heart and I see his work in my life.

Mark My Word
Acts 10:38
Hebrews 13:8

The Bible In A Year

Morning
Deuteronomy 5
Psalm 88

Evening
Isaiah 33
Revelation 3

Faith Or Chaos?

Today's Scripture
That you may be sons of your Father in heaven; for He makes his sun rise on the evil and on the good, and sends rain on the just and on the unjust. (Matthew 5:45)

Daily Power!
I take great comfort in knowing that my faith in God is based on his Word.

Mark My Word
Psalm 97:7
Matthew 5:45

The Bible In A Year

Morning
Deuteronomy 6
Psalm 89

Evening
Isaiah 34
Revelation 4

There is no substitute for faith in God. History rings the warning bells. Without the knowledge of the Lord God, nothing ever made sense. The ancients – even the most brilliant thinkers – produced the wildest ideas, superstitions, and speculations. Mystery clothed nature. They were sure of nothing, not even of the weather or the seasons. To make the sun rise, they worshipped it. To make it rain, they offered divine worship. Rivers had to be persuaded to run and not dry up. Everyone had his own god. *"Let all be put to shame who serve carved images, who boast of idols."*

Therefore, the prophets were raised up and inspired with a burning realization of God's reality and his will. The concept of God as the Father of all was unknown. Conflicts and family blood-feuds took place, and war was the glory of men. But Israel's prophets taught their people not to fear the signs of the Heavens, to work and not to war. God would faithfully look after all his creatures. They should not worry about harvests, like the heathens around them. Jesus himself clearly taught this*: "That you may be sons of your Father in heaven; for he makes his sun rise on the evil and on the good, and sends rain on the just and on the unjust."*

It is easy to sit and watch TV, and casually say that you do not believe in God. But the consequences are eternal. They fertilize corruption, bribery, violence, terrorism, and crime. Atheists claim that they can live decent lives without believing in God, but they forget that the very idea of decency comes from Christianity. Before Christ, it was a different story and a far crueler world. In fact, we do not know what is good or bad without faith in God. A totally unbelieving world would be like a lunatic asylum taken over by its patients. If you do not trust God, you soon trust nobody. Resolve today to wear your faith in God like an emblem on your sleeve.

Wonderful Knowledge

The real point of the story of Jonah – and it speaks to every evangelist who ever went out to do God's work – is that he had preached judgment, but no judgment came. That was just what he feared would happen. In fact, Jonah had never wanted to preach against the city, for the very reason that if his preaching were successful, God would change his mind about judgment! Afterwards, he protested, saying:

> "Ah, LORD, was not this what I said when I was still in my country? Therefore I fled previously to Tarshish; for I know that you are a gracious and merciful God, slow to anger and abundant in lovingkindness, One who relents from doing harm."

Jonah had profound insight into the character of God. In all thirty-nine books of the Old Testament, this statement of the prophet stands out as something exceptional. **Jonah knew that God had a heart of unparalleled goodness.** More than that, he knew that the mercies of the Lord extended beyond the borders of Israel into enemy territory, embracing even the Gentiles.

Few in Israel would have believed that this could be true. In that age of spiritual darkness, only the Holy Spirit could have shown this to the prophet. He somehow knew that God could be as gracious with Gentiles as with Israel, even with the worst sinners on earth. That is why he went - and why he did not want to go. Part of him wanted this wicked nation to get what it really deserved, but, at the same time, he knew that God was not like that. Jonah wanted vengeance, but God was, and still is, a God of forgiveness.

You and I may look at our world with dismay and revulsion at the evidence of sin – greed, hatred, inequality – but when we choose to look at the world through God's eyes, we see lost souls dying without him. Our hearts are filled with compassion. Ask God to give you a fresh vision for souls today. Ask him to let you see others the way that he sees them.

Today's Scripture
The Lord is very compassionate and merciful.
(James 5:11)

Daily Power!
God is gracious, even with the worst sinners on earth, for he saved me.

Mark My Word
Psalm 116:5
Jonah 4:1-11
James 5:11

The Bible In A Year

Morning
Deuteronomy 7
Psalm 90

Evening
Isaiah 35
Revelation 5

4

Truth, And People Who Reflect It

The prophet-evangelist Jonah knew the compassion of God, but he had no compassion himself. Any man who stands up to speak of Christ knows very well what Jonah knew. It is common knowledge among the saved that God is loving, gracious, merciful, and compassionate. But do we personally harbor such feelings for the lost?

Jonah had none at all — he preached only out of duty or obedience. There could not be a more serious shortcoming for anyone who preaches the Word of God. Evangelism is not a matter of simply mouthing words of God's pitying love, or spelling out theology. An evangelist's heart should beat in tune with the heartbeat of God, expressive of his heart's longings and compassion. The need in evangelism is twofold: the truth, and the people who reflect it. Some people say that preaching the right thing is enough. It is not! The Holy Spirit has a part in this, placing the missing ingredient in our own hearts: *"The love of God has been poured out in our hearts by the Holy Spirit who was given to us."* The love of God in Christ is more than a piece of systematic theology, and it is meant to come alive in those who declare it. We can preach with tongues of fire only when we have his fire in our hearts! How do you get those fires burning? Get to know the Word of God for yourself. It is God's Word to you and for you!

Jonah was a rare preacher and prophet in that he did not want to succeed. He hoped that nobody in Nineveh would take notice of the message he preached. Yet even the king on his throne became alarmed about his sins and decided to do something about it. If we take the Word of God upon our lips, we should know what we are doing. This is major firepower that no one should play with! Ask God today to give you a fresh outpouring of his compassion for the lost.

Today's Scripture
Then Jesus, moved with compassion, stretched out his hand and touched him, and said to him, 'I am willing; be cleansed.'
(Mark 1:41)

Daily Power!
Father, teach me your love for the lost.

Mark My Word
Jonah 3:1-10
Mark 1:40-45
Romans 5:5

The Bible In A Year

Morning
Deuteronomy 8
Psalm 91

Evening
Isaiah 36
Revelation 6

"Our Father"

We should all seek to perceive God's true position – he is infinitely superior to us. But the invitation to call him "Father" brings him close to us, and makes him approachable. Readers of the Book of Hebrews, still emerging from the old dispensation of the Law, had to be taken by the hand and led into this new relationship. They were told:

> "'Seeing then that we have a great high priest … Jesus, the Son of God … let us then come boldly to the throne of Grace … Having boldness to enter the Holiest by the blood of Jesus, by a new and living way which he consecrated for us, through the veil, that is, his flesh.'"

When Jesus taught his disciples to pray, it made them a new breed … praying always and about everything. He told them: *"And whatever you ask in my name, that I will do, that the Father may be glorified in the Son. If you ask anything in my name, I will do it.'"*

In a way, to call on God is instinctive. Who does not – especially when in distress? There is a story told about an atheist who was fishing on a lake, when suddenly the Loch Ness Monster rose up out of the water and opened its jaws to swallow him. The atheist cried: "Oh God, help me!" Then he heard a voice saying: "So now you believe in me?" To which the atheist replied desperately: "Come on, give me a break! I didn't believe in the Loch Ness monster either until a second ago!"

Christ taught us the right way to go about it – to pray in his name. his mighty works mark a new road to God. He has opened heaven's door. Enter! You will be received! That's a promise for you today.

Today's Scripture
Most assuredly I say to you, whatever you ask the Father in my name he will give you. Until now you have asked nothing in my name. Ask, and you will receive, that your joy may be full. (John 16:23-24)

Daily Power!
My key to Heaven's door is to pray in the name of Jesus.

Mark My Word
John 16:23-24
Hebrews 4:14-16;
10:19-20.

The Bible In A Year

Morning
Deuteronomy 9
Psalms 92 and 93

Evening
Isaiah 37
Revelation 7

6

Today's Scripture
And the Word became flesh and dwelt among us, and we beheld his glory, the glory as of the only begotten of the Father, full of grace and truth.
(John 1:14)

Daily Power!
I serve a most unusual God, who does impossible things !

Mark My Word
1 Kings 10:7
Matthew 11:27
John 1:14
Revelation 1:1-20

The Bible In A Year

Morning
Deuteronomy 10
Psalm 94

Evening
Isaiah 38
Revelation 8

In the first chapter of Revelation, God revealed the nature of his Son, Jesus Christ, by twice referring to him in three tenses: *"Grace to you and peace from him who is, and who was, and who is to come* (verse 4) and *'I am the Alpha and the Omega, the Beginning and the End,'* says the Lord, *'who is and who was and who is to come, the Almighty'"* (verse 8). These are unusual words, for it says: *"Who is to come,"* when we would have said, "Who will be" – the same verb, "to be." God uses it twice in "Who was, and who is," then switches to a different verb, "to come." Anybody can see this is unusual. Why this peculiar way of putting it?

The reason is that God is unusual. He baffles grammar and syntax, and the language has to be pushed around when we speak of him! Christ himself was a mystery: *"Nor does anyone know the Father except the Son,"* and to talk about him in ordinary language always leaves something out. When it comes to the Lord, human language is never good enough. The first Christians had to give new meanings to many words, and even coin new words, because Jesus did new things and was a new kind of person. God himself did not communicate about himself with mere words, such as Mohammed's "Final Testament" or Joseph Smith's Mormon "Revelations." God simply presented himself with his actions, and to describe him we often need a bigger alphabet. It is like angel's music that needs a new notation. When we speak of God, we can lack the words and feel like the Queen of Sheba seeing Solomon's court: *"Not even half was told me."*

God never relied on mere words to inspire our faith in himself. To show us who and what he is, he came! *"The Word became flesh and dwelt among us and we beheld his glory ... full of grace and truth."* Is it not a wonderful privilege to be able to say: "My God has come to live with me!"

The Continual Promise

"I am the Alpha and the Omega, the Beginning and the End ... who is, and who was, and who is to come, the Almighty." A grammar teacher would notice that this sentence – this eternal promise from God – contains three verbs: *"am"*, *"was"* and *"come."* Why did God change verbs? Why did he say He is coming? It means He is everlastingly breaking in upon us! We get the same thing in Matthew where Christ was called "the coming One." What he will be, he is now and always has been: the eternal unchanging One. He is already perfect. *"I am the Lord. I change not."*

Yes, but it is different for us as individuals. We are always finding something new in him. Suppose you stand in the water at the edge of the Mississippi River. You are at the river ... yet the river keeps coming toward you. And the water we stand in today will be the same river that somebody else may stand in tomorrow further downstream as the waters flow. God is like that. We come to him ... He is there ... and yet he keeps coming to us. He is not just "being God" somewhere – like the Sphinx, just being mysterious. *"We will come to you,"* Jesus said, and he never stops coming, not now nor ever.

The Old Testament prophet caught a glimpse of this:

> "This I recall to my mind, therefore I have hope. Through the Lord's mercies, we are not consumed, because his compassions fail not. They are new every morning, great is Your faithfulness. 'The Lord is my portion,' says my soul, 'Therefore I hope in him.' The Lord is good to those who wait for him, to the soul who seeks him. It is good that one should hope and wait quietly for the salvation of the Lord."

Later, Peter testified to this continual renewal of the presence of God: *"Repent therefore and be converted, that your sins may be blotted out, so that times of refreshing may come from the presence of the Lord."* Our God never stops being, and never stops coming to refresh you!

Today's Scripture
Through the Lord's mercies, we are not consumed, because his compassions fail not. They are new every morning; great is Your faithfulness. (Lamentations 3:22-23)

Daily Power!
Each day, when I meet my Lord, He is ever the same and always refreshing.

Mark My Word
Lamentations 3:21-26
Malachi 3:6
Matthew 11:3
Acts 3:19
Revelation 1:8

The Bible In A Year

Morning
Deuteronomy 11
Psalms 95 and 96

Evening
Isaiah 39
Revelation 9

8

Overcomers

Today's Scripture
The battle
is the Lord's.
(1 Samuel 17:47)

Daily Power!
I am more than a
conqueror through
Jesus my Lord.

Mark My Word
1 John 5:4
1 John 2: 17

The Bible In A Year

Morning
Deuteronomy 12
Psalms 97 and 98

Evening
Isaiah 40
Revelation 10

Seven letters to seven churches, with seven promises by the Lord to those who "overcome" – that is certainly impressive (Rev 2 and 3). Obviously "overcoming" is not a spare-time hobby, but something touching the very heart of life. So, what, or whom, should we overcome?

When I looked into it, I was staggered. It seemed to me such a sweeping concept. One thing I knew already was that anything we do is worthwhile as we abide in Christ. We do it in and through him. So I decided to take **his** victory as my starting point, for there is no victory without him.

If we ask how we overcome, the answer is in every way, every day: *"This is the victory that has overcome the world, even our faith."* The moment we trust Christ and he takes over in our lives, we are living in victory. Overcoming is not a mere question of overcoming habits like biting our fingernails, or of keeping our temper, but of resisting the ways of the world which are motivated, even dominated, by false loves, such as money, power, success and fame. The Christian has one driving force, which is faith in Christ.

Life is not a losing battle full of constant struggle and anxiety. We live in Christ's victory even when we are spiritually "little children". Victory is for beginners as well as fathers. By faith in him our defeats drop away like dead leaves in autumn. When we allow Jesus to take over our responsibilities, *"the world and its desires pass away."*

Faith Is A Decision

The great Swiss theologian, Dr. Emil Brunner, summed up his thinking in four words: "Faith is a decision." He took it from Jesus, who always talked that way. Jesus praised believers … and blamed unbelievers. Just as we can see, hear, feel, taste, smell, so too can we believe. That is our "sixth sense" or faculty. It is spiritual eyesight, an ear to hear, or a hand to take God's blessing. Believing is not beyond anybody. "I'm not made that way," they plead, but we all are. Some think of faith as money – a good thing if you have some. Faith is not what you have but what you do. We can all rise to the heights – if we want to.

Paul, the master apostle, understood that everyone has faith, but some are more proficient in its use than others:

> "Receive one who is weak in the faith, but not to disputes over doubtful things. For one believes he may eat all things, but he who is weak eats only vegetables. Let not him who eats despise him who does not eat, and let not him who does not eat judge him who eats, for God has received him … For if we live, we live to the Lord; and if we die, we die to the Lord. Therefore, whether we live or die, we are the Lord's."

Who wants unbelief? It is a blind alley, the way to "no land, no water, and no love." To get out of it, turn around. Or in Bible language, **repent** – decide to believe instead of not believing. Doubt is deadly. Choose to live. *"Repent and believe the gospel."* Faith produces good works, but good works do not produce faith – just as milk produces butter, but butter does not produce milk.

Faith, mighty faith the promise sees
And looks to that alone
Laughs at impossibilities
And cries, "It shall be done."

Today's Scripture
Therefore let us not judge one another anymore, but rather resolve this, not to put a stumbling block or a cause to fall in our brother's way. (Romans 14:13)

Daily Power!
I will not waver at the promises of God through unbelief, but will be strengthened in faith, giving glory to God.

Mark My Word
Romans 4:20; 14:1-13

The Bible In A Year

Morning
Deuteronomy 13 and 14
Psalms 99 to 101

Evening
Isaiah 41
Revelation 11

10

The Size Of Faith

Today's Scripture
Having then gifts differing according to the grace that is given to us, let us use them; if prophecy, let us prophesy in proportion to our faith.
(Romans 12:6)

Daily Power!
If I have faith as small as a microchip, I can still move mountains!

Mark My Word
Isaiah 40:31
Luke 17:5-6
Romans 12:6

The Bible In A Year

Morning
Deuteronomy 15
Psalm 102

Evening
Isaiah 42
Revelation 12

The apostles said to the Lord, *"Increase our faith."* Christians have wanted that ever since – faith in bulk! What was the reply of Jesus? *"If you have faith as a mustard seed, you can say to this mulberry tree, 'Be pulled up by the roots and planted in the sea,' and it would obey you."* That must have puzzled the apostles. They wanted big faith, but he spoke of the smallest thing they knew. He did not refer to the mustard seed because it was very small – the issue was the contrast between massive faith, and small, but living, seed. He wanted to hammer home that faith is never a matter of size. Size is the wrong word. Faith has neither bulk nor weight. What shape is a thought? Believing is what you do! It is an action, not a substance. Scripture speaks of the "proportion of faith" – it is proportionate to the job at hand, linked to the need. Like running and needing more air, your intake increases automatically.

Size loses its meaning even for the task when it is a faith-task. The height of a hill, a house and a molehill are all one to a bird flying over them. By faith *"we mount up with wings like eagles"* and nothing is insurmountable. Active faith needs impossibilities. Religious faith, faith just in church, does not have enough impossibility. Robust faith grows in the outside weather, or it will be a sickly plant.

Perhaps you have never seen a mustard seed? You may need your glasses for one! But the people to whom Jesus spoke knew seeds. It was an agricultural world. Jesus spoke their farming language. Today we are a "high-tech" society, and our expressions are scientific. Jesus spoke the language of the people, and today our expressions come from technology. No doubt today Jesus would use our common speech. Two thousand years ago, Jesus spoke about the *"mustard seed,"* a small thing with mighty potency. Maybe today he would talk about a microchip or fuse to illustrate his teaching: "If you have faith as small as an electric fuse, you could transplant trees from soil to sea." Like the mustard seed, the value of a fuse is not in breadth or length. The key is conductivity. Your faith transfers the power of God to wherever it is needed.

"Righteous Anger" And Right Priorities

In the intriguing story of Jonah, God spoke to him through a plant that grew up over him and then withered. Jonah was staying outside the city for awhile, waiting to see what would happen. The sun was very hot, and so Jonah had made himself a shelter. A plant provided by God grew up over Jonah to give him even more protection from the heat, but then it withered overnight. Its root had been destroyed by some kind of worm.

Jonah was furious. God said, *"Is it right for you to be angry about the plant?"* Well, Jonah claimed to be angry enough to die. So God stated his case – the last words of the Book of Jonah are the words of the Lord:

> "You have had pity on the plant for which you have not labored, nor made it grow, which came up in a night and perished in a night. And should I not pity Nineveh, that great city, in which are more than one hundred and twenty thousand persons who cannot discern between their right hand and their left – and much livestock?"

To Jonah, the plant seemed more important than the lives of people. This has a lesson to teach us about what is important to us. There are plenty of righteous causes around today. Europe is particularly known for its powerful lobbies affecting legislation on several great moral issues, such as concern for the environment. Some Christians may find themselves involved in such matters politically or professionally … and why not? The question is: "What are we choosing to be most angry about?"

> "My sheep hear my voice, and I know them and they follow me. And I give them eternal life, and they shall never perish, neither shall anyone snatch them out of my hand. My Father, who has given them to me, is greater than all, and no one is able to snatch them out of my Father's hand."

Jesus himself exhibited anger when people were polluting his Father's house, but he was also quick to restore peace. Let that be your goal: to be a restorer of God's peace to the world.

Today's Scripture
But Jesus said, "Let her alone. Why do you trouble her? She has done a good work for me. For you have the poor with you always, and whenever you wish you may do them good; but me you do not have always." (Mark 14:6-7)

Daily Power!
The spreading of the gospel of Jesus Christ into all the world must become my top priority.

Mark My Word
Jonah 4:1-11
Mark 14:3-9
John 10:27-29

The Bible In A Year

Morning
Deuteronomy 16
Psalm 103

Evening
Isaiah 43
Revelation 13

Christ "For Us"

Today's Scripture
I am the Good
Shepherd. The Good
Shepherd gives his
life for the sheep.
(John 10:11)

Daily Power!
Out of his love he
died for me. In his
love I now live.

Mark My Word
John 10:7-18
1 Peter 2:24
1 John 1:7; 3:16

The Bible In A Year

Morning
Deuteronomy 17
Psalm 104

Evening
Isaiah 44
Revelation 14

"By this we know love, because he laid down his life for us."

Christ's earthly life was very brief. He was crucified at thirty-three years of age, and was in the public eye for only three-and-a-half years. Jesus Christ was a gift to mankind. his whole life was entirely for us. We were his exclusive concern. his life is a flawless example of dedication to mankind. He was totally free of self-interest, and he had only one purpose for being here: we, the people.

He did not serve by being a humanitarian, political or social activist. He never gave anybody one penny, simply because he never had any money. Once, when he needed a penny for a sermon illustration, someone had to lend him one. But he gave people all he had – and that was himself, his very heart. *But if we walk in the light as he is in the light, we have fellowship with one another, and the blood of Jesus Christ his Son cleanses us from all sin.*

Out of his hands flowed healing. When he had nothing left and he could not give anymore, he finally gave his own life's blood – the blood of Redemption; the price of our salvation. What he gave was far more than material things, or even healing. **He gave himself.** In absolute abandon, He met the needs of mankind with himself: *Who himself bore our sins in his own body on the tree, that we, having died to sins, might live for righteousness – by whose stripes you were healed.*

When they had no shepherd, he became the Good Shepherd. When they had no physician, he became the Great Physician. When they had no teacher, he became the Truth. When the crowds were in the darkness, they found him to be the Light of the world. This same Jesus Christ of two thousand years ago is the same One today, for you and for me!

Overcoming Love

The gospel is a message of love – and love is not presented by reason, but by loving. If you fell in love and wanted to ask a lovely girl to marry you, would you ask a lawyer to come and present your case to her? Imagine it! Would that win any woman? Marriage is either love, or it is not marriage. The gospel is both power and life, or it is not the gospel. Preaching is not a three-point homily. Preaching is a man burning in the pulpit for everybody to see. A sermon may be a neatly turned and engineered presentation – like the casing of an armour-piercing shell – but it needs filling with explosive, or it will bounce off the case-hardened minds of unbelievers. Their prejudices are fortified with argument, but the explosive power in a sermon filled with the Holy Spirit can demolish it.

When Peter stood up to preach that day in Jerusalem, he recounted instances from the ancient holy Scriptures which illustrated what was currently happening. He also sharply pointed out that the same Jews who had called for the death of Jesus, were being offered an opportunity to repent of their great sin:

> "'Therefore let all the house of Israel know assuredly that God has made this Jesus, whom you crucified, both Lord and Christ.' Now when they heard this, they were cut to the heart … Then Peter said to them, 'Repent, and let every one of you be baptized in the name of Jesus Christ for the remission of sins; and you shall receive the gift of the Holy Spirit. For the promise is to you and to your children, and to all who are afar off, as many as the Lord our God will call.'"

The gospel is always a surprise attack. It gets at people from a direction they never planned to defend. They are prepared for argument, but the gospel does not argue. They are prepared for sentiment, but the gospel is not sentimental. On the day of Pentecost, the Holy Spirit was outpoured, and that transformed the disciples totally. Man power had been filled with God's power – and that is your secret for your life … even today.

Today's Scripture
For the promise is to you and to your children, and to all who are afar off, as many as the Lord our God will call.
(Acts 2:39)

Daily Power!
Only the compassion of Christ can present the gospel with the love of God.

Mark My Word
Acts 2:17-39

The Bible In A Year

Morning
Deuteronomy 18
Psalm 105

Evening
Isaiah 45
Revelation 15

14

Power Demonstrated

Today's Scripture
There are diversities
of gifts, but the
same Spirit There
are differences of
ministries, but the
same Lord. And there
are diversities of
activities, but it is the
same God who
works all in all.
(1 Corinthians 12:4-6)

Daily Power!
Lord, show me today
how to manifest your
power and love to a
hurting world.

Mark My Word
1 Corinthians 12:1-31

The Bible In A Year

Morning
Deuteronomy 19
Psalm 106

Evening
Isaiah 46
Revelation 16

The power of the gospel is manifest power: *"The manifestation of the Spirit is given to each one for the profit of all."* His power should be seen, be manifested. There should be effects – physical or personal – that can be attributed to the power of God – people's lives should be affected in some tangible way. The Holy Spirit is not a theory, a statement about what goes on in some distant world of which we are not aware. his power is power made manifest.

There are two forms of power, and the one most Christians speak of is "dunamis." We can identify with that word because we use it so much in English: dynamo, dynamite, dynamics. But actually those words express "power under wraps." Dynamite is simply a grey substance, which you can carry in your briefcase. Be careful though! It is a power pack. It is latent power, power stored up. Paul also uses another word, "energema" – energy. When the power of dynamite is released, it becomes energy. Energy is power let loose. In 1 Corinthians 12, the same word is translated "activities" – power in operation. The "working of miracles" later used is a combination of both words – "power operating in energy."

To be blunt, Christianity is either supernatural, or nothing at all. We had – and still have – a supernatural Jesus, with a supernatural ministry, creating a supernatural church, with a supernatural gospel, and a supernatural Bible. Take the miraculous away, and you have taken Christianity's life away. The church becomes an ethical society, or a social club, when it is intended to be the grid system for transmitting the power of God into this powerless world. You and I are conductors of God's power to the world!

A World Vision

Among the Old Testament prophets, Jonah was the only one to leave Israel and actually preach the Word of the Lord openly in the streets of a foreign land. There was a kinship between Jonah and Jesus. Jonah was the only prophet with whom Jesus personally associated himself. He spoke of him as "the sign to Israel." Jonah had a God-given burden for a Gentile city. The next to carry such a burden was Jesus Christ himself. his heart was big enough to hold the whole of Israel, and the whole Gentile world!

No other prophet of Israel ever carried the Word of the Lord to the outside world except when they themselves were carried away as captives of war. In Babylon, some maintained their witness to the Lord, the God of Israel. We read of these in the books of Daniel and Esther. But the northern tribes were absorbed into the Assyrian Empire and lost. In the Book of Psalms, we are told, *"And those who plundered us requested mirth, saying, "Sing us one of the songs of Zion!" How shall we sing the LORD'S song in a foreign land?"* What a pity – those songs could have introduced the living God to the outside world.

The concern of God for his creatures extends to all equally, even to the most renegade and wicked. However, Jonah did not feel the same way at all and was out of sympathy with his commission. He tried to get away from God. But God was determined that he should go, and sent a storm at sea as Jonah tried to flee. It was God's storm of protest at Jonah's attitude, devoid of any pity.

God made Jonah a remarkable exception. He coerced him into doing what Israel was supposed to do, but never did. God had raised up Israel to make the name of the Lord known throughout the whole earth! Even the original church was entirely Jewish for maybe twenty years. Perhaps Jonah was, despite his shortcomings, one of the greatest of all the prophets! Today, allow God to speak to your heart about your own responsibility to a dying world.

Today's Scripture
Therefore he is also able to save to the uttermost those who come to God through him, since he always lives to make intercession for them.
(Hebrews 7:25)

Daily Power!
Dear Lord, please remind me that in everything I say, in everything I do, I represent you to a sinful world.

Mark My Word
Psalm 67, 96, 137:3-4
Ezekiel 36:23
Jonah 1:1-17; 2:1-10
Matthew 12:39
Hebrews 7:25

The Bible In A Year

Morning
Deuteronomy 20
Psalm 107

Evening
Isaiah 47
Revelation 17

16

Today's Scripture
No one can serve two masters; for either he will hate the one and love the other, or else he will be loyal to the one and despise the other. You cannot serve God and mammon [money]. (Matthew 6:24)

Daily Power!
I want to be "rich in good works, ready to give, willing to share, storing up for myself good foundation for the time to come, that I may lay hold on eternal life."

Mark My Word
Jonah 1:1-17
Matthew 6:24
Luke 16:13
Ephesians 4:11
1 Timothy 6:17-19
2 Peter 3:9

The Bible In A Year

Morning
Deuteronomy 21
Psalms 108 and 109

Evening
Isaiah 48
Revelation 18

Evangelism Is God's Initiative

The initiative to save Nineveh came from God, not from Jonah. *"The Lord is … not willing that any should perish but that all should come to repentance."* The initiative for evangelism comes from God, and God both calls and equips us for this work. It was he who gave some to be evangelists. At first, Jonah acted on his own initiative and went in the opposite direction – to Tarshish – instead of going East. God responded by sending a ferocious storm! God has promised to bless and support his own divine plans. There is no divine blessing upon our own plans, only upon his.

So where was Jonah going? Where is Tarshish? Various experts have studied this, trying to find out. The word "tarshish" is linked closely with the smelting of ore, silver, gold, and tin. The ships of Tarshish were treasure ships – famous for the expensive cargo they carried. They became symbols of wealth, power and pride. For Jonah, Nineveh represented only sacrifice. It was a stark choice: Nineveh, with its menace, or Tarshish, with its money.

"No servant can serve two masters, for either he will hate the one and love the other, or else he will be loyal to the one and despise the other. You cannot serve God and mammon." Are we "for hire" – where the biggest salary is offered? Is cash to be the deciding factor in our calling? Mammon and ministry do not mix too well. He profits most who serves best:

> "Command those who are rich in this present age not to be haughty, nor to trust in uncertain riches but in the living God, who gives us richly all things to enjoy. Let them do good, that they be rich in good works, ready to give, willing to share, storing up for themselves a good foundation for the time to come, that they may lay hold on eternal life."

So make the decision today … to serve God … to put him first … to make him your number one priority. And then you will see every other area of your life fit into place.

Low Resistance

A fuse is made of a metal, such as silver wire, which offers low resistance to current. Low resistance means high conductivity. Translated into the spiritual, the lower our resistance to the Word of God, the higher the power rating. The higher our resistance in obedience to the Word, the lower the operational power of God. A fuse with high resistance would either carry no power at all, or else soon blow. When we resist the Word by unbelief, the power of God cannot come through. If we say that we believe in the Word but disobey it, we negate our faith. It blows the fuse. The power of God is little when the Word of God means little to us.

Christianity is a power religion, or it is nothing. Liberals, teachers of rationalist doctrine, rely on logic. The apostles relied on the power of God: *"The world through wisdom did not know God, it pleased God through the foolishness of the message preached to save those who believe."* Reasoning is too uncertain an instrument for vital personal relationships, especially with God. When people turn to science with its philosophic deductions to approve religious faith, it is ridiculous. Science has no equipment to handle relationships with God.

How do we believe, or not believe, in anybody? By mathematics? Have you ever felt that you could not trust somebody, but you were unable put your finger on why not? It is a gut feeling under your skin. A higher self, intuition, is at work and triggers off an alarm. But we believe in somebody else for the same reason … and what that is, we may not know. Instinct never warns us against Jesus. When we "get wise" to him, we want to come closer. Knowing him better, we heart-warm to him. *"We love him because he first loved us."* What unbelievers say means no more than what the barometer says. The proper way, the only possible way, is to trust him. Remember: the effective center of true life … your life … is your heart, not your brain.

Today's Scripture
For with the heart man believes unto righteousness, and with the mouth confession is made unto salvation. (Romans 10:10)

Daily Power!
The lower my resistance to the Word of God, the higher my power rating!

Mark My Word
Romans 10:10
1 Corinthians 1:21
1 John 4:19

The Bible In A Year

Morning
Deuteronomy 22
Psalms 110 and 111

Evening
Isaiah 49
Revelation 19

18

Believing

Today's Scripture
Take heart, for I
believe God that it
will be just as it was
told me.
(Acts 27:25)

Daily Power!
On Christ the solid
rock I stand.

Mark My Word
Acts 27:25-26

The Bible In A Year

Morning
Deuteronomy 23
Psalms 112 and 113

Evening
Isaiah 50
Revelation 20

Faith is not just "believing" with nothing special in mind – it is believing unto something and for something. The Word of God gives point, direction and purpose. Without the Bible, it is like "an arrow shot into the air that fell to earth I know not where." In fact, it is the only book that gives faith a positive goal. One wonders what some religions propose to do for people who believe. They become a religious treadmill, believing for the sake of believing.

The apostle Paul was aboard a sinking ship, but he said, *"I believe God."* It was not a kind of defiant sentiment. It was specific:

> "Now when neither sun nor stars appeared for many days, and no small tempest beat on us, all hope that we would be saved was finally given up … Then Paul stood in the midst of them and said … 'I urge you to take heart, for there will be no loss of life among you, but only of the ship. For there stood by me this night an angel of the God to whom I belong and whom I serve, saying, "Do not be afraid, Paul … indeed God has granted you all of those who sail with you." Therefore take heart, men, for I believe God that it will be just as it was told me. However, we must run aground on a certain island.'"

It was rather different for a man who was crossing the Atlantic Ocean in a storm. The captain tried to reassure him, saying, "Sir, we are in the hands of God." The man replied, "Is it as bad as that?" Please hold this truth deep in your heart today – "when God gives you a promise, then you can stand securely upon it!"

One-Drink

Jesus said that when the Helper has come: *"He may abide with you forever."* This is where the blessing of speaking with tongues is seen. We cannot speak unless the Holy Spirit gives utterance. If he does, then he is there. By that sign, we can go out and conquer, for he is with us. Our feelings are not a reliable indicator of the Holy Spirit's power within us. In the 19th century, before tongues were commonly heard, the problem was knowing when the Spirit had come. People would pray a great deal – "tarrying" – believing that power could be measured by the time spent in prayer, an idea quite foreign to the Bible. By the 20th century, it was taught for the first time that the sign of tongues was the assurance of the baptism in the Spirit. This immediately triggered the greatest movement of the Holy Spirit of all time. My own faith was energized by the initial sign of tongues, which led me into this present ministry of evangelism.

Paul spoke about the importance of speaking in tongues, yet put it into perspective:

> "Pursue love, and desire spiritual gifts, but especially that you may prophesy. For he who speaks in a tongue does not speak to men but to God, for no one understands him; however, in the spirit he speaks mysteries. But he who prophesies speaks edification and exhortation and comfort to men. He who speaks in a tongue edifies himself, but he who prophesies edifies the church. I wish you all spoke with tongues, but even more that you prophesied; for he who prophesies is greater than he who speaks with tongues, unless indeed he interprets, that the church may receive edification."

When Jesus spoke to the woman at the well in Samaria, he referred to *"whoever drinks."* The Greek tense He used (aorist) means to drink once only, not to keep coming back with an empty water pot. That is the very thing the woman at the well of Sychar understood, for she said: *"that I may not thirst, nor come here to draw."*

The one-drink results in *"a fountain of water springing up into everlasting life."* Water is frequently used as a symbol of the Holy Spirit in Scripture, just as it is here. Oh, come to that fountain again today, and every day, and drink of the well that will never run dry!

Today's Scripture
If you knew the gift of God, and who it is who says to you, 'Give me a drink,' you would have asked him, and he would have given you living water.
(John 4:10)

Daily Power!
The gift of speaking in tongues enables me to speak secrets to God.

Mark My Word
John 14:1-24; 1 Corinthians 14:1-5

The Bible In A Year

Morning
Deuteronomy 24
Psalms 114 and 115

Evening
Isaiah 51
Revelation 21

20

Identified By Miracles

Today's Scripture
And as you go, preach, saying, "The kingdom of heaven is at hand." Heal the sick, cleanse the lepers, raise the dead, cast out demons. Freely you have received, freely give. (Matthew 10:7-8)

Daily Power!
The kingdom of God is identified by miracles.

Mark My Word
Matthew 10:7-8
Mark 16:17-18

The Bible In A Year

Morning
Deuteronomy 25
Psalm 116

Evening
Isaiah 52
Revelation 22

When I was in Brazzaville, the capital of the West African country of Congo, God gave me a word of knowledge for a couple otherwise unknown to me, somewhere among the tens of thousands present in the service. The wife had been in a coma for three days, and had been carried into the meeting by her husband. By faith and obedience to God's prompting, I told the vast audience what the Spirit of the Lord had made known to me. As I spoke, the unconscious woman – though not hearing – came out of her coma and was healed. Mind over matter? Impossible! The patient knew nothing of what was going on until she revived.

> "And these signs will follow those who believe: in my name they will cast out demons; they will speak with new tongues; they will take up serpents; and if they drink anything deadly, it will by no means hurt them; they will lay hands on the sick, and they will recover."

Another lady present needed urgent surgery. Her unborn baby had died in her womb, and the hospital had arranged for the baby to be removed the next day. When prayer was offered for all the needy ones in the service, the baby in her womb leaped. She rushed forward to the platform tearfully to testify – and just in time too – because straight afterward, she went into labor! She later gave birth to a bouncing baby boy.

> "And as you go, preach, saying, 'The kingdom of heaven is at hand.' Heal the sick, cleanse the lepers, raise the dead, cast out demons. Freely you have received, freely give."

These were not the only wonders that happened. They left me unable to sleep for excitement and joy. Most important of all, for six days the Holy Spirit swept through the crowd like a heavenly dam-burst, carrying one hundred thousand precious Congolese on a wave of blessing into the kingdom of God! That joy is yours today!

Acts Today

21

The book of Acts reads better than any modern novel. It has clearly defined characters, some in leading roles, others in support roles. It has action, adventure, triumphs, tragedies. The scenes change from Jerusalem to Damascus to Antioch to Rome, from prison cells to shipwrecks. Yet the marvelous thing about it is that it is completely true!

See how the love of Jesus came into the life of Saul, the angry persecutor of Christians, and transformed him into the most powerful apostle of all. That rings true! Read about the arguments between the Jews-only faction and the Gentiles-too group. That rings true too, for so many churches still squabble among themselves. The miracles of healing, the explosive growth of the early church, government leaders baffled and chagrined by the boldness of these ignorant peasants, these are all quite believable, and even applicable to our own day.

Sometimes people have suggested that "The Acts of the Apostles" ought to be re-named "The Acts of the Holy Spirit." Perhaps. The Book describes the acts of the apostles, as its title indicates, but it certainly does not give an exhaustive account of all the acts of the Holy Spirit. He did not cease to operate at the end of chapter 28! The acts of the apostles carry on uninterrupted into the acts of the early church, and then on into the acts of God's people today. The book of Acts tells of the day of small things, which paved the way for the acts of today. It is a book that is still being written! I carry on with the work that the apostles began – together with you. We are partners and co-workers with Christ on God's harvest fields. Together, let us make history for Christ!

Today's Scripture
Preaching the kingdom of God and teaching the things which concern the Lord Jesus Christ with all confidence.
(Acts 28:31)

Daily Power!
Lord, may my chapter in the modern-day book of Acts be one that completely honors you.

Mark My Word
Acts 28:1-31

The Bible In A Year

Morning
Deuteronomy 26
Psalms 117 and 118

Evening
Isaiah 53
Matthew 1

22

God Raises The Dead

Today's Scripture
To open their eyes, in order to turn them from darkness to light, and from the power of Satan to God, that they may receive forgiveness of sins and an inheritance among those who are sanctified by faith in me.
(Acts 26:18)

Daily Power!
Lord, give me the words to say that will persuade others to open their eyes, and turn from darkness to light, and from the power of Satan to God.

Mark My Word
Acts 26:1-32.

The Bible In A Year

Morning
Deuteronomy 27 to 28:19
Psalm 119:1-24

Evening
Isaiah 54
Matthew 2

When preaching to King Agrippa, one of the most scholarly rulers of his day, Paul boldly proclaimed Jesus Christ crucified and resurrected – a fact hard to accept by the intellectual king. Paul asked: *"Why should it be thought incredible by you that God raises the dead?"* He continued with his testimony – how he had formerly persecuted his own people whom he considered to be blaspheming renegades, but was transformed by a divine appointment on the road to Damascus. He proclaimed that he was sent:

> "To open their eyes, in order to turn them from darkness to light, and from the power of Satan to God, that they may receive forgiveness of sins and an inheritance among those who are sanctified by faith in (Christ)."

Eventually, the king responded: *"You almost persuade me to become a Christian."*

Some people brush the resurrection aside. They say it is just another wonder from an unsuspicious and superstitious age. However, the news of the resurrection of Jesus did not fade and die. Hundreds testified that they had seen him alive! Authorities were alarmed. Believers were threatened, beaten and imprisoned, but they could not be silenced. They convinced thousands. Then, as others believed, they also had glorious experiences. There was only one explanation for it: Jesus Christ was walking the earth again, and as a result, history was changed! Today, these things still happen. Thousands discover that Jesus is alive. They stake their soul on it, build their lives on it, and they are never let down. So remember today to be active in this on-going, end-time resurrection harvest of souls.

No Matter Where We Run

Aboard the ill-fated ship to Tarshish, the crew did not know Jonah was a prophet, nor did they know his God. The sailors were heathens, but they rebuked the prophet of God for sleeping on the job. *"What do you mean, sleeper? Arise, call on your God; perhaps your God will consider us, so that we may not perish."*

The people of this world expect a prophet to speak up, whether they agree with what he says or not. Maybe they do not want to adopt Christian morals, or the way of the Lord for themselves – yet they still believe morality is a good thing for other people to practice. If we do not preach what they know we believe, they feel cheated and let down. The church must never fail to sound a clear note on what is right and wrong.

When backed into a corner, Jonah admitted who he was. This startled and even terrified the crew. These men were potential converts – they already recognized the power and authority of his God. Despite Jonah's poor testimony, they came to believe in Jonah's God: *"Then the men feared the LORD exceedingly, and offered a sacrifice to the LORD and took vows."* Here was a man who knew the marvelous truth about God, and yet they had to ask him who his God was. With Jonah aboard their ship, who his God was should have been clear. Now ask yourself this hard question: "Do people know who **my** God is?" Why not make sure that they do!

> "There was a man sent from God, whose name was John. This man came for a witness, to bear witness of the Light, that all through him might believe"

> "The God of our fathers has chosen you that you should know his will, and see the Just One, and hear the voice of his mouth. For you will be his witness to all men of what you have seen and heard."

Has God been good to you? Have you seen and heard his marvelous works? Then be a witness of that to all men … and they will know who is your God!

Today's Scripture
For I am not ashamed of the gospel of Christ, for it is the power of God to salvation for everyone who believes.
(Romans 1:16)

Daily Power!
In every thought, word, and deed, dear Lord, let me be Your representative to this world.

Mark My Word
Jonah 1:1-16
Acts 22:14
Romans 1:1-32

The Bible In A Year

Morning
Deuteronomy 28:20
Psalm 119:25-48

Evening
Isaiah 55
Matthew 3

24

True Spirit Of Evangelism

Today's Scripture
You are the salt of the earth, but if the salt loses its flavor, how shall it be seasoned? It is then good for nothing but to be thrown out and trampled underfoot by men. You are the light of the world. (Matthew 5:13-14)

Daily Power!
Lord, let me be Your epistle written in the hearts of men, known and read by all men, and a clear signpost to you.

Mark My Word
Jonah 1:1-3
Matthew 5:13-14;
7:22-23; 10:16-26
John 15:26
1 Corinthians 2:4
2 Corinthians 3:2

The Bible In A Year

Morning
Deuteronomy 29
Psalm 119:49-72

Evening
Isaiah 56
Matthew 4

Jesus told his disciples that the Spirit of God is the Spirit of witness. Today we often talk about "power evangelism" – signs and wonders to confirm the gospel. But Jesus said that even wicked people would work miracles although he never knew them. Paul also talked about the demonstration of the Spirit.

However, one cannot help but be impressed by the way the apostle manifested the reality of the gospel in his daily life. He told the Corinthians that their lives were *"epistles … known and read by all men."* Looking at us, will people be able to say, "So, that is what your God is like"?

Evangelism means to recommend Jesus. The evangelistic method taught by Jesus was that we should recommend him by our lives, as well as by our words. We should be "Jesus people" … or more precisely, "Jesus-of-the-gospel people." We are *"the light of the world"* – there should be no other options.

> "And as you go, preach, saying, 'The kingdom of heaven is at hand.' Heal the sick, cleanse the lepers, raise the dead, cast out demons. Freely you have received, freely give … You will be brought before governors and kings for my sake, as a testimony to them and to the Gentiles. But when they deliver you up, do not worry about how or what you should speak, for it will be given to you in that hour what you should speak; for it is not you who speak, but the Spirit of your Father who speaks in you."

Jonah fled from the presence of the Lord, but he carried a light in his soul that somehow shone through. He concealed his testimony from the captain and crew of the ship that he boarded at Joppa. But Jonah knew God – and that came across even when he tried to run away from God. The crew of a storm-tossed ship sensed it … and caught the vision.

This is God's call to you and me today: to catch his vision for the world, and to be his tools to bring the lost to Christ.

Personal Presence

One thing has always amazed me: the disciples did not weep when Christ left them. They never showed any nostalgia for "the good old days." Luke tells us that after he ascended out of sight, they *"returned to Jerusalem with great joy, and were continually in the temple praising and blessing God."* Why did they display such a remarkable reaction to the departure of Jesus? The answer is the coming of the Spirit! When Christ was present, they were only eyewitnesses of his power. But when the day of Pentecost came, they were more than eyewitnesses – they possessed power themselves, and experienced the divine presence personally. It was different from when Christ was with them. That personal sense of the presence of God is nowhere said to be just for the disciples alone, as if they were some kind of elite band. Peter said: *"The promise is to you and to your children, and to all who are afar off, as many as the Lord our God will call."* He quoted the promise from the prophet Joel, where God said: *"I will pour out my Spirit on all flesh."* Wesley observed that this promise is not only for the day of Pentecost – it described the **normal** Christian experience, as does the whole book of Acts.

Another curious fact is that, although Jesus told the disciples to take bread and wine in memory of him, they never used the language of "remembering." One does not "remember" a person with whom he or she lives. He is a living and abiding presence by the Spirit. *"From now on, we regard no one according to the flesh. Even though we have known Christ according to the flesh, yet now we know him thus no longer."* To be filled with the Spirit makes us alive to Jesus, which is even better than being alive when Jesus was on earth. Note too, that the Spirit does not come to talk about himself, but to reveal Jesus. Paul said that he preached Christ crucified in the power and demonstration of the Spirit. If we only preach the power of the Spirit without the cross, we short-circuit the very power we preach about. The Spirit's primary interest is in the cross. We do not preach power, but the gospel of the cross, which is the power of God by the Spirit.

Today's Scripture

And suddenly there came a sound from heaven, as of a rushing mighty wind, and it filled the whole house where they were sitting. Then there appeared to them divided tongues, as of fire, and one sat upon each of them. And they were all filled with the Holy Spirit.
(Acts 2:2-4)

Daily Power!

Lord, help me to show to others the cross of Christ and the power of the Holy Spirit in my life.

Mark My Word

Joel 2:28;
Luke 24:52-53;
John 16:15;
Acts 2:17-39; 2
Corinthians 5:16.

The Bible In A Year

Morning
Deuteronomy 30
Psalm 119:73-96

Evening
Isaiah 57
Matthew 5

26

Today's Scripture
You are of God, little children, and have overcome them, because he who is in you is greater than he who is in the world.
(1 John 4:4)

Daily Power!
The gospel of Christ, is the power of God to salvation for everyone who believes!

Mark My Word
Isaiah 53:11
1 John 4:4.

The Bible In A Year

Morning
Deuteronomy 31
Psalm 119:97-120

Evening
Isaiah 58
Matthew 6

Since my earliest attempts as a missionary in Africa, what we are seeing God do today is breathtaking. Following the footsteps of giants, we reap with joy where they had sown in tears. We came to Bukavu, first visited by missionary C.T. Studd, and still remote in the rain forests of Zaire. There we saw 70,000 people respond to the call of God's love. David Livingstone prophesied that where he hardly saw a convert, later there would be thousands – so it was. At Blantyre, Malawi – named after the town in Scotland where Livingstone was born – several hundred thousand responded to the call of salvation.

Today, witchcraft, occultism and evil make the gospel as vital as a gun in a snake pit. Jesus sets the captives free, wholesale. Cool and casual Christianity will do nothing. Nations urgently need the flaming message of the cross now, not at our leisure. Sometime ago, our northerly thrust reached almost to the Sahara Desert at Ouagadougou, capital of Burkina Faso (formerly Upper Volta), a country noted for its occultism. Gatherings totaled 800,000 people in six meetings, with almost a quarter-million people in the culminating service. Most of them professed Jesus Christ, including many Muslims and animists. Similarly later on, in the Nigerian city of Kaduna, 500,000 people gathered in a single service – a total of 1.67 million in six meetings. And then to top it all, at our Millennium Great gospel Crusade in Lagos, Nigeria, where we preached the gospel to over 6 million precious souls, 3.4 million filled out decision cards. 1.6 million people gathered on the last day of this six-day crusade. The response to the power-gospel is absolutely awesome!

For over 20 years I had a divine promise in my heart that we would see one million souls converted in a single meeting. We acquired sound systems to reach crowds bigger, perhaps, than ever before addressed by one man face-to-face. Arrogant presumption? If the Crucified One is to *"see the labor of his soul, and be satisfied,"* dare we think in smaller terms? Would he be "satisfied" with anything less? Dare to have big faith! Yes, we saw one million souls saved in a single service in Lagos. God's promise has been fulfilled and we are moving forward with God's gospel "combine harvester" gathering souls to him en masse.

The God Who Creates

Twice in the first chapter of Revelations, God called himself, *"he who was."* "The God that was" is how half the world thinks of him: the One who created heaven and earth … and has done very little ever since. Limited to that idea, people may as well have faith in Pharaoh Tutankhamun. Could a God of such creative imagination settle down to being a God of long ago, the past, sitting in heaven with his hands folded in his lap? He filled the empty skies with unsurpassing beauty … and then went to sleep? If we do not see further than that, we are not very perceptive. Could any of us build even a house and abandon it? Could God ignore his own universe?

"In the beginning God created the heavens and the earth." So what? Well, the question naturally is, "Why should God do any such thing?" He did not do it to please anybody – there was nobody else, only himself! He pleased himself when he did it. He was not obliged to do so. He was not pressured. What someone does because they want to do it, shows what they are. If I sat down in my room, shut the door and played the organ, it would be for my own pleasure. It would tell people that it was me, because I am musical. I would do that. God brought the glittering stars and the planets into being because that is what he wanted to do. *"The heavens declare the glory of God; and the firmament shows his handiwork."* So begins Psalm 19, and the writer is thrilled. But it is the aurora of God – not the splendor of the universe – that he is excited about. He is distracted from Creation by the Creator!

Modern science takes everything apart, like taking a violin apart to see what makes the sound. I imagine God standing by, pensive, watching us like children opening their Christmas stockings, while he is waiting to love us. But then, fathers are often forgotten for the sake of Christmas toys! God pulled a blank sheet of paper across his desk, thought, then designed everything that we see around us. Its substance was shaped out of his own grandeur – he himself must be absolutely, eternally breathtaking! And this is the God who **loves you!**

Today's Scripture
The law of the Lord is perfect, converting the soul; the testimony of the Lord is sure, making wise the simple.
(Psalm 19:7)

Daily Power!
Nothing, but nothing shall be able to separate us from the love of God which is in Christ Jesus our Lord.

Mark My Word
Genesis 1:1
Psalm 19:1-14
Romans 8:39
Revelation 1:4, 8

The Bible In A Year

Morning
Deuteronomy 32
Psalm 119:121-144

Evening
Isaiah 59
Matthew 7

28

The Good God

Today's Scripture
For the Lord is good; his mercy is everlasting, and his truth endures to all generations
(Psalm 100:5)

Daily Power!
My God is an awesome God who reigns with wisdom, power and love.

Mark My Word
Genesis 1:31
Job 38:7
Psalm 100:3
John 3:16
Romans 8:28

The Bible In A Year

Morning
Deuteronomy 33 and 34
Psalm 119:145-176

Evening
Isaiah 60
Matthew 8

God delights in activity, in color, beauty, wonder and life, and much more. He made us – why? Why do we long for children? As an opportunity for our instinct of love – God made us that way. He is like that himself. What he is must come out as long as God exists, on and on. *"Then God saw everything that he had made, and indeed it was very good."* his idea of what was good was a material world, not just an abstract spiritual principle of goodness. God does not deal in abstractions. He is pragmatic, the God of earth and sea, animals, trees and birds, fishes … and people. *"We are his people."* He made it all, and made us and was happy about it. He loved it: *"God so loved the world."* He molded this beautiful globe, and said "Good! Good! Good!" seven times in Genesis chapter one. He clapped his hands with pleasure, and the morning stars sang together for joy. The whole process works towards good. Evil fights it, but it will never work out: *"… all things work together for good to those who love God."* God is good.

When things are wrong, we ask, "Why?" Of course we do. God put that in us. We hate evil because he does. God put that "Why?" in our souls. Even Jesus asked: "Why?" when he experienced the utmost agony on the cross. A good God is the God of true faith. That is the God of the Bible. That is where the idea came from – the Bible. The pagans had not the remotest idea of a good God.

"God said let there be … and there was." Creation was the first and greatest of all miracles. If God could extrude the Himalayas and the Rockies through his cupped hands, and with his finger scoop out the hollows for the Pacific and the Atlantic, and cap the poles with miles-thick ice, then what is the problem about God healing deaf ears, or blind eyes? Are miracles possible? What a question! How dull can we be? But then, doubt does dull our thinking. It is absurd for anybody to say that miracles cannot happen. To know that, we would have to know everything about everything and about God. Nobody knows enough to declare that it cannot be. You can rest in the assurance of God's love for you.

Jonah's Problem

Jonah knew in his very bones what God was like: He was gracious! How could he – Jonah – preach judgment to Nineveh when he knew perfectly well that God was so kind and merciful? He would forgive their wickedness at the drop of a hat … or rather, at the first sign of repentance. So he fled from the presence of the Lord. To be where God was, meant carrying the scent of grace in his clothes. The atmosphere was infected by compassion, and Jonah did not want to feel compassionate. He had no inclination for smiling kindly toward monsters like the lords of Nineveh.

Evangelism means deliverance from judgment. But Jonah strongly felt that Nineveh deserved judgment. his attitude was understandable, I suppose. Jonah's feelings are often echoed in the Book of Psalms.

When Jesus was traveling through Samaria with his disciples, He wanted to stay one night in a village. But the local inhabitants were hostile to the Jews, and would not accommodate the party. The disciples had been enjoying the experience of using God's power to heal, through the authority vested in them by Jesus. They knew that Elijah had brought fire down from heaven upon soldiers sent to arrest him, so they proposed doing the same to wipe out this unfriendly village – after all, God had done it to Sodom and Gomorrah! But Jesus said to them: *"You do not know what manner of spirit you are of. For the Son of Man did not come to destroy men's lives but to save them."*

Let compassion be your guiding word today, even as Jesus had compassion toward the most hardened sinner. You can have compassion on those he brings across your path.

> "I will have mercy on whomever I will have mercy, and I will have compassion on whomever I will have compassion. So then it is not of him who wills, nor of him who runs, but of God who shows mercy … For this very purpose I have raised you up, that I may show my power in you, and that my name may be declared in all the earth."

Today's Scripture
For the Son of Man did not come to destroy men's lives but to save them.
(Luke 9:56)

Daily Power!
Lord, teach me to move with compassion, as you did when you saw the needy.

Mark My Word
2 Kings 1:8-14
Psalm 18:37-45
Jonah 1:1-3
Luke 9:15-62
Romans 9:15-17

The Bible In A Year

Morning
Joshua 1
Psalms 120 to 122

Evening
Isaiah 61
Matthew 9

30

Our Ultimate Objective

Today's Scripture
It is not for you
to know times or
seasons which the
Father has put in his
own authority. But
you shall receive
power when the Holy
Spirit has come upon
you; and you shall be
witnesses to me in
Jerusalem, and in all
Judea and Samaria,
and to the ends
of the earth.
(Acts 1:7-8)

Daily Power!
I am empowered
by the Holy Spirit
to carry out the
Great Commission,
however near or far,
large or small.

Mark My Word
Jonah 4:1-11
Acts 1:3-8

The Bible In A Year

Morning
Joshua 2
Psalms 123 to 125

Evening
Isaiah 62
Matthew 10

Social, environmental, and moral issues are not trifles to be dismissed lightly. We ought to be angry about many of the abominations perpetrated by modern society. But what about the issue of eternal salvation? Pro-life people fight (rightly) for the lives of unborn babies … but what are we doing about the souls of the millions of people walking our city streets?

We cannot all be preachers or evangelists. There must be people who do all sorts of different jobs in order to keep society and our churches functioning. Yet, whatever our concern with the fabric of mortal life, and the issues of society, **the call of Christ to preach the gospel to all creatures must still be our ultimate objective.**

To put it another way, we can be like Jonah, whose most immediate problem was the loss of shade that had been provided by his now-dead plant, or so he thought. Are we more disturbed about endangered species in the North Atlantic than by the eternal danger in which Christ-rejecters stand?

When Jesus had risen from the dead, and was about to ascend into heaven, he gave the disciples extensive teaching about the kingdom of God. They asked him: *"Will you at this time restore the kingdom to Israel?"* That was not only their priority, but also their interpretation of "the kingdom of God" – a nationalistic issue. They were interested in times and seasons. Jesus answered:

> "It is not for you to know times or seasons which the Father has put in his own authority. But you shall receive power when the Holy Spirit has come upon you; and you shall be witnesses to me in Jerusalem, and in all Judea and Samaria, and to the end of the earth."

Those were the last words of Jesus on earth. True, not everybody can give up their fishing boats to fish for men. But the Great Commission must still remain the top priority for all believers … including you and me. Please accept the Great Commission as your opportunity to shine in this dark and dying world. Shine brightly today!

Sickness is not the ultimate evil,
therefore healing is not the ultimate good.
Sin is the ultimate evil and salvation is the ultimate good.
Yet salvation and healing go hand in hand.

The practice of the supernatural
without the message of Calvary is very dangerous!

John never called miracles miracles,
but called them signs,
because they were pointing at something.

Future Evangelism

The world can be evangelized sooner than most believe, even as we have begun the new millennium. There were only a few thousand believers when Jesus left this world – perhaps one Christian follower for every twenty thousand people. Yet within three hundred years, the entire Roman Empire became officially Christian.

Today, it is estimated there are more than six hundred million born-again Christians on earth. That is one in every ten people! If we are distracted by other issues and devote our time, money and energy to mere political and social concerns, the gospel witness will decrease. It must increase! We need one final, all-out effort to reach the other nine-tenths of the world!

> "Now to him who is able to establish you according to my gospel and the preaching of Jesus Christ, according to the revelation of the mystery kept secret since the world began, but now made manifest, and by the prophetic Scriptures made known to all nations, according to the commandment of the everlasting God, for obedience to the faith."

When the gospel has been preached in the entire world as a witness to all nations, the end will come at last.

Now we come to that part when you and I must ask ourselves: "What kind of an evangelist am I? Do I want to preach judgment – like Jonah or John the Baptist – and see God's wrath come against greedy, evil people? Am I more concerned about side-issues – even as Jonah was angry about the plant that withered and died – than I am about millions of lost and dying souls? Do I have the capacity to preach compassion and mercy – as Jesus did – and offer Good News to people? And what am I prepared to do about evangelism?"

These are important questions, and it is our responsibility to find the answers … and then make them stick!

Today's Scripture
This gospel of the kingdom will be preached in all the world as a witness to all the nations, and then the end will come.
(Matthew 24:14)

Daily Power!
Lord, give me the ability to preach, and to show compassion and mercy as you did.

Mark My Word
Matthew 24:14
Romans 16:25-26

The Bible In A Year

Morning
Joshua 3
Psalms 126 to 128

Evening
Isaiah 63
Matthew 11

2

A Modern Man

Today's Scripture
And be kind to
one another,
tenderhearted,
forgiving one another,
even as God in Christ
forgave you.
(Ephesians 4:32)

Daily Power!
Father, you showed
no partiality in
choosing me. Let me
not show partiality to
others.

Mark My Word
Mark 16:15
Acts 10:34
Ephesians 4:1-32

The Bible In A Year

Morning
Joshua 4
Psalms 129 to 131

Evening
Isaiah 64
Matthew 12

The apostle Paul lived a modern man in his own times. his writings were filled with references and word-pictures that were clearly evident to his contemporaries. Therefore, in his letter to the church at Ephesus, a city well-influenced by Rome's power, he taught principles with vivid images that would truly appeal to, and be understood by, the Ephesians. Yet his imagery continues to inspire people throughout the centuries – and even today.

> "I therefore, the prisoner of the Lord, beseech you to walk worthy of the calling with which you were called, with all lowliness and gentleness, with long-suffering, bearing with one another in love, endeavoring to keep the unity of the Spirit in the bond of peace. There is one body and one Spirit, just as you were called in one hope of your calling: one Lord, one faith, one baptism; one God and Father of all, who is above all, and through all, and in you all. But to each one of us grace was given according to the measure of Christ's gift."

Here, Paul was writing to Christians who were slaves and free, lowborn and highborn, poverty-stricken and wealthy. Each person was treated exactly the same, as there are no favorites with God – *"In truth I perceive that God shows no partiality"* – and each person had the same responsibilities as a Christian to fulfil. What we learn today from Paul's ancient writings is that God expects the same of each of us – even as he expected it of those Christians who were yet to be martyred for their faith, persecuted for their beliefs, stripped all of possessions for the sake of the gospel. The number one assignment that they were given is the same assignment that was given to the apostles as they watched the resurrected Lord and Savior Jesus Christ ascending into heaven – *"Go into all the world and preach the gospel to every creature!"* That same assignment is yours and mine today!

Maxims Of Faith

Here are some basics of faith:

- To be believers, we should know what we believe and who we believe.
- The most basic lesson is we must take the Word of God at its face value.
- Without knowing God's will, faith is impossible.
- The Word is the eternal will of God.
- To question scripture is to question the only guide we have … and to question God.
- The Word of God is an ultimatum, not an option for discussion.
- Democratic vote or consensus does not decide Bible truth. It is *"settled in heaven forever."*
- The Bible is the Constitution of the kingdom of God, and no two-thirds majority of any parliament on earth can change it.

The Bible makes no bones about it and insists a thousand times on its own divine authority. The prophets who spoke, for example, were not offering their private political opinions, but *"holy men of God spoke as they were moved by the Holy Spirit."* They used the phrase: *"Thus says the Lord."* The Jewish conception was of a God of awful holiness, and they trembled before his awesome greatness.

Unless they had an overwhelming sense that God had sent them, no prophet of Israel would dare to claim to be the mouthpiece of this Almighty Being. Only absolute certainty would open their mouths. Moses reluctantly got into a lengthy argument with God when he commissioned him to return to Egypt for the liberation of his people. Jeremiah declared, *"I will not make mention of him, nor speak anymore in his name."* But his word was in my heart like a burning fire shut up in my bones; I was weary of holding it back, and I could not."*

The Word of God is alive and real and powerful in your life today!

Today's Scripture
Then I said, "I will not make mention of him, nor speak anymore in his name." But his Word was in my heart like a burning fire, shut up in my bones; I was weary of holding it back.
(Jeremiah 20:9)

Daily Power!
The Word of God is alive, real, and powerful in my heart and life today.

Mark My Word
Exodus 3:1-22; 4:1-17
Psalm 119:89
Jeremiah 20:9
2 Peter 1:21

The Bible In A Year

Morning
Joshua 5 to 6:5
Psalms 132 to 134

Evening
Isaiah 65
Matthew 13

4

Power Anywhere

Today's Scripture
Rejoice because
your names are
written in heaven.
(Luke 10:20)

Daily Power!
Father, give me
opportunities to
display your power by
the light that I shine.

Mark My Word
Matthew 17:20
Luke 10:20
John 11:40

The Bible In A Year

Morning
Joshua 6:6
Psalms 135 and 136

Evening
Isaiah 66
Matthew 14

Great power-lines stretch across a whole country. Day and night, the huge power turbines are feeding the vast system, harnessing the forces of coal, water, oil, or nuclear fusion, housed in towering buildings. All that! Then, at home a tiny sliver of wire fails, and everything in your house stops, without power. The greatness of God … the greatness of the work of Christ … the greatness of the Word of God are all there. But without faith, as small as a fuse wire, none of that greatness avails. The circuit is broken, the Power Bridge is down. If the faith-fuse fails, the dynamic of God is defused … and will be refused by those to whom we preach; indeed, they could be confused! Take the Word, put in the faith-fuse … and the power of God comes through – there will be light, warmth, energy, salvation, healing, strength, and blessing.

I once went into a very smart hairdressing salon where two ladies worked, and one of them began to cut my hair. Typically of hairdressers, she talked while she worked and asked me whether I was a businessman. My reply was: "I am a man of God." It was perhaps a good hard knock – but it broke the ice, and we were launched. In a short time, I was leading both these ladies to Christ. They knelt in the shorn hair on the floor while they prayed the prayer of salvation. When I left the shop, I heard one with tears in her eyes saying to the other: "That man of God came in for a haircut – what a glorious day!" I went out very happy and moved. Then I met my colleague, Peter van den Berg. I said to him: "Peter, I see you need a haircut too. Go and get your hair cut in that salon. I've led two women to Christ in there. Go and do the follow up!"

"If you have faith as a mustard seed," Jesus said – so little! Our faith is no towering sensation that everybody sees and gasps. It is the hidden fuse. But by it, the energies of heaven flow into the world. God uses fuses, but never subterfuge. Wherever we are, the hidden attitude of our hearts is God's missing link: *"If you would believe you would see the glory of God."* Wherever you go in your life, take the power of God with you – and be a conduit of that power to change lives.

In One Word – Compassion

Christ's gift to the world was not a new religion, or a new theory about life, or a new formula for heaven. He gave himself for us, *"the just for the unjust, that he might bring us to God."* Christianity is not a religion – it is Jesus! We can form doctrines around him, but Jesus did not come to bring us theology. He came just to be here, available, never to leave or forsake us, personally.

One of the Old Testament names for God was "El Shaddai" – it means God All-Sufficient. That God came to earth in the person of Jesus. He gave all of himself … and he is all we need! Another Old Testament title was "Jehovah Shammah" – it means the Lord is there. If he is there, that is all we want. Peter said: *"Therefore, to you who believe, he is precious."*

Jesus refused to live to benefit himself. his motives could be summed up in the word *compassion*. He was driven by love – never by fear, gain or popularity.

> "And Jesus, when he came out, saw a great multitude and was moved with compassion for them, because they were like sheep not having a shepherd. So he began to teach them many things."

He lived absolutely for us. When he left the carpenter's bench in Nazareth, he first faced fierce temptations in the wilderness. In every instance, he was tempted to think about himself. One test was to feed himself by a miracle; another to receive all the kingdoms on earth as a gift; the other to perform a wonderful sign that would have everybody acclaiming him as Messiah. The Lord was repelled by the very suggestion. He went hungry; he was crucified instead of crowned; and he was charged with blasphemy instead of being deified. Jesus' love for you and for me is overwhelming at times, but it is true! Let that love motivate you today. Let Christ's compassion drive you to action!

Today's Scripture
For Christ also suffered once for sins, the just for the unjust, that he might bring us to God, being put to death in the flesh but made alive in the Spirit.
(1 Peter 3:18)

Daily Power!
I desire to be filled with the compassion that motivated Jesus Christ.

Mark My Word
Mark 6:34;
1 Thessalonians 5:10
1 Peter 2:7; 3:18

The Bible In A Year

Morning
Joshua 7
Psalm 137 and 138

Evening
Jeremiah 1
Matthew 15

6

Christ The Giver

Today's Scripture
I have been crucified with Christ; it is no longer I who live, but Christ lives in me; and the life which I now live in the flesh I live by faith in the Son of God, who loved me and gave himself for me.
(Galatians 2:20)

Daily Power!
The relationship which I have in Christ Jesus is the one that gives me life.

Mark My Word
John 3:6; 4:3-26
Galatians 2:20

The Bible In A Year

Morning
Joshua 8
Psalm 139

Evening
Jeremiah 2
Matthew 16

When the people of Christ's day applauded him, he wept for them. They tried to make him King by force, but he chose the cross. Going to his death, He told the women of Jerusalem to weep for themselves, not for him – they were his last thought. Christ was not thinking of himself at all … and even if it meant death, he would bear it **for us**. He was ready to save us from hell by going through that hell of torment himself.

> "Jesus answered and said to her: 'If you knew the gift of God, and who it is who says to you: 'Give me a drink,' you would have asked him, and he would have given you living water.'"

He met a woman at a well, and asked her for a drink. In a couple of sentences, He became concerned just about her. Jesus was far more interested in giving her a drink at the fountain of eternal life than quenching his own natural thirst. In fact, did she ever bring him that drink? We never read that she did. That little episode lights up for us what Jesus was.

Christ lived for us to be one of us. A Christian is somebody related to God, in the family of God. They are born-again by the Spirit of God. It is not a case of having a religious experience one day, or a vision, or feeling good or happy. It is a relationship – a closeness, a family tie. Christ lived for us, in order to belong to us. If Christ belongs to me, then I am saved. If he belongs to you, then you are saved. Christ gave himself for us, and gave himself to us. Salvation means being united with him. Jesus does not send salvation: he **is** salvation. He does not send forgiveness: **he brings it**. He forgives us and lives with us. Doesn't that thrill your soul to know that, today … you are living with Christ!

Resurrection – An Impossible Hoax?

Some people think that resurrection is impossible. But how do they know that resurrection is impossible? Nobody knows enough to declare with absolute certainty that something is impossible. We would have to be God to know what God cannot do. We are limited, and can be wrong.

Look at the past. Until this century, television seemed impossible. If anybody had said, two or three hundred years ago, that a person would be seen and heard all round the globe at the same moment, he would have been thought mad. The moon was considered unreachable ... men could never fly ... never travel faster than a horse ... never live at the bottom of the ocean. All these were firmly believed to be impossible, but everybody was wrong. Television, aeroplanes and fast cars are now part of everyday life – we know that they are not figments of the imagination.

Christ has risen also, so we know that it is possible. By definition, God is the Almighty. So if God is God, there is no problem with the resurrection.

> "And with great power the apostles gave witness to the resurrection of the Lord Jesus. And great grace was upon them all."

The disciples were not the sort of characters who would be hoaxers. They did not treat life as a huge joke. At first sight of the resurrected Jesus, they were frightened. Later, they were all persecuted – and some were killed – simply because they said Jesus that was alive. Nobody dies to hoax people. Hoaxers do not lie to ruthless emperors. Hoaxers do not stand being tortured, being burned alive, or torn to pieces by wild beasts. The disciples simply could not deny the truth, no matter what. Let us be truth-tellers today as well.

Today's Scripture
I am the resurrection and the life. He who believes in me, though he may die, he shall live. And whoever lives and believes in me shall never die. Do you believe this?
(John 11:25-26)

Daily Power!
Lord Jesus, I believe in Your resurrection, therefore I too shall be resurrected!

Mark My Word
John 11:1-27
Acts 4:32

The Bible In A Year

Morning
Joshua 9
Psalms 140 and 141

Evening
Jeremiah 3
Matthew 17

Regeneration And Resurrection

8

Today's Scripture
Let the weak say:
"I am strong."
(Joel 3:10)

Daily Power!
Jesus Christ is alive
in me – I am made
strong in him!

Mark My Word
Joel 3:10
John 1:12
2 Corinthians 5:17;
Galatians 6:14,18
1 Peter 3:18

The Bible In A Year

Morning
Joshua 9
Psalms 142 and 143

Evening
Jeremiah 4
Matthew 18

We hear about evolution and revolution, but Christianity is regeneration and resurrection. The early Christians said that they were a *"new creation."* The Creator has started work again, doing something even greater. *"Therefore, if anyone is in Christ, he is a new creation; old things have passed away; behold, all things have become new."* A higher order than the human biological order has come into existence. We are the children of God, born from above*: "For Christ also suffered once for sins, the just for the unjust, that he might bring us to God, being put to death in the flesh but made alive by the Spirit."* When God made Adam, he did not ask Adam's permission. Nobody is asked if they want to be born. But it is up to us whether we want to be born again and belong to the new order. Now is the time to choose: *"As many as received him, to them he gave the right to become children of God."* Resurrection life – eternal life – flows to those who do.

> "But God forbid that I should boast except in the cross of our Lord Jesus Christ, by whom the world has been crucified to me, and I to the world. Brethren, the grace of our Lord Jesus Christ be with your spirit."

These new people astonished the Roman world. Rome tried to destroy them, but its policy of annihilation only served to multiply them. The Romans gloried in strength; the Christians gloried in their weakness. The Romans believed in hatred and revenge; the Christians believed in love and forgiveness. The Romans believed in imperial authority; the Christians said, *"Jesus Christ is Lord."* The Romans believed in the sword; the Christians said they would conquer the world with love. And praise God, they did … and still do! From where does that kind of strength come? From the most glorious fact of all: Jesus is alive! And he is alive in you and in me today!

Join The Orchestra!

"Why does God want us to do anything at all when he has all power?" Because he loves us, and he likes to share his pleasures and joys with us. You may feel that you are a very small instrument, but each of us is vital in the full orchestra. The Lord of all the earth has big things in mind, and they call for millions of helpers with varied gifts and capabilities. *"We have this treasure in earthen vessels, that the excellence of the power may be of God and not of us."*

Since I began to move in the power of the Holy Spirit – even as a young boy – I have learned that *"I can do all things through Christ who strengthens me."* In Christ, we have the resources of God. To fulfill God's purpose, we should think of ourselves as humble conduits for his Word and Spirit to flow through. A copper pipe cannot boast of the water that flows through it to the tap in our homes. We are to let living waters flow – and just stay unblocked. Whatever gifts or talents we lay at his feet, the Master can use them all. They become accessory parts, shaping the conduit through which God does what he wants.

This is a lesson that we must take deep into our hearts as the foundation for everything else we learn or do. God has given me my job. Many times I have been asked: "When did you begin to see miracles in your ministry?" or "Why do so many turn to Christ when you preach?" The answer is: "God gives us the power to do what he commands." That power comes through the baptism with the Holy Spirit. I experienced that wonderful baptism – and it has stayed, charging and surging within me. I spoke with tongues also, and it was such a marvelous thing to me that I have never doubted since that miracles are for today. The Word itself has always stirred my faith. Then – when the promise of the Spirit was fulfilled for me, and became an ongoing constant filling – the whole experience boosted my faith like supercharging a car engine. The Bible confirmed what was happening. What God has done for others (based upon his Word) he will do for you. If God has commanded you to do something … ask his power to help you do it!

Today's Scripture

For if I preach the gospel, I have nothing to boast of, for necessity is laid upon me; yes, woe is me if I do not preach the gospel!
(1 Corinthians 9:16)

Daily Power!

I lay everything upon Your altar, for you to use as you desire.

Mark My Word

2 Corinthians 4:7
Philippians 4:13

The Bible In A Year

Morning
Joshua 11
Psalm 144

Evening
Jeremiah 5
Matthew 19

10

God Is Not Who Some Think He Is

We cannot get away with ignorance or unbelief – they both have effects. Faith in God brings obvious benefits, switching the light on. Unbelief releases the acid of cynicism. *"And even as they did not like to retain God in their knowledge, God gave them over to a debased mind."* We would do better to ignore creation than the Creator.

Paul the apostle said: *"I know whom I have believed."* It was not just anybody. Paul hated Christ, until he met him. Multitudes have been like that, not even looking for somebody to believe in, and then meeting Jesus. They would not believe very much in anything otherwise. But having met him in some way, they have to believe in him. It is easy not to believe in Jesus when you do not know him. It takes no cleverness! But when Christ approaches or touches you, not believing is nearly impossible. No argument ever yet invented can nullify that experience.

Nobody can understand what it is like to meet Jesus until they do. Then they know why millions say as Paul said: *"For me to live is Christ;"* or, as John said: *"This is eternal life: that they may know you, the only true God, and Jesus Christ."* It has happened like that, from the time that he first appeared. The sex-obsessed woman of Samaria described in John chapter 4 met Jesus for five minutes, and could not get over it. She roused the whole town in her excitement, and then when the men met him, they felt the same. They did not become "religious enthusiasts" – in fact, they stopped being that. They became followers of Jesus, the Savior of the world. Modern Christians are like that too. They have found him: the One whose presence makes heaven the wonderful place that it is. That is the Jesus who lived and died for you.

Today's Scripture
And this is eternal life, that they may know you, the only true God, and Jesus Christ whom you have sent.
(John 17:3)

Daily Power!
Nobody can understand what it is like to meet Jesus – until they do.

Mark My Word
John 4:5-43; 17:3
Acts 9:1-22
Romans 1:28
Philippians 1:21
2 Timothy 1:12

The Bible In A Year

Morning
Joshua 12-13
Psalm 145

Evening
Jeremiah 6
Matthew 20

Ammunition!

11

The Holy Spirit is God in earthly activity, just as Jesus had been. The baptism in the Spirit is not meant to be a single emotional event: it envelops believers permanently. The Spirit is their environment, the very air that they breathe, feeding their Christian faith. When we bombard the world with the artillery of the gospel, our ammunition is the explosive power of the Holy Spirit. The Spirit animates believers, their teachings, their preaching, their prayer, their service, and their very lives. The Spirit is the dynamic life force of the faith. Without the life of the Holy Spirit, Christianity would be another lifeless religious system that can only be kept going by human effort. But nothing can compete with the Holy Spirit! We cannot replace the Holy Spirit with organization, magnificent churches, or anything else.

God himself teaches us when we obey him. The Holy Spirit, God in action, leads us into action. There are higher activities than church celebrations, and worship choruses alone will never save the world. Songs that do not mention the name of Jesus, or have any gospel content are especially powerless. Praise is not the power of God unto salvation – the gospel is. We must not flatter ourselves into thinking that we can build a throne for God with lots of new song books. Our contract with God contains the clause: "Preach the Word." *"It pleased God through the foolishness of the message preached to save those who believe."* We should do more than celebrate – we must communicate. As noted scholar, Richard John Neuhaus once observed: "It is not our securities and satisfactions we celebrate, but the perilous business of love, of that supreme love that did not and does not turn back from the cross."

Today's Scripture
But we preach Christ crucified ... Christ the power of God and the wisdom of God; because the foolishness of God is wiser than men, and the weakness of God is stronger than men.
(1 Corinthians 1:23-25)

Daily Power!
When we bombard the world with the artillery of the gospel, our ammunition is the explosive power of the Holy Spirit.

Mark My Word
1 Corinthians 1:21-25

The Bible In A Year

Morning
Joshua 14 and 15
Psalms 146 and 147

Evening
Jeremiah 7
Matthew 21

12

Today's Scripture
Delight yourself also in the Lord, and he shall give you the desires of your heart. Commit your way to the Lord, trust also in him, and he shall bring it to pass.
(Psalm 37:4-5)

Daily Power!
The effective, fervent prayer of a righteous man avails much.

Mark My Word
Psalm 37:4-5
Acts 27:29
Romans 1:9; 5:2
James 5:16
3 John 2

The Bible In A Year

Morning
Joshua 16 and 17
Psalm 148

Evening
Jeremiah 8
Matthew 22

The New Testament has an astonishing array of references to prayer. The main word for "prayer" (Greek: proseuche) is used over 120 times. God gives many things without being asked – rain, sunshine, winter, summer – but He planned that we should receive other things by asking for them. The list is long: salvation, the Holy Spirit, guidance, equipment for spiritual battles, the Gifts of the Spirit, power to witness, strength, effectiveness, boldness, relief from anxieties, our *"daily bread"*, the kingdom to come, the will of God to be done, relief from trial and temptation, healing – and more. We are even to pray for our enemies.

Communicating with God is the Christian distinction. Jesus forbade *"vain repetition."* The disciples opened their hearts to God about everything, including their innermost feelings. They wrote letters which changed the usual good wishes and pleasantries into prayers. Paul wrote to Christians in Rome: *"Without ceasing I make mention of you always in my prayers."* To believers in Corinth, Galatia, Ephesus, Philippi, Colossus, Thessalonika, and to Timothy, he wrote: *"Grace to you and peace from God our Father and the Lord Jesus Christ."* Some letters appear to be just extended prayers.

"If wishes were horses, beggars would ride," it is said, but the first Christians addressed "wishes" to the Father in the name of Jesus – and did receive! Praise God! The unbeliever wishes – the believer **prays**. In the book of Acts, the soldiers and crew of a ship were in danger and *"all hope that we would be saved was finally given up."*

Paul prayed – and they were saved! James prayed in the Christian way: *"Pray for one another that you may be healed."* Like John writing to Gaius: *"I pray that you may prosper in all things and be in health."* Prayer expects an answer. The unbeliever sighs, "If only …" The believer rejoices *"in hope of the glory of God."* Today, pray … and expect him to hear and answer!

Blood That Speaks

I have repeatedly seen a divine vision of a blood-washed Africa. I now desire nothing more than to see that gloriously fulfilled. I vowed to God that I would preach the message of the blood of Jesus wherever he sends us. By the grace of God, we have made good progress over the years, seen many nations in Africa shaken by the power of the gospel, and millions of precious souls receiving Jesus Christ as their Savior.

Hebrews 12 says that the blood of Jesus Christ *"speaks better things than that of Abel."* What better things? Abel was murdered by his brother, Cain. What did his blood say ... and what does the blood of Jesus Christ say? *"The voice of your brother's blood cries out to me from the ground. So now you are cursed from the earth, which has opened its mouth to receive your brother's blood from your hand."* Abel's blood cried out death and murder, and called for revenge.

The blood of Christ also discolored the dust. But what better words does it say? It speaks **life**, not death! Abel's blood is death-blood, but the blood of Jesus is Life-blood. Abel's blood called for revenge, but the blood of Jesus speaks **forgiveness**.

Cain was punished for Abel's death, but nobody suffered for Christ's death. Instead, Christ suffered death for us. The assassination of the Archduke Ferdinand started World War I, but Christ made *"peace through the blood of his cross."* When soldiers used a hammer and nails to spike Jesus Christ's living flesh to the timber gallows, his blood splashed them. They literally had the blood of Christ on their hands. Yet Jesus kept on praying: *"Father, forgive them, for they do not know what they do."* If God forgave the sin of those soldiers, it was only by the same blood which they had caused to flow. *"Without shedding of blood there is no remission",* and that only by the blood of Jesus. You have received that forgiveness already – rejoice in that wonderful fact today!

Today's Scripture
To Jesus the Mediator of the new covenant, and to the blood of sprinkling that speaks better things than that of Abel.
(Hebrews 12:24)

Daily Power!
The blood that Jesus shed for me will never lose its power.

Mark My Word
Genesis 4:10-11
Luke 23:34
Colossians 1:20
Hebrews 12:24

The Bible In A Year

Morning
Joshua 18 and 19
Psalms 149 and 150

Evening
Jeremiah 9
Matthew 23

14

"To The Glory Of God The Father"

Anyone reading the Bible finds it full of "glory" words. There are, in fact, nearly 600 of them, but some are words of key revelatory importance. Christians are familiar with many of the "glory" texts but sometimes we know them so well that we miss what they are showing us – like looking through a window and clouding it with our breath.

When we serve the Lord, we talk about bringing him glory, giving to the Lord *"the glory due his name."* As Moses did in his song, when we join together in praise and worship, we testify to the glory of God: *"Ascribe greatness to our God."* That, however, is what *we* do, not what *he* does.

Whether we give glory to God or not, his glory is real. The burning bush that Moses saw in the desert was God exhibiting his very essence. The fire was inextinguishable because our God is a consuming, eternal fire. Yet the glory of God is more than radiance. We might describe one of our friends as being "full of life" or "the picture of health" – and it shows in his or her bright eyes and glowing complexion. Well, God is full of life – and it shows! But more than this, he *is* life and the life brings light, as we read in John 1:4: *"In him was life, and the life was the light of men."*

In the gospels three disciples saw Jesus on the Mount of Transfiguration emanating pure brilliant splendour. *"Lift up the light of your countenance upon us,"* is the Psalmist's prayer, because the glory of his face will fill us with joy. The light of life is available for all to see in Jesus: *"The Word became flesh and dwelt among us and we beheld his glory."*

This is the greatest reality, pulsating non-stop throughout history and through all of creation.

Today's Scripture
The son is the radiance of God's glory and the exact representation of his being.
(Heb1:3)

Daily Power!
I am being changed from glory to glory, because the light of Jesus shines into my life.

Mark My Word
1 Chronicles 16:29
Deut 32:3
Psalm 4:6
John 1:14

The Bible In A Year

Morning
Joshua 20 and 21
Acts 1

Evening
Jeremiah 10
Matthew 24

Fish In The Sea Of Nations

The disciples were not anglers sitting on a serene riverbank, trying this bait or that fly. They were sea fishers, using nets. Galilee was their sea – and a treacherous one it was. Winds swept down the hills and almost scooped the waters out of their bed. A storm on the Sea of Galilee was frightening even for experienced sailors. In their minds, the sea was always a foreign element – an abyss where monsters and devils lurked, where winds shrieked and wailed like lost souls. The sea awoke every superstition. The sea is mentioned nearly five hundred times in Scripture, usually as a fearsome place. The Psalms talked about men calling upon God to save them, tossed high on the waves and brought low into the depths. The sea represented uncontrolled forces. It was the haunt of primeval elements, ghosts and demons, the place of the dead. The fishermen-apostles braved the Sea of Galilee, but it was a battle to wrest a living from the deep.

In scripture, the sea represents **the nations**. Jesus refers to the sea and the waves roaring, the people in uproar, in war, and in distress. The sea symbolizes the masses of the godless. *"The wicked are like the troubled sea … whose waters cast up mire and dirt."* The sea was terrifying and menacing. Putting that all together: the apostles were sent to fish in the raging nations, amidst enormous dangers in uncharted waters. They had caught fish from the angry Sea of Galilee – but now they would be fishers of men from the angry seas of the nations. There would be storms and casualties. The winds and currents of the world would be contrary to them. Sometimes mountainous waves would threaten to swallow them up. All that, but they would be still fishers of men! And you and I are so commissioned by him today.

Today's Scripture
Then (Jesus) said to them, "Follow me, and I will make you fishers of men."
(Matthew 4:19)

Daily Power!
Thank you, Lord, that you have called me to be a fisher of men.

Mark My Word
Isaiah 57:20;
Matthew 4:18-19;
Luke 21:25.

The Bible In A Year

Morning
Joshua 22
Acts 2

Evening
Jeremiah 11
Matthew 25

The Lord Of The Seas Of Nations

Today's Scripture
Then (Jesus) called his twelve disciples together and gave them power and authority over all demons, and to cure diseases. He sent them to preach the kingdom of God and to heal the sick.
(Luke 9:1-2)

Daily Power!
Lord, enable me to be obedient to your commands.

Mark My Word
Psalm 2:1-4, 8
Luke 5:4,9:1-2
Acts 1:8

The Bible In A Year

Morning
Joshua 23
Acts 3

Evening
Jeremiah 12
Matthew 26

Jesus demonstrated to his disciples that they could have a miraculous catch from the Sea of Galilee. He was teaching them that they could have a miracle-catch in the Sea of Nations as well. They would have a great haul of fish if they put their nets down at Christ's command. When Jesus said: *"Let down your nets,"* somehow half the fish in Galilee felt disposed to jump in. When Jesus said: *"I will make you fishers of men"* – half the world could be netted!

The nations were a troubled sea, but Jesus could handle the raging elements. He literally walked on the waters. The sea may have been a monster, but Jesus trod it underfoot. When the elements frothed and foamed against him – whipped into a frenzy, howling like dogs of hell, opening wide their dribbling mouths to engulf him – he rebuked them. Like whimpering hounds, they cowered at their Master's heels. Make no mistake about it – **Jesus Christ is Lord**.

> "Why do the nations rage, and the people plot a vain thing? The kings of the earth set themselves, and the rulers take counsel together, against the Lord and against his Anointed, saying, 'Let us break their bonds in pieces and cast away their cords from us.' He who sits in the Heavens shall laugh; the Lord shall hold them in derision. 'Ask of me, and I will give you the nations for your inheritance, and the ends of the earth for your possession.'"

Jesus himself used similar language in Acts: *"You shall be witnesses to me … to the end of the earth."* He is the Lord of heaven and earth, of the sea and the sky. He makes the very seas his own, and scoops from them their wealth. Go and teach all nations. You and I are part of God's equation. So, please, as one of his laborers, continue to trawl the Sea of Nations for Jesus Christ today!

Compelling Evidence

With the compelling evidence of the gift of salvation freely provided by Jesus Christ, it is a strange thing then that even some church members seem unsure about their fate. They do not expect to learn its outcome until the great Day of Judgment! They use the words "perhaps" and "hope." God says:

> "He who believes in the Son of God has the witness in himself; he who does not believe God, has made him a liar, because he has not believed the testimony that God has given of his Son. And this is the testimony: that God has given us eternal life, and this life is in his Son. He who has the Son has life; he who does not have the Son of God does not have life. These things I have written to you who believe in the name of the Son of God, that you may know that you have eternal life, and that you may continue to believe in the name of the Son of God."

Note that these reassuring Scriptures do not say that you **will** have eternal life, but they say that you **already have it**! These are powerful promises which the apostle John received from the Holy Spirit. They contain the key elements about the assurance of salvation: written … believe … Son of God … know … have … eternal life. These keys are given in the Word of God, which means you must read what is written in the Word.

The Biblical principle is that every matter must be established by the testimony of two or three witnesses: *"One witness shall not rise against a man concerning any iniquity or any sin that he commits; by the mouth of two or three witnesses the matter shall be established."* This was well-known in Bible days, but in our world today, "circumstantial" evidence is not admissible – only "corroborative" evidence: two or three witnesses stating the same fact independently. However, assurance is so important that God has given it a double anchorage in the rock of two faultless witnesses, both divine: the Word of God and the Spirit of God. That is God's Word to you today!

Today's Scripture
And this is the testimony: that God has given us eternal life, and this life is in his Son.
(1 John 5:11)

Daily Power!
I know, by the Word and the Spirit, that I am the recipient of eternal life through Jesus Christ.

Mark My Word
Deuteronomy 19:15
Matthew 18:16
2 Corinthians 13:1
1 John 5:10-13

The Bible In A Year

Morning
Joshua 24
Acts 4

Evening
Jeremiah 13
Matthew 27

18

The Eternal Mark

The blood-mark of Jesus is eternal. The blood-mark does not rub off. It outlasts Time. We need to appreciate our salvation, though, and keep on following Jesus. The blood of Jesus is no license to sin. But God has given us everlasting salvation, and we are his forever, not just when we feel well. Hallelujah! All heaven will be filled with the blood-marked saints, and not one will be in hell – not even by accident.

Somebody said that the blood of Jesus has "reduced the devil." The Bible says that Satan is *"like a roaring lion."* He comes in the darkness and tries to frighten the children of God with his mighty roar. But when you switch on the light of the Word of God, you discover that there is no lion – there is only a mouse with a microphone!

John Bunyan said that the lion at the side of the path has neither fangs nor claws. Christ pulled them out at Calvary. At Calvary, that nailed-scarred foot of Jesus came down on Satan's head – and crushed it. Since that moment, the devil has suffered some kind of "brain-damage." He cannot think the things of God. In the Garden of Eden, God already knew that the blood of his mighty Son would destroy the works of the devil.

It was no empty promise that Jesus gave his disciples, which includes you and me: *"He … gave them power over unclean spirits …and to heal all kinds of sickness and all kinds of disease."* He could do that because Jesus has power over the devil. Jesus' power leaves nothing untouched – body, soul, mind, spirit, heart. It reaches right to the depths of our being. his blood is the secret of victory. Let Jesus mark you, internally, externally, eternally, and you will be a child of God, a member of the royal household of the Lord!

Today's Scripture
Be sober, be vigilant; because your adversary the devil walks about like roaring lion, seeking whom he may devour. Resist him, steadfast in the faith, knowing that the same sufferings are experienced by your brotherhood in the world.
(1 Peter 5:8-9)

Daily Power!
As a member of the royal household of God, I am marked internally, externally and eternally by the blood-mark of Jesus Christ.

Mark My Word
Genesis 3:15
Matthew 10:1; 16:23
1 Peter 5:8

The Bible In A Year

Morning
Judges 1
Acts 5

Evening
Jeremiah 14
Matthew 28

From Faith To Faith

They say that the great Greek writer, Homer, wandered from town to town begging his bread, and telling his stories of the siege of Troy. Storytellers did make a living that way. There were no theaters, dramas, books, or television, and everybody loves a good story. Scripture uses that method to teach us. It is not a book of academic theology. But with a divine author, there is all the subtle character drawing that creates faith in God. Let's look at some gospel incidents.

There was the nobleman mentioned in John chapter 4. He showed faith in Christ's powers by coming all the way from Capernaum to Cana (a day's journey) to ask Christ to go to his house and heal his son who was dying. Jesus said a strange thing to the poor man: *"Unless you people see signs and wonders, you will by no means believe."* It was strange because he had believed enough to come to see Christ, but Jesus had another kind of faith in mind. The man was not put off by this apparently "cold" reception. He still believed and said: *"Sir, come down, before my child dies!"*

Jesus simply responded to the man: *"Go your way. Your son lives."* This meant extra faith. He had believed that Jesus could heal his son if he came. Now he had to believe Jesus was bigger than that. The official departed and we read: *"The man believed the word that Jesus spoke to him."* It was the **next day** before he arrived. All that way, all the man had was this brief word from Jesus, every step and every minute. But when he discovered a miracle had taken place, then John records that real faith came: *"He himself believed, and his whole household."* It was not the miracle they believed; that was there to see, not just to be believed. They believed in the way John always talks about believing: **commitment to Christ**.

You may have only a single word of Jesus to cling to – but that one word contains all the explosive resurrection power you will ever need!

Today's Scripture

For assuredly I say to you, whoever says to this mountain, "Be removed and be cast into the sea," and does not doubt in his heart but believes that those things he says will be done, he will have whatever he says.
(Mark 11:23)

Daily Power!

I believe, therefore I am committed to Christ.

Mark My Word

Mark 11:23
John 4:46-54

The Bible In A Year

Morning
Judges 2
Acts 6

Evening
Jeremiah 15
Mark 1

20

Today's Scripture
Now we know that God does not hear sinners; but if anyone is a worshipper of God and does his will, he hears him. (John 9:31)

Daily Power!
Let this be my daily motto: "Lord, I believe!"

Mark My Word
John 9:1-34

The Bible In A Year

Morning
Judges 3
Acts 7

Evening
Jeremiah 16
Mark 2

John chapter 9 tells a story that demonstrated developing faith. Without even asking, Jesus healed a blind man. He plastered mud across his eyes and sent him to wash – the man came back with good sight. When questioned, the formerly blind man replied: *"A man called Jesus made clay and anointed my eyes and said to me, 'Go to the pool of Siloam and wash.' So I went and washed, and I received sight."* Then they said to him, *"Where is he?"* The once-blind man did not know where Jesus had gone. Dissatisfied, the authorities decided, *"This Man is not from God."*

However, faith began to arise. They queried: *"How can a man who is a sinner do such signs?"* Who was Jesus? The man who was healed replied: *"He is a prophet."* But the authorities had already agreed to excommunicate from the Temple anybody who said that Jesus was the Christ. Faced with such a fact as a man born blind now seeing, they tried to prompt him to state that Jesus was a sinner. But he would not, declaring instead: *"Now we know that God does not hear sinners; but if anyone is a worshiper of God and does his will, he hears him … If this Man were not from God, he could do nothing."*

his faith was developing. For this, he suffered persecution, and was victimized as a disciple of Jesus. Jesus then found the man. He had been thrown out of the Temple – typical of a world which rejects those who testify to the goodness of God. He had one important question to ask the man: not whether he felt grateful, or if he had started to work, but: *"Do you believe in the Son of God?"* The man was puzzled: *"Who is he, Lord, that I may believe in him?"* He had enough faith in Jesus to feel his way to the pool of Siloam when blind because Jesus told him to go. That brought him physical sight. But another kind of faith could bring him far greater illumination: and his faith had not yet reached that point. Then Jesus replied: *"You have both seen him and it is he who is talking with you."* The man looked at Christ, and his faith exploded – he had no problem accepting Christ's declaration. He answered: *"'Lord, I believe!' And he worshiped him."* Faith was complete.

Christ Is Our Home

Christ *"dwelt among us."* He made his home with us – or rather, He made a home, and when we believe, we cross the doorstep and walk in. God is our true home. Away from him, we are away from home. That is why Christ lived for us. He wants to be with us, and us with him – at home.

> "And the Word became flesh and dwelt among us, and we beheld his glory, the glory as of the only begotten of the Father, full of grace and truth."

The Bible is full of references to "home." The prodigal son came home. Jesus went into many homes. He talked about the eternal home: *"In my Father's house are many mansions; if it were not so, I would have told you. I go to prepare a place for you."*

Christ lived for us to show us how to live. The Bible speaks of Christ as being without sin. He lived the perfect life for us, leaving us an example. What was his perfection? It was very simple: **obedience to God**. He did not live by a set of rules to govern every action of his life. He was not a walking encyclopedia of the Law, which he consulted every second from getting up in the morning to going to sleep again at night. He simply did what he knew would please the Father.

That is how we should live. All that is wanted is to please God. We may have great moral problems, and we do not know which is the right thing to do. Well, there is only one reason why we should be good at all, and that is to be like Jesus, and to please God! Choose to live to please God today.

Today's Scripture
In him was life, and the life was the light of men.
(John 1:4)

Daily Power!
Christ showed me how to live. I want to be like Jesus, and to please God.

Mark My Word
John 1:4, 14; 14:2

The Bible In A Year

Morning
Judges 4
Acts 8

Evening
Jeremiah 17
Mark 3

22

The Glory Of The Lamb

Today's Scripture
He who loves his life
will lose it, and he
who hates his life in
this world will keep
it for eternal life. If
anyone serves me, let
him follow me;
and where I am, there
my servant will be
also. If anyone serves
me, him my Father
will honor.
(John 12:25-26)

Daily Power!
It is my desire to
always glorify my
Father.

Mark My Word
Mark 14:24
John 1:14; 2:1-11
12:23-24; 13:31-32
Hebrews 10:10
Revelation 5:12

The Bible In A Year

Morning
Judges 5
Acts 9

Evening
Jeremiah 18
Mark 4

The "glory of princes" is public adulation, and military display. The glory of man is conquest, the honor of a world, which has false gods and false desires. The glory of Christ is not triumph over slaughtered armies. We read in the account of the first miracle at Cana in Galilee, that Jesus *"manifested his glory"* in simple red wine! This speaks to us through Christ's words at the Last Supper: *"This is my blood of the new covenant, which is shed for many for the remission of sins."*

In the first chapter of his gospel, John wrote: *"We beheld his glory."* We appreciate what that glory really was in chapters 12 and 13. It had nothing to do with the heroic ring by which the world recognizes its kind of glory, but rather pointed to the horror of an ugly, but necessary, death. *"The hour has come that the Son of Man should be glorified ... Unless a grain of wheat falls into the ground and dies, it remains alone."*

We continue reading in the account of the Last Supper to the point when Judas Iscariot went out to betray Jesus: *"So, when he had gone out, Jesus said, 'Now the Son of Man is glorified, and God is glorified in him. If God is glorified in him, God will also glorify him in himself, and glorify him immediately.'"*

That glory of Jesus broke forth at Calvary – the true glory. The glory of heaven was revealed in those streams of abounding mercy – water and blood from his heart – twin rivers of cleansing and love. *"By that will we have been sanctified through the offering of the body of Jesus Christ once for all! ... Worthy is the Lamb who was slain to receive power and riches and wisdom, and strength and honor and glory and blessing!"* Honor the Lamb of God today, and you will see his glory!

Rivers!

When speaking about the Holy Spirit, the Scriptures repeatedly use the word rivers. This "ideal" for believers – rivers of the Holy Spirit – was anticipated by Isaiah: *"You shall be like ... a spring of water, whose waters do not fail."* For many people in our reserved Western culture, exuberance is embarrassing. For those who stand within the kingdom of God, however, this matters little – they shout for joy!

The Septuagint (Greek version of the Old Testament) uses a surprising word about the Spirit of God acting in the lives of Samson and Saul: it says the Spirit "leapt" upon them. This rare word "allomai" is used twice in Acts 3: leaping up (exallomenos) and leaping (allomenos). It is not surprising when people who have not been in the Upper Room of Pentecost deride Spirit-filled people as "fanatics." Even the apostles had critics. Some onlookers in Jerusalem – completely ignorant of the facts – thought that the apostles were drunk.

> "When the day of Pentecost had fully come, they were all with one accord in one place. And suddenly there came a sound from heaven, as of a rushing mighty wind, and it filled the whole house where they were sitting. And they were all filled with the Holy Spirit and began to speak with other tongues, as the Spirit gave them utterance. And there were dwelling in Jerusalem Jews, devout men, from every nation under heaven. And when this sound occurred, the multitude came together, and were confused, because everyone heard them speak in his own language. Then they were all amazed and marveled, saying to one another, 'Look, are not all these who speak Galileans? And how is it that we hear, each in our own language in which we were born?' ... Others mocking said, 'They are full of new wine.'"

How mistaken the world is when they only stand on the banks of the river to describe the genuine flow of the Holy Spirit in your life. Remember, it is a river flowing through you. Go with the current. Let it lift you up and carry your load. The world may describe it differently ... but they will soon stand amazed when they see what that river can do in your life.

Today's Scripture
We hear them speaking in our own tongues the wonderful works of God.
(Acts 2:11)

Daily Power!
I shout for joy because I stand within the kingdom of God!

Mark My Word
Isaiah 58:11
Acts 2:1-13; 3:8
Ephesians 3:16

The Bible In A Year

Morning
Judges 6
Acts 10

Evening
Jeremiah 19
Mark 5

24

Today's Scripture
The message
of the cross ... is
the power of God.
(1 Corinthians 1:18).

Daily Power!
Believers are the light
of the world, but they
need the Holy Spirit
to switch them on.

Mark My Word
John 17:4-5

The Bible In A Year

Morning
Judges 7
Acts 11

Evening
Jeremiah 20
Mark 6

The Cross, And Kingdom Miracles

The power of the kingdom, the Holy Spirit, and the gospel of the cross are welded together. The work of Christ, especially in his death, tore down the wall between this world and the other world of God's kingdom. Since then, the Holy Spirit has invested everything in the crucified Christ. He works his wonders solely on redemption ground. The Spirit supports the gospel only, always and everywhere. What more do we need? One man filled with the Spirit is better than a hundred committees which "keep minutes but lose hours." When God so loved the world, He did not form a committee – he sent his Son. When his redemptive work was done, the Son sent the Spirit. Christ said believers are the light of the world, but they need the Holy Spirit to switch them on.

No doubt many people are eager for miracles, but it will save many from disillusionment if they know that miracles belong only to the gospel – nothing else. No marvels for the sake of marvels. God is not in the business of supplying marvels to bring fame to any strutting egotist. The Holy Spirit, in league with the crucified Christ, has one goal: to defeat the devil through the gospel. The gospel is totally comprehensive, leaving nothing untouched – earth, hell or heaven.

As a Christian, I knew that the cross had a spiritual effect in my life, but when I spoke with tongues, it reached me as an earthly person. The Father in heaven and the Son on earth are both concerned with redemption, each in his own sphere, as Jesus expressed: *"I have glorified You on the earth. I have finished the work which you have given me to do. "And now, O Father, glorify me together with Yourself, with the glory which I had with you before the world was."*

Christ's work on earth affected earth, and the Father's work affected glory. Jesus came here – for here. If it was only to get us an entrance into heaven, He might have arranged it in heaven – but salvation had to be produced on earth for earthly purposes. My baptism in the Spirit touched both my spirit and my body, typical of the true nature of the Christian faith. Open your heart to the Spirit today!

Fear Not The Future

What the future holds for anybody depends very much on themselves. When Dumah asked the prophet Isaiah: *"Watchman, what of the night?"* the prophet replied: *"The morning comes, and also the night."* This was not ambiguous – it simply pointed out that the answer depended on Edom's response to God. If Edom turned to God, it would be day – if not, it would be night. Similarly Jesus spoke of the latter days, with *"men's hearts failing them from fear,"* adding, *"when these things begin to happen, look up and lift up your heads, because your redemption draws near."* For those whose hands are not in the hand of Jesus, the landscape of tomorrow is full of fearful specters. But for those who have come to him, the future is the province of a victorious Christ.

The scythe of Father Time will cut short the days of many. Many are concerned about the future. Again for those who know the Lord, *"Neither death nor life ... nor things present nor things to come ... shall be able to separate us from the love of God that is in Christ Jesus our Lord."* No born-again Christian fears the future. Several times Jesus said: *"Fear not",* and because he said so, we certainly *"fear not"* – otherwise, where is our faith? We look for the coming of Christ – it identifies believers. his coming is not doomsday, except for those who reject him. We read that when he comes, the godless will try to hide. How badly they must have treated him to fear him! For those who know Jesus, the future is full of his glory. It lights the dawn of every day for those with eyes to see. And you have those believer's eyes!

Today's Scripture

For I know that my redeemer lives, and he shall stand at last on the earth.
(Job 19:25)

Daily Power!

No true believer in the Lord Jesus Christ fears the future, but looks forward to his coming.

Mark My Word

Isaiah 21:11-12
Luke 21:26, 28
Romans 8:38-39

The Bible In A Year

Morning

Judges 8
Acts 12

Evening

Jeremiah 21
Mark 7

26

Today's Scripture
But you shall receive power when the Holy Spirit has come upon you.
(Acts 1:8)

Daily Power!
God's power is given only to enable me to be his witness.

Mark My Word
Acts 1:1-14

The Bible In A Year

Morning
Judges 9
Acts 13

Evening
Jeremiah 22
Mark 8

"Get It Straight, Boys!"

When we read the opening verses of the book of Acts, we see why Jesus twice stressed the coming of the power of the Holy Spirit, in his last conversation on earth:

> "And being assembled together with them, he commanded them not to depart from Jerusalem, but to wait for the Promise of the Father, 'which,' he said, 'you have heard from me; for John truly baptized with water, but you shall be baptized with the Holy Spirit not many days from now.' Therefore, when they had come together, they asked he, saying, 'Lord, will you at this time restore the kingdom to Israel?' And he said to them, 'It is not for you to know times or seasons which the Father has put in his own authority. But you shall receive power when the Holy Spirit has come upon you; and you shall be witnesses to me in Jerusalem, and in all Judea and Samaria, and to the end of the earth.' Now when he had spoken these things, while they watched, He was taken up, and a cloud received him out of their sight."

Jesus had given his final instructions to the apostles after his resurrection, and told them to wait for the Promise of the Holy Spirit. That seemed fine – surely they had got the point and knew what was going to happen. But no! In verse 6, they were floundering again in the old notion that Jesus had spent three years trying to get out of their system: that of political triumph for Israel led by Jesus as the Warrior-Lord. Jesus had to correct them, and insist that their interests were not to lie in the direction of restored political power for Israel.

They were to go beyond Israel and preach the gospel to all nations! The power He would give would not be for political victory, but to achieve a far more significant result: the moral and spiritual victory of the kingdom of God. Today you and I must continue to preach and proclaim the gospel to the nations in our own way.

A Mission for Africa

CfaN CHRIST FOR ALL NATIONS

Countries in which CfaN crusades have already been held

Countries in which a CfaN crusade has not yet been held

CfaN CfaN office   As of May 2003

In pursuit of the vision of an Africa washed in the blood of Jesus, the ministry of Christ for all Nations preaches the gospel message across the length and breadth of the continent.

Anni & Reinhard Bonnke and the CfaN International Planning Team.

GOD'S LOGOS IN LAGOS, NIGERIA

1.6 million people in one single meeting!
3.4 million souls saved within five days.

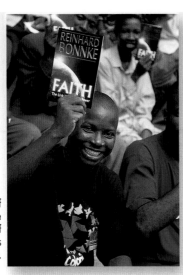

Each delegate of the Fire Conference received a free copy of Reinhard Bonnke's 'Faith' book.

God opened her ears!

80,000 delegates gathered at the Fire Conference in Lagos.

68 year old woman was healed from cancer.

4 million 'Now that you are Saved' booklets were handed out to the responders.

300 hired busses brought people in from surrounding areas.

8,000 Fire Conference delegates heard the word of God.

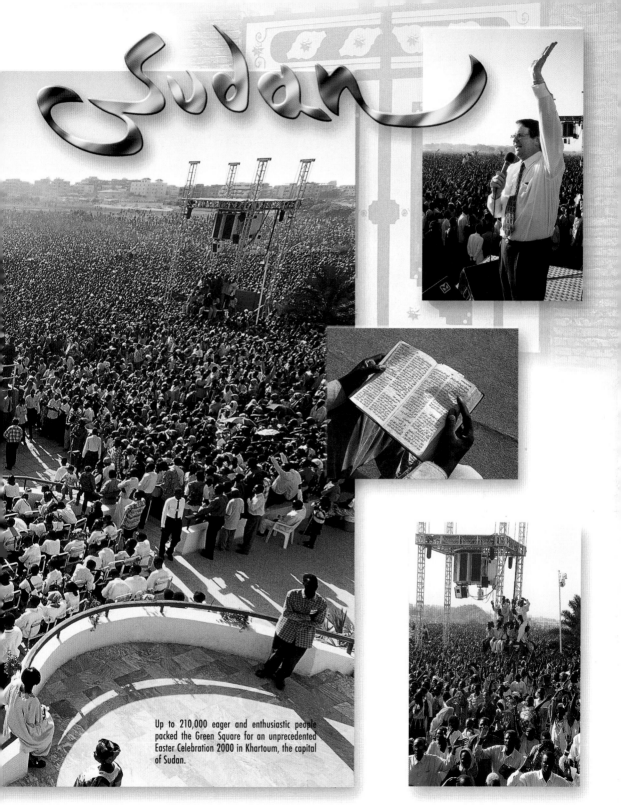

Up to 210,000 eager and enthusiastic people packed the Green Square for an unprecedented Easter Celebration 2000 in Khartoum, the capital of Sudan.

This mans barren wife conceived after prayer in the 1987 crusade and
this beautiful girl was born.

All sorts of fetishes and
even a human skull were
burned in public.

Nigeria

ABA

600,000 people in one service.

She was paralysed for 10 months.
Now she can walk!

God touched this little girl
and healed her body.

Where aeroplanes once took off and landed, the Gospel of Christ was proclaimed. Over four million people came to the old airport in Ibadan over five days of meetings, heard the Good News of salvation, and were amazed by the signs and wonders that followed.

Mr Matthew Kolawole - full of joy over his restored sight.

74,000 delegates at the Fire Conference.

Salvation Power

Ibadan, Nigeria

Seven-year-old Akintayo Akintola demonstrates his healing from paralysis and blindness.

Mrs Binat Aiyegsusi with her baby which she conceived after prayer at the *Millennium Crusade* in Lagos a year previously.

BENÍN CÍTY

In 1999, for the first time in almost a decade, the CfaN Gospel Campaign returned to Nigeria, and held a series of meetings in the Garrick School Park, where up to half a million people gathered on the final night to hear the Gospel.

Nigeria

Blind for many years, but now "Jesus has opened his eyes"!

She can hear and speak for the very first time!

1,758,144 people
make a decision to follow Christ

Every available advantage point is filled to capacity.

Reaping Days in Ogbomosho

Nigeria

Above: 15-year-old Adunbola can now hear a whisper after ten years of deafness in his right ear.
Right: Healed from an acute bladder problem.

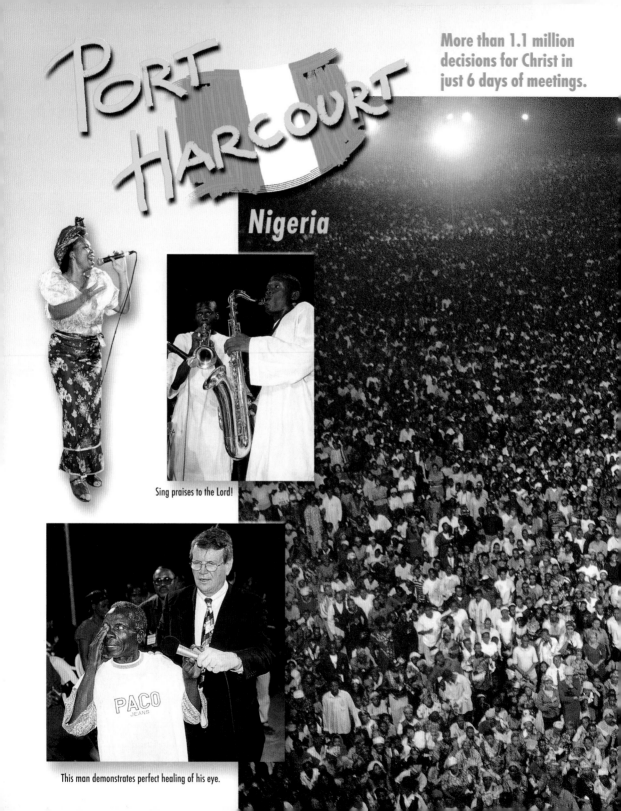

PORT HARCOURT

Nigeria

More than 1.1 million decisions for Christ in just 6 days of meetings.

Sing praises to the Lord!

This man demonstrates perfect healing of his eye.

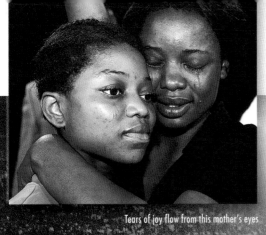

Tears of joy flow from this mother's eyes

Now he can walk without these crutches.

Global Outreach

CfaN's literature arm has seen 155,000,000 books and booklets distributed in 141 languages to many nations of the world.

Millions of copies of the book "Evangelism by Fire" have been printed in over sixty languages and distributed amongst Bible School students and Church leaders throughout the world.

Jesus Corrects Us

After being with him for three years of miracle-ministry, what the disciples wanted to know from Jesus at the last was this: *"Lord, will you at this time restore the kingdom to Israel?"* In other words, they were asking, "What are you going to do, Lord?" Jesus, in effect, replied, me? What am I going to do? You really have missed the point! It is **you! You** shall be my witnesses!"

We are all praying for worldwide revival. The more we see it taking place, the more we are encouraged to keep praying for it. But are we simply saying to God, "Lord, you do it. You send revival. Lord, you must enter the field. Lord, you take over. Lord, bring in the kingdom"? Jesus corrects all that. He says, "I give **you** the power, **you** must get on with the job. Evangelize! Preach! Work! Heal! Get going with **your** part." Once you and I go through the gate, we will get the tools, the power equipment. God never does our job for us; but he knows what we need to enable us to do it.

It is the same all the way through the New Testament:

> "And when they had prayed, the place where they were assembled together was shaken; and they were all filled with the Holy Spirit, and they spoke the Word of God with boldness ... And with great power the apostles gave witness to the resurrection of the Lord Jesus. And great grace was upon them all" ... "For I am not ashamed of the gospel of Christ, for it is the power of God to salvation for everyone who believes, for the Jew first and also for the Greek."

Preaching releases the power of God. You cannot pray for power, and then keep it in the deep freeze. Preach it, and it is manifested! Receive God's power in your life today.

Today's Scripture
But when the Helper comes, whom I shall send to you from the Father, the Spirit of truth who proceeds from the Father, he will testify of me. and you also will bear witness. (John 15:26-27)

Daily Power!
God has given me an assignment: to preach his Word with the power of the Holy Spirit.

Mark My Word
John 5:39; 15:26-27
Acts 1:6; 4:31, 33
Romans 1:16
1 Corinthians 2:1-4

The Bible In A Year

Morning
Judges 10 to 11:11
Acts 14

Evening
Jeremiah 23
Mark 9

28

We Cannot Escape

Our rebellion and wickedness in no way changes God's mind about his love for us, for *"while we were still sinners, Christ died for us."* The object was that *"in Christ Jesus you who once were far off have been brought near by the blood of Christ."* The Son of God, our Lord, Jesus Christ, could bear our sins and die for us simply because of the live link between Creator and creature. We are *"bound in the bundle of the living with the Lord our God."* We cannot escape what happens to God, and God cannot escape what happens to us.

Jesus became Man and walked this very earth to restore the God-and-man family relationship. He did not come to us as aliens, a race of unknown parentage, to adopt us. He had fathered us. We were prodigals, *"sons of disobedience."* The opening chapters of the Bible present the shock of Cain murdering his brother Abel. God's reaction showed it as the antithesis and disruption of God's fundamental purpose. It broke the life-bond of family.

This throws open the tremendous truth that this very day the Spirit of sonship is at work, constantly working to bring many glory. He is creating again – not another Adam – but new creatures, endued with eternal life. We do not know God's final purposes. But one thing is certain: the mark of heaven will be his eternal fatherly embrace for his children. His plan is that *"in … the fullness of the times he might gather together in one all things in Christ, both which are in heaven and which are on earth – in him … Now we are children of God; and it has not yet been revealed what we shall be."* Rejoice in that today!

"Bondage Is Truth Corrupted"

People mock those who "bury themselves in religion." But Christianity is Christ; and you cannot call Christ a religion! He is the Resurrection and the Life. Christ said: *"If you abide in my word, you are my disciples indeed. And you shall know the truth, and the truth shall make you free."* He is no deceiver. Millions have found themselves gloriously free through the gospel. his words do not stifle us with rules and commandments. his yoke is easy and his burden is light. The Sermon on the Mount describes what Christians are naturally, what they want to do, not what people should be like.

There is a warning that Christ repeatedly gave us, and one which is very relevant: *"Beware of false prophets."* They are not all in the cults either, although there are over five thousand sects in the United States. Many are a threat to the concept of liberty. By definition, a cult means control. *"By their fruits you will know them."* Once they get hold of you, they keep you under their thumb, control your money, what you do, where you go, what you think, and who your friends are. Their evil effect is to destroy self-reliance, and breed dependency. Their leaders are not shepherds – they are wardens, religious policemen.

> "Beware of false prophets, who come to you in sheep's clothing, but inwardly they are ravenous wolves. You will know them by their fruits. Do men gather grapes from thorn bushes or figs from thistles? Even so, every good tree bears good fruit, but a bad tree bears bad fruit. A good tree cannot bear bad fruit, nor can a bad tree bear good fruit. Every tree that does not bear good fruit is cut down and thrown into the fire. Therefore by their fruits you will know them."

Some teach the scriptures, but turn Bibles into chains, standing truth on its head, like the scribes and pharisees. They use the gospel of deliverance to bind their converts, falsifying the very spirit and purpose of the message. There are sad souls who lack true faith and accept handcuffs to gain a sense of security. Please guard your heart and do not become one of them.

Today's Scripture
Enter by the narrow gate; for wide is the gate and broad is the way that leads to destruction, and there are many who go in by it. Because narrow is the gate and difficult is the way which leads to life, and there are few who find it.
(Matthew 7:13-14)

Daily Power!
Lord, help me always stay true to your Word and to bear good fruit.

Mark My Word
Matthew 7:13-20
John 8:32

The Bible In A Year

Morning
Judges 12
Acts 16

Evening
Jeremiah 25
Mark 11

30

Leaps Of Faith

Today's Scripture
But the hour is
coming, and now
Is, when the true
worshipers will
worship the Father
in spirit and truth; for
the Father is seeking
such to worship him.
(John 4:23)

Daily Power!
Lord, I believe that
you are the Christ, the
Savior of the world.

Mark My Word
John 4:1-42

The Bible In A Year

Morning
Judges 13
Acts 17

Evening
Jeremiah 26
Mark 12

The woman of Samaria in John chapter 4 teaches a powerful lesson on faith. It is an illustration of a sinner taking a leap of faith into the supernatural. She came to draw water from a well when Jesus was resting there from a long, hot walk. He asked her for a drink of water, which astonished her. She thought that he was an odd Jew to be so free, breaking all the rules by speaking to a Samaritan; even more so when he said that He could give her a drink of water that would be *"a fountain of water springing up into everlasting life."* At that point, she decided to humor him, thinking him slightly irrational; she joked: *"Sir, give me this water, that I may not thirst, nor come here to draw."* She certainly expected nothing of the kind. Jesus simply answered: *"Go, call your husband, and come here."* With an air of innocence, she replied that she had no husband. Jesus then shattered her with a recitation of her sullied life, and her Hollywood-like record of husbands. The woman replied, shocked: *"I perceive that you are a prophet."* She had advanced in perception and faith.

Next Jesus shook her ideas about worship. She retorted a four-hundred-year old argument – but Christ's reply was totally new. Worship had nothing to do with the place or time: worship was anywhere, everywhere and always. God wanted those whose worship was not confined to a local spot or fixed schedule. She felt lost in such theological depth, so she tried to edge around it, saying such matters would be settled when the Messiah came. The woman was getting closer – then Jesus revealed: *"I, who speak to you, am he."* Her faith soared! She looked at this Man who saw her past like a filmed record and swept her out of her depth with his profound teaching. Excited, she rushed into the town telling everybody about Jesus: *"Could this be the Christ?"* Many went to see this Man who had so affected her. They too fell under his divine magnetism, inviting him to stay. For two days, He was among them, with the result that they declared: *"This is… the Savior of the world!"* The woman had believed, sinful as she was, and that is all that Christ asks of you and of me – *"believe."*

Faith Embrace

The Bible stories of the blind man healed by Christ; the Samaritan woman who met him at the well ; the nobleman who traveled a great distance to receive healing for his dying son; each showed that the development of faith was swift and always ended with a commitment, a relationship, and taking hold of Jesus personally. A believer in God has a long way to go. But the gap can be leapt. One minute far from God, the next bound to him eternally through faith, *"one with Christ."* We become, in a moment, as he said about the disciples to the Father, *"They are yours … and yours are mine, and I am glorified in them … and none of them is lost."*

The Greek expression used for faith **in** Christ means moving close to him in trusting love. It is an embrace. This kind of loving embrace between man and his Maker comes only through Christ. Jesus is the great beloved One. The dry, loveless religious world of the Jews had no spiritual experience that corresponded to this love relationship. Any passionate embrace between heaven and earth was unknown, until Jesus came. He is Love personified … and we are those he came to love.

A woman emptied a flask of priceless ointment upon the head of Christ in holy adoration. A street-girl washed his feet with the water of her eyes and toweled them with her hair. A hard-hearted tax collector went wild with joy and wanted to give his money away. Jerusalem had never seen anything like that. They had seen fanatical fury burning murderously in men's eyes, but not this adoring wonder. But then, he began it himself, for we read, *"Having loved his own who were in the world, he loved them unto the end … knowing … that He had come from God and was going to God, rose from supper and … began to wash the disciples' feet."* Jesus was the Lord God whom everyone could fling his or her arms around. his mother Mary did. So did Mary Magdalene, and so can you and I – by faith!

Today's Scripture
And this is eternal life, that they may know you, the only true God, and Jesus Christ whom you have sent. (John 17:3)

Daily Power!
Jesus Christ came to earth to love me.

Mark My Word
John 13:1-5; 17:3; 9-12

The Bible In A Year

Morning
Judges 14
Acts 18

Evening
Jeremiah 27
Mark 13

God brings changes,
but he never changes himself.

When Jesus said: "I am with you always"
he did not make a promise, he stated a fact!

Peter did not walk on the water.
He walked on the word "come!"

"This Same Jesus"

The glory of Christ will be revealed again when he comes again. It will not be the glory of overpowering might, but of the all-conquering cross. He comes with the honor of the Father encircling his thorn-torn brow. When he comes again, it will be *"this same Jesus"* who went away to heaven with pierced hands and feet. That Christ is the Christ who will return – not a "healed Christ" whose death for sinners has been forgotten: but a Christ who bears the still-active marks of indelible grace. Heaven and earth know him forever as the Crucified One: *"The Lamb slain from the foundation of the world."* **The Lamb on the throne will be King!**

Who else bore our sins in agony and blood? What other Savior could there be but he who carried our transgressions and suffered the penalty for our sin? At last, that which was foolishness to the Greeks and a stumbling-block to the Jews – which people could never grasp – is revealed. What glory!

If Christ's glory had been that of mere dazzling splendor, it would have been overwhelmed in the darkness of Calvary. If it had been fame, success, wealth, or achievement, it all would have ended in that awful catastrophe of crucifixion. But the glory of Christ can never die. Put him in a manger in a limestone cave among cattle, and kings fall down before him. Send him out as a wandering preacher walking the dusty village roads of a barren land, and his glory breaks upon all who come near. Herod is troubled, the rulers take counsel together against him; but the masses of common people hear him gladly and want to make him King. They have seen glory in this Carpenter-Preacher.

Take the time. Open your heart. Look for his glory today!

Today's Scripture
Blessing and honor and glory and power be to him
who sits on the throne, and
to the Lamb, forever and ever!
(Revelation 5:13)

Daily Power!
Salvation and glory and honor and power belong to the Lord our God!

Mark My Word
Zechariah 13:6
Acts 1:11
Revelation 13:8; 19:1

The Bible In A Year

Morning
Judges 15
Acts 19

Evening
Jeremiah 28
Mark 14

2

Time To Grow Up!

Today's Scripture
And I, brethren, could not speak to you as to spiritual people but as to carnal, as to babes in Christ. I fed you with milk and not with solid food; for until now you were not able to receive it, and even now you are still not able.
(1 Corinthians 3:1-2)

Daily Power!
Lord, help me to accept, and carry out my responsibilities as a mature Christian.

Mark My Word
Acts 20:8
1 Corinthians 3:1-2
Ephesians 5:8
Philippians 2:15

The Bible In A Year

Morning
Judges 16
Acts 20

Evening
Jeremiah 29
Mark 15

Jesus was not a spiritual policeman. He did not discipline the disciples. That is not what "disciple" means. He never ordered them about. They came and went as they wished. It was all left to their wisdom and discretion. That is how Christ deals with us. Give Jesus our lives, and he makes them our own. If we blindly obey a church leader, we are still responsible before God for what we do. No man should appropriate to himself authority over others. Christ is your master. Truth comes from the Word of God, which sets us free. God is a Deliverer. Laws, like the Sabbath, were made for us, not us for the laws.

The disciples came with various personality differences and outlooks on life. There was Peter: impetuous, courageous; Matthew: thoughtful, faithful; James and John: competitive, tenacious. Each had faults and strengths. Each had to learn to understand and accept the Messiah coming to them in their day … and then learn how to communicate the wonder of the Son of God and the Son of Man in one person, the ultimate sacrifice. We have hindsight to our advantage, so we automatically think, "Yes, of course I would have recognized that Jesus was the Son of God, and I would have been faithful to the end without hesitation." But put ourselves in a hostile environment – such as the early Christians experienced in Jerusalem or Rome – and we quickly discover that our character is tested and tried! Too often we fall back on the letter of the Law to hide our own deficiencies, rather than open ourselves to the discipline of the Holy Spirit, and grow in he. Or we are lazy, and resign the responsibility for our own spiritual growth to church leaders, even as we too readily turn over the Christian education of our children to Sunday School teachers. It is time that Christians grew up, and accepted their duties to be bright shining lights in a darkened world! **Let your light shine today!**

Dynamic Power Points

3

"I did not come with excellence of speech or of wisdom declaring to you the testimony of God. My speech and my preaching were not with persuasive words of human wisdom, but in demonstration of the Spirit and of power, that your faith should not be in the wisdom of men but in the power of God."

The Holy Spirit and the gospel of Christ's redeeming love are inseparably tied together in the bundle of life. If you want to see the power of God, then ignore all the techniques, manipulation and psycho-suggestion, and simply preach the Word! That is where the power of God is released, right in the gospel. I do not take only one thing out of God's treasure chest. I proclaim the whole gospel, which contains everything that we human beings need – salvation, healing, peace, hope and deliverance.

"The Gentiles should be fellow heirs, of the same body, and partakers of his promise in Christ through the gospel, of which I became a minister according to the gift of the grace of God given to me by the effective working of his **power**.

Now to him who is able to do exceedingly abundantly above all that we ask or think, according to the **power** that works in us, to him be glory in the church by Christ Jesus to all generations, forever and ever. Amen."

These are only two of many texts, which use the word **power,** but in fact, the whole New Testament could illustrate that power. It is the essence of Christian witness. It is not "a gospel accessory." It is not the bell on a bicycle – it is the whole machine! There is never the slightest hint that some disciples would be powerless. If you are a believer, then power is available. Paul spent three and half years preaching the whole counsel of God to the Ephesians. Yet he had to write to them later: *"I make mention of you in my prayers that … the eyes of your understanding being enlightened; … you may know … what is the exceeding greatness of his power toward us who believe."* God empowers those he sends – you and me.

Today's Scripture
And he said to them, "Assuredly I say to you that there are some standing here who will not taste death till they see the kingdom of God present with power" (Mark 9:1)

Daily Power!
Lord, help me to know the exceeding greatness of your power towards me.

Mark My Word
1 Corinthians 2:1-5
Ephesians 1:18-19;
3:6-7, 20-21

The Bible In A Year

Morning
Judges 17
Acts 21

Evening
Jeremiah 30 and 31
Mark 16

4

"Proving" Salvation

Today's Scripture
Nor is there salvation in any other, for there is no other name under heaven given among men by which we must be saved.
(Acts 4:12)

Daily Power!
The Holy Spirit himself assures me that I am a child of God.

Mark My Word
John 5:24;
Acts 3:24; 4:10-12, 8:16
Romans 3:24
Revelation 12:10-11

The Bible In A Year

Morning
Judges 18
Acts 22

Evening
Jeremiah 32
Psalms 1 and 2

The subject of salvation is important to me – and it occupies the entire Bible! Liberal people today like to rationalize that it is impossible to know you possess salvation, and we will have to wait until the afterlife (if there is such a thing, some say) to discover whether salvation had indeed provided eternal life. But Jesus made it very clear that we **can know** that we are saved. That confidence can inspire us to share our salvation with others:

> "Let it be known to you all, and to all the people of Israel, that by the name of Jesus Christ of Nazareth, whom you crucified, whom God raised from the dead, by him this man stands here before you whole. This is the 'stone which was rejected by you builders, which has become the chief cornerstone.' Nor is there salvation in any other, for there is no other name under heaven given among men by which we must be saved."

However, Satan still tries to undermine that confidence in the gift of salvation provided by Christ Jesus on the cross. We must guard against his lies and accusations:

> "Now salvation, and strength, and the kingdom of our God, and the power of his Christ have come, for the accuser of our brethren, who accused them before our God day and night, has been cast down. And they overcame him by the blood of the Lamb, and by the word of their testimony, and they did not love their lives to the death."

Being saved is not a casual experience, something that you would hardly notice. When you repent, believe and come to the Lord and Savior Jesus Christ, he receives you, and you are cleansed in his precious blood! Salvation is absolute and complete. How ridiculous to think that Jesus would find you and receive you, but would not want you to know this! In fact, he does not keep it from you: *"The Spirit himself bears witness with our spirit that we are children of God."* There is something greater still: you are *"justified freely by his grace."* What a divine promise for you to hold onto today!

Critics Do Not Get It

As we learn more about the activities of the Holy Spirit, we should never be worried by critics. No great work of God has ever remained unchallenged by those who thought they knew better. Theologian Ronald A. Knox showed contempt for John Wesley by describing him as a mere "enthusiast" – an overwrought or unbalanced person. Father Knox may be an example of cool scholarship, but from his book, "Enthusiasm", it is clear that he would not have been with the one hundred and twenty on the day of Pentecost. The intellectual bishop of Bristol, Joseph Butler, told Wesley that he considered charismatic experiences to be quite "horrid." O.T. Dobbin came to Wesley's defense in 1848: "We admit that Wesley was an enthusiast, but only to the degree in which a man more than ordinarily filled with the Holy Ghost would be an enthusiast." Wesley's first rule for stewards of the Methodist Society, quoting Ephesians 3:16, was: *"to be strengthened with might through his Spirit in the inner man."* George Whitefield, the great evangelist, was another man full of the Holy Spirit.

The question we must ask is this: if Christ did exactly what he promised and baptized people in the Holy Spirit and fire, what would they be like? Cool? If they had currents of divine radiance coursing through them, would they sit as though made of stone? The emblem of God is fire, not stone. What is more ridiculous – people dancing for joy with the vision of God, or people as immovable as the Sphinx, which remained unmoved even when Napoleon fired a cannon at it? We cannot experience the Spirit and show no sign of that experience. What we have in earthen vessels is *"treasure"* which reveals that this all-surpassing power is from God. This power will seem totally strange to minds alienated from God. As Festus said to Paul: *"You are beside yourself! Much learning is driving you mad!"* Why should it be any different today when people experience the original brand of Christianity, instead of some diluted version? *"You he made alive,"* we read in Ephesians – not "You hath he stiffened!"

Today's Scripture
And you he made alive, who were dead in trespasses and sins.
(Ephesians 2:1)

Daily Power!
We cannot experience the Holy Spirit, and show no sign of that experience.

Mark My Word
Acts 26:24
2 Corinthians 4:7
Ephesians 2:1

The Bible In A Year

Morning
Judges 19
Acts 23

Evening
Jeremiah 33
Psalms 3 and 4

6

The Spirit's Difference

Today's Scripture
His divine power has
given to us all things
that pertain to life and
godliness, through
the knowledge of
him who called us by
glory and virtue.
(2 Peter 1:3)

Daily Power!
I received power
when the Holy Spirit
came upon me.

Mark My Word
Matthew 7:7
Acts 1:9
2 Peter 1:3

The Bible In A Year

Morning
Judges 20
Acts 24

Evening
Jeremiah 34
Psalms 5 and 6

The prophets struggled in vain to bring Israel back to God. But when Spirit-filled Peter preached, then three thousand people surrendered to God. Without the Holy Spirit, Christianity is reduced to religion. Jesus said: *"You shall receive power when the Holy Spirit has come upon you."* Without that vitality, we have a rationalized, harmless religion. Mystical contemplation bears no resemblance to New Testament dynamism. Quietism is for Buddhists, not Christians.

Before the charismatics arrived, there were those who were fired up and Spirit-filled, or "pneumatized." Whatever chill may have frozen the church, however much "enthusiasm" was disapproved of, and even when Christianity was only "churchianity," there were always some lively Spirit-filled people around. The springs of spiritual waters in this century came from rains which fell centuries before. Some trace them to Wesley and his teaching, which he called "perfect love." But whatever it was called, the vision and experience Wesley had came from earlier men and women of God.

All the Scriptural terms, such as "coming upon," "being filled," "drinking," and "anointing" describe the same divine gift of the Spirit. Christ said we should *"Ask … Seek … Knock."* This applies to receiving the baptism of the Spirit also. The *"baptism in the Holy Spirit"* is a New Testament expression used by both John the Baptist and Jesus. The personal experience of millions conforms to the New Testament promise whether it is called baptism or anything else. If it looks like such a baptism, and operates like it, then what else is it? If you do what the apostles did and you get what the apostles got, its name does not matter.

Ghostly Terrors

Unbelief populates the future with giant fears. The "millennium bug" created widespread panic, with some even preparing underground shelters. To gain admission, applicants at one shelter were required to have a gun, a thousand rounds of ammunition and enough food for a year. Such terror inspired by a ghost!

"The wicked flee when no one pursues," but God whispers secret assurance to those who love him. He has the future in hand for us. Unbelievers exist in the permanent shadow of uncertainty and anxiety. In times gone by, the heathen were terrified by stellar events, but Jeremiah said: *"Do not be dismayed at the signs of heaven, For the Gentiles are dismayed at them. He is the Maker of all things … the Lord of Hosts is his name."* The phrase "fear not" is a special Biblical feature, occurring sixty-six times, but the Bible deals positively with fear over five hundred times!

The one certainty about the future is Christ's Second Advent. I am aware that expectations of Jesus' return to earth have reached fever pitch at various different times in the past. The 17th century Puritans who founded settlements in America were filled with anticipation that Christ would soon appear, and great men like Milton and Newton shared these expectations. Indeed, it was the sustaining hope of the earliest Christians. However, mistakes and questions do not in the slightest diminish the truth that he is coming again. The signs are all in place. Watch for him!

Today's Scripture
It is not for you to know times or seasons which the Father has put in his own authority. But you shall receive power when the Holy Spirit has come upon you; and you shall be witnesses to me ... to the end of the earth. (Acts 1:7-8)

Daily Power!
Christ has promised: I will come again and receive you to myself; that where I am, there you may be also.

Mark My Word
Proverbs 28:1
Jeremiah 10:2, 16
John 14:3
Acts 1:7-8

The Bible In A Year

Morning
Judges 21
Acts 25

Evening
Jeremiah 35
Psalms 7 and 8

8

Sure Of Salvation

Today's Scripture
If we confess our sins, He is faithful and just to forgive us our sins and to cleanse us from all unrighteousness
(1 John 1:9)

Daily Power!
I have repented; I have received Jesus; therefore I have everlasting life!

Mark My Word
John 3:3-6; 5:24
Hebrews 10:23
1 John 1:9; 3:2

The Bible In A Year

Morning
Ruth 1
Acts 26

Evening
Jeremiah 36
Psalm 9

To be sure of salvation, you do not need to be sure of everything, but only of God, who *"is faithful and just to forgive us our sins, and to cleanse us from all unrighteousness"* and *"He who promised is faithful."*

Let me use a simple illustration. I am Reinhard Bonnke, whether I feel like it or not. If I am asleep, I do not think about it, yet I am still Reinhard Bonnke. Even if I should suffer from a loss of memory, my identity remains the same. my birth certificate states that I am who I am, and that settles it!

So it is with the Word of God. If you have received the Lord Jesus Christ as your personal Savior, you have been born into the family of God. You have been *"born again."* The Bible is your birth certificate. If you cannot believe that, then you will not know who you are. It is that simple!

> "Most assuredly I say to you, unless one is born again, he cannot see the kingdom of God … Unless one is born of water and the Spirit, he cannot enter the kingdom of God. That which is born of the flesh is flesh, and that which is born of the Spirit is spirit."

John said: *"Beloved, now we are children of God; and it has not yet been revealed what we shall be … but we shall be like him."* What we shall be we do not yet understand, but we know who we are – children of God. Jesus said: *"Most assuredly, I say to you, he who hears my word and believes in he who sent me has everlasting life, and shall not come into judgment, but has passed from death into life."*

That is powerful! It says that if you have repented and have received Jesus as your own Savior, then you have everlasting life and have crossed over from death to life. Praise the Lord!

Switch On The Light!

When the apostle Paul preached in Corinth, he did not feel physically robust and full of vigor. He was weak and trembling. In fact, he even talked about despairing of life sometimes. his preaching was simple and direct. He did not rely on brilliant speech but preached in *"demonstration of the Spirit and of power."* The effects were mighty, and many repented and received salvation. What did he preach to have such effects? The secret is this: he said: *"For I determined not to know any thing among you, save Jesus Christ, and him crucified."* Salvation does not rest in mere words, but on what happened: *"Christ died for our sins according to the Scriptures."*

If you want assurance that today God smiles upon you, is on your side, and that one day you will be welcomed in heaven, this is how it happens. First, you hear or read the gospel that Christ died for your sins. Next, you believe the gospel and repent, and the power of God applies the benefits of Christ's redeeming death to your heart. Then, something wonderful happens: the Word of God quickens your dead spirit, and you become alive in God, cleansed and made whole. What Jesus did for you on the cross, the Holy Spirit transfers into your life.

Let me illustrate this: you may have electricity in your home. The house is wired and connected to the power plant. If you go home at night, you press the switch, and have instant light and warmth. Believing Christ died for you is like turning the switch on. Everything is ready. The gospel message is like the wires connected to the power station, Calvary's cross. Lines of truth have already been laid. The power is there waiting. Then you believe, which turns the spiritual switch on, and the saving power flows to you, giving you light. **You are saved.**

Today's Scripture
Christ died for our sins according to the Scriptures.
(1 Corinthians 15:3)

Daily Power!
Christ died for me – I believe it – I am saved!

Mark My Word
1 Corinthians 1:8; 2: 2-4; 15:3.

The Bible In A Year

Morning
Ruth 2
Acts 27

Evening
Jeremiah 37
Psalm 9

10

Life Blood

The blood of Jesus brings life. He said so himself: *"Whoever eats my flesh and drinks my blood has eternal life, and I will raise him up at the last day."* "Drinking" is, of course, a figure of speech, not literal, for Jesus was still alive when he spoke these words. It means taking God's forgiveness through the blood of Jesus by faith, and spiritually applying his blood to our need. Now the true heights of Calvary's mountain soar before us. When the spear opened the veins of Jesus, and blood and water came forth, the veins of God opened too. When life-streams flowed on the cross, an eternal fountain of life and mercy began.

After Abel's murder defiled the ground, another killing, by Lamech, is recorded. The weapon forged by Tubal-Cain and the wicked deed – glorified in music by Jubal – prompted more and more bloodshed. Abel's blood that had cried in solo from the earth swelled to a mighty choir of voices, which God heard. We read that finally: *"The earth also was corrupt before God, and the earth was filled with violence."* So God declared: *"And behold, I myself am bringing floodwaters on the earth."* God called Noah into the Ark, and *"all the fountains of the great deep were broken up, and the windows of heaven were opened."* Swirling waters covered the earth to the mountain tops. Was the earth washed clean? Indeed not. Immediately after the Flood, God told Noah that only blood can cleanse sin. God had much to teach mankind: *"Whoever sheds man's blood, by man his blood shall be shed."* There was only one way: *"Behold! The Lamb of God who takes away the sin of the world!"* and *"The blood of Jesus Christ his Son cleanses us from all sin."* His blood removes it all.

Some people think that the waters of baptism can cleanse their souls. As they pass through the waters, they imagine that the religious ceremony has taken their sin away. But it simply cannot do that. If the waters of baptism could remove our sin, Jesus Christ would never have needed to die such a cruel death – but there was no alternative. Be free in Christ – your sins are forgiven and you have his new life!

The Precious Oil

The Bible uses a very striking illustration for the principle of unity: oil! Oil in Scripture always represents the working of the Holy Spirit, whether it is about oil in lamps, anointing oil, cosmetic oil or perfumed oil. The idea originates from Psalms: *"How good and pleasant it is for brethren to dwell together in unity! It is like the precious oil upon the head."* This was referring to the ceremony of pouring special perfumed oil upon the head of the high priest of Israel.

Why is unity like oil? Because the Holy Spirit is oil, and he brings unity. Unity through the oil of the Spirit poured upon us is like the oil poured on the head in Psalm 133:

> "It is like the precious oil upon the head, running down on the beard … of Aaron, running down on the edge of his garments. It is like the dew of Hermon, descending upon the mountains of Zion; for there the Lord commanded the blessing – life forevermore!"

Notice this oil was poured lavishly, running all the way down to the hem of Aaron's robe. Unity has wide-reaching effects. The purpose of this outpouring of Holy Spirit oil is *"for the equipping of the saints for the work of ministry … till we all come to the unity of the faith."* So faith also comes into it – faith, the Holy Spirit, and in unity, all play their parts.

Now Scripture says: *"keep the unity of the Spirit in the bond of peace."* Unity **does** exist – we only have to maintain it. That unity is the presence of the Holy Spirit in every believer. You are one in him from the moment you believe.

Today's Scripture
Till we all come to the unity of the faith and of the knowledge of the Son of God, to a perfect man,
to the measure of the stature of the fullness of Christ.
(Ephesians 4:13)

Daily Power!
The oil of the Holy Spirit flowing in my life enables me to walk in unity with my brothers and sisters in Christ.

Mark My Word
Psalm 133:1-2
Ephesians 4:3, 13; 4:12-13.

The Bible In A Year

Morning
1 Samuel 1
Romans 1

Evening
Jeremiah 39
Psalms 13 and 14

12

Commitment

Today's Scripture
If we live in the Spirit,
let us also walk in the
Spirit.
(Galatians 5:25)

Daily Power!
Can two walk
together, unless they
are agreed?

Mark My Word
Amos 3:3
Luke 22:42
John 10:30
Galatians 5:25; 6:2
Ephesians 4:4; 6:11

The Bible In A Year

Morning
1 Samuel 2
Romans 2

Evening
Jeremiah 40
Psalms 15 and 16

Nobody can have unity by himself. You cannot be married by yourself. There is no such thing as an independent believer. You cannot have unity by belonging nowhere. Some say that they belong to the universal church, but are committed nowhere particularly. Well, that means nobody can rely upon these people. Churches cannot be built on floaters.

Every born-again believer is *"in Christ"* together with all others. *"There is one body and one Spirit"* – a great body of believers in heaven and on earth. Everything in the New Testament points to unity. We are to bear one another's burdens, for example: *"Bear one another's burdens, and so fulfill the law of Christ."* How can we do that if we have nothing to do with other Christians?

The New Testament always assumes that all believers are attached to one another locally. The epistle to the Ephesians is all about the church, and everything said is to the whole church, not to isolated individuals. It is the whole church, for example, which must have *"the whole armor of God,"* for it is a fighting force, an army. Certainly there are people who like to imagine themselves as one-man armies, single-handedly combating the enemy, ripping through communities and nations, usually leaving a path of destruction behind. Even as Christ Jesus himself was accountable to his heavenly Father, *"nevertheless not my will, but yours, be done"*, so are we, the church today, accountable to each other for our actions. That is why we must live in the community of churches.

The Holy Spirit is the Spirit of unity. He is the bonding element. This bonding is a wonderful effect of faith in Christ. It is creative. It brings about a new kind of oneness not even known in the closest of earthly families.

Only God Can Reveal God

Unless God allowed it, we could never know him. Only God can reveal himself. Scholars deny his miracles and resurrection, reducing Jesus to their own eye-level. Human imagination is very limited, and cannot reach God. But Christians know the Jesus whose face is the glory of God!

The experience of Christ is beyond those who are strangers to it. *"Eye has not seen, nor ear heard, neither has entered into the heart of man the things which God has prepared for them that love him."*

Isaiah mocked those who tried to make images of their gods. A block of wood cannot become like the Creator of heaven and earth. Every attempt to portray God comes up against the depravity of the human mind. The gods of the Greeks and Romans were lustful and treacherous.

Our only ideas come from the Bible, and only the Bible has the right to tell us how to get to heaven, or who will get there. The Bible itself describes it as a place where only those cleansed in the blood of Jesus dare enter. If we turn elsewhere to know God, we feel depressed. The sacred writings of India, China, or Islam bring fear but little cheer.

Open the Bible, and see wonderful light stream out! The more you understand that Book, the more your mind opens to its revelations, as flowers to the rising sun.

The power that inspired it, designed your soul to receive it.

Today's Scripture
Eye has not seen, nor ear heard, Nor have entered into the heart of man The things which God has prepared for those who love him.
(1 Corinthians 2:9).

Daily Power!
The experience of Christ is beyond those who are strangers to it.

Mark My Word
1 Corinthians 2:9

The Bible In A Year

Morning
1 Samuel 3
Romans 3

Evening
Jeremiah 41
Psalm 17

Today's Scripture
Your Father in heaven
makes his sun rise
on the evil and on the
good, and sends rain
on the just and
on the unjust.
(Matthew 5:45)

Daily Power!
All my needs are
covered by faith in
God's promises.

Mark My Word
Genesis 8:22; 9:10
Matthew 5:45;
6:28-29; 7:7-11.

The Bible In A Year

Morning
1 Samuel 4
Romans 4

Evening
Jeremiah 42
Psalm 18

Divine Promises

It is human nature to depend on people's promises until we are disillusioned. Tricksters and con men trade on it. We trust people when they give us their word. We should be able to trust God as he has given us his Word. A hundred generations have proved him, and he has given us the same reason for relying upon him, express declarations of what he will undertake to do for us. Somebody went through the whole Bible and counted – finding 7,874 promises that God made to us! That glittering array covers our understanding of God and what we can expect of him.

Outside these promises is possibly outside the Word of God. Nevertheless, there is no hard boundary to the kindness of God. He is gracious. Experience shows that he may allow beyond the fringe of his precise Word. When that happens, it is not to be taken as setting a precedent for others to demand the same of him. But the scope of 7,874 promises should be wide enough for all circumstances that need God's help. Many of the promises come in the form of a covenant.

God does a lot for us without our asking him: *"Your Father in heaven … makes his sun rise on the evil and on the good, and sends rain on the just and on the unjust."* God is good, and good to all. Millions give him no credit, although they are quick to blame him when bad things hit them. The processes of nature seem unchangeable and regular. To this day, nobody has shown that God has no part in this. He keeps his promises to *"every beast of the earth, on every bird of the air, on all that move on the earth"* … *"As long as earth remains, seedtime and harvest, cold and heat, summer and winter, and day and night shall not cease."* Jesus took it further and included the flowers, saying: *"Consider the lilies of the field, how they grow; they neither toil nor spin, and yet … even Solomon in all his glory was not arrayed like one of these."* Rejoice in God's loving kindness and caring faithfulness. Even his creation declares his miraculous provisions for you.

The Golden Gift Of Faith

One minute, we do not believe - the next moment, faith is suddenly there! Perhaps in a less than dramatic fashion, we step over a border, and we believe. We just know who Jesus is. It does not always come framed in all the right words, or it may not conform to a classic conversion experience, but within our souls, there is intuition. We see it. We know that he is the One who should come if this world is to have any meaning. He is the key, the answer to the riddle of existence, the focus. Jesus Christ crystallizes people's ideas about God.

In the Old Testament, revelation came to people about God, but it seemed to be only to rare individuals, such as Abraham, Jacob, and the prophets. The mass of people moved very slowly – often backwards. God used various circumstances to help them to have faith. But the coming of Jesus has swept the world. Somehow, Calvary does what the awesome manifestations of Sinai could not do. Jesus is the great Faith-Creator. Looking back over the long, cheerless world history of uncertainty and doubt, we can see when it changed. It came with the gospel. It awakened sleeping trust. The dawn had come. *"I am the way, the truth and the life. No one comes to the Father except through me … The words that I speak to you I do not speak on my own authority, but the Father who dwells in me does the works. Believe me that I am in the Father and the Father in me."*

Jesus said: *"No one comes to the Father except through me."* It was a pragmatic, simple fact. There are religions enough, pointing a thousand different ways, but Christ **is** the way. He does not point to a way. He is the door, and flings heaven wide open: *"Come unto me … and you will find rest"* … *"Fear not."* These are his promises to all mankind!

Today's Scripture
Come to me, all you who labor and are heavy laden, and I will give you rest. Take my yoke upon you and learn from me, for I am gentle and lowly in heart, and you will find rest for your souls. For my yoke is easy and my burden is light.
(Matthew 11:28-30)

Daily Power!
Living with Jesus Christ in my heart gives meaning and hope to my life.

Mark My Word
Matthew 11:28
Luke 12:32
John 14:5-11

The Bible In A Year

Morning
1 Samuel 5 and 6
Romans 5

Evening
Jeremiah 43
Psalm 19

16

Faith In Three Tenses

Today's Scripture
He who has begun a
good work in you will
complete it.
(Philippians 1:6)

Daily Power!
Lord, your Word is
true. I read what you
have done, so I know
what you will do.

Mark My Word
Psalm 27:3
John 2:17
Philippians 1:6
1 Timothy 4:8

The Bible In A Year

Morning
1 Samuel 7 and 8
Romans 6

Evening
Jeremiah 44
Psalms 20 and 21

Today, "Yesterday" knocks on our door, telling us about "Tomorrow." What we believe will be, comes from what was. Like the weather, life is a matter of probabilities – except one thing: the will of God. God is not affected by changes. God's will is the key to bring order from chaos. This business of faith is needed for the whole business of life. We have to take it on trust that the water from our taps is not toxic. Making money or making a living are the same. But my concern is living itself: we can make a mess of it, or a good job. We can fail in living while being successful in making a living. *"Godliness is profitable for all things, having promise of the life that now is and of that which is to come."*

Faith can snap us out of our snug little burrows and get us going for God. God gave me a world-sized job – to publish and distribute a first-class gospel booklet for every home in many nations. I had no money for such a fantastic scheme, but I had faith. Now I have seen God meet the need in many countries, with the "Minus to Plus" booklet. At present, our other books and booklets are translated into 142 different languages and dialects, and so far we have printed over 152 million copies of them!

What God has done before indicates to me what will happen next. No matter with whom we deal, we do not know what they will be like. We take it on trust that if they have been trustworthy in the past they will be trustworthy now. Even circumstances change, and we have to take a chance. There is no other way. Faith is a fact of life, like the need to breathe. I trust God because he has a proven track record, as they say. He has always handled things well, very well indeed, in my work.

There are three tenses of faith: *"Being confident of this very thing, that he who has begun a good work in you will complete it until the day of Jesus Christ."* The Christian confidence is that what God was, he is and will be. *"Though war should rise against me, in this I will be confident."* His will cannot be challenged or changed – it shapes the future. In his will, we are secure.

The Source Of Oil

The great National Temple in Jerusalem had a famous golden lamp-stand, the seven-branched menorah described in Exodus chapters 25, 35, 37, and 39. The Romans carried it off when they plundered Jerusalem in AD 70, and it is depicted on the Arch of Titus seen daily by tourists in Rome. The menorah is the badge of modern Israel. This lamp-stand – or lamp standard – had neither joint nor weld, being made out of a single piece of gold. Each arm had a lamp, a mere wick, and the oil came from a single source in the central stem. The seven lights shone as one light and had no shadow of itself. Jesus talked about oil in lamps, a symbol of the Holy Spirit.

In the Book of Revelation, the apostle John described Christ standing among seven golden lamp-stands, each lamp standard representing a church:

> "I was in the Spirit on the Lord's day, and I heard behind me a loud voice, as of a trumpet, saying, 'I am the Alpha and the Omega, the First and the Last,' and 'What you see, write in a book and send it to the seven churches which are in Asia' … Then I turned to see the voice that spoke with me. And having turned I saw seven golden lamp-stands, and in the midst of the seven lamp-stands One like the Son of Man."

Also, he said that before the throne, seven lamps were blazing. These are the seven Spirits of God. The seven flames of each candelabrum had a single fuel source: the Spirit of God, casting a single light. There is one Spirit as we read, although manifested in many gifts, ministries and operations.

If believers shine and bring a little brightness into our drab world, it is by the Holy Spirit – otherwise they are dead wicks. A wick cannot shine without fuel, no matter how hard it tries. Christ sets hearts aglow, and we can blaze for God. Nobody just believes – if you believe, you shine!

Today's Scripture
But the manifestation of the Spirit is given to each one for the profit of all.
(1 Corinthians 12:7)

Daily Power!
The Source of oil in my lamp is the Holy Spirit of God.

Mark My Word
Exodus 25:1-40;
35:1-35; 37:1-29;
39:1-43
1 Corinthians 12:4-11
Revelation 1:10-13;
4:5

The Bible In A Year

Morning
1 Samuel 9
Romans 7

Evening
Jeremiah 46
Psalm 22

18

Today's Scripture
For where two or three are gathered together in my name, I am there in the midst of them. (Matthew 18:20)

Daily Power!
Your word is a lamp to my feet and a light to my path. As I go, I can see clearly!

Mark My Word
Psalm 119:105
Mark 16:17-18;
John 14:23

The Bible In A Year

Morning
1 Samuel 10
Romans 8

Evening
Jeremiah 47
Psalms 23 and 24

Faith in God seems to be a vague sentiment, but it soon solidifies into reality. We can "cast ourselves upon the ocean of the unknown" with wonderful assurance. Jesus said: *"If anyone loves me, he will keep my word; and my Father will love him."* The major lesson that I personally had to learn when arriving in Africa from Germany was to unlearn the business of questioning God. We question politicians – but believe God! For example, Christ said: *"These signs will follow those who believe … they will lay hands on the sick and they shall recover."* It is not for me to consult intellectuals for their approval, but simply to obey the Word. I do what God says, and then he does what he said. God changed the polarity of my heart and spirit, and then began to use me to shake whole nations! God used the rod of Moses, and so he uses us when we follow his orders. I see his power at work time after time. My faith-fuse has held, and the currents of blessing have flowed through my life to millions of precious people to redeem their souls by the blood of the Lamb.

You cannot generate power by anything you do, for instance by music, worship, or atmosphere. As soon as two or three gather in his name, Christ is there! Immediately, the throne is built, and you do not need to take an hour of worship to build it. It is impossible for Christians even to meet in his name without Christ being there in power! Every day, plug into the power that is yours in Christ Jesus!

Flash Flood!

God said: *"For the earth will be filled with the knowledge of the glory of the Lord, as the waters cover the sea."* How do the waters cover the sea? So thoroughly that there is not a single dry spot on the bottom of the sea! This clearly illustrates God's plan: the knowledge of his glory, power and salvation will be spread across the world like a flash flood. There will not be a single dry spot, no ignorant country, city, town, village, family, or individual. *"The whole earth is full of his glory!"* cried the seraphim to the prophet Isaiah.

This knowledge of God comes through his own Son, Jesus Christ:

> "There shall come forth a Rod from the stem of Jesse, and a Branch shall grow out of his roots. The Spirit of the Lord shall rest upon him, the Spirit of wisdom and understanding, the Spirit of counsel and might, the Spirit of knowledge and the fear of the Lord ... For the earth shall be full of the knowledge of the Lord as the waters cover the sea."

We must see the culmination of global evangelism and revival, the consummation of the toils and tears of former generations of God's anointed. The church is a life-boat, not a pleasure-boat. Entertainers are not needed or wanted. From the captain to the cook, all hands are needed on deck for soul-saving. The church that does not seek the lost is lost itself. Some excuse themselves saying that in today's pluralistic societies, the Christian half can never penetrate the other half. But was not our situation anticipated by God? People ask: "What is God saying to the church today?" Why is that a problem? Does God speak so inaudibly? **He says nothing today that is not in his Word already.** I know one thing that God is saying – and if our prophets are true, they will be voicing the same urgency as Jesus Christ, and echoing the same Great Commission: *"Go into all the world and preach the gospel to every creature."* That is God's command to you today.

Today's Scripture

And in that day there shall be a Root of Jesse, who shall stand as a banner to the people; for the Gentiles shall seek him, and his resting place shall be glorious.
(Isaiah 11:10)

Daily Power!

The church is a life-boat, not a pleasure-boat, to bring the news of salvation to the lost.

Mark My Word

Isaiah 6:3;
11:1-2, 9-10
Habakkuk 2:14
Mark 16:15

The Bible In A Year

Morning

1 Samuel 11
Romans 9

Evening

Jeremiah 48
Psalm 25

Miracles Characterize The Kingdom

20

Today's Scripture
God also bearing witness both with signs and wonders, with various miracles, and gifts of the Holy Spirit, according to his own will.
(Hebrews 2:4)

Daily Power!
I will love you, O LORD, my strength.

Mark My Word
Psalm 18:1
Daniel 4:34, 37
Luke 10:8-9
1 Corinthians 13:13
Hebrews 2:4

The Bible In A Year

Morning
1 Samuel 12
Romans 10

Evening
Jeremiah 49
Psalms 26 and 27

Miracles are normal for the kingdom. Jesus sent his disciples out and said: *"Whatever city you enter, and they receive you, eat such things as are set before you. And heal the sick there, and say to them, 'The kingdom of God has come near to you.'"* Before Christ, miracles were rare, being historic visitations of God. There were no gifts of healings for the blind, crippled or deaf. Outstanding people – such as David, Ezra, Nehemiah, Jeremiah, and Esther – never once witnessed a physical wonder, and some never experienced anything that they could call supernatural. Ezra never felt the moving of the Spirit – he never had a vision, a call, a voice or even an appointment as a prophet. He could trust the Word alone. Generally, the few signs and wonders that were seen, were demonstrations to reprove rulers, such as the despotic lords of Egypt, Babylon and Israel. These wonders were aimed at humbling them, as they did with Nebuchadnezzar. He was forced to admit that God's *"dominion is an everlasting dominion, and his kingdom is from generation to generation … I, praise and extol and honor the King of heaven."*

Usually such events were judgments, like the plagues of Egypt, But the higher qualities of kingdom power were kindness and mercy. John the Baptist, the last of the Old Testament prophets, expected harsh judgment when the Messiah came. He spoke of the fire cleansing and burning up the chaff. But when Jesus baptized with fire rather than destruction and judgment, the blaze of love came. Jesus healed the sick. Jesus sent John the Baptist a message to show that his fire was his rage against the evils men suffered. He was the One who should come. The gifts of the Spirit are benevolent and kind.

"And now abide faith, hope, love, these three; but the greatest of these is love." Walk joyfully in God's love today.

His Greatest Work

Salvation is the Holy Spirit's greatest work. It does not bring about only minor results, like patching you up, making you religious or tuning you in to nature. The creation of heaven and earth took God just six days, but he spent centuries preparing for mankind's salvation. He worked in different locations: Egypt, Israel, Babylon, Rome; through good men and bad, throughout history, until in *the fullness of the time"* Jesus came. It affected everything and everyone, even God. God's Son, torn from his side, depriving angels of their joy, faced life from a humble stable in Bethlehem. Then he faced death on Calvary, making war on Satan. In that struggle, the earth was shaken, the rocks rent, the sun blackened out of the sky.

> "Now from the sixth hour until the ninth hour there was darkness over all the land … And Jesus cried out again with a loud voice, and yielded up his Spirit. Then, behold, the veil of the temple was torn in two from top to bottom; and the earth quaked, and the rocks were split, and the graves were opened; and many bodies of the saints who had fallen asleep were raised … So when the centurion and those with him, who were guarding Jesus, saw the earthquake and the things that had happened, they feared greatly, saying, 'Truly this was the Son of God!'"

Cowed by such awesome scenes, his enemies, who had howled like wolves for his blood, crept away in fear. Hell felt the impact. Jesus Christ broke out of the granite of the sealed tomb, unhinging the gates of death, leading out captives and ascending far above all authorities to present his wounds to the Father. Wounded for you and me! These are the mighty events which made your salvation and mine possible. It is too big a thing for you not to know you are saved! It is not just being hopeful or optimistic – the Word says it. Have confidence in Christ, that you have indeed received his greatest gift. Thank him for that Gift. Walk in it. Share and enjoy it: and apply it to your challenges today.

Today's Scripture

For this reason I also suffer these things; nevertheless I am not ashamed, for I know whom I have believed and am persuaded that he is able to keep what I have committed to him until that day.
(2 Timothy 1:12)

Daily Power!

He was wounded for our transgressions, he was bruised for our iniquities; the chastisement for our peace was upon him, and by his stripes we are healed.

Mark My Word

Isaiah 53:5
Matthew 27:45-56
Galatians 4:4
2 Timothy 1:12

The Bible In A Year

Morning

1 Samuel 13
Romans 11

Evening

Jeremiah 50
Psalms 28 and 29

22

No Imitations

Today's Scripture
You are of God, little children, and have overcome them, because he who is in you is greater than he who is in the world.
(1 John 4:4)

Daily Power!
I am persuaded that he is able to keep what I have committed unto him until the day of his appearing.

Mark My Word
Matthew 7:16
Romans 8:16
2 Timothy 1:12; 2:19
2 Peter 1:4
1 John 3:14

The Bible In A Year

Morning
1 Samuel 14
Romans 12

Evening
Jeremiah 51
Psalm 30

"The solid foundation of God stands, having this seal: 'The Lord knows those who are his' and 'Let everyone who names the name of Christ depart from iniquity.'" There is a false confidence which shows in arrogance, boasting of an experience of salvation which never shows in a person's character, behavior and life style: *"you will know them by their fruits."* Such people are phony Christians. *"We know that we have passed from death to life, because we love the brethren. He who does not love his brother abides in death."* There is a subtle danger. People can be imitators and live like Christians, but not be saved.

Some people have pet parrots. Parrots are born mimics. A friend of mine has a fine African gray named Polly, who can repeat what people say, seemingly in their own voices. Sometimes it is hard to tell who is speaking. The bird talks as if it were one of the family, and uses a human-sounding voice. It tries to join in the conversation quite often. But alas, poor Polly, although it talks like a human being, and maybe even thinks that it is one, it is still only a parrot. Plenty of people live like Christians by imitation. They do what Christians are supposed to do. They parrot all the words – but not the music – none of that glorious song of the redeemed responding to heaven. Their lives are all works and effort. They might also be pretty good mimics, doing better than real Christians sometimes. But are they Christians? Christians are born-again from above; their true spiritual Father is in heaven. *"The Spirit himself bears witness with our spirit that we are children of God."* When you are truly his, you should know it.

Now we will all fall, but salvation goes on working in us to overcome our weaknesses. Our desires to please the Lord must be true, at least until the day when our redemption is completed and we see his wonderful face. Until then, whatever comes, we can say as Paul said: *"I ... am persuaded that he is able to keep what I have committed unto him until that day."* Agree with that today!

Boast Only In Christ

Nobody can take away Christ's glory, and age cannot dim it. It is there in himself, and is not produced by artificial pomp or outward circumstance. He needs no brilliant display. his glory shines through his peasant's garment. Put him on a cross, and it can destroy nothing of him. He triumphs over it, transforming this thing of shame into the greatest symbol of glory on earth.

Jesus Christ was crucified on a rough wooden cross – the cruelest form of execution yet known to man. He was stripped naked (unlike the dressed-up pictures that we are accustomed to seeing), the ultimate humility, and hung for hours without any protection from the elements, or from shame.

> "So (Thomas) said to them, 'Unless I see in his hands the print of the nails, and put my finger into the print of the nails and put my hand into his side, I will not believe' … Then (Jesus) said to Thomas, 'Reach your finger here and look at my hands, and reach your hand here and put it into my side. Do not be unbelieving, but believing … Blessed are those who have not seen and yet have believed.'"

The ugliest instrument of human torture and hate – sticky with blood and guts – is so transfigured until a former enemy had to call out: *"God forbid that I should boast except in the cross of our Lord Jesus Christ"* There is no way to destroy his glory. The more you attack him, the more his mercy, his compassion, and his patience appear. The one who is his enemy only gives him an opportunity to forgive, to seek, to save, and to display the eternal glory of his indestructible love. Let us shout, "Hallelujah, what a Savior!"

Today's Scripture
But God forbid that I should boast except in the cross of our Lord Jesus Christ, by whom the world has been crucified to me and I to the world. (Galatians 6:14)

Daily Power!
I will boast in the cross of our Lord Jesus Christ, for to us who are being saved it is the power of God.

Mark My Word
Isaiah 22:23
John 19:1-42;
20:24-39
Galatians 6:14.
1 Corinthians 1:18

The Bible In A Year

Morning
1 Samuel 15
Romans 13

Evening
Jeremiah 52
Psalm 31

24

Today's Scripture
Wash me, and I shall be whiter than snow. Make me hear joy and gladness, that the bones you have broken may rejoice. Hide your face from my sins, and blot out all my iniquities. Create in me a clean heart, O God, and renew a steadfast spirit within me. (Psalm 51:7-10)

Daily Power!
My Jesus, my Savior, has washed me completely from my sins; now I wear his righteousness.

Mark My Word
Isaiah 53:1
John 13:1-17; 19:37

The Bible In A Year

Morning
1 Samuel 16
Romans 14

Evening
Lamentations 1
Psalm 32

Who is the greatest in the kingdom of God? Maybe the unknown: but certainly, the one who serves without an ulterior motive. Undoubtedly, the greatest of all is the One who took a towel and washed the disciples' feet; and when water would not do, he poured out his life's blood for humanity's cleansing. Jesus Christ, what a Servant, who came to wash the hearts and feet of all mankind!

> "Jesus, knowing that the Father had given all things into his hand, and that he had come from God and was going to God, rose from supper and laid aside his garments, took a towel and girded himself. After that, he poured water into a basin and began to wash the disciples' feet, and to wipe them with the towel with which he was girded … So when he had washed their feet, taken his garments, and sat down again, he said to them, 'Do you know what I have done to you? You call me Teacher and Lord, and you say well, for so I am. If I then, your Lord and Teacher, have washed your feet, you also ought to wash one another's feet.'"

He is the One we shall see: *"They shall look on him whom they pierced."* That is his special identity – he is *"the pierced One."* And *"He shall see the labor of his soul, and be satisfied."* his coming in glory will be with his saints, the blood-washed ones. Not the name-droppers, the collectors of wealth and awards, cups and medals – but the redeemed ones. He redeemed them, sought them, found them, and glorified them!

What glory! He has perfumed the odious with grace. The polluted are now clothed in righteousness. The unclean have been washed with his tears, prayed for under the olive trees of Gethsemane, where Jesus sweated drops of blood.

Determine today (afresh and anew) that you will **never** forget to honor and value Jesus Christ, the Lamb of God.

Power Conductors

25

If it were **our** work to produce the power of God, **we** would be the power generators. But **Christ gave us power.** We are not called to go into the entire world with our own little power plant, so that people will think how wonderful we are. We could parade our own charisma and make the sparks fly for an hour; but soon our power-plant would run out of fuel. We are not generators – but conductors. *"… the church, which is his body, the fullness of him who fills all in all."* We are channels, not the source. *"As the branch cannot bear fruit of itself, unless it abides in the vine, neither can you, unless you abide in me."*

God does not need any of our energy dynamos. He has his own: the cross, and the empty Tomb. Power flows forever from those sources. There is no fluctuating flow *"from the Father of lights, with whom there is no variation or shadow of turning."*

> "That I may know him and the power of his resurrection, and the fellowship of his sufferings, being conformed to his death, if, by any means, I may attain to the resurrection from the dead."

Here is our full equipment: the spiritual energies of the cross and the resurrection; the power-lines of the Word of God; the fuse of our faith, the vital link. They give us power for every need: to change lives; to break vicious habits; to heal the sick; and to light the storm-darkened highway of life. No power known on earth created in test-tubes or in industry, can do any of those things. The power of God is the great force on earth to deal with the intractable problems of living! Tap into that power today!

Today's Scripture
That I may know him and the power of his resurrection.
(Philippians 3:10)

Daily Power!
Father, I pray that my faith will not be in the wisdom of men but in the power of God.

Mark My Word
John 1:16; 15:4
1 Corinthians 2:5
Ephesians 1:23
Philippians 3:10-11
James 1:17

The Bible In A Year

Morning
1 Samuel 17
Romans 15

Evening
Lamentations 2
Psalm 33

26

Plugged In

At a conference, I overheard some young people say: "We must be switched on for Jesus. All it takes is to be switched for him." I turned to them: "Yes, it is good to be switched on for Jesus – but it is more important to be **plugged in**. Switching on for Jesus will be useless unless we are plugged in. We must be connected first." Being switched on to ourselves produces no current.

The power of God coming through the Word reaches the faith-fuse first, and that could be the preacher. That tiny bridge of power can become very warm. A preacher of the Word is the first to feel that warmth. He burns with the charge. He is likely to show it, and he should. He is a communicator, not of his own thoughts, but of the power of God. He should be a live wire.

A preacher is a man having an experience with God in public. If he represses his exuberance, and puts polish, elegance and propriety first, then he should remember they are not the fruit of the Spirit – but joy is. *"The joy of the Lord is your strength"* not your weakness.

If an experienced electrician touches a bare wire and gets a shock, he may just say: "Ouch!" But anybody having an electric shock for the first time is likely to react in more dramatic fashion: "Wow!" God's power is not fiction but fact. It is the greatest reality we know.

If God does manifest himself, what would one expect? A graveyard, or a resurrection? Dynamic life may seem unseemly at first, but when people experience the flowing current of divine blessing, they will appreciate why it is dynamic. Nobody knows what it is like to meet Jesus Christ until they do. One exuberant preacher was told: "Please restrain yourself!" He replied: "I **am** restraining myself!" Do not let the cares of this world, or appearances, or pride, let you be anything less than joyful about your life in Christ!

Today's Scripture
Behold, God is my salvation, I will trust and not be afraid; 'For YAH, the LORD, is my strength and song; he also has become my salvation.'
(Isaiah 12:2)

Daily Power!
Lord, In your presence is fullness of joy. What more can I ask?

Mark My Word
Nehemiah 8:10
Psalm 16:11
Isaiah 12:2

The Bible In A Year

Morning
1 Samuel 18
Romans 16

Evening
Lamentations 3
Psalm 34

The Welcoming Face Of Faith

Often afflicted people are thought to be less intelligent. The Bible is not like that. An example is the leper mentioned in Matthew 8. He was outstanding in acumen and saw what few others ever expressed. He met Jesus and said: *"If you are willing, you can make me clean."* Many put the cart before the horse, saying: "If you **can**, you **will**." That is human thinking, not revelation, and certainly not Bible talk. God always can, but will he?

For the leper, it was a revelation. He saw that everything depended on Christ's will. The leper's faith was reasonable: *"If you are willing, you can."* The Bible was not written to tell us what God can do – we all know that. God is Almighty or we would not call him God. The Bible is here to tell us what he will do; that is what we want to know. So, what is he willing to do? The answer is: "his Word is his will" – a short answer, but it comes in a long book: sixty-six books, in fact. Each book gives us special help: it builds our understanding of God and his character. Then we know what he will do.

Christ taught us to pray: *"Your kingdom come. Your will be done on earth as it is in heaven."* The will of God is certainly not done always on earth now. God's goodness continues, but the devil is permitted freedom for the time being, and complicates every issue. If this were a perfect world, faith would not be needed. When we get to glory, faith will not apply. Everything in heaven will be secure: faith becomes sight, and evil is excluded. But this world is imperfect. Sin and the devil produce uncertainties. Logically, logic cannot produce hope. Logic cannot predict the next five minutes. It has to be faith in God.

The key words are: *"I will."* God is the God of goodwill. When we come to him, we find his arms open with a willing welcome: *"All day long I have stretched out my hands."* His face shines upon you!

Today's Scripture

Behold, I stand at the door and knock. If anyone hears my voice and opens the door, I will come in to him and dine with him, and he with me. (Revelation 3:20)

Daily Power!

By faith, I hear God knocking on the door of my heart, and I willingly open my heart to him.

Mark My Word

Matthew 6:10; 8:2; 12:18 Romans 10:21

The Bible In A Year

Morning
1 Samuel 19
1 Corinthians 1

Evening
Lamentations 4
Psalm 35

28

Purely From The Word

Today's Scripture
The hand of our God
is upon all those for
good who seek him;
but his power and
his wrath are against
all those who
forsake him.
(Ezra 8:22)

Daily Power!
Your Word I have
hidden in my heart,
that I might not sin
against you.
(Psalm 119:11).

Mark My Word
Judges 6:1-40;
7:1-25;
8:1-35
The book of Ezra
Psalm 119:11

The Bible In A Year

Morning
1 Samuel 20
1 Corinthians 2

Evening
Lamentations 5
Psalm 36

The Book of Judges tells us about Gideon, who had heard about the great things that God had done when he brought his people out of Egypt, and wanted to see the same God at work in his day. He believed that the mighty arm of two centuries before, had not lost its strength. Gideon rightly asked: *"Where are all his miracles which our fathers told us about?"* God showed him! The story of Gideon tells how a great triumph came about without human prowess and power. God delivered little Israel again, as he had delivered them before from Egypt, by soundly defeating the largest army of desert people ever mustered in those days that they never recovered to invade Israel again. Gideon only knew God from the past until then.

Some years later, we read about the faith of Ezra, who belonged to the Jewish priestly caste, and was brought up in Babylon as a palace officer, and highly thought of by the emperor of Medo-Persia. He brought nearly six thousand of his exiled people back home, traveling through countryside infested with lawless tribesmen who ruthlessly preyed on travelers. The Emperor wanted Ezra and his people to travel under military protection during their five months' journey. But Ezra boasted that God, who had looked after Israel for forty years in the wilderness, and brought them out of Egypt, could take care of them very well for five months. That sounds very religious: but the truth is that neither Ezra, nor anybody else at that time, had ever seen a vision, ever heard God's voice, witnessed a healing, or miracle, or had any sign from God whatever. Ezra was not a prophet: Ezra had nothing but the scriptures. But he believed God, resting purely upon the written scriptures. He put the whole project into operation under the wings of the Lord. This kind of raw faith, based purely on the Word of God, is available to you today!

Quickened By The Spirit

Being filled with the Spirit is shown to have had a dynamic and energizing effect or "power" (dunamis) in the New Testament, and in the lives of millions of people since then. There is very little Scripture to suggest that the Holy Spirit comes upon men like a quiet breath, unobtrusive and unnoticed. It is usually very noticeable. Manifestations of the Spirit include fire, wind, noise, wonders, outward signs, powers, and visible effects. God does not give his gifts to the unconverted nor his Holy Spirit to the world. But when we are born-again, we are encouraged to be filled, just as Paul admonished the churches.

I must emphasize again that we are looking at what Scripture says about these things. Some turn to church history, to try and prove that apostolic power died out with the apostles. church history, not the Bible, settles their doctrine. They could have wondered why it died down at the end of the apostolic age (although it did not completely vanish). But there is not a single scrap of biblical evidence to indicate that this happened. A true scholar would want to know why. If we have learned anything from church history, we know that unbelief and spiritual decline set in, and that the power of the Spirit was therefore unlikely to be manifested widely.

Christianity was never intended to be anything but an outpouring of the Holy Spirit. It is a reviving, quickening, renewing energy. Revival is not an extraordinary work above and beyond normal Christianity. Christianity is revival. The Spirit of God took the field long ago, and has never withdrawn from the battle! He does not "visit" now and then: he came to stay permanently. Having put his hand to the plow, he did not look back. Revival is always there when the Word is preached, and the Spirit is present. Always be on the lookout for the impact of those components in your own life!

Today's Scripture
But if the Spirit of him who raised Jesus from the dead dwells in you, He who raised Christ from the dead will also give life to your mortal bodies through his Spirit who dwells in you. (Romans 8:11)

Daily Power!
The Word and the Spirit are present and active in my life.

Mark My Word
Ephesians 5:18

The Bible In A Year

Morning
1 Samuel 21 and 22
1 Corinthians 3

Evening
Ezekiel 1
Psalm 37

30

Intercession

Today's Scripture
Take heed to the ministry which you have received in the Lord, that you may fulfill it.
(Colossians 4:17)

Daily Power!
Because Christ intercedes for me, I will intercede for others.

Mark My Word
Ezekiel 22:30
Romans 8:26-28
Colossians 4:17
1 Timothy 2:1
Hebrews 7:26-28
2 Peter 1:4

The Bible In A Year

Morning
1 Samuel 23
1 Corinthians 4

Evening
Ezekiel 2
Psalm 38

Intercession is a special form of prayer for believers. But what exactly does it involve? First, it is a special assignment for believers. We are called to a special work, not just to ask for things for ourselves, but to stand before God for others. This is a vital feature of the superstructure of world redemption. Christ is the great Intercessor, and we are called to a similar role. Christ's intercessory work is on a different level from ours, but he is still our role model:

> "For such a high priest was fitting for us, who is holy, harmless, undefiled, separate from sinners, and has become higher than the heavens; who does not need daily, as those high priests, to offer up sacrifices, first for his own sins and then for the people's, for this he did once for all when he offered up himself. For the law appoints as high priests men who have weakness, but the word of the oath, which came after the law, appoints the Son who has been perfected forever."

Intercession needs knowledge of those for whom we intercede, and of the One to whom we address our prayers: this is a dual knowledge. Jesus took our nature on himself, and also carried the nature of God in perfection: he was fully human, and fully divine. He identified himself with us, and with God. We are human but have received "the divine nature." We have kinship with both God and man. And so we are fitted for the work to which God has appointed us:

> "Likewise the Spirit also helps in our weaknesses. For we do not know what we should pray for as we ought, but the Spirit himself makes intercession for us with groanings which cannot be uttered. Now he who searches the hearts knows what the mind of the Spirit is, because he makes intercession for the saints according to the will of God. And we know that all things work together for good to those who love God, to those who are the called according to his purpose."

What a powerful promise for you. Think of it: because you love God, every detail in your life is being worked out for your ultimate good!

Christ-Like Compassion

We need more than just determination to enter into true intercession. Our role model, Jesus, poured out a flood of compassion. This was his sole motivating force. The effective power of intercession derives from a spontaneous outflow of concern and love. Normally speaking, it is, naturally, for our own family and friends. Now it must embrace all the world! Although the Christian basis of prayer is not in the Old Testament, it is there that we find some great examples of intercession. Abraham interceded for Abimelech, and for the doomed cities of Sodom and Gomorrah. Moses, Solomon, Elijah, Hezekiah, Daniel, Ezra, Esther, Jeremiah, and the prophets all interceded for the nation of Israel. There are even intercessory Psalms!

As an evangelist, I am called to stand before very big crowds: but I dare not preach unless I know that intercessory prayer has ascended for those very people. Workers go out to the crusade area in advance and spend several weeks there, specifically to prepare the ground through intercession. Christians are recruited locally and instructed to storm heaven with pleadings for the souls of men and women. Indeed, when these teams of intercessors knock on heaven's door, it adds weight to the prayers of tens of thousands of people around the whole world that the souls of those in the crowd may be delivered and saved!

During our evangelistic crusades, a spirit of prayer and intercession soaks my soul, often making me jump out of bed at three o'clock in the morning. Hundreds – sometimes thousands – of intercessors uphold me in prayer while I am ministering on the platform. This provides my spirit with "lift" like a powerful thermal for an eagle. I glance across a sea of faces, and rejoice that the devil's hand has been struck off their shoulders.

This is the most important thing that you can ever do for me: **Intercede prayerfully !** Thank you for being my prayer partner!!!

Today's Scripture
Likewise the Spirit also helps in our weaknesses. For we do not know what we should pray for as we ought, but the Spirit himself makes intercession for us with groanings which cannot be uttered. (Romans 8:26)

Daily Power!
I am committed to daily prayer and intercession for Evangelist Reinhard Bonnke and his team, because I want to be a partner in this vast harvest of souls!

Mark My Word
Romans 8:26-28

The Bible In A Year

Morning
1 Samuel 24
1 Corinthians 5

Evening
Ezekiel 3
Psalm 39

The rich must foot the bill
for the poor to hear the gospel.
That is divine social justice.

I do not want to be a dollar millionaire,
but a soul millionaire.

I cannot purr like a cat
when millions are perishing every day.
I want to roar like a lion!

Endurance

The Spirit-filled life is not an experience to be cultivated in special conditions, like house plants. Christians are not flowers. During the early expansion of the industrial cities of England, some clergymen could not be persuaded to take a parish among the hordes of unwashed workers, because they said it might spoil their "spirituality." The Holy Spirit makes believers tough specimens for all conditions. They carry perpetual springtime in their souls and are "winterized," just as homes are prepared for the cold weather.

The apostles discovered a new resilience, a new strength within them, power that operated in their weakness and sent them out into a brutal pagan world to demolish its idol establishment and change history. That is a true mark of the Spirit-filled life.

> "We are bound to thank God always for you, brethren, as it is fitting, because your faith grows exceedingly, and the love of every one of you all abounds toward each other, so that we ourselves boast of you among the churches of God for your patience and faith in all your persecutions and tribulations that you endure, which is manifest evidence of the righteous judgment of God, that you may be counted worthy of the kingdom of God, for which you also suffer."

Things like that are happening today. A new age of persecution is testing the church throughout the world. We may have to lay down our physical lives, but we are proving that the baptism in the Spirit makes people undefeatable.

> "Who shall separate us from the love of Christ? Shall tribulation, or distress, or persecution, or famine, or nakedness, or peril, or sword? As it is written: 'For Your sake we are killed all day long; we are accounted as sheep for the slaughter.' Yet in all these things we are more than conquerors through him who loved us."

Today's Scripture
But he who endures to the end shall be saved. And this gospel of the kingdom will be preached in all the world as a witness to all the nations, and then the end will come.
(Matthew 24:13-14)

Daily Power!
Nothing shall separate me from the love of God which is in Christ Jesus. (Romans 8:39).

Mark My Word
Matthew 24:13-14; Romans 8:35-39; 2 Thessalonians 1:3-5.

The Bible In A Year

Morning
1 Samuel 25
1 Corinthians 6

Evening
Ezekiel 4
Psalms 40 and 41

When Arson Is Not A Crime

2

Today's Scripture
I indeed baptize you with water unto repentance, but he who is coming after me is mightier than I, whose sandals I am not worthy to carry. He will baptize you with the Holy Spirit and fire.
(Matthew 3:11-12)

Daily Power!
Let me burn on for Thee, dear Lord.

Mark My Word
Exodus 3:2
Matthew 3:11-12.

The Bible In A Year

Morning
1 Samuel 26
1 Corinthians 7

Evening
Ezekiel 5
Psalms 42 and 43

God sets driftwood on fire. Dry old sticks can burn for God, just like Moses' bush did: *"And the Angel of the LORD appeared to him in a flame of fire from the midst of a bush. So he looked, and behold, the bush was burning with fire, but the bush was not consumed."* Hallelujah! I do not pray: "Let me burn out for Thee, dear Lord." I do not want to be an ash heap. The amazing feature of the bush was that it did not burn out. Too many of the Lord's servants are burning out. The cause of that is some other kind of fire. I say instead: "Let me burn on for Thee, dear Lord." The altar flame should never go out.

Without fire, there is no gospel. The New Testament begins with fire. The first thing said about Christ by his first witness concerned fire. John the Baptist, himself a shining light, declared: *"He will baptize you with the Holy Spirit and fire. his winnowing fan is in his hand, and he will thoroughly clean out his threshing floor, and gather his wheat into the barn; but he will burn up the chaff with unquenchable fire."*

John the Baptizer introduced Jesus the Baptizer, the Baptizer with a vast difference. John used water, a physical element, but Christ was to use a spiritual element: holy fire. Water and fire: what a contrast! Not that John the Baptist had a "watery" religion (although there is plenty of that around, often combined with ice!). John the Baptist stood in the cold waters of Jordan baptizing – but Jesus the Baptizer stands in a river of liquid fire!

The notable work of John was baptism. He announced the notable work of Jesus as baptism also. Baptism is the Lord's present great work. Jesus, the Baptizer in the Holy Spirit. This is Christ's major experience for you after you become a born-again believer.

An Infectious Faith

3

People talk about the evangelistic gift and debate what it really means. Simply put, the evangelistic gift is an infectious faith. To enthuse others we must be enthused ourselves.

There are people we could describe as "unbelieving believers." They are sound in doctrine but have no trust. They preach what they call the gospel, but it is lifeless. When a man describes the beauty of a lovely girl, he can do so quite clinically. But if he is in love with her, then he makes her sound like a very alive person.

Preaching must in itself be a believing act, fully reliant on God. The truth of Christ is the seed we must sow. But without faith it is seed that has never been fertilized. The gospel won't germinate, spring up, blossom or produce fruit unless it is preached with faith. To have faith in the faith once delivered to the saints (see Jude 3) is very important, but it is not sufficient. Faith should be fruitful, life-generating—*"by believing you may have life in his name."* It is a vibrant, living process. You **are** believing, you **are** receiving, you **are** knowing, you **are** seeing, you **are** abiding in him.

Evangelism calls for that kind of active believing. It is testifying, witnessing, seeing, knowing and doing. **The gospel is not truth on ice, but truth on fire!**

Today's Scripture
When I preach the gospel, I cannot boast, for I am compelled to preach. Woe to me if I do not preach the gospel! (1 Corinthians 9:16)

Daily Power!
Father, may my faith be fruitful and life-generating!

Mark My Word
John 20:31
Romans 10:14

The Bible In A Year

Morning
1 Samuel 27
1 Corinthians 8

Evening
Ezekiel 6
Psalm 44

4

Today's Scripture
Blessed be the Lord who daily loads us with benefits, the God of our salvation! Selah. Our God is the God of salvation; and to God the Lord belong escapes from death.
(Psalm 68:19-20)

Daily Power!
As for me and my house we will serve the Lord.

Mark My Word
1 Samuel 25:29
Acts 16:25-34

The Bible In A Year

Morning
1 Samuel 28
1 Corinthians 9

Evening
Ezekiel 7
Psalm 45

Household Salvation

"Yet a man has risen to pursue you and seek your life, but the life of my lord shall be bound in the bundle of the living with the Lord your God; and the lives of your enemies he shall sling out, as from the pocket of a sling."

If you want your family to keep together and know the Lord, you are on a winning ticket, with everything going for you. For example, look at this famous incident:

"But at midnight Paul and Silas were praying and singing hymns to God, and the prisoners were listening to them. Suddenly there was a great earthquake, so that the foundations of the prison were shaken; and immediately all the doors were opened and everyone's chains were loosed. And the keeper of the prison, awaking from sleep and seeing the prison doors open, supposing the prisoners had fled, drew his sword and was about to kill himself."

The apostles Paul and Silas were in jail at Philippi when a midnight earthquake sprang the prison doors open and the jailer expected he had lost his prisoners. The discipline consequences were so terrifying to him that he was about to commit suicide. However, Paul, with typical presence of mind, shouted to reassure the poor man they were all still there. The reply of that jailer became classical: *"Sirs, what must I do to be saved?"*

Now the jailer had called them, "Sirs" and Paul saw a chance for a witty play on words. "Sir" in Greek is the same word as "Lord" (Greek: "kurios"). When the jailer asked, *"Sirs, what must I do to be saved?"* – Paul's answer was, *"Believe on the Lord Jesus Christ, and you will be saved, you and your household."* The jailer had called on Paul and Silas as kurioi, (which can mean lords), but they could not save him. The only one was "The Lord Jesus." Remember today: salvation is not in a host of lords, but in the Lord of Hosts!

Working Out His Will

We are privileged to learn from the experience of those who first ventured on the faith road, the pioneers: *"These things … were written for our admonition upon whom the ends of the ages have come."* The people of the Bible struggled with God's goodness and with the problems of evil. Their stories help us in the good fight of faith. We should remember that they had the same human nature, lived in the same world, and had the same God as we do. James reminds us, *"Elijah was a man with a nature like ours."* In fact, the world was a far more frightening and mysterious place for them than for us with our advanced knowledge – but they learned to lean on God! Israel was the most harried and persecuted race on earth, yet it was Israel who gave us the most glorious recommendation to trust in God: *"When you pass through the waters, I will be with you; and the rivers they shall not overflow you. When you walk through the fire, you shall not be burned … for I am the Lord your God, the Holy One of Israel, your Savior."* After three thousand years, Israel is still around!

The story of the three Hebrews who were cast into a furnace alive and came out alive – is a picture of their race. For twenty-five hundred years, the Chosen People have gone through the furnace of affliction but emerged, and occupy newspaper columns every day! No wonder the Psalmist wrote: *"If it had not been the Lord who was on our side [let Israel say] … the swollen waters would have gone over our soul."*

The Bible message of faith comes to us out of the crucible of suffering, and yet it is the happiest Book ever written. It contains six hundred fifty-three references to joy and gladness! Some people can believe anything, even if it took place a long time ago, or will take place a long time ahead. They can accept a promise like: *"All things work together for good to those who love God,"* which might mean eternity; but they find it harder to believe: *"I am the Lord who heals you."* They believe in the God of Moses and Elijah, that Jesus did work miracles, that the Holy Spirit empowered the disciples: but that is hollow believing unless it transfers to today, believing that he will carry on the good work! Be a present-tense believer!

Today's Scripture
Our help is in the name of the Lord, who made heaven and earth.
(Psalm 124:8)

Daily Power!
My time on earth is finite, but my life with God is eternal.

Mark My Word
Exodus 15:26
Isaiah 43:2-3
Psalm 124:1, 5
Romans 8:28
1 Corinthians 10:11

The Bible In A Year

Morning
1 Samuel 29 and 30
1 Corinthians 10

Evening
Ezekiel 8
Psalms 46 and 47

6

Action Words

Today's Scripture
Blessed be the God and Father of our Lord Jesus Christ, who has blessed us with every spiritual blessing in the heavenly places in Christ.
(Ephesians 1:3)

Daily Power!
I want to be right in the middle of God's action!

Mark My Word
Exodus 3:1-22; 4:1-31; 6:5
Ephesians 1:3

The Bible In A Year

Morning
1 Samuel 31
1 Corinthians 11

Evening
Ezekiel 9
Psalm 48

About eight centuries after Abraham, God said that he had not forgotten his covenant with Abraham, the father of all who believe. He spoke to Moses, telling him what he was doing. Look at these action words:

"The Lord **said**, see what I **will do** ... I **appeared** ... I **have established** my Covenant ... I **have heard** ... I **have seen** ... I **am come down** ... I **know** ... I **will send** thee ... I **will be with** thee ... I **will stretch out** my hand ... I **have remembered** ... I **will rid** you out of their bondage ... I **will redeem** you with an outstretched arm ... I **will take** you to me for a people ... I **will be** to you a God ... I **did swear** to give, and I **will give**."

That is a swift pen-sketch of the God of the past. One could build on that picture through the Scriptures when God became the God of Israel ... Samuel ... David ... Isaiah ... and then *"the God and Father of our Lord Jesus Christ."* That is the God that used to be. However, for some people, God stays as a used-to-be God. Millions get no further, and God for them is perhaps around, somewhere, but he generally seems to have gone into retirement. Or they say, "Jesus did wonderful things, was crucified, raised and taken to heaven, end of the episode." Full stop. Their God is firmly anchored in history, Christ beyond the blue, never to be active again.

There is a book that claims God withdrew from the Bible. But since Jesus came, God becomes more and more vivid in the Bible, and in the world to this very day. It took three hundred forty-eight pages for this writer to put his theory together, but just one miracle demolishes the idea! If anybody thinks that God has dwindled away, or done the vanishing trick, let them come to Africa. I have seen him there, manifested in greater power than anywhere in the Old Testament, expelling demons, restoring the sick, healing the blind, the cripples and the deaf. God is shaking cities and nations. Perhaps that is where God disappeared to, among people who believe him! This is a fact of your Christian faith: your God is alive and real today, as much as he ever was, or ever will be!

The Proof Of Jesus

The church of Pentecost demonstrated that Jesus is alive. The proof that Jesus is alive should be in the church itself – demonstrated by its energy, love and vitality. I am alive. I do not know anybody who is trying to prove that I am alive – it is not necessary. Living people tend to show up! All Jesus wants is a chance to show that he is alive in the church. When the church spends its time trying to prove that Jesus was resurrected, people naturally think: "If Jesus is alive, why do they have to devote so much effort and reason to proving it? It should be obvious." Compassion for the suffering, and that matchless quality of Christ-like goodness that only he can impart must be there, clearly in evidence.

> "So Jesus answered and said, 'Assuredly I say to you, there is no one who has left house or brothers or sisters or father or mother or wife or children or lands, for my sake and the gospel's, who shall not receive a hundredfold now in this time – houses and brothers and sisters and mothers and children and lands, with persecutions – and in the age to come, eternal life.'"

When Jesus gave the Great Commission, he was talking to twelve men only – twelve ordinary men. It must have sounded an outrageous assignment! No king, no tyrant ever expected so much of so few. But Jesus did. **You can know the true Jesus because he demands the impossible.** That is how you can identify him. That is Jesus every time, telling you to do what is beyond your natural abilities. Kill Goliath! ... Be a giant, not a grasshopper! ... Move mountains! ... Be perfect! ... Walk on the waves! ... Cleanse the lepers! ... Raise the dead! ... Teach all nations! ... Preach the gospel to **every** creature! The idea of being saddled with the task of the Great Commission without the power of Pentecost is (in my opinion) ridiculous. Whenever Jesus demands the impossible, he is there – the living Christ – to make it possible. That is the principle of a life with Jesus – all the glory goes to God! Hallelujah!

Today's Scripture
But Jesus looked at them and said: "With men it is impossible, but not with God; for with God all things are possible." (Mark 10:27)

Daily Power!
When God asks me to do the impossible, I know he will equip me with his power and ability to fulfill the task.

Mark My Word
Mark 10:23-31

The Bible In A Year

Morning
2 Samuel 1
1 Corinthians 12

Evening
Ezekiel 10
Psalm 49

8

A Conquest Of Christ

Today's Scripture
I, therefore, the prisoner of the Lord, beseech you to walk worthy of the calling with which you were called, with all lowliness and gentleness, with long-suffering, bearing with one another in love, endeavoring to keep the unity of the Spirit in the bond of peace.
(Ephesians 4:1-3)

Daily Power!
I will grow in my faith in Christ, and share my faith with others.

Mark My Word
Ephesians 3:1-21;
4:1-32

The Bible In A Year

Morning
2 Samuel 2
1 Corinthians 13

Evening
Ezekiel 11
Psalm 50

"When he ascended on high, he led captivity captive, and gave gifts to men." In his letter to the Ephesians, Paul used a word-picture that was all too familiar to the Ephesians, long accustomed to Roman domination. When Roman armies subdued some new part of the world, they brought back prisoners-of-war and paraded them through the streets of Rome in triumphal processions. The conquering general was celebrated and exalted on high. Prisoners were his booty, and he proudly gave captives as gifts to eminent Romans. They became captive slaves of Romans – "captivity was led captive" – or the captives had new masters. Paul thought of himself as one of Christ's conquests, once a slave of sin. He called himself *"the prisoner of Christ,"* and added, *"indeed you have heard of the dispensation of the grace of God which was given to me for you … I became a minister according to the gift of the grace of God given to me by the effective working of his power."* Notice that he says, "God's grace … was given to me **for you**" – he was **given** the gift in order **to be** a gift.

Everyone whom Christ conquers is given a gift in order that they may be a gift. No man is saved for himself alone. Paul mentions five gifts: apostles, prophets, teachers, evangelists, and pastors. But I think we should be very clear about this: they are not the only gifted ones; others are needed too. That becomes more obvious when we know what the aim is. Paul describes it: *"…for the edifying of the body of Christ, till we all come to the unity of the faith and of the knowledge of the Son of God, to a perfect man, to the measure of the stature of the fullness of Christ."* That is the aim.

If you have believed that accepting Christ's gift of salvation is the same as buying a heavenly insurance policy and that is it, then you have been deceived by the enemy, who wants to keep you powerless and ineffective in God's kingdom. Being a Christian entails a responsibility to share your faith in Jesus Christ, to reach others with his loving, life-changing power, to grow in your faith, using the gifts which God has placed within you for his glory! Amen!

Miracle Challenge To Faith

The supreme miracle in the New Testament was the raising of Lazarus from the dead. This story from John chapter 11 provides some classic lessons in faith. When Christ arrived, Martha met him, saying: *"If you had been here, my brother would not have died."* In other words, she displayed a marvelous faith for **yesterday**: "If you had been here five days ago, I believe there would have been a miracle." "If" was her word – a favorite word for believers believing for the past. Anything could have happened yesterday "if." Old faith is like the old manna from yesterday described in the books of Exodus and Numbers. If they kept yesterday's manna, it would breed worms and stink. Faith has to be today's faith. Jesus assured Martha, *"Your brother will rise again,"* and Martha replied, *"I know he will rise again, in the resurrection at the last day."* Martha had faith for **tomorrow**: the last day. It is so often like that: "There will be a miracle sometime … in God's good time … when revival comes … when things are different."

> "Then many Jews who had come to Mary and had seen the things Jesus did, believed in him. But some of them went away to the Pharisees and told them the things Jesus did. Then the chief priests … gathered a council and said, 'What shall we do? For this Man works many signs. If we let him alone like this, everyone will believe him, and the Romans will come and take away both our place and nation.'"

Christ worked miracles in the common streets of villages and cities: but according to the scholars of his day, it was the wrong time. It was only to happen when the apocalyptic world dawned. They believed one day the lame would leap like the hart and the blind would see: but not now, with Roman soldiers occupying the holy city! The miracles they saw in Jerusalem or Galilee could not be genuine. "It must be the devil at work," those old rabbis thought. Today, we are still inundated with skeptics: but we have a firm, unshakable faith in Christ Jesus our Lord! So give him praise from your heart today.

Today's Scripture

Did I not say to you that if you would believe you would see the glory of God? (John 11:40).

Daily Power!

Faith for today is powerful faith.

Mark My Word

John 11:1-57

The Bible In A Year

Morning
2 Samuel 3
1 Corinthians 14

Evening
Ezekiel 12
Psalm 51

10

Faith Breakthrough

Today's Scripture
But without faith it is impossible to please him, for he who comes to God must believe that he is, and that he is a rewarder of those who diligently seek him. (Hebrews 11:6)

Daily Power!
The faith which God has given to me is vital to my everyday life.

Mark My Word
Matthew 6:33
Luke 8:14; 12:27
Hebrews 11:6
James 4:3

The Bible In A Year

Morning
2 Samuel 4 and 5
1 Corinthians 15

Evening
Ezekiel 13
Psalms 52 to 54

God plans for nothing to be ordinary. Jesus pointed to the lilies as examples of superb beauty: *"Consider the lilies, how they grow; they neither toil nor spin, and yet I say to you, even Solomon in all his glory was not arrayed like one of these."*

In the kingdom of God, the extraordinary is so common that it is ordinary. There is a story told about a rich man who somehow managed to persuade God to allow him to bring with him a suitcase filled with gold bars when he died and went to heaven. Proud of his earthly accomplishments of wealth and riches, this man opened up the suitcase when he arrived at the Pearly Gates. St. Peter scratched his head and asked, "Why are you bringing pavement?" Even the streets of heaven are paved with gold!

More importantly, each person is special. The shepherd with a hundred sheep searches for one gone astray. The boy David, the young outsider in Jesse's warrior family, was chosen to be anointed as the future king. Christianity is the religion of the unwanted. Faith is the fertile ground in which God grows his plants and trees. He plants qualities in the man or woman of faith, which presently become admired anywhere. Little people take on stature by faith in Christ. They have zest, a grip on life, and tackle difficulties with determination and confidence. It is common practice for believers to perform beyond their natural capacity. Jesus said to the unlearned fishermen on Galilee, *"I will make you fishers of men!"* They switched direction … and also elevation.

That is very good, but some say, "I'm not a faith person." Well, here is bad news and good news. The bad is that: *"Without faith it is impossible to please God."* The good is that we can all be "faith people!" Faith is so vital that God intends nobody to be faithless. The road to faith is wide open. You can have faith today!

Laser Beams

11

In Western churches, comparatively few unbelievers venture to expose themselves to evangelism. Usually they are brought to a meeting by somebody who has sought God on their behalf, perhaps for years, and the ground is watered with tears and prepared. What about the teeming populations of Africa, Asia, China, India, Japan, and Indonesia? How many are ever named personally before the Lord? These great unprayed for masses are struggling human beings like ourselves, however remotely acquainted we are with them. If we do not intercede for them, who will?

Everyone who calls, "Help, God!" gets help. But how can people call for help if they do not know who to trust? And how can they know who to trust if they have not heard of the One who can be trusted? And how can they hear if nobody tells them? And how is anyone going to tell them, unless someone is sent to do it? That is why Scripture exclaims: *"How beautiful are the feet of those who preach the gospel of peace, who bring glad tidings of good things!"*

In the darkness of a bedeviled world, our prayers cut through the darkness like lasers, becoming channels through which God's blessing may reach earth, and transmitting the power-currents of Calvary and the resurrection: *"The effective, fervent prayer of a righteous man avails much."* Intercession jams the wavelengths of the devil: *"Resist the devil and he will flee from you."* Certainly the devil will resist, and the world will howl in protest. The works of Satan are many, but they must go: *"For this purpose the Son of Man was manifested, that he might destroy the works of the devil."*

Remember: the prayers that you pray today will not help and bless you. They will be used by God to help dismantle the works of the devil, in ways you may never see with your eyes. Keep praying!

Today's Scripture
Let your light so shine before men, that they may see your good works and glorify your Father in heaven.
(Matthew 5:16)

Daily Power!
Father, envision me with your love of the lost.

Mark My Word
Matthew 5:13-16
Romans 10:13-18
James 4:7; 5:16
1 John 3:8

The Bible In A Year

Morning
2 Samuel 6
1 Corinthians 16

Evening
Ezekiel 14
Psalm 55

The Distinction Of Intercession

Today's Scripture
Therefore I exhort
first of all that
supplications,
prayers, intercessions,
and giving of thanks
be made for all men,
for kings and all
who are in authority,
that we may lead
a quiet and
peaceable life in
all godliness
and reverence.
(1 Timothy 2:1-2)

Daily Power!
Intercession touches
the heart of God.

Mark My Word
2 Kings 4
2 Samuel 12:20, 23
Ezekiel 22:30
1 Timothy 2:1-2

The Bible In A Year

Morning
2 Samuel 7
2 Corinthians 1

Evening
Ezekiel 15
Psalms 56 and 57

Intercession honors those for whom we pray, better than recommending them for an "Honors List." In 2 Kings, we read about a woman of Shunem who was designated as notable. She was not famous, nor did she want to be. She gave quiet hospitality to Elisha the prophet, and in order to thank her, he asked: *"Do you want me to speak on your behalf to the king or to the commander of the army?"* She declined, high circles did not attract her, but she did want God to grant her a son. He did so, and this began the thrilling miracle story of the birth of her long-awaited son, his tragic death, and eventually his being raised to life again! Elisha prayed for her to the Lord, and it brought her immortal fame.

Praying brings distinction to ourselves, and to those for whom we pray. It highlights them, and makes "nobodies" into "somebodies" before God. He turns his attention to them – just think of that! *"So I sought for a man among them who would make a wall, and stand in the gap before me on behalf of the land, that I should not destroy it; but I found no one."* Politicians, talkers, musicians: but not one intercessor. If he had found a man, his name would be in The Book, immortalized. To intercede means we join an elite company.

It may be the only practical thing that we can do for some people. Elisha could only pray for his hostess. To omit prayer from our activities is loveless, and grieving to the Spirit of God. It is not difficult for us to think of individuals who need our prayers. But we should never forget the awesome power of interceding for nations.

"Pray for the peace of Jerusalem: May they prosper who love you." (Psalm 122:6)

Your prayers make a difference.

God And His Children

13

God has many good things in store for his children. The promise is: *"Seek and you shall find,"* for they are obtainable only by direct application. Actually, they are promised and most of them are listed in Scripture: *"No good thing will he withhold from those who walk uprightly."* When we come to the end of natural provision, Jesus said: *"Ask and you shall receive"* … *"Everyone who asks receives … If you then … know how to give good gifts to your children, how much more will your Father who is in heaven give good gifts to those who ask him!"* If we ask for good, he will not send evil, never! *"Every good gift and every perfect gift is from above, and comes down from the Father of lights, with whom there is no variation or shadow of turning."*

The exercise of faith in prayer is a healthy activity. The bird in the nest must learn to fly, and gather what is available. Having to ask is an excellent reminder to us of our dependency on God, and is arranged to bring us to seek him. It gives birth to a spirit of childlikeness, looking to our heavenly Father at all times. It is fellowship – family fellowship with our Father.

Jesus described this family relationship clearly – after all, he lived in a human family himself! The parallels between human and heavenly families are obvious: the nurturing Father, the kids just learning to get along:

> "Our Father in heaven, hallowed be Your name. Your kingdom come. Your will be done on earth as it is in heaven. Give us day by day our daily bread. And forgive us our sins, for we also forgive everyone who is indebted to us. And do not lead us into temptation, but deliver us from the evil one."

"Ask, and it will be given to you; Or what man is there among you who, if his son asks for bread, will give him a stone?" It is our Father's desire that you have a healthy relationship with him, and with the others in his great family.

Today's Scripture
Ask, and it will be given to you; seek, and you will find; knock, and it will be opened to you. (Matthew 7:7)

Daily Power!
Having to ask in prayer is an excellent reminder of our dependency on God, and is designed to make us seek him.

Mark My Word
Psalm 84:11
Matthew 7:7-11
Luke 11:2-4, 11-13
John 16:24
James 1:17

The Bible In A Year

Morning
2 Samuel 8 and 9
2 Corinthians 2

Evening
Ezekiel 16
Psalms 58 and 59

Interdependent

God could have arranged to do everything for us: but the object is to teach a child to stand on its own two feet. God's ultimate purpose is that we will not be helpless dependents, like babes at the breast, but his co-workers. At present, prayer is our sole access if we wish to be useful to him. It is so often forgotten that he actually created the kind of world in which prayer would be necessary. Prayer was not an afterthought when the devil upset things. Even Jesus prayed.

To help the ongoing affairs of the kingdom of God, prayer is essential. A lot goes on that God does not want, but we should pray that his will shall be done. We ask, then he performs. He planned that we should cooperate in that way, just as he put Adam *in the garden of Eden to tend and keep it.* That is how to read the promise: *"If you ask anything in my name, I will do it."* We ask for whatever is necessary for the will of God on earth to be fulfilled. *"If you ask anything in my name, I will do it."* We are his collaborators. The world and the people in it need care, and the promise that Christ will do whatever we ask is for the fulfillment of that purpose, not to get the moon or half a dozen Rolls Royce cars.

It is obvious that the apostle James (the half-brother of Jesus) grew up in an all-too-human family, with all the tugs and pulls of siblings. His description of human family life – and how God wants us to learn to view him as our Father – rings so true:

> "Where do wars and fights come from among you? Do they not come from your desires for pleasure that war in your members? You lust and do not have. You murder and covet and cannot obtain. You fight and war. Yet you do not have because you do not ask. You ask and do not receive, because you ask amiss, that you may spend it on your pleasures."

God is not going to wet-nurse us. He feeds the sparrows … but does not throw food into their nests. If you want God to work, you must work in prayer, with right motivation.

Today's Scripture
If you ask anything in my name, I will do it. (John 14:14)

Daily Power!
If we want God to work, we must work in prayer, with right motivation.

Mark My Word
Genesis 2:15
John 14:13-14
James 4:2-3

The Bible In A Year

Morning
2 Samuel 10
2 Corinthians 3

Evening
Ezekiel 17
Psalms 60 and 61

Fire-Starters

15

The gospel is a fire lighter. The Holy Spirit is not given just to help you preach eloquent sermons. He is given to put a flame into human hearts. Unless Christ sets you alight, you can bring no fire to earth: *"Without me, you can do nothing."* Jesus instructed the disciples not to do anything until they received *"power from on high."* When that power came, the Spirit revealed himself as tongues of flame sitting upon each one of them.

Previously, Jesus had sent the disciples out in pairs. It reminds me of Samson sending foxes out two-by-two, as the animals carried torches for an arson raid on the enemy's corn fields and vineyards. The disciples also were sent out two by two, carriers of the divine torch, fire-starters for God, scorching the devil's territories with the fire gospel. They were new Elijahs bringing fire from heaven.

Until the fire falls, evangelism and church activities can be very routine and unexciting. Pulpit essays, or preaching about how you think the economy of the country should be run – all that is glacial work. No divine spark brings combustion to ice. No one goes home ignited. In contrast, the two who listened to Jesus on the Emmaus road sat at home and said to each other: *"Did not our hearts burn within us while he talked with us on the road, and while he opened the Scriptures to us?"*

Jesus came *"to send fire on the earth."* The mission of Jesus is not a holiday picnic. Satan is a destroyer. The Lord sends out his servants with a warning of physical dangers: *"And do not fear those who kill the body but cannot kill the soul. But rather fear him who is able to destroy both soul and body in hell."* What is mere physical hurt, compared to a life ablaze with the joy and zest of Jesus? What is bodily danger compared to the crown of life or to the wonderful work he gives us to do? *"Heal the sick, cleanse the lepers, raise the dead, cast out demons. Freely you have received, freely give."* Allow the Holy Spirit to set your heart alight today!

Today's Scripture
Whatever I tell you in the dark, speak in the light; and what you hear in the ear, preach on the housetops. And do not fear those who kill the body but cannot kill the soul. But rather fear him who is able to destroy both soul and body in hell.
(Matthew 10:27-28)

Daily Power!
What is mere physical pain, compared to a life ablaze with the joy and zest of Jesus?

Mark My Word
Judges 15:1-8
Matthew 10:8, 28
Luke 10:1; 12:49; 24:49
John 15:5

The Bible In A Year

Morning
2 Samuel 11
2 Corinthians 4

Evening
Ezekiel 18
Psalms 62 and 63

16

Two Courtroom Dramas

Today's Scripture
My little children,
these things I write
to you, so that you
may not sin. And if
anyone sins, we have
an Advocate with the
Father, Jesus Christ
the righteous. And
he himself is the
propitiation for our
sins, and not for ours
only but also for the
whole world.
(1 John 2:1-2)

Daily Power!
This is my blood of
the new covenant,
which is shed
for many for the
remission of sins.

Mark My Word
Matthew 26:28
Colossians 2:13-14

The Bible In A Year

Morning
2 Samuel 12
2 Corinthians 5

Evening
Ezekiel 19
Psalms 64 and 65

What a relief to know that Jesus Christ acts as our own Advocate in the Court of heaven, bringing our case before the Most High and Mighty Judge - God the Father. Imagine it: the courtroom of heaven, with serious-looking officials, uniformed police, the prosecutor (Satan himself), and the judge. Having reviewed the evidence – we were all born in sin, none were righteous – the prosecutor makes his summation and rests his case. After a brief interval, the jury returns with a verdict: "Guilty as charged." The defendant stands in the dock condemned. He must suffer the penalty, pay the price. If he asked to be justified, the solemn court would burst into disbelieving laughter.

Now picture a different scene: a sinner stands before the highest Judge of all. The accuser, Satan, is there, and dazzling ranks of sinless angels look on. The sinner knows he is guilty. The Judge of all the earth must act justly. The sinner's Advocate, Jesus, appears and challenges the accuser, "Where is your evidence?" That causes quite a stir! The accuser is embarrassed. He cannot produce any evidence, not a single scrap of proof. What has happened to it?

I will tell you: our sinful evidence has been destroyed! Christ Jesus gathered it all unto himself and carried it into the fires of divine judgment which swept across Calvary. During those awful hours, the record was consumed, leaving no trace. Colossians 2 describes it:

> "You … he has made alive together with him, having forgiven you all trespasses, having wiped out the handwriting of requirements that was against us, which was contrary to us. And he has taken it out of the way, having nailed it to the cross."

Those sins are yours and mine – not just crossed out, but wiped out, because of the blood of Jesus!

"Made Innocent!"

In the Court of heaven, Jesus the Advocate makes his sensational claim: "There is no evidence against this man." Then the throne of Justice becomes the throne of Grace. Satan the accuser retires in baffled rage. The Judge beckons the accused and hands him a document called "The New Covenant." He opens it. There he sees that it carries the red seals of the sprinkled blood of Jesus. It is a royal exoneration declaring, "This court finds no evidence and therefore no case against you." *"There is therefore now no condemnation to them who are in Christ Jesus."* The Judge has signed it saying: *"Their sins and their lawless deeds I will remember no more."*

The prisoner is free, justified by grace. Then the whole court rises and applauds, for there is joy in heaven over one sinner who repents. When you are justified by grace, God the Judge wants you to know it. Those who wait for the Day of Judgment to discover whether they are saved or damned, do not understand salvation at all. Knowing the promise of Jesus – *"Most assuredly, I say to you, he who hears my word and believes in him who sent me has everlasting life, and shall not come into judgment, but has passed from death into life"* – is part of salvation. He lifts that fear from you when you get saved. The word "judgment" in that Scripture is the Greek word "krisis", from which the word "crisis" is derived. So you can say that a born-again believer will never know such a "crisis" hour, standing in the judgment, waiting to find out whether he is saved or lost. The matter was settled at Calvary.

> "Therefore let it be known to you, brethren, that through this Man is preached to you the forgiveness of sins; and by he everyone who believes is justified from all things from which you could not be justified by the law of Moses."

Today's Scripture

There is therefore now no condemnation to those who are in Christ Jesus, who do not walk according to the flesh, but according to the Spirit. (Romans 8:1)

Daily Power!

I once was lost, but now I'm found; was blind, but now I see.

Mark My Word

Luke 15:7
John 5:24
Acts 13:38-39
Romans 8:1
Hebrews 10:17

The Bible In A Year

Morning
2 Samuel 13
2 Corinthians 6

Evening
Ezekiel 20
Psalms 66 and 67

18

Today's Scripture
So that they should seek the Lord, in the hope that they might reach out for him and find him, though he is not far from each one of us.
(Acts 17:27)

Daily Power!
The importance of families in God's grand design is never to be underestimated.

Mark My Word
Psalm 127:3; 128:1-4
Acts 17:25-27

The Bible In A Year

Morning
2 Samuel 14
2 Corinthians 7

Evening
Ezekiel 21
Psalm 68

Family Salvation

When we pray and plan for the salvation of our own families, we are moving in the stream of divine activity. God especially wants to be in our families. The Bible anticipates the "*the whole family in heaven and earth.*" The family is not just a human idea to help strengthen society; its value is more than just social. It is the way God planned that the world should be run! It is part of his eternal objective.

The secular world talks about the families being the "building blocks" of society. They are, but they need building together, not left lying around. Families can structure society only when cemented together. There is one element on earth to do this: not patriotism, but the gospel. It explains the church, the family of God:

> "He has made from one blood every nation of men to dwell on all the face of the earth, and has determined their preappointed times and the boundaries of their dwellings."

With biblical truths like this behind us, we can plan for the salvation of our household. blood is thicker than water. If we pray especially for our loved ones, it is natural – the way God meant it – and we have everything going for us. In Acts 16, Paul showed that if the jailer was saved, the whole family was on the way to salvation.

One of the wonderful possibilities and blessings of godly parents is that children will not break their hearts and wreck their own lives. Churches are so often composed of family generations – a wonderful stabilizing and assuring thing, children honoring godly parents.

> "Blessed is every one who fears the Lord, who walks in his ways ... You shall be happy and it shall be well with you. Your wife shall be like a fruitful vine in the very heart of your house, your children like olive plants all around your table ... Behold, children are a heritage from the Lord."

It does not take long to show. It may seem a youthful blip when a teenage girl becomes interested in a boy; but if he is a born-again child of God, it can mean the start of another new godly dynasty to last for generations.

No Alternative

Scripture stresses the importance of children brought up in the fear of God, not yoked with unbelievers. This is more than a social category, such as training children to become good Methodists, but a matter of children learning the critical necessity of following Christ, putting God before prestige, living by a spiritual code and for the gospel of Christ. Nothing in the world is important except that which ties in with the gospel. The rest will vanish.

There is no alternative. Children either have a spiritual basis or no basis, either a guiding light or no light. The world, the great illusion, will compete for their hearts: and it has a magnetic and immediate appeal. Secular pressures bear down powerfully upon everyone, and inexperienced children should be shown the other side: eternal and spiritual realities. Time and place should be given to the counter-measure of the things of the Spirit, and their minds protected with the Word of God. It forms a watertight bulkhead against the greatest ocean.

One text from the devil's credo: "Don't push religion down our throats!" This is a cynical, breathtaking remark and downright hypocritical! Godlessness is pushed down our throats without apology. People openly sneer at Christians with no other intention but godlessness. Another satanic maxim: "Don't foist your own religious prejudices upon children. Let them feel free to believe with an unprejudiced mind." Free? The world leaves nobody free and unprejudiced:

> "And you he made alive, who were dead in trespasses and sins, in which you once walked according to the course of this world, according to the prince of the power of the air, the spirit who now works in the sons of disobedience, among whom also we all once conducted ourselves in the lusts of our flesh, fulfilling the desires of the flesh and of the mind."

How much godly influence really touches us day by day? In our secular cities, the day is likely to be completely devoid of any spiritual influence, but the pressures will be an environment of godlessness, blasphemy, corruption, unbelief and cynicism.

Make godly living your daily bread!

Today's Scripture
Do not be unequally yoked together with unbelievers. For what fellowship has righteousness with lawlessness? And what communion has light with darkness? (2 Corinthians 6:14)

Daily Power!
Lord, let your ways be done in my life and family, not the ways of the world.

Mark My Word
2 Corinthians 6:14-18
Ephesians 2:1-3

The Bible In A Year

Morning
2 Samuel 15
2 Corinthians 8

Evening
Ezekiel 22
Psalm 69

20

A Warning About Faith

For all the wonderful things we know about faith, it is also important to know that faith is not for the gold-digger. God, who made all wealth, is not against wealth: but those whose god is gold can expect no help from heaven!

There has been an epidemic of people who have deliberately misused the message of faith to disguise their pursuit of wealth: shame on them! These people are idol worshipers, placing false doctrines and other things ahead of their relationship with God, and their lives are bound to fall into ruin:

> "The idols of the nations are silver and gold, the work of men's hands. They have mouths, but they do not speak; eyes they have, but they do not see; they have ears, but they do not hear; nor is there any breath in their mouths. Those who make them are like them; so is everyone who trusts in them."

Stay away from these people who hide their unrighteousness behind a facade of teaching true faith!

Jesus' Parable of the Sower uses a word which has passed into the English language: "hedonism" (Greek: "hedonon"), the pursuit of pleasure. *"Now the ones that fell among thorns are those who, when they have heard, go out and are choked with cares, riches, and pleasures of life, and bring no fruit to maturity."* The same plain words address us in James: *"You ask, and do not receive, because you ask amiss, that you may spend it on your pleasures."* A life-aim of riches is stupid, because at the end, we cannot take it with us. But it is eternal profit to follow Christ's directions: *"Seek first the kingdom of God and his righteousness, and all these things shall be added to you."* You line your faith up with the pure Word of God – and it cannot fail.

Today's Scripture
But seek first the kingdom of God and his righteousness, and all these things shall be added to you. Therefore do not worry about tomorrow, for tomorrow will worry about its own things. Sufficient for the day is its own trouble.
(Matthew 6:33-34)

Daily Power!
Without faith there can be no riches. By faith we have treasure in earthen vessels.

Mark My Word
Psalm 135:15-18
Matthew 6:33
Luke 8:14
2 Corinthians 4:7

The Bible In A Year

Morning
2 Samuel 16
2 Corinthians 9

Evening
Ezekiel 23
Psalms 70 and 71

Divine Principle Of Action

The absolute ABC of faith is that as we act, God acts. We respond to him by faith, and he responds to us for faith. Paul found that it operated like the blood flowing through his veins. *"It is no longer I who live; but Christ lives in me: and the life, which I now live in the flesh, I live by the faith of the Son of God."*

Here are some examples from Scripture: *"They were all filled with the Holy Spirit and began to speak with other tongues as the Spirit gave them utterance."* They spoke and the Spirit gave them language. *"Work out your own salvation with fear and trembling. For it is God who works in you both to will and to do for his good pleasure."* This has a play on words: "God is in you to do his good will" or, "He puts the desire in us to do his desire." That is what "being led of the Spirit" means: *"Holy men of God spoke as they were moved by the Holy Spirit."* Jesus said: *"But when they deliver you up, do not worry about how or what you should speak. For it will be given to you in that hour what you should speak; for it is not you who speak, but the Spirit … in you."* *"The steps of a good man are ordered by the Lord"* – we walk and God steers us. *"O Lord, I know the way of man is not in himself: it is not in man who walks to direct his own steps."* Three times we read, *"He makes my feet like deer's feet"* – which is what Isaiah meant: *"They shall run and not be weary; they shall walk and not faint."*

God does not want you to be like a pair of gloves, uselessly waiting to be picked up off the shelf, lifeless. People pray, "Use me, O Lord" – but do nothing. There is the idea that being used of God means being another Luther, Wesley, or Livingston. But you are alive to get on with the task at your elbow! Today, purpose to be used by God.

Today's Scripture
Those who wait on the Lord shall renew their strength; they shall mount up with wings like eagles, they shall run and not be weary, they shall walk and not faint.
(Isaiah 40:31)

Daily Power!
Being used by God is his plan for me.

Mark My Word
2 Samuel 22:34
Psalm 18:33; 37:23
Isaiah 40:31
Jeremiah 10:23
Habakkuk 3:19
Acts 2:4
Philippians 2:12-13
Galatians 2:20
2 Peter 1:21

The Bible In A Year

Morning
2 Samuel 17
2 Corinthians 10

Evening
Ezekiel 24
Psalm 72

22

Today's Scripture
Men always ought to
pray and not
lose heart.
(Luke 18:1)

Daily Power!
God speaks to us
anytime he wants. He
does not wait
until we pray.

Mark My Word
Habakkuk 2:1
Luke 18:1-8

The Bible In A Year

Morning
2 Samuel 18
2 Corinthians 11

Evening
Ezekiel 25
Psalm 73

God Speaks Anytime, Anywhere

Prayer is the act of speaking to God, not God speaking to us. God speaks to us anytime he wants: he does not wait until we pray. In fact, nobody in the Bible seemed to be praying when God spoke to them. God is close to us and can speak at all times. It may be that sometimes we cannot hear him, because we are clamoring for him to say something different. Prayer is basically a time to pour out our hearts to him. Listening is another thing. We should constantly be ready, for he speaks at any time. It is no use rising from our knees and saying he has not spoken. We cannot demand that he should speak at that precise time, like switching on the radio. We should never be switched off. He may interrupt our own program with specific personal instructions at any time.

It may seem strange to Christians today that there is nothing in Scripture about praying in order to hear from God, for guidance or anything else. There is plenty about hearing his voice, but almost nothing about waiting to hear – except when Habakkuk stood at his watch to hear from God: "*I will stand my watch and set myself on the rampart, and watch to see what he will say to me, and what I will answer when I am corrected.*" If we pray and wait to hear, we may hear, but whatever voice speaks, we need to know who it is. The dangers are obvious. It is a fact of our nature that our desires can sound like divine commands. Shout long enough about what we already want to do, and the echo will come back sooner or later: but it is our own voice, not the voice of God.

People talk of how they wrestled with God over a decision. Looked at honestly, that is an invidious procedure. Is God like that? In fact, **they are wrestling with their own will, not God.** They want him to agree. Do we really imagine we must wrestle with God to pry the secret out of him about what he wants us to do? Surely he would just tell us without an all-out wrestling match. It is ridiculous to approach God that way, as if he were unwilling to tell us his will. The business of asking God for directions suggests he has neglected to guide us as he said he would. God never shuts his children out – that means he always hears you!

Three Pillars Of Wisdom

23

God uses manpower; man needs God's power; God works when people work. These are three pillars of wisdom. To unfold these principles, I shall begin with the basics. Millions of sermons are preached and heard by hundreds of millions of people, but the effect is not so great. Preachers complain: "The people don't do what I say." That is just it, of course. Of all those who listen, how many feel like exerting themselves, putting themselves out to serve the Lord, while the rest are content only to sing, worship and enjoy a good sermon? God wants us to be *"doers of the Word, and not hearers only."* I am not passing on mere knowledge, but trying to lead everybody into the dynamic power and blessing of God.

Let me encourage you first. You can be absolutely sure that God has something for you to do now, and a special privileged place in which to put you. You are perhaps already there: but just have not realized it. Many think that God has some great thing for them to do – one day. Perhaps he has, but what you are doing now is important too, if you are obeying him. There is a job to suit you, and a job for which you are being prepared. If you think that you are not in on these things, it is not true. Do not deprive yourself of your right and proper place in the glorious scheme of God.

Once you realize that first point – that **God uses manpower** – you can move on. If God wants you to do something, he will give you the ability to do it. Very likely it may stretch you beyond what you have done before. He wants you to grow. Whatever lies before you, God put it there. You can move mountains. Say this to yourself: "God means me to be more than I thought I was." Do not measure what you should do by your gift – measure the gift by what you should do. It will match. God specializes in the impossible. He wants this fact to show in the lives of those who belong to him. He commands the impossible, and then makes it possible, to his glory. My purpose is to reveal to you the ways to his power.

Today's Scripture
I thank Christ Jesus our Lord who has enabled me, because he counted me faithful, putting me into the ministry.
(1 Timothy 1:12)

Daily Power!
I am in partnership with my heavenly Father to fulfill his work on earth.

Mark My Word
1 Timothy 1:12
James 1:22

The Bible In A Year

Morning
2 Samuel 19
2 Corinthians 12

Evening
Ezekiel 26
Psalm 74

24

Powers Of A New Order

Today's Scripture
There are some
standing here who
will not taste death till
they see the kingdom
of God present
with power.
(Mark 9:1)

Daily Power!
I have been
transplanted into
God's kingdom of
light and power..

Mark My Word
Matthew 4:17
Mark 9:1
Luke 11:20

The Bible In A Year

Morning
2 Samuel 20
2 Corinthians 13

Evening
Ezekiel 27
Psalms 75 and 76

I have seen countless mighty wonders and unclean spirits cast out by the finger of God. Christ explained it: *"If I cast out demons with the finger of God, surely the kingdom of God has come upon you."* We must look carefully at that explanation. *"The kingdom"* – what is it? If we are to catch the real secret of the faith, we must understand the kingdom. Jesus talked about it all the time. He knew what he was talking about, whereas the pharisees tried to accuse him of representing the kingdom of Satan! We only need to consider it from one angle at this point.

We have had different historical ages: the Stone Age, the Bronze Age, the Dark Ages, and so on. These time periods were given special names to show their main features. We also have the Christian Age. We even register our calendars and clocks by designating Anno Domini – "in the year of our Lord." Is this just another division of history? No. This Age is unique. During the Christian Age, another age also broke in: "the kingdom of God." Jesus began to preach: *"Repent, for the kingdom of heaven is at hand."*

The kingdom is the realm of God in which God's power is supreme. When Christ came, he introduced the activity of God – the Holy Spirit – into our mundane affairs. It was a new resource: not physical power like water, wind or nuclear energy, for these are all part of the natural world. This was the power of a world with laws far above the laws of nature.

Read this sentence carefully:

> In the beginning, God made this world by the power
> of another world.

In Christ Jesus, he re-introduced the powers of that creative world into the earthly scene. That is the kingdom of God. And that is where you and I live today!

A Million-Candlepower Light

25

When Paul the apostle was preaching in an upstairs room in Troas, *"there were many lights"* there. The Bible writers had a way of saying that kind of thing with conveying a spiritual truth. There were two kinds of lights there: the oil lamps, and the room full of Christians who were the true "many lights." This is what believers are. *"You were once darkness, but now you are light in the Lord."* Believers are stars – unbelievers are black holes from which light never escapes. Faith makes *"children of God without fault in the midst of a crooked and depraved generation, among whom you shine as lights in the world."*

A Christian believer needs a church, just as a candle needs a candlestick and a tree needs soil. Without a candlestick, a candle cannot stand, and without soil, a tree cannot grow. Neither can you. Without fellowship, a Christian can neither stand nor grow.

Jesus does not put you on the shelf. He has a special niche especially for each of us in his edifice. He said: *"You are the light of the world"* – single lamps, and also many lights together. It was a single lamp when he said it should be *"put …on a lampstand, and it gives light to all who are in the house."* One-candlepower for one house. But he also said: *"You are the light of the world. A city that is set on a hill cannot be hidden."* A city is not one-candlepower but a million-candlepower. When Christ said: *"You are the light of the world,"* it was a plural *"you."* He brings *"many lights"* together, people combining, mingling flame with flame. The *"city set on a hill"* is a church. In Troas, there were *"many lights"* together because it was a big room. The world is a big place, and many lights are needed. The children's hymn said: "You in your small corner and I in mine", but there is more than a dark corner: there is an entire dark planet. There is no light where there is no faith in God. If you have a living faith in God, always remember that the whole globe needs your light. Let others see your light wherever you go!

Today's Scripture
On this rock I will build my church, and the gates of Hades shall not prevail against it.
(Matthew 16:18)

Daily Power!
It is my heart's desire to shine as brightly as I can for Christ, for as long as I can, to as many people as I can.

Mark My Word
Matthew 5:14-15

The Bible In A Year

Morning
2 Samuel 21
Galatians 1

Evening
Ezekiel 28
Psalm 77

26

Business In Great Waters

Today's Scripture
Oh, that men
would give thanks
to the Lord for his
goodness, and for his
wonderful works to
the children of men!
Let them sacrifice
the sacrifices of
thanksgiving, and
declare his works
with rejoicing.
(Psalm 107:21-22)

Daily Power!
Lord, whatever the
task, no matter
how small, I will
do my best.

Mark My Word
Genesis 1:1-31
Psalm 46:3; 107:23;
146:9
Matthew 16:18
Acts 1:8; 5:28; 17:6
2 Corinthians 4:6

The Bible In A Year

Morning
2 Samuel 22
Galatians 2

Evening
Ezekiel 29
Psalm 78:1-37

Spiritually, the world today is like it was at the very beginning: *"darkness was upon the face of the deep."* But: *"God said, 'Let there be light,' and there was light."* Today, God still says: *"Let there be light!"* *"God, who commanded light to shine out of darkness, who has shone in our hearts, to give the light of the knowledge of the glory of God in the face of Jesus Christ."*

After Christ rose from the dead, the disciples began brightening up the world with the light of the gospel. We should do the same. The establishment complained that they had *"filled Jerusalem with [their] doctrine,"* and a little later it was said: *"These who have turned the world upside down have come here too."* That is exactly what God said he would do: *"The way of the wicked he turns upside down."* The way of unbelief is upside down, but God turns it the right way up. That is my job and your job. We are God's agents for putting a topsy-turvy world upright.

When Christ beckoned to his first followers, they were unknown, quietly getting on with their own business, fishing on a lake. But he sent them out *"to the ends of the earth."* In Scripture, the sea represents nations: the waves roaring and turbulent. Christ once stilled the storm on the waters. He sends us to fish in every nation, though the waters of the world *"roar and be troubled."* The Lord speaks peace to the nations.

Jesus does not call us just to sit in church and vegetate as if in a rest home. We have a job to do, not a hobby, and the biggest job of all is to change the world! It is a joint-effort, together and with Christ. He said: *"I will build my church."* So whatever he asks you to do, even if it seems to be something simple and small, do your best to do your part in building his church today.

Before-And-After Heroes

Here are certain before-and-after attributes of biblical heroes of faith:

Abraham – This pioneer is notable because *"Abraham believed God, and it was accounted to him for righteousness. And he was called the friend of God."* Abram in Ur was in terrible shape, possibly idolatrous. Faith came to him quite late in life, but it made him the most dominant character that the Middle East has ever known, except for Christ.

Jacob – The grandson of Abraham. At first, Jacob did not even claim that he belonged to God. Then came a night when God wrestled with him, and Jacob experienced a breakthrough. It changed him so much that God changed his name to Israel.

Gideon – A young, frustrated son of the local chief who rose literally overnight to be a national leader. He began with very shaky faith, even complaining about God. God nurtured Gideon's faith. He faced an invading army five hundred times bigger than his, unarmed, and *"turned to flight the armies of the aliens"* – a classic operation of faith.

Jehoshaphat – he was a nervous king, not always pleasing to God. When he and the nation were in danger, God's Spirit fell upon a man in prophecy, bringing a breakthrough. Jehoshaphat's expectations soared, leading to a victorious episode in the annals of Israel.

Thomas the Twin (better known as "Doubting Thomas") – he said: *"I will not believe."* He was a practical-minded type, of the kind who needs hard evidence: but even he experienced a faith breakthrough when he saw Jesus!

Dare to do the impossible through God and for his glory!

Today's Scripture
Now faith is the substance of things hoped for, the evidence of things not seen
(Hebrews 11:1)

Daily Power!
Through faith in Christ I can do the impossible to the glory of God!

Mark My Word
Genesis 32:28
Judges 7:1-25
2 Chronicles 20:1-37
John 20:25; 21:1-25
Romans 4:11
Hebrews 11:34
James 2:23

The Bible In A Year

Morning
2 Samuel 23
Galatians 3

Evening
Ezekiel 30
Psalm 78:38

28

Eye-Opening Prayer

Today's Scripture
I pray that the God of our Lord Jesus Christ, the Father of glory, may give to you the spirit of wisdom and revelation in the knowledge of him, the eyes of your understanding being enlightened; that you may know what is the hope of his calling, what are the riches of the glory of his inheritance in the saints.
(Ephesians 1:17-18)

Daily Power!
Even as a small child trusts his parents, so I trust my heavenly Father.

Mark My Word
Ephesians 1:17-19

The Bible In A Year

Morning
2 Samuel 24
Galatians 4

Evening
Ezekiel 31
Psalm 79

I wish people would be more exact when searching Scripture. Take Ephesians 1:17-19, where Paul prays for believers to experience a breakthrough:

> "I pray that the God of our Lord Jesus Christ, the Father of glory, may give to you the spirit of wisdom and revelation in the knowledge of him, the eyes of your understanding being enlightened; that you may know what is the hope of his calling, what are the riches of the glory of his inheritance in the saints, and what is the exceeding greatness of his power toward us who believe, according to the working of his mighty power."

In the matter of power, Paul – neither here nor anywhere else – ever prays for power. The New Testament never talks about a new infilling or another Pentecost, even if the convention speakers do. He prayed only that *the eyes of (their) understanding (be) enlightened"* – that is, to see what resources lay at their very finger tips! We pray for power when Christ has all power: and that is all that matters. It follows that as we obey his command, he will back us without our having to spend half our time begging him to do so. The power breakthrough for the Ephesians was a faith breakthrough in realization of what was theirs already in Christ. We take it by faith, not through merit by the labors of prayer.

We talk of "big believers" with "great faith" – but some event encouraged them. They took their opportunity, changed their attitude and believed. God honors such a holy resolve. Jesus commended one or two for their *"great faith,"* but not one of them arrived at that happy position by a long and arduous process. They met Jesus. That was all and enough. Faith is just that: faith in him. What Jesus commended was the quality of their faith, not its scope. Ever-increasing faith is not some kind of trapeze act. It is as a little child who trusts his parents more as he grows older. Be childlike in faith!

The Fire Age

Why was Jesus exalted to the right hand of God? Christ's ascension seems to be a neglected study. Is it of such little importance? Jesus declared his ascension to be expedient. He told us that unless he went to the Father, a most essential experience would never be ours. Without the Lord's ascension, we could never be baptized into the Spirit. Look back upon all that Jesus did. John writes that his works were so many that, if they were all written, the whole world could not contain the books. So what could there be that he did not do when he was on earth? There was one thing, the very thing which John the Baptist said he would do: baptize in fire and in the Holy Spirit! He did not do that when he was on earth. Jesus came from heaven and had to return there, via the cross and the tomb, before the final part of his mission could begin.

Nothing Jesus did on earth could be described as baptizing with the Holy Spirit and with fire. In none of his mighty works, his preaching, his teaching, his healing or in his death and resurrection did he baptize with the Holy Spirit. Jesus did much for his disciples: he gave them authority to carry out healing missions; but he went away without baptizing them into the Holy Spirit. Such a baptism could not have happened until he went to the Father. Indeed, the Lord not only said it, but he emphasized it. He entered glory to take up this brand new office, the office of the Baptizer into the Holy Spirit. This is the reason he ascended to the Father! The Old Testament knows nothing of such a baptism. It is God's "new thing." Jesus brings us many other blessings now, of course. He is our high priest, our advocate, our representative. But he himself did not name these works. He only described the sending forth of the Spirit. After he ascended, not before, the Spirit came and *divided tongues, as of fire, and one sat upon each of them.* Years before, the altars of the Tabernacle of Moses and the Temple of Solomon had been set ablaze by the pure fire from heaven. The flames in the Upper Room of Pentecost came from the same heavenly source. Jesus has all power at his command. He is in the control room; and you are in the palm of his hand.

Today's Scripture
It is to your advantage that I go away; for if I do not go away the Helper will not come to you; but if I depart, I will send him to you. (John 16:7)

Daily Power!
The Holy Spirit is given to me to continue the work that Jesus began.

Mark My Word
John 16:7; 21:25
Acts 2:3

The Bible In A Year

Morning
1 Kings 1
Galatians 5

Evening
Ezekiel 32
Psalm 80

30

Today's Scripture
Let not your heart be troubled; you believe in God, believe also in me.
(John 14:1)

Daily Power!
As God's servants, we can only save one generation. Let us diligently set to work!

Mark My Word
Ezekiel 48:35
John 14:1,3

The Bible In A Year

Morning
1 Kings 2
Galatians 6

Evening
Ezekiel 33
Psalms 81 and 82

Reunited

Christ is coming back to bring heaven and earth together. Jesus said: *"I will come again … that where I am, there you may be also."* It is not wishful thinking taken from a few Scripture verses, not a minor event: but the culmination of all time, and the purpose of Creation itself! God's purposes revolve around this planet. his Son came here, not to some other world. Earth is the battlefield where evil and Satan will be overthrown in the sight of all those whom he has deceived. Our calling is not only heavenly but also earthly. God loves this world. He never said he loved heaven as he loves the world, although he made both heaven and earth. Jesus was born on earth, and became a man who breathed, lived, and died. He was raised again as man, and now appears in glory as the First Man, the Son of Man. To come back to this world as man is what it is all about. Jesus loves people – not just souls – and has a future for this old world, when his presence will be sensed on every square yard. What we sometimes enjoy now will be experienced vividly by all. His coming is his "parousia": that is, his presence. Ezekiel said that in the Temple, the Lord's name is "Shammah" – *"the Lord is there"* – but when Jesus comes again, this will be said of the whole earth.

John's actual Greek says: *"It is the last hour"*, which is God's viewpoint. With the Lord, one day is like a thousand years, and represents his patience as he waits for the world to turn back to him. John and Peter both spoke as if they were in the last days, and they were – just as we are. Now two thousand years have moved along, we can only speak of the last hours. If anybody thinks delay means that it was all a mistake about Jesus coming back, and he or she can just live it up, they are living in a fool's paradise. No generation lives forever. For every generation there is a last hour. As God's servants, we can only save one generation. We do not have the third millennium to save the world. Most people alive today will be gone soon after it begins. *"The last hour"* is an expression for the swift shuttle of mortal existence. Live in each minute, each second, of this last hour, this last day!

When you seek the saved, you produce conferences,
When you seek the lost, you produce crusades.

Evangelism must lead into the local church.
An evangelist brings his nets and
borrows the pastor's boats, and together
they go out and bring in a catch of souls.
Then the evangelist shakes out every fish
into the church, and moves on
to the next potential harvest.

I want one thing, "Hell empty and Heaven full."

Consumed By Fire

Baptism in the Holy Spirit means that everything to do with him and with the gospel should be characterized by fire! It should burn. There should be fire in those who witness and work ; fire in those who preach. Fire in the Truth we preach: *"Is not my word like a fire?"* Fire in the Lord we preach: *"For our God is a consuming fire."* Fire in the Spirit by which we preach: *"..the Holy Spirit and fire"!*

There were two sacrifices on Mount Carmel: one was performed by the priests of Baal, the other by Elijah. The sacrifice to Baal never burned – it was fireless. The sacrifice was there, the sacrificers were intensely earnest: they prayed to Baal all day, and they cut themselves with knives to show how desperate their sincerity was. They put everything they had into it, yet their sacrifice brought no fire. If the devil could have brought up a spark or two from hell to make a blaze, Satan would have: but the altar just stayed cold.

Fire did not fall just because Elijah set up a sacrifice either. It came when **Elijah prayed and believed!** Elijah followed the instructions of Moses to the letter, but no fire resulted purely from his obedience. Faith brought the blaze. God sent the fire on the sacrifice only. There would be no point in sending the fire without the sacrifice. Armchair Christians receive no fire. There is no such thing as an "anointed couch-potato." Sometimes people pray for fire when they are not yielded to God at all, and subsequently do little for him. They give up little time or money, and render no effort. If they had God's fire, what would they do with it? Sit at home and just enjoy it? The fire is not to save us trouble in winning the world – it is to empower us to preach the gospel in spite of trouble. Tap into that fire today!

Today's Scripture

Since we are receiving a kingdom which cannot be shaken, let us have grace by which we may serve God acceptably with reverence and Godly fear. For our God is a consuming fire. (Hebrews 12:28-29)

Daily Power!

Holy Spirit fire is to empower us to preach the gospel.

Mark My Word

1 Kings 18:1-46
Jeremiah 23:29
Matthew 3:11
Acts 2:3
Hebrews 12:29

The Bible In A Year

Morning

1 Kings 3
Ephesians 1

Evening

Ezekiel 34
Psalms 83 and 84

2

Faith Breakthrough

Today's Scripture
And the power of the Lord was present to heal them.
(Luke 5:17)

Daily Power!
When faith breaks through, you glorify God and have power and boldness.

Mark My Word
Luke 5:17-26

The Bible In A Year

Morning
1 Kings 4 and 5
Ephesians 2

Evening
Ezekiel 35
Psalm 85

Four men had a literal breakthrough of faith:

"As [Jesus] was teaching, there were Pharisees and teachers of the Law sitting by, out of every town of Galilee, Judea and Jerusalem. **And the power of the Lord was present to heal them**. Then men brought on a bed a man who was paralyzed, whom they sought to bring in and lay before him. And when they could not find how they might bring him in, because of the crowd, they went up on the housetop and let him down with his bed through the tiling into the midst before Jesus. When he saw **their** faith, he said to him, 'Man, your sins are forgiven you.' And the scribes and the pharisees began to reason. ... He said to the man who was paralyzed, 'I say to you, arise, take up your bed, and go to your house.' Immediately he rose up before them, took up what he had been lying on, and departed to his own house, glorifying God. And they were all amazed, and they glorified God and were filled with fear, saying, 'We have seen strange things today!'" (Emphasis mine).

Christ was in a house crowded with people, believers and unbelievers alike. Many had physical troubles, and *"the power of the Lord was present to heal them";* but none of these religious people were healed. Then four men brought a paralyzed man on a stretcher, and because they could not get through the crowd they went up the outside stairs of the flat-roofed house, pulled apart the coverings and lowered the man down right in front of Jesus. Seeing **their** faith, he restored this man to health. It was a double breakthrough. They (physically) broke through the roof, and they (spiritually) broke through the unbelief of the crowd, which had kept them back from Christ. *"They were all amazed ... and were filled with fear."* Fear is one of Satan's favorite tricks to try to undermine miracles. It is also possible to lose your healing if you allow unbelief to undermine what God has done. But when faith breaks through, it causes **you** to glorify God, it brings a power, a certainty, a boldness that enables **you** to withstand fear and unbelief, and empowers *you* to be a stronger witness than ever before.

Faith Giants

3

Every time somebody is healed, it breaks through the unbelief of the world. It has to, or we will never get near Jesus at all. Believe God! It will please some people, and amaze everybody else. Jesus dealt with people's varying degrees of faith. Some tried to keep theirs hidden, like the sick woman who crept through the crowd to touch the hem of his garment, but did not want others to know. He healed her anyway. Some had "risky" faith, like the four friends who wanted healing for their paralytic friend (whose faith was it anyway, that brought healing to the sick man – that sick man's, or that of his friends?). That miracle caused rejoicing in believers, but fear in the hearts of the unbelievers. Or there was faith based on authority: such as the centurion (probably a pagan) who yet believed that Jesus was more than capable of healing by his word, and who received Jesus' commendation: *I have not found such great faith, not even in Israel!* as well as healing for his servant.

We are surrounded every day by doubters. Godlessness is the order of the day. Newspapers, radio, television, all of them push godlessness down our throats for breakfast, dinner, tea, and supper. If we want faith, we should try a different diet than all this rationalistic chaff. Feed on the Bible, prayer, Christian encouragement, and faith-building reading. Come hopefully, exercising faith (however nervously) and you will get more faith! The believer is destined to be a giant, walking tall, riding high above the spiritual poverty of the world, the representative of a greater order of creation, a strength and a pillar:

> The loss of wealth is much
> The loss of health is more
> The loss of faith is such
> That nothing can restore.

Be one who is known as having **great faith**!

Today's Scripture

Then Jesus answered and said to her, "O woman, great is your faith! Let it be to you as you desire." And her daughter was healed from that very hour.
(Matthew 15:28)

Daily Power!

I intend to be a giant among pygmies, riding high above the spiritual poverty of the world.

Mark My Word

Matthew 8:5-13; 9:19-26; 15:28
Mark 2:1-12

The Bible In A Year

Morning
1 Kings 6
Ephesians 3

Evening
Ezekiel 36
Psalm 86

"Born Again"

When Christ Jesus bridged the gulf between the natural world and the spiritual, one of the possibilities he opened up for us was to be *"born again."* This Greek expression can also be translated *"born from above."* Men and women can be made new – new creatures – by the power of heaven, the kingdom power of God, as the Bible tells us. Obviously, people "born from above" would never be satisfied with a world which was only material. They need spiritual links as well as physical ones. The present world, with its limited scientific laws, is not big enough for a converted Christian anymore than a cage is for an eagle. It needs extending, and that extension goes beyond our three-dimensional world into the fourth dimension of the Spirit. We *"walk in the Spirit,"* and we *"sit together in the heavenly places in Christ Jesus."*

The book of Acts shows the disciples drawing upon new resources as they moved through the world blessing the people with salvation and healing. The first new people in Christ, these new creatures of the kingdom, were sent out to bring others into the same kingdom order with new instincts, new powers and new laws written on their hearts.

After I was baptized in the Spirit and spoke with tongues, it did not take me long to realize that this gift opened up new possibilities. If I spoke with tongues through the Spirit, then there could be other wonders through the Spirit. I have learned to live in the Spirit. I am on new ground where signs and wonders happen. Praise God! If it were not for that, nothing could happen as it does. Vast multitudes come to my meetings. They represent an intimidating accumulation of needs. But I am baptized in the Holy Spirit. I know the powers of the coming age and how to tap those resources. A great conviction grips me that God has something for them. That is not only my secret, but it is also the conviction of hundreds of millions today. If I have any other "secret," it is the message itself. I am confident of its effectiveness. It is *"the power of God to salvation."* You too can be confident in this.

Today's Scripture
Most assuredly I say to you, unless one is born again, he cannot see the kingdom of God (John 3:3)

Daily Power!
There are limitless wonders to be learned and experienced through the Holy Spirit.

Mark My Word
John 3:3
Romans 1:16
Galatians 5:16;
Ephesians 2:6
Hebrew 8:1-13

The Bible In A Year

Morning
1 Kings 7
Ephesians 4

Evening
Ezekiel 37
Psalms 87 and 88

My First Missionary Efforts

As a young missionary in Africa, I sometimes preached to five people. Beyond our mission there were 450 million souls in Africa, most of them ignorant of salvation through Jesus Christ. Yes, they could all be evangelized by the way we were tackling it: but only if they stayed alive for about 5,000 years! However, small audiences did not dismay us. After all, revival could come, and save us a lot of trouble! This hope kept us patient and starry-eyed, for had not our spiritual great-grandfathers banked upon this with unquestioning faith? Later it struck me that **the gospel is not Good News to people who do not hear it. An unpreached gospel is no gospel at all.** Another small ray of illumination penetrated my heart: in the New Testament, we never read about God going forth on his own, but that, *"They went out and preached everywhere, the Lord working with them."* God acted when they acted. So, he was waiting for us and – I could not get away from it; that included me!

I set up a Bible correspondence course, and 50,000 people enrolled. So many! Like a periscope from a submarine, it revealed that I was submerged in an ocean of salvation-hungry humanity. Additionally, a vision followed me: night after night, I saw the entire African continent washed in the blood of Jesus, country after country. We had waited for revival, thoroughly and patiently, through a hundred long years of earnest prayer. Surely God must answer now? Seemingly on a wild impulse (which proved to be of God), I booked a 10,000-seat stadium for a campaign with a church of forty members … and ten thousand people came! The first ripe wheat! For the first time, I witnessed thousands running forward to respond to the call of salvation. God opened my eyes and I actually saw a mighty wave of Holy Spirit power arrive in the stadium, invisible to earthly sight. A mass baptism in the Holy Spirit, accompanied by many healing miracles, took place. I wept like a boy, and vowed to the Lord that in obedience, I would move across all of Africa to bring the vision to pass. I reasoned that if God can do that to 10,000 people, he could do it to 450 million. That is the kind of aggressive evangelistic faith I hope to impart to you today.

Today's Scripture

And they went out and preached everywhere, the Lord working with them, and confirming the Word through the accompanying signs. Amen.
(Mark 16:20)

Daily Power!

The gospel is not Good News to people who do not hear it, and an unpreached gospel is no gospel at all.

Mark My Word

Mark 16:20

The Bible In A Year

Morning
1 Kings 8
Ephesians 5

Evening
Ezekiel 38
Psalm 89

6

Invasion!

Our world has been invaded, and the authority of the kingdom of God has drawn near to us. It is a superior, miracle order that overarches natural or scientific order. Just as higher laws can overrule physical laws, the spiritual can overrule the material. That happens in the baptism of the Holy Spirit, and when his gifts operate.

John's gospel says that all things were made by the Word: that is, by the Son of God, *"All things were made through him, and without him nothing was made that was made."* He who is the source of everything that we see came into his own creation. He *"came down from heaven."* That very important statement means that he became the bridge reaching from the higher, invisible world to the visible. Jesus later portrays himself as a Jacob's ladder set up between heaven and earth. There are two orders, with their own forces or powers. Jesus is the link between them, the heavenly and the earthly order. The power of heaven is the creative power of God, by which the earth was made. Through Christ, the link with heaven, things are possible on earth which were not possible before he came. He is called the *"new and living way."* Through Jesus Christ, by the Holy Spirit, commerce has begun between earth and heaven. The angels of God are coming and going.

Because of Christ in our world, God can exercise his will here, through our prayers. It is a case of God wanting manpower, and our needing God's power, for Jesus taught us to pray, *"Your will be done on earth as it is in heaven."* He has not shut himself out of any part of his universe. He is Lord. He applies greater forces, and the natural laws obey the Spirit of God. We call that a miracle. God is dealing with us in a new way. There is, of course, a grand purpose behind it. The object is not to pull off a few sensational wonders, like stage tricks, but the redemption of the world. You can tap into that power today!

Today's Scripture
In the beginning was the Word, and the Word was with God, and the Word was God. He was in the beginning with God. All things were made through him, and without him nothing was made
that was made.
(John 1:1-3)

Daily Power!
He who is the source of everything, dwells in me by his Spirit.

Mark My Word
Matthew 6:10
John 1:1-3, 14, 51;
3:13,6:38 Hebrews
10:20

The Bible In A Year

Morning
1 Kings 9
Ephesians 6

Evening
Ezekiel 39
Psalm 90

Natural And Spiritual Laws

Every time you move, you bring natural laws under your authority. Left to nature, rocks would not fly, but we human beings introduce a higher law: that of our will. We can throw rocks and make them fly. We are not the slaves of the laws of nature: they are our slaves. We can use scientific laws to leave this planet altogether. We can move into a state of weightlessness or even fly to the moon. Better still, we can move, and act, and minister in the Word of God!

When people say that miracles are contrary to the laws of nature, they completely ignore the fact that where there is a superior will and superior power. With man, as well as omnipotent God, laws of nature can be overridden. The difficulty arises when people do not believe in God. Bring God into it, and nothing is impossible. And that is what has happened. The kingdom of God is among us: therefore, devils are cast out; the sick are healed; and we speak with tongues.

Human beings are both flesh and spirit. God linked us to two worlds, the earthly and the spiritual. By our five senses, we are aware of this world; and by our spirits, we sense the nonphysical world; and, on occasion, fear it. But something has gone wrong. A great calamity has befallen us: sin has almost destroyed the link between body and spirit! After the fall of Adam, only occasional flashes of the supernatural were seen, until Jesus came. Only a breakthrough now and then is recorded in the Old Testament. Sometimes God exercised his sovereignty and initiated a spate of wonders, as he did with Moses and the Elijah-Elisha ministries. God's power and his authority were rarely seen directly.

Then a radical change came about: Christ's marvelous coming – God in the flesh – opened up the resources of creative power. He was, and is, Lord of all things. He announced it himself, saying: *"The kingdom of God is near."* That is the kingdom that you and I live in!

Today's Scripture
When you see these things happening, know that the kingdom of God is near.
(Luke 21:31)

Daily Power!
The God-ordained link between heaven and earth is through his Son, Jesus Christ.

Mark My Word
Mark 1:14
Luke 21:31

The Bible In A Year

Morning
1 Kings 10
Philippians 1

Evening
Ezekiel 40
Psalm 91

8

Today's Scripture
If you abide in me, and my words abide in you, you will ask what you desire, and it shall be done for you. By this my Father is glorified, that you bear much fruit; so you will be my disciples. (John 15:7-8)

Daily Power!
The primary aim of prayer is to bring about the revealed will of God.

Mark My Word
Matthew 6:10
Mark 16:15
Luke 2:45-49
John 15:7
1 John 5:14

The Bible In A Year

Morning
1 Kings 11
Philippians 2

Evening
Ezekiel 41
Psalms 92 and 93

If God has anything to say to the church as a whole, it is what Christ said when he left this world: *"Go into all the world and preach the gospel."* Until that commission is completed, God has no afterthoughts or overriding concerns to get us busy about side issues, such as church structures and organizations.

Even as a young boy, Jesus had a burning in his heart to fulfill his mission on earth as the Messiah. He came to win the lost, even willing to suffer a brutal death for our sakes. But in the years prior to that, he longed to be busy with his Father's work:

> "Now so it was that after three days, they found him in the Temple, sitting in the midst of the teachers, both listening to them and asking them questions. And all who heard him were astonished at his understanding and answers. So when they saw him, they were amazed, and his mother said to him, 'Son, why have you done this to us? Look, your father and I have sought you anxiously.' And he said to them, 'Why did you seek me? Did you not know that I must be about my Father's business?'"

From the beginning, Jesus intended to preach the gospel of the kingdom to the world! He did not get sidetracked, not even once.

God has a revealed will, so, *"If we ask anything according to his will, he hears us."* That is why Christ gave us the petition, *"Your will be done on earth as it is in heaven."* Jesus said again: *"If … my words abide in you, you will ask what you desire, and it shall be done for you."* The primary aim of prayer is not for **our** will to be done, but to bring about the revealed will of God; not to persuade God to our way of thinking, or to force his hand. his expressed will is that God desires all men to come to repentance. Everything in the New Testament spells that out clearly. If we ask according to that will, God hastens to answer. It is expressed in the prayer, *"Your kingdom come, Your will be done on earth as it is in heaven."* It is the gospel that will achieve it. **You** have a part to play in that kingdom today!

Evoking Thoughts Of God

Anointing was like a perfume. Paul quoted David:

> "Your throne, O God, is forever and ever; a Scepter of righteousness is the scepter of Your kingdom. You have loved righteousness and hated lawlessness; therefore God, Your God, has anointed you with the oil of gladness more than your companions"… 'All Your garments are scented with myrrh and aloes and cassia'" (in referring to Christ).

Cassia came from the distant Far East. Israel probably obtained it from passing traders. It provided a distinctive fragrance associated only with the dwelling place of God and its priests – it evoked thoughts of God.

Scripture calls Jesus the Anointed One: *"Simon Peter answered and said, 'you are the Christ (the Anointed One), the Son of the living God.'"* Jesus is as exclusively anointed as he was exclusively the Son of God. "Christ" is from the Greek christos, which translates as the Hebrew "Messiah." Everything denoted by the anointing of the Tabernacle and priests and kings is fulfilled in Jesus. Christ is our priest-king: *"Your garments are scented."* He carried the purity and odor of heaven, that evocative and subtle beauty of spirit which makes him the Anointed One, distinguished from all others. He drew people, not merely by power or "charisma" in the popular sense, but by love, moving in the atmosphere of his own holiness which people had never breathed before. If we can put it this way: Jesus was God's "Alabaster Box," broken for us on the cross; and now filling the world with his fragrance!

We have opportunity to "participate" in Christ's anointing, even as Mary did: *"Then Mary took a pound of very costly oil of spikenard, anointed the feet of Jesus, and wiped his feet with her hair. And the house was filled with the fragrance of the oil."* Our most intimate acts of worship, where we humble ourselves at his feet and give our best to him, causes his anointing to spill over into our lives. We carry the fragrance of Jesus upon us: our "odor" is associated with the dwelling place of God. It is true that Christ-like fragrance extends beyond you into the whole world.

Today's Scripture
And they realized that they had been with Jesus.
(Acts 4:13).

Daily Power!
We carry the fragrance of Jesus upon us.

Mark My Word
Psalm 45:6-8
Matthew 16:16
John 12:3
Acts 4:13
Hebrews 1:8-9

The Bible In A Year

Morning
1 Kings 12
Philippians 3

Evening
Ezekiel 42
Psalm 94

Nobody Is A "Nobody"

Today's Scripture
Brethren, my heart's
desire and prayer to
God for Israel is that
they may be saved.
(Romans 10:1)

Daily Power!
The ultimate aim
of intercession is
evangelism.

Mark My Word
Genesis 37:30
Luke 22:44; 23:34
John 3:16; 8:39-44
1 Timothy 2:1-4

The Bible In A Year

Morning
1 Kings 13
Philippians 4

Evening
Ezekiel 43
Psalms 95 and 96

To God, nobody is a "nobody." Each individual has a value beyond computation. Our prayers should be in direct proportion to the desperate wickedness from which people need saving. The worse the wickedness, the greater the intercession. Nobody should have to go through life without somebody praying for him (or her).

"Therefore I exhort first of all that supplications, prayers, intercessions, and giving of thanks be made for all men, for kings and all who are in authority, that we may lead a quiet and peaceable life in all godliness and reverence. For this is good and acceptable in the sight of God our Savior, who desires all men to be saved and to come to the knowledge of the truth."

So the ultimate aim of intercession is evangelism: *"God so loved the world that he gave his only begotten Son, that whoever believes in him should not perish but have everlasting life.* Intercession is not a say-so, but a heart-cry. Not "Lord, bless me and everybody everywhere, Amen!" Our Lord Jesus prayed for us until he sweat drops of blood! He even prayed for the soldiers hammering nails through his quivering flesh.

Pray for all men, for Christ-lessness is terrible. There is only one Savior, and if he is rejected, what can people do? Their cry is like Reuben's when he found Joseph had gone: *"And I, where shall I go?"* There is nowhere to go. So people just drift along, perhaps together, perhaps alone, unknowingly heading for hell. Christ-less religion is hell on earth! Religious leaders killed Christ. We see it today in terrorism, murder, and oppression in the name of God. Jesus said:

"If you were Abraham's children, you would do the works of Abraham. But now, you seek to kill me … Abraham did not do this … You are of your father, the devil… He was a murderer from the beginning."

Intercession is urgent. Intercession brings divine intervention. We have one generation in which to save a generation – not a century! That is God's challenge to you and to me! Do your part **today**, and you will help pave the way for others who will soon follow.

See And Believe!

Some people seem to know all about the cross. They wear a cross or carry a crucifix. But it is merely a superstition which does nothing for them. Knowing all about a power station can still leave you in the cold and dark. You can touch the very walls of a nuclear power plant, but still be freezing. Yet you can plug in to the power of God because the wiring system is completed by the preaching of the gospel, the truth! When you hear it and believe it, you are tapping into the resources of God, which are inexhaustible. Then you **know** that you are saved.

There were people actually at the foot of the cross while Jesus hung there, who were not saved. The Bible describes some who *"Sitting down, they kept watch over him there."* That is all they did, so they were not saved. Today, thousands of people do the same thing. They are just onlookers, curious perhaps, or even pitying, feeling sorry about Christ's death, but never receiving what he died to give them: an assurance of God's forgiveness and his acceptance of them.

When faith comes, assurance comes. You cannot separate them, and sometimes in Scripture the two words are exactly the same. I want to show you how this can be. We read in Mark 15 *"And those who passed by blasphemed him, wagging their heads and saying… 'Let the Christ, the King of Israel, descend now from the cross, that we may see and believe.'"* They actually saw Jesus dying for them, but they did not believe and were not saved. **See and believe!** Mark had his answer to that. He wrote that one man, a Roman captain, was different. *"So when the centurion, who stood opposite him, saw that he cried out like this and breathed his last, he said, "Truly this man was the Son of God!"*

This soldier had seen the whole thing: and with a more perceiving eye, saw the truth. He did not need to see a miracle, like Christ detaching himself from the nails and walking around, or Elijah coming to release Jesus, as some had hoped. He was seeing the true wonder: the love of God, the greatness of Christ. He saw the glory of God in the face of Jesus Christ. **See and believe!**

Today's Scripture
Truly this man was the Son of God!
(Mark 15:39)

Daily Power!
My faith in Jesus Christ gives a rock-solid assurance of salvation.

Mark My Word
Matthew 27:36
Mark 15:29-39

The Bible In A Year

Morning
1 Kings 14
Colossians 1

Evening
Ezekiel 44
Psalms 97 and 98

12

Today's Scripture
Two are better than one, because they have a good reward for their labor. For if they fall, one will lift up his companion ... Again, if two lie down together, they will keep warm; but how can one be warm alone? Though one may be overpowered by another, two can withstand him, and a threefold cord is not quickly broken. (Ecclesiastes 4:9-12)

Daily Power!
Team work! That will bring about the kingdom of God faster than solo-play.

Mark My Word
Ecclesiastes 4:9-12
Romans 1:11.

The Bible In A Year

Morning
1 Kings 15
Colossians 2

Evening
Ezekiel 45
Psalms 99 to 101

The Ax And The Orchestra

The church is Christ's battle-ax. Every ax has a handle, a head and a cutting edge: a handle for the handler; a head for weight; and a sharp edge to do the work. Whether we make God's work possible by the support jobs that must be done; give weight to the work by our support; or are on the attacking-and-cutting-edge of evangelism; we are **all** vitally needed! I, Reinhard Bonnke, have no churches. But I depend on churches. They give the weight to what I do, and my team looks after the endless matters that must be organized – yet we are one tool in the hand of the Master.

The church is also Christ's orchestra. I never attempt anything alone. A soloist needs accompaniment, perhaps a whole orchestra. All of our work has to be arranged, whether campaigns, literature, TV, films, books, or whatever. There are thousands of back-up players in tune with my aims, with special gifts, abilities, or with their prayers and gifts; and we work with the same purpose. Every melody needs harmonizing, and is enriched by the qualities of other instruments. I never go to any country except when groups of churches ask me to go. We must all work together.

No man seemed stronger in faith than the apostle Paul did. When he heard that Christians had appeared in Rome, he wrote to them: *"For I long to see you, that I may impart to you some spiritual gift, so that you may be established; that is, that I may be encouraged together with you by the mutual faith both of you and me."* – mutual faith. Each of us is like one sheet of paper that cannot stand up on its own edge alone. But a ream of paper is a block of five hundred sheets – all able to stand on edge comfortably together, supporting one another. Every believer needs support. The world will not help. The world is no friend to the friends of Jesus. So wherever you are, whatever you do, remain in fellowship with other believers, and stand up for Jesus.

Evangelists Sought!

There are thousands of evangelists in church jobs to which God never called them. It is time for the body of Christ to boldly reaffirm the office of Evangelist! God's concern today, as at Calvary, is the salvation of souls. And when Jesus Christ ascended into heaven, he established the work of evangelists within the church to help accomplish this great work.

The past holds tragedies. When doors opened, some Christian workers were found jealously guarding their monopoly, as gold miners did their claims. Sometimes rivalries ruined revivals. The harvest must not go unreaped while reapers merely defend their "own" flock. Christ did not die to give people a career, but to save the lost. I do not preach "means and methods," but spiritual principles. God will give you resourcefulness. There are as many methods as he directs. We need more imaginative approaches, rather than people doing things by tried and proved methods. Plodding along mechanically might be called faithfulness, but our primary concern in evangelism is effectiveness, not a twisted type of faithfulness.

During my years as an evangelist and missionary, I have discovered a number of limiting factors hindering the gospel. I know from experience that many of the traditional methods of evangelism have remained unchanged for generations. Others are doctrines which tell us to "leave it all to God." Some insist God's way is revival, but they fail to carry out the Great Commission in the meantime. Some think that if people are to be saved, they will be saved anyway. I know this is not true, and I trust you will come to understand that too.

Today's Scripture
Do you not say, "There are still four months and then comes the harvest"? Behold, I say to you, lift up your eyes and look at the fields, for they are already white for harvest! (John 4:35)

Daily Power!
Christ did not die just to give people a career, but to save the lost.

Mark My Word
Ephesians 4:8-16

The Bible In A Year

Morning
1 Kings 16
Colossians 3

Evening
Ezekiel 46
Psalm 102

14

Singleness Of Heart

Today's Scripture
Therefore God also has highly exalted him and given him the name which is above every name, that at the name of Jesus every knee should bow, of those in heaven, and of those on earth, and of those under the earth, and that every tongue should confess that Jesus Christ is Lord, to the glory of God the Father.
(Philippians 2:9-11)

Daily Power!
We dare not neglect the task of evangelism.

Mark My Word
Philippians 2:9-11; 2 Timothy 4:5.

The Bible In A Year

Morning
1 Kings 17
Colossians 4

Evening
Ezekiel 47
Psalm 103

We dare not neglect the task of evangelism. I would rather use a method despised by man but approved by God, than a method approved by man which gets no results. I make no apology for this: I desire to share God's anointing on all those who are ready to step out in faith. My perspective runs hot; very hot. Its flames can scorch. Some who read these pages would do well to take out fire insurance, for I guarantee many old concepts will be set to the torch!

My message comes from a singleness of heart. I hammer away at the Great Commission, for I know it cannot be overemphasized. I cry to God day and night for greater effectiveness in winning our generation for him. **Evangelism by Fire** is the only feasible solution. I look for other anointed men and women who may take up this challenge of the Word of God for Holy Spirit evangelism. I believe the best is yet to be. The time is coming soon when the whole world will resound with the praises of our God and Savior. In all nations and in every language, the day is almost here when every tongue will confess that *"Jesus Christ is Lord, to the glory of God the Father."*

God has taught me many things, has allowed me to experience much over the years. I am sharing this with you today for one reason alone: to inspire *you* to *"Do the work of an evangelist."* I have laid out the principles necessary for any Holy Spirit ministry. Read this – not to discover how **I** operate in my evangelistic crusades – but to discover how God operates through **anyone** willing to follow his plan; and that means you.

A Gospel That Is Not

The gospel has sometimes been reinterpreted in ways that take the heart out of it, and out of us. Liberal and rationalistic thought is based on the shifting sands of biblical criticism, and philosophy. No assured grounds for the frightened millions have ever been offered by this new thought. It is a theology of chaff for those hungry for God. Too many scholars have made truth depend on questions that can never have any certain answers, doing nothing for lost nations and devil-stricken masses. If God is the only Savior, he cannot save by a message of "perhaps" or "if" or "it is my opinion." The world needs people with a live link to heaven!

For all people, cultured or primitive, there is one word of truth – the cross – to the wise, the barbarian, the Greek, the Jew. The gospel is the power of God. The gospel preacher is an ambassador demanding surrender to the kingdom of heaven. It is God's ultimatum. He shows us the way things are. The gospel is neither a theory nor an abstraction, but the reality behind everything. We either recognize it, or perish.

When you grasp what I am saying here, then you join the army with the battering ram of the Word and of the cross. It will pulverize the strongholds of the devil. It is the thundering drum roll of God's invincible army on the march. When God filled me with his Spirit and opened my lips to speak with tongues, he opened my ears to hear the triumphant blast of the trumpet announcing that Jesus has all power in heaven and on earth. What a gift! Be certain that the gospel you follow is one of life and power.

Today's Scripture
For this reason the gospel was preached also to those who are dead, that they might be judged according to men in the flesh, but live according to God in the spirit.
(1 Peter 4:6)

Daily Power!
The gospel of Christ, is the power of God to salvation for everyone who believes.

Mark My Word
Romans 1:16
1 Peter 4:6

The Bible In A Year

Morning
1 Kings 18
1 Thessalonians 1

Evening
Ezekiel 48
Psalm 104

16

Marching Orders

Both David and Isaiah prayed, *"Bow down your heavens, O Lord, and come down."* It happened when Jesus came. Therefore, New Testament believers need never pray it again. Christ tore the heavens and came down to us. He then returned through the heavens, ensuring that they remain open. The rent heavens have been opened forever, and have never been sewn up again. Through that open heaven, the Holy Spirit then began to descend: the *"latter rain."* Hell cannot impose sanctions and blockade the kingdom of God, nor deprive its citizens. The new and living way is established beyond enemy control.

In his book, "Joy Unspeakable", the great teacher D. Martyn Lloyd-Jones concluded that revival is the baptism in the Holy Spirit. He laid down firm proof that there is a Scriptural reception of power after conversion, that it is the baptism with the Spirit, and that it is revival. Since 1901, when that truth was recovered, the restoration of Bible signs and wonders has brought hundreds of millions into the kingdom of God.

No New Testament Christian confined himself to religious meditation. Mystics usually ended up with erroneous teachings. The apostles were activists. Smith Wigglesworth was right: "The Acts of the Apostles were written because the apostles acted." They did not visit shrines or keep the relics of holy men. They were in vital contact with God themselves through the Spirit. They went directly to him, not through saints and their bones.

The entire Christian life is *"in the Spirit."* By the Spirit, the Son of God was the Anointed One. This set the pattern. Just as he went about doing good because he was anointed with the Spirit, so must you. Like Jesus, you and I are told to walk in the Spirit, pray in the Spirit, love in the Spirit, live in the Spirit, be filled with the Spirit, sing in the Spirit, and have the fruit of the Spirit.

Today's Scripture

I will pray with the Spirit, and I will also pray with the understanding. I will sing with the Spirit, and I will also sing with the understanding.
(1 Corinthians 14:15)

Daily Power!

My life in the Spirit is filled with his fruit – love, joy, peace.

Mark My Word

Psalm 144:5
Isaiah 64:1

The Bible In A Year

Morning
1 Kings 19
1 Thessalonians 2

Evening
Daniel 1
Psalm 105

The Authority Of Christ

God spoke, and heaven and earth materialized: *"He spoke, and it was done. He commanded, and it stood fast."* Then John's gospel makes the tremendous assertion that *"the Word became flesh."* The same Voice that created all things now spoke to us. What he said comes with absolute authority. It is the Word of the Lord.

When Christ spoke, he said that heaven and earth would pass away, but not his words. He was not like the prophets: they spoke **for** the Lord, but Christ spoke **as** the Lord. The prophets said: *"Thus says the Lord,"* but Christ said: *"Most assuredly, I say to you."* The Jews listened to Moses, but Jesus went beyond Moses: *"Moses said … but I say."* There was something else different. The prophets were sent **with** a message, but Jesus **is** the message. The prophets spoke **about** the Lord, but Jesus spoke about **himself**. He not only brought the Word of God, but he **is** the Word of God. He did not point to the way: he **is** the way. Jesus was not one of the roads that led to God: he was where the road led!

That is why we have no right to doubt the Word of God. If we do so, *"Lord, to whom else shall we go? You have the words of eternal life"*, as the apostle Peter recognized. We either obey or die. Using our technology language, we blow the fuse and suffer a lifelong power failure. The heating fails, the lights go out, communications cease, and cold eternal night settles in. Liberal teachers scorn people like us. They say we have an authoritarian religion. But do they teach without any authority? All learning is based on authority, either divine or human. Some trust in the authority of scholarship, but nothing is less trustworthy. Their arguments are steps in sand. Scholars never agree with one another. Remember: the Word of God has been a light to a hundred generations, and that lamp has never flickered.

Today's Scripture
By the Word of the Lord the heavens were made, and all the host of them by the breath of his mouth … Let all the earth fear the Lord; let all the inhabitants of the world stand in awe of him. For he spoke, and it was done; he commanded, and it stood fast.
(Psalm 33:6-9)

Daily Power!
Gladly I place myself under the authority of Jesus Christ, the Son of God.

Mark My Word
Psalm 33:9
Matthew 19:8-9; 24:35
John 1:14; 6:68

The Bible In A Year

Morning
1 Kings 20
1 Thessalonians 3

Evening
Daniel 2
Psalm 106

18

Today's Scripture
Jesus said to him, "I am the way, the truth, and the life.
(John 14:6)

Daily Power!
I am baptized with the Holy Spirit and fire.

Mark My Word
Isaiah 4:5
John 5:35; 14:6
Acts 7:38

The Bible In A Year

Morning
1 Kings 21
1 Thessalonians 4

Evening
Daniel 3
Psalm 107

Fire Comes By Faith

It is Holy Spirit fire that matters. Laying out and setting up a sacrifice is not enough. God will not save souls and heal the sick until we lay our all on the altar for him: that is true. But our sacrifice is not why he does it: he performs his wonders of salvation and healing because of his mercy and grace. Elijah's godliness did not generate the awesome lightning that burned up everything on the altar. The fire did not come from his holiness. Your tithes and offerings cannot buy a tiny candle flame of the celestial flame. The fire of God comes – not because of our sacrifice – but because of Christ's sacrifice. Therefore, thank God, the fire is for all! Revival fire is not a reward for good people. It is God's gift. Why struggle for it? People talk about "paying the price" but fire comes in response to faith.

We can insist on the "body of truth," but it may be a cold corpse. Jesus did not merely say: "I am the way and the truth" – he said: *"I am the way, the truth and the life."* God said he would put in Zion *"the shining of a flaming fire."* Jesus testified that John the Baptist was *"the burning and shining lamp."* These are images of light and heat. The gospel is a hot gospel, no matter how much the silly world smiles at it. I do not know how to preach the *"living oracles"* of God without being lively. The gospel is a fire. To preach the gospel coolly and casually would be ridiculous.

One day a lady told me that there was a demon sitting on her, although she was a born-again Christian. I said to her: "Flies can only sit on a cold stove, and they can sit very long on a cold stove! Get the fire of the Holy Spirit into your life, and that dirty demon will not dare to touch you, lest he burn his filthy fingers." The gospel provides its own fiery power. It is natural, therefore, for a preacher to be fired-up. And it should be natural for you to walk in that fire too!

Biblical Anointing

"Anointing" is sometimes taken as one of the latest things for those seeking a higher stratum of spirituality, but it is not new. In the Old Testament, all who served God had to be anointed. In the New Testament, this was replaced by the baptism of the Holy Spirit for all believers. There was actually an Old Testament practice of oiling the head of sheep for their protection: but the anointing of the Spirit, or the baptism with the Spirit, is much more than a protective measure. It refers to the anointing of the Spirit, or the baptism with the Spirit.

In the house of Simon the Pharisee, Jesus used similar language to that in Psalm 23, saying, *"You did not anoint my head with oil."* It was the social welcome for guests to anoint them with fragrant oils and greet them with the double kiss on the cheeks, as is still the practice in the East. Jesus compared Simon with an unknown woman, who had poured perfumed oil upon his feet and continued kissing his feet, while Simon had done nothing. Simon had been too casual, showing Jesus no such respect. The social anointing of guests was meant to impart a pleasant smell to the guests and to help their appearance by making their faces shine, which was considered admirable in those days. Jesus accepted the anointing from this woman who lavished upon him the best ointment that money could buy.

Mary Magdalene also anointed Jesus. Her ointment was spikenard, a very rare and precious preparation of nard brought from northern India at great expense and prepared with the secret art of the perfumer. Sold in long, slender alabaster containers, it kept for years, and would even improve in quality and value. When filled with ointment, they were kept as an investment, a household treasure. The fragrance of Mary's oil was so rich we are told it pervaded the whole house. It was a tremendous sacrifice, an act of love's bountiful extravagance. It speaks of the love of God through Jesus Christ, which brings us the priceless gift of the anointing of the Holy Spirit. It is no cheap experience. It is God's best. Holy Spirit anointing is God's gift for you!

Today's Scripture
The earth is satisfied with the fruit of your works... Wine that makes glad the heart of man, oil to make his face shine, and bread which strengthens man's heart.
(Psalm 104:13-15)

Daily Power!
The anointing of the Holy Spirit is God's gift for me.

Mark My Word
Psalm 23:5; 104:15
Luke 7:36-50

The Bible In A Year

Morning
1 Kings 22
1 Thessalonians 5

Evening
Daniel 4
Psalms 108 and 109

True Anointing

Today's Scripture
It shall come to pass
in that day that his
burden will be taken
away from your
shoulder, and his
yoke from your neck,
and the yoke will be
destroyed because of
the anointing oil.
(Isaiah 10:27)

Daily Power!
I am anointed by
the Holy Spirit.

Mark My Word
Exodus 30:1-38
Esther 2:12
Song of Solomon 3:6
Matthew 1:17

The Bible In A Year

Morning
2 Kings 1
2 Thessalonians 1

Evening
Daniel 5
Psalms 110 and 111

The most common ingredient of cosmetic ointment was myrrh, which was refined from a perfumed, resinous substance from the small commiphora myrrha nees tree. The girl loved by Solomon had fingers dripping with sweet-smelling myrrh. Solomon himself came from the dusty wilderness, *"perfumed with myrrh and frankincense."* Part of Esther's beauty treatment for presentation to King Xerxes was six months with oil of myrrh. Value was shown when the Magi brought myrrh to the baby Jesus as a special gift. Taken medically, myrrh was used as an opiate. Jesus refused it on the cross.

The special anointing oil described in Exodus 30 was used only for the Lord's tabernacle and priests, to ordain them for service. Kings were also anointed. Most commentaries also say prophets were anointed. But from what I can see in Scripture, not one of them ever was. They were independent men of God, not socially appointed. God chose and gave them the real anointing with the Spirit. Nobody made prophets: they were God's men. By divine command, Elijah should have anointed Elisha, but failed to do so. God himself anointed Elisha with the Spirit.

It was the habit to call the Spirit of God by the name of a prophet - *"the spirit of Moses"* or *"the spirit of Elijah"* – as a personal and rare distinction. The spirit of Moses was to be put upon the elders of Israel, and Elisha wanted a double portion of the spirit of Elijah. When God anoints believers today, it is with *"the spirit of the prophets."* The true anointing is always by the Lord. Oils, unguents, and ointments were poured upon priests and kings as mere symbols that God's Spirit had chosen to rest upon them. God was the originator, and such men were therefore called *"the anointed of the Lord"* – especially Christ (from "Messiah" or "anointed"), who is *"the Anointed of God."* Today among believers, the anointing is a sovereign act of God, which he desires to lavish upon you.

How Big Is Hell?

The angel who appeared to Cornelius in Acts chapter 10 was not allowed to mention the name of Jesus, or to speak about salvation to the man. That high and holy privilege was – and is – reserved for men: people like you and I. All the angel was allowed to say was: *"Now send men to Joppa, and send for Simon whose surname is Peter."* This mighty seraphim from heaven had to bow to Peter's higher privilege. It has always pleased God to call and to send people like us. God used four evangelists: Matthew, Mark, Luke, and John to write down the story of the gospel of Jesus Christ. Such a pattern is linked, in my mind, to the four men in Old Testament times who carried the Ark of the Covenant. Carriers of the gospel change from generation to generation: but the gospel remains the same. Now we are here … and today it is our turn! God has called you and me. The gospel needs to be taken to the ends of the earth. This is the Great Commission of the Lord to us; and the King's business requires haste.

I do not believe that God's plans call for hell to be bigger than heaven. Although Scripture speaks about *"many"* who are on their way to destruction, these same people must be intercepted – by men and women preaching the original gospel. Provision has been made to bring *"many sons to glory."* Praise God! The Book of Revelation speaks of a successful conclusion! Jesus commanded: *"Go … and make disciples of all the nations."* There is no alternate plan in case the gospel fails because it will not! More people are being saved, healed, and baptized into the Holy Spirit today than ever before in man's history. The tempo is increasing, leading to but one conclusion: **Jesus is coming soon!** That is your greatest hope.

Today's Scripture
But in every nation, whoever fears him, and works righteousness, is accepted by him.
(Acts 10:35)

Daily Power!
I am called, commanded and commissioned.

Mark My Word
Matthew 7:13; 28:19
Acts 10:1-48
Hebrews 2:10
Revelation 7:9

The Bible In A Year

Morning
2 Kings 2
2 Thessalonians 2

Evening
Daniel 6
Psalms 112 and 113

22

Dummy Ammunition

Today's Scripture
For whoever desires
to save his life will
lose it; but whoever
loses his life for
my sake will find it.
(Matthew 16:25)

Daily Power!
Your word is a lamp
to my feet, and a light
to my path.

Mark My Word
Leviticus 10:1-2
1 Kings 18:24
Psalm 119:105
Isaiah 55:8-9
Matthew 16:23

The Bible In A Year

Morning
2 Kings 3
2 Thessalonians 3

Evening
Daniel 7
Psalms 114 and 115

Fire is the ensign of the gospel, the sign of the Son of Man. When we see fire, that is evidence that Jesus, and nobody else, is at work. It is the identifying hallmark of his activity, the true outburst of Christian faith. Elijah made the same point: *"The God who answers by fire, he is God!"* What does your spiritual thermometer read? Does it even register? There are theologies and teachings as fire-proof as asbestos, religious books that provide heat only if put in a bonfire. Such faith-chilling items have nothing to do with the Christ of Pentecost. Whatever he touches catches fire. Church efforts to whip up enthusiasm are, spiritually, as pitiful as rubbing two sticks together.

Only the fire of God was allowed on the altar of Moses, not fire produced by human means. Nadab and Abihu made fire themselves and lit their incense with it. It was labeled *"profane fire":* then divine fire gushed from the tabernacle, swallowing up the false fire, and bringing death to the rebel priests. Today, we have profane fire being offered: strange gospels which are not a gospel at all, but theologies of unbelief, the thoughts of men and their philosophies, criticisms and theories. They bear no trace of the glory-heat from heaven. Nothing in them produces any combustion except controversy. What lies behind all this is what Jesus said: *"Get behind me, Satan! You are an offense to me, for you are not mindful of the things of God, but the things of men."*

There are the thoughts of God and those of man. Satan thinks as men think. The fact is that Satan simply cannot grasp God's outlook. That is strange when you remember that he was originally Lucifer, a throne angel of God. Jesus bruised the serpent's head, and I think he inflicted some kind of brain damage upon the devil! Once Satan was full of wisdom. But today that *"prince of the power of the air"* is baffled by what God is doing, and especially by what the Lord did at the cross! This type of confusion is brought on by sin. You have been "enlightened" by the entrance of the pure Word of God.

"Crazy Joy"

The disciples were crazy with joy when they cast out devils, but Jesus said that was nothing:

> "Then the seventy returned with joy, saying, 'Lord, even the demons are subject to us in Your name.' And he said to them, 'I saw Satan fall like lightning from heaven. Behold, I give you the authority to trample on serpents and scorpions, and over all the power of the enemy, and nothing shall by any means hurt you. Nevertheless do not rejoice in this, that the spirits are subject to you, but rather rejoice because your names are written in heaven.' In that hour Jesus rejoiced in the Spirit and said, 'I thank you, Father, Lord of heaven and earth, that you have hidden these things from the wise and prudent and revealed them to babes. Even so, Father, for so it seemed good in your sight. All things have been delivered to me by my Father, and no one knows who the Son is except the Father, and who the Father is except the Son, and the one to whom the Son wills to reveal him.' Then he turned to his disciples and said privately, 'Blessed are the eyes which see the things you see; for I tell you that many prophets and kings have desired to see what you see and have not seen it, and to hear what you hear and have not heard it.'"

We are so privileged to see and hear what the Lord Jesus Christ does today!

Peter heard Christ say those words, and he took in that lesson; later he wrote this about believers: *"Whom having not seen you love. Though now you do not see him, yet believing, you rejoice with joy inexpressible and full of glory, receiving the end of your faith – the salvation of your souls."* Rejoice in undertones? Worship in whispers? That is not what the word "rejoice" means in this Scripture. It means "to exult, shout, be rapturous" – **Crazy Joy**! Try doing that without emotion, without fire! The fire of the Holy Spirit is real. It must flow through the church of Jesus Christ like blood through the veins. God's people on fire, and the church as a whole on fire, will win our lost generation for him. Let your inhibitions go: let the fire of God run through you!

Today's Scripture
That the genuineness of your faith, being much more precious than gold that perishes, though it is tested by fire, may be found to praise, honor and glory at the revelation of Jesus Christ.
(1 Peter 1:7)

Daily Power!
The fire of the Holy Spirit must flow through the church like blood through the veins.

Mark My Word
Luke 10:17-24
1 Peter 1:7-9

The Bible In A Year

Morning
2 Kings 4
1 Timothy 1

Evening
Daniel 8
Psalm 116

24

Today's Scripture
Jesus Christ, the faithful witness, the firstborn from the dead, and the ruler over the kings of the earth.
(Revelation 1:5)

Daily Power!
Speaking the truth was a key attribute of Jesus Christ – he is trustworthy.

Mark My Word
John 8:13-14; 18; 14: 1 Revelation 1:1-29

The Bible In A Year

Morning
2 Kings 5
1 Timothy 2

Evening
Daniel 9
Psalms 117 and 118

One man entrusted with the message of a past, present, and future faith was John the apostle. When he was up against the whole Roman Empire, he wrote a marvelous and triumphant book. He wrote: *"I, John, both your brother and companion in the tribulation and kingdom and patience of Jesus Christ, was on the island that is called Patmos for the Word of God and for the testimony of Jesus Christ."* John was close to Jesus. It was a unique friendship. He also suffered for Christ. John was the man who saw what things meant. He read the signs with prophetic insight. What he saw was difficult to explain. It was new on earth. Nobody had thought of it, especially in one sentence. So let us look at what he said: *"Grace to you and peace from he who is and who was and who is to come, and from the seven Spirits who are before his throne, and from Jesus Christ, the faithful witness, the firstborn from the dead, and the ruler over the kings of the earth."*

How can Jesus be a "faithful witness"? We are witnesses to Christ, but to what does Christ witness? This scripture refers to another passage, where the Pharisees were arguing: *"You bear witness of Yourself; Your witness is not true."* Jesus answered and said to them, *"Even if I bear witness of myself, My witness is true, for I know where I came from and where I am going; … I am One who bears witness of myself, and the Father who sent me bears witness of me."* Jesus witnessed to himself. He said: *"Believe in God; believe also in me."* By his life and mighty deeds, he has shown us what he is: faithful to what he told us he is.

He does not disappoint us. If he were different now, he would not be a faithful witness. He is consistent with what he said and did. The life of Jesus spells hope for sinners and the sick, and concern for everybody. He writes, "Yours faithfully, Jesus Christ." Our Lord Jesus is always faithful to you and to me, praise his name!

Read Carefully

"On the last day, that great day of the feast, Jesus stood and cried out, saying, "If anyone thirsts, let him come to me and drink. He who believes in me, as the Scripture has said, out of his heart will flow rivers of living water."

That is, rivers of living water will flow from anyone who *"believes in me as the scripture has said."* It is not living waters that Jesus says the Scripture talks about – but himself and those who believe on him. People have not found which Scripture Jesus had in mind when he spoke of waters, although we have suggested Isaiah 58:11. The promise of living water originates with Jesus himself, and as Peter preached, *"The promise is to you and to your children, and to all who are afar off, as many as the Lord our God will call."*

It is important to look at John 3:34 again. *"For he whom God has sent speaks the words of God, for God does not give the Spirit by measure."* God gives his Spirit to us all, as John 1:16 tells us *"Of his fullness we have all received."* Literally we are filled without measure.

Fullness lies in Christ Jesus and flows out of him to fill us. He is the Source. So long as Christ is full, we shall "be being filled." He is *"full of grace and truth,"* and out of him we receive *"grace for grace"* or grace constantly being renewed.

Today's Scripture
To know the love of Christ which passes knowledge, that you may be filled with all the fullness of God. (Ephesians 3:19)

Daily Power!
Because I believe rivers of living waters will flow out of my heart.

Mark My Word
Isaiah 58:11
John 1:14-16;
3:34; 7:37-38
Acts 2:39

The Bible In A Year

Morning
2 Kings 6
1 Timothy 3

Evening
Daniel 10
Psalm 119:1-24

26

True Faith

We pray for Christian revival – why? To see the church full, pay the bills, ease the labors of evangelism, as a religious duty? Look at the pitiful attempts of Christ-less people to save themselves, making their own impotent gods. Let us weep for them. Let us cry out to God:

> "Gird yourselves and lament, you priests; wail, you who minister before the altar; come, lie all night in sackcloth, you who minister to my God. For the grain offering and the drink offering are withheld from the House of your God. Consecrate a fast, call a sacred assembly. Gather the elders and all the inhabitants of the land into the House of the Lord your God, and cry out to the Lord … 'Now, therefore,' says the Lord, 'turn to me with all your heart, with fasting, with weeping, and with mourning.' So rend your heart, and not your garments; return to the Lord your God. For he is gracious and merciful, slow to anger, and of great kindness; and he relents from doing harm."

God is moved when our hearts – not just our mouths – are moved.

A true intercessor has faith. All the great prayers of intercession in Scripture were triggered heavenward from the launch-pad of faith. Faith is assurance of the changeless character of God's goodness, believing he is faithful to what he says he is. If prayer is controversial, then everything is. If all answers to prayer were printed, they would fill the Atlantic depths.

Faith is faith in God, not just in some miracle happening. The great intercessors in the Bible did not always see what they asked for. God heard Abraham, but in the end, the cities of Sodom and Gomorrah were destroyed. Pray on: and leave matters in God's hands to do whatever he knows is good.

The Real Anointing

27

Disciples and apostles were never anointed with oil. In the New Testament, Christians received the Spirit for their work of service. Oil was never poured upon Jesus: except by a woman for his burial, as he said. Before the day of Pentecost, priests were anointed and carried the fragrance with them. But since the day of Pentecost, believers have carried the aura of Jesus: *"They realized that they had been with Jesus."* The real anointing had come!

Anointing with oil was retained only for the healing of the sick in the New Testament. Our anointing flows out of Christ's anointing, and we receive it only from him: *"Of his fullness we have all received."* To John the Baptist, it was revealed that *"Upon whom you see the Spirit descending, and remaining on him, this is he who baptizes with the Holy Spirit.'* He identified the source: Jesus Christ, the giver and the authority of the giving.

> "God anointed Jesus of Nazareth with the Holy Spirit and with power, who went about doing good and healing all who were oppressed by the devil, for God was with him."

We may pray and lay hands on people to be baptized in the Spirit, as the apostles did: but we must realize that a man cannot and need not give his anointing to someone else. It is out of Christ's fullness, not somebody else's fullness. I want my own anointing from God, not a second-hand anointing. To bestow an anointing, even as a temporary effect, is foreign to biblical thought. God alone is the Baptizer. The blessings of God may flow in many ways through our lives as rivers of living water from Christ, but that is very different from doing what only Jesus can do: impart the Spirit. The virgins refused to share their oil and were counted wise. Value the anointing that God gives you; treasure it and allow it to empower you to be a blessing to others.

Today's Scripture
God anointed Jesus of Nazareth with the Holy Spirit and with power, who went about doing good and healing all who were oppressed by the devil, for God was with him.
(Acts 10:38)

Daily Power!
I want my own anointing from God, not a secondhand anointing.

Mark My Word
Matthew 25:7-10
John 1:16, 33
Acts 4:13; 8:17; 10:38
James 5:14

The Bible In A Year

Morning
2 Kings 8
1 Timothy 5

Evening
Daniel 12
Psalm 119:49-72

28

Today's Scripture
"Do not touch my anointed ones, and do my prophets no harm."
(Psalm 105:15)

Daily Power!
The anointing which I have received from him abides in me.

Mark My Word
1 Samuel 16:1-13
Psalm 105:15
1 John 2:27

The Bible In A Year

Morning
2 Kings 9
1 Timothy 6

Evening
Hosea 1
Psalm 119:73-96

"Anointing" has acquired a broader meaning among believers today, signifying a general blessing. When people offer to bring anointing by laying their hands upon us, we need not object. Scripturally, there is no such thing as "an anointing" – only "**the** anointing." But we need not be pedantic about the use of a word: providing, of course, that it does not convey bad theology; or that the exclusive sense of giving the Holy Spirit is not intended; but only a prayer for help, strength or any other need.

Once, by divine leading, I found myself far from where I should have been, staring at a house in Clapham, London. A board outside referred to George Jeffreys, whom many consider to have been the greatest British revivalist since John Wesley. He filled the greatest halls, pioneered in the face of universal opposition, and proclaimed the glorious message of Jesus Christ, Savior, healer, Baptizer, and coming King. I could hardly believe it; I had just read one of this great man's books! Was he really there? I dared to go and ask; he heard my voice and invited me in. There he prayed with me, and it was as if his mantle had come upon me (to use a scriptural expression). God heard that man's prayer for me. I was already baptized in the Spirit – anointed – but sometimes we lack language to describe all that God does. I know that making contact with George Jeffreys and hearing his prayer for me had been a special experience, which brought me a sense of equipping and readiness for service. Earlier that day, I had left the Bible college at Swansea to begin my full-time service for God. God had already called me to his work: and now this special experience seemed to cover me.

David was anointed by Samuel as king, which David took to mean that he was *"the Lord's anointed."* Later, the elders of Israel also anointed him as their assurance of his call to them as king. Anointings are not to be expected every time we meet a special evangelist or teacher. For me it was only once, after my call, when I met a man who had done the same work as God wanted me to do. It was like Elisha following Elijah. Seek God's anointing for your own life!

Satan's Chess Game

Satan thinks as men think – this means men think as the devil thinks. They too find the cross foolishness, and cannot grasp the things of God, as the apostle Paul remarked. Paul also could not see it at first. Cold fury against the believers ate away in his heart. He was a "dragon man," breathing out threats and slaughter. Full of zeal, his brain was full of clever unbelief. Scales fell from his eyes when he believed.

I wonder if hell would like to send espionage agents into the kingdom of God, just to see what secrets are there? The demons would not understand these secrets anyway. Hell is completely baffled. To Satan, Christ's sacrifice is a deep-rooted plot devised by God for his own advantage. The devil devours people: that is his evil nature. If we would fight the devil on the level of human thought, we must remember that he thinks as men think. Satan invented a human chess game, and has played this game for thousands of years. The devil anticipates our every move, and he will checkmate us ten moves ahead. Satan has experience from the time of Adam onward, and he knows every trick of human ingenuity on the board. You cannot produce faith by the wisdom of words. The devil always has a counter-statement for whatever you say.

The gospel did not come out of somebody's head. We have to move into the divine dimension, where the enemy cannot follow us. The devil is no match for the mind of the Holy Spirit. If we plan, preach, witness and evangelize as men, Satan will foil us. He can handle psychology and propaganda. The answer is: move in the Spirit and preach the gospel as it is. Then the arch-confuser becomes confused, and he cannot follow the game at all. It is so good to know that you are on God's team.

Today's Scripture
Be sober, be vigilant; because your adversary the devil walks about like a roaring lion, seeking whom he may devour. (1 Peter 5:8)

Daily Power!
The devil is no match for the mind of the Holy Spirit.

Mark My Word
1 Peter 5:8

The Bible In A Year

Morning
2 Kings 10
2 Timothy 1

Evening
Hosea 2
Psalm 119:97-120

30

God's Fire In Jesus

Today's Scripture
Have you never read,
"Out of the mouths
of babes and nursing
infants you have
perfected praise"?
(Matthew 21:16)

Daily Power!
God's fire ignites
human passion.

Mark My Word
Psalm 69:9
Matthew 20:17; 21:
1-17
Mark 10:32

The Bible In A Year

Morning
2 Kings 11 and 12
2 Timothy 2

Evening
Hosea 3 and 4
Psalm 119:121-144

In human experience, God's fire translates into passion: the type of passion that we saw in Jesus. Perhaps he was not only passionate in his words. When Jesus was going to Jerusalem for the last time, we read that he was walking ahead of his disciples, and they saw how he urged himself onward: *"Now they were on the road, going up to Jerusalem, and Jesus was going before them; and they were amazed. And as they followed, they were afraid."* Why? Somehow the fires in his soul were evident in the way he walked.

When they arrived, Jesus saw the desecration of the Temple. The disciples then had further evidence of his passionate feeling: his reaction turned him into an awesome figure! The disciples were reminded of the Psalm: *"Because zeal for your house has eaten me up."* But it was a love-anger, not a cold fury. Jesus was not a frenzied fanatic: he loved his Father's house, that is all. It was his desire to see people in the Temple, worshiping with freedom and happiness. But commercialism in the Temple had spoiled all that, and his heart overflowed like a volcano; the fire in his soul made him cleanse the Temple. his actions were frightening, and many fled from the scene because of them.

The children, the blind, and the lame stayed, however, and he healed them. That was what he had wanted to do anyway, and that was the reason his anger achieved furnace heat. his indignation aimed for joy. Jesus got the children singing, *"Hosanna!"* This was the only occasion in scripture where excitement about God was rebuked; the only time a hush was demanded in the courts of the Lord. The silence was demanded by the Pharisees; the praise of the Lord was drowning the tinkling of their commercial tills. "Money music" was muted! This was all part of the picture of the fire of the Lord. Purpose to have that fire alive in your heart today.

Parakletos

Before Christ, nobody had been "baptized in the Spirit." This term means something different from the "attachment of the Spirit" to Old Testament men and women. Samuel took the horn of oil and anointed David, and the Spirit of the Lord *came upon David from that day forward.*" But such experiences are never described as a baptism, for the Holy Spirit's relationship with blood-washed, born-again believers is new. *"The Spirit of truth … dwells with you and will be in you."* That is why a new expression is used; it describes a new kind of experience. To deny Christians the right to use the phrase "baptized in the Spirit" leaves them limited to the same kind of experience as in the Old Testament dispensation.

The Old Covenant people knew nothing of speaking with tongues, casting out demons, or healing by the laying on of hands. These signs were reserved for the age of the Spirit. A new kingdom, a new covenant with new features, a new gospel for spirit and body describe the Christian age. Jesus used a new word for the Holy Spirit – "parakletos". It is used four times in John's gospel, and is translated "Helper."

> "And I will pray the Father, and he will give you another **Helper**, that he may abide with you forever the Spirit of truth, whom the world cannot receive, because it neither sees him nor knows him; but you know him, for he dwells with you and will be in you."

> "But the **Helper**, the Holy Spirit, whom the Father will send in my name, he will teach you all things, and bring to your remembrance all things that I said to you."

> "My little children, these things I write to you, so that you may not sin. And if anyone sins, we have an advocate (**Helper**) with the Father, Jesus Christ the righteous."

> The Helper is here today to help you!

Today's Scripture

And I will pray the Father, and he will give you another Helper, that he may abide with you forever. (John 14:16)

Daily Power!

"The baptism in the Holy Spirit" describes the New Testament experience.

Mark My Word

1 Samuel 16:13
Mark 16:17
Luke 11:13
John 14:16-18, 26; 15:26; 16:17
Acts 1:4-5
Romans 8:14
James 1:27
1 John 2:1

The Bible In A Year

Morning

2 Kings 13
2 Timothy 3

Evening

Hosea 5 and 6
Psalm 119:145-176

Christians should not run from the devil:
the devil should run from them.

People who look back are prone to turn back.

Those eternally seeking the will of God
are overrun by those who do the will of God.

Dead, Boring Christians

A burning message, and nothing less, was supposed to be presented to the world. It does not need fireworks. Firebrands do not need to be hotheads. Everything about the church, however, should reflect the warm light of God, to the very highest steeple. Not only evangelists: but witnesses, ministers, church officials, leaders, workers, teachers, and administrators should all glow with the Holy Spirit, like torches in a cold street. The business meeting should see Holy Spirit fire just as much as the revival meeting (perhaps even more so).

A fish has the same temperature as the water in which it swims. Too many Christians are like fish: they have no more warmth of spirit than the cold, unbelieving world around them. Men are warm-blooded creatures: that is the way the Lord made us. That is also the way he chose us to take the Good News: with warmth! The Lord does not send us out because we have cool heads and dignity. Nor does he choose us because of our self-composure. He sends us out with live coals from the altar, as witnesses to the Resurrection, to testify that we have met the God of Pentecost. I have heard sermons that were like lectures on embalming the dead. Would such a talk remind anyone of the living Jesus? Neither Jesus, Peter nor Paul left congregations sitting like marble statues in a museum.

Logic can be set alight and still be logic, like the logic of Isaiah or Paul, for example. Logic need not belong to the glacial period. Fire implies fervor, not ignorance. Learn by all means: but not if it puts your fire out. Remember: **radiance before cleverness**: *"You shall love the Lord your God with all your heart, with all your soul, and with all your mind, and with all your strength."* The Lord wants you to have an burning heart, and to radiate joy, compassion and love. Set your heart on fire today!

Today's Scripture
And you shall love the Lord your God with all your heart, with all your soul, with all your mind, and with all your strength. This is the first commandment (Mark 12:30)

Daily Power!
Today, I will to radiate joy, compassion and love to those around me.

Mark My Word
Psalm 29:9
Mark 12:30

The Bible In A Year

Morning
2 Kings 14
2 Timothy 4

Evening
Hosea 7
Psalms 120 to 122

2

The Height Of Human Experience

Today's Scripture
I say to you that
likewise there will be
more joy in Heaven
over one sinner
who repents than
over ninety-nine just
persons, who need
no repentance.
(Luke 15:7)

Daily Power!
Lord, you died for me;
I will rejoice lavishly
in you.

Mark My Word
Luke 19:40

The Bible In A Year

Morning
2 Kings 15
Titus 1

Evening
Hosea 8
Psalms 123 to 125

Human dignity takes on a new meaning when people are rapt in praise to God. Have you ever seen fifty thousand people weeping, waving, jumping, and shouting in gladness to God? What else would you expect to happen when a mother stands on our platform, testifying that her child has just been healed of congenital blindness; or deafness; or perhaps, of twisted limbs? I have seen these miracle testimonies so often. It is a glorious scene; the height of human experience. It is not to our credit when we keep perfectly cool as the lame walk, or the blind see. Such reserve is not clever: it is foolish. Dance – now that is more in keeping with such moments! We should take joy in the presence of the Lord! Jesus said that, at such times, even the stones would cry out.

I look at the precious men and women – black or white, many who were so sad earlier – standing in a meeting, hands pressed together in emotion or lifted in worship, eyes glistening with glad tears, faces turned up to God, lips moving in wondering thankfulness. I say to myself, "How beautiful they are!" In such moments, I wish I was an artist. When dignity comes before our delight in God, that is a catastrophe! If God does not touch our feelings, the devil will. How can God convict sinners, and help them come to repentance, unless they feel moved? How can he grant them the joy of sins forgiven, without giving them any sensation in their souls? I believe that an evangelist's job is to light a fire in the human spirit. Getting people saved is more than getting their names on a dotted line. Christianity is not a club that they are joining. Salvation is spiritual surgery. What is the forgiveness that we proclaim? What sort of forgiveness did Jesus give? It was the real kind of mercy. This forgiveness made a cripple walk again; it melted a street woman's hardness, causing her to wash his feet with tears. It was the sort of forgiveness to make people love much. It made them do something extravagant – like throw a party, as Levi did. This forgiveness caused Mary to break open a box of spikenard worth a small fortune; and Zacchaeus to give away lots of money. When you remember what God has done for you, you will rejoice lavishly!

Live Ammunition

When we open up our evangelistic meetings to the Holy Spirit completely, the results are thrilling. Whole nations are challenged by the mighty power of Christ! Where false religion and doctrines of demons previously have prevailed, they are shaken and broken! No preacher could do this, no matter how popular or clever. Such success happens only when God does it his way. When he enters the field, there is a mighty victory. He can, will, and does succeed – every time we allow him to take over. These breakthroughs are part of the End Time blessings that the Lord promised. The day of Pentecost continued: it did not stop at Jerusalem, but is for *"the ends of the earth."* I offer this challenge: let anybody begin to work on the level of the Holy Spirit; and see if he experiences anything less than the Lord's own rescue and deliverance. This kind of evangelism will break Satan's back worldwide, and he will be routed. It is this Holy Fire which cannot be imitated.

When a gun is loaded with blanks, the bang is the same as with live ammunition. A difference can be observed in the use of live ammunition and blanks, but not in its noise. The dummy ammunition makes no mark on the target, because it never reaches it. The real bullet can hit its mark. We are not interested in mere bang and recoil, excitement and spectacular gospel displays, even if those draw hundreds of thousands of people. We want to see something live hitting the bull's-eye! The crowds may come, but we must, by faith, let loose a true broadside of Holy Spirit fire-power in order for something to be accomplished. Multitudes are born again, lives are completely changed, churches are filled, hell is plundered and heaven is populated. Hallelujah!

Today's Scripture
"And he commanded us to preach to the people, and to testify that it is he who was ordained by God to be Judge of the living and the dead. To him all the prophets witness that, through his name, whoever believes in him will receive remission of sins." While Peter was still speaking these words, the Holy Spirit fell on all those who heard the Word. (Acts 10:42-44)

Daily Power!
Our faith is the victory that has overcome the world.

Mark My Word
Acts 1:8; 10:42-44
1 John 5:4

The Bible In A Year

Morning
2 Kings 16
Titus 2

Evening
Hosea 9
Psalms 126 to 128

4

Eternal Purposes

Today's Scripture
Watch therefore, for you know neither the day nor the hour in which the Son of Man is coming.
(Matthew 25:13)

Daily Power!
The Holy Spirit gives me power to witness, even to my neighbor!

Mark My Word
Mark 16:15
1 Corinthians 9:16

The Bible In A Year

Morning
2 Kings 17
Titus 3

Evening
Hosea 10
Psalms 129 to 131

The fire of God is not sent just for the enjoyment of a few emotional experiences; though it does have that glorious side effect. Holy Spirit power produces lively meetings! But just being happy does not satisfy God's design: the Holy Spirit works for eternal purposes. I think of this when I see the now almost-extinct old steam engines puffing away. These "iron horses" are like living creatures, breathing steam with fire in their bellies. The fireman's job is to stoke the fire and get a full head of steam going. When the steam pressure is up, the driver can do one of two things: he either can pull the whistle lever; or he can turn the lever that directs power onto the pistons. The whistle will blow off steam until there's none left, making itself heard for miles around. However, if power is directed onto the pistons, the steam can turn the wheels with far less fuss, drawing no attention to itself. The train then rolls away, carrying its load across the land. Thank God for the train whistle! It is important. But if blowing a whistle was all that steam could do, making a fire under the boiler and stoking it up would not be worthwhile.

The fire of the Holy Spirit brings power. Never mind the noise: let us apply this power to get on the move! Thunder is justified after lightning has struck. The proper purpose of Pentecost is to get the wheels rolling for God in every church, thereby transporting the gospel across the face of the whole Earth: *"Go into all the world and preach the gospel to every creature."* The church is a "Go" church, not a "Sit" church. Look outward to where our Lord is moving across the continents. Some are looking inward, everlastingly examining their own souls, incapacitated by introspection. Jesus is saving you – do not worry! Start helping him to save others! If the Holy Spirit has come, then be up and going. He does the work, not you or me. *"Woe is me if I do not preach the gospel!"* And woe to those to whom we fail to preach it. Let us be busy for Christ, not lazy.

Worship And Praise

A true intercessor delights in worship and praise. Throughout the intercessory Psalms, there is not a single instance of honor to God being omitted in some shape or form. But intercession rises to God on the wings of worship. Requests and praise are two sides of the same coin.

> "Be anxious for nothing, but in everything by prayer and supplication, with thanksgiving, let your requests be made known to God ... As you have therefore received Christ Jesus the Lord, so walk in him, established in the faith, as you have been taught, abounding in it with thanksgiving. Beware lest anyone cheat you through philosophy and empty deceit, according to the tradition of men, according to the basic principles of the world, and not according to Christ. ... Rejoice always, pray without ceasing, in everything give thanks ... Let the heart of those rejoice who seek the Lord!"

Intercessors do not come to God being offended about what he has not done. Moaning is not praying. Our burden for the world's needs is lifted as we pray in remembrance and thanks for what he can, and will do. Often, our prayers of intercession are based on knowing that what God has done for ourselves, he will do for others too:

> "You have lifted me up, and have not let my foes rejoice over me. O Lord my God, I cried out to you, and you healed me. O Lord, you brought my soul up from the grave; you have kept me alive, that I should not go down to the pit. Sing praise to the Lord, you saints of his, and give thanks at the remembrance of his holy name. ... You have turned for me my mourning into dancing; You have put off my sackcloth and clothed me with gladness, to the end that my glory may sing praise to you and not be silent. O Lord my God, I will give thanks to you forever."

The Lord's Prayer begins: *"Our Father in heaven, hallowed be Your name."* That is the beginning of all true intercession ... and the end is: *"For Yours is the kingdom and the power and the glory forever. Amen."* Make that the beginning and the end of your prayers today; and see your prayer life rise up to a new level of effectiveness.

Today's Scripture

Rejoice always, pray without ceasing, in everything give thanks, for this is the will of God in Christ Jesus for you.
(1 Thessalonians 5:16-18)

Daily Power!

I will rejoice, pray and give thanks to the Savior of my soul.

Mark My Word

Psalm 30:1-12; 105:3
Matthew 6:9-13
Philippians 4:6
Colossians 2:6-7; 4:2
1 Thessalonians 5: 16-18

The Bible In A Year

Morning
2 Kings 18
Philemon

Evening
Hosea 11
Psalms 132 to 134

6

Faith And Knowing

Today's Scripture
But now the
righteousness of
God apart from the
Law is revealed ...
through faith in Jesus
Christ, to all and on
all who believe ...
being justified freely
by his grace through
the redemption that
is in Christ Jesus ...
that he might be just
and the justifier of the
one who has faith in
Jesus.
(Romans 3:21-26)

Daily Power!
I know whom I have
believed and am
persuaded that he
is able to keep what
I have committed to
him until that Day.

Mark My Word
Romans 3:21-26
2 Timothy 1:12

The Bible In A Year

Morning
2 Kings 19
Hebrews 1

Evening
Hosea 12
Psalms 135 and 136

Faith means to place confidence in something. That does not mean that anything at all will do; whatever we trust must be **trustworthy**. Christian faith is faith in Christ: this is not irrational. "Blind faith" is careless and irresponsible, like putting your money into the hands of somebody you know nothing about. A Christian brother felt sorry for people who had been in jail, so he employed men who had been in prison in order to give them a new start. He showed his confidence in one man by making him his general manager. Secretly, the man robbed him, and his thefts almost ruined the business. Later, he learned that the reason for this trusted employee's previous sentence was embezzlement! Blind faith!

All over the world, people are putting faith in an endless variety of religions, systems, gods, theories, cults, and self-proclaimed messiahs. Only a fool would trust an unknown deity: but fools do when techniques and strong emotional pressures are applied. They have, in recent times, committed mass suicide in their deluded hopes. The vast majority of "faiths" (or religions) – old as well as new – promise nothing this side of eternity, but "pie in the sky when you die." The late Ayatollah Khomeini sent young teenagers into mined battlefields with the promise that, if they died killing infidels, they would go straight to paradise. How can killing people make anybody fit for heaven? Who would believe it? But it is an example of the deceitfulness of satanic influence. The Spanish Emperor at the time of the Inquisition was stricken with anxiety about his own salvation because he thought he had not burned enough Jews and others who were not Catholics! Few "faiths" are like the common experience of Christian believers: in fact, no real experience of God at all. There is no miracle, no forgiveness, no victory over sin, no strength in adversity, no peace with God, no joy. Some of them promote resignation to fate as a great virtue. But Christian believers overcome fate. They do not bow to the inevitable. Know what your faith **in Christ** means to you!

False Faiths

Most religions impose rules, prayers to pray, practices to observe, and offer (as a reward) some kind of future hope. This is a day of suicidal fanaticism, violent assertion, screaming threats, and murder, but Abraham – the father of three present-day religions – indulged in no raving demonstrations. In Christ's day, there were those claiming to be children of Abraham who fumed with hate and wanted to kill Jesus. He said: *"If you were Abraham's children, you would do the works of Abraham. But now, you seek to kill me … Abraham did not do this. You do the deeds of your father (the devil) … he was a murderer from the beginning."* People who know the truth do not get into a demented rage. When critics arise, they let the truth prove itself. The very method for spreading Christian truth shows what kind of gospel it is: no threats, no swords, nor intimidation. *"It pleased God by the foolishness of the message preached to save those who believe."* The first Christians said, "We will conquer the world by love", and they did.

We are commonly told to keep an open mind about religion and never be dogmatic. That is the liberal view. If we keep an open mind about it, we brush aside all Christ's wonderful promises, and enjoy nothing that he promises. Christians do not keep an open mind: they embrace the positive blessings of Christ! Their minds are settled, not open. How many would board an aircraft if the pilot kept an open mind about flying, the destination and how to get there? Passengers want a very dogmatic pilot! He must be dead sure they will not end up dead! Keeping an open mind about our journey through life is equally perilous. The Bible does not encourage anybody to be dogmatic – but its language is always that of a sure and certain hope. "We know" is a typical New Testament expression. The simple attitude of Christians is to be sure of tomorrow and of God: what he has done, he will do; what he is, he will be. *"I know whom I have believed, and am persuaded that he is able to guard what I have entrusted to him for that day."* That kind of certainty is no more than we would expect from any God worth calling God. You can have that assurance today.

Today's Scripture
For this reason I also suffer these things; nevertheless I am not ashamed, for I know whom I have believed and am persuaded that he is able to keep what I have committed to him until that Day.
(2 Timothy 1:12)

Daily Power!
I am a child of God through faith in Christ Jesus.

Mark My Word
John 8:39-41, 44
1 Corinthians 1:21
Galatians 3:26
2 Timothy 1:12

The Bible In A Year

Morning
2 Kings 20
Hebrews 2

Evening
Hosea 13
Psalms 137 and 138

8

Anointing And Appointing

Today's Scripture
You are a chosen
generation, a royal
priesthood, a holy
nation; his own
special people, that
you may proclaim
the praises of him
who called you out
of darkness into his
marvelous light.
(1 Peter 2:9)

Daily Power!
God has established
me and anointed me!

Mark My Word
Judges 14:6
1 Corinthians 12:
23-24
2 Corinthians 1:21
1 Peter 2:9

The Bible In A Year

Morning
2 Kings 21
Hebrews 3

Evening
Hosea 14
Psalm 139

Some experiences which we may call "anointings" (for lack of a better expression) may come as the assurance of God to a particular call, like that of the elders of Israel, David and Elisha. To some they have come when listening to some other man of God, when they knew God was thrusting them forward as what Paul calls *"the more honorable"* members of the body of Christ. My colleague, George Canty, had been put off by the methods of some healing evangelists and was critical of such activity. God had been pressuring him for some time, asking him: "Where are all your mighty miracles?" One day, he sat listening as a healing evangelist spoke. As soon as the man quoted his text, George felt a sudden spiritual elevation to a new plane. He knew he would do what the preacher had done and heal sick people. The impression was so vivid he had to look around to assure himself that the building was real, because it seemed such a visionary and transcendent moment. He knew he was different from that moment on.

Anointing and appointing go together. The only people anointed were those selected for a particular task, especially that of priest or king. It was not an experience for mere emotional enjoyment. Anointing did not signify that a special level of holiness had been attained. The anointing was given solely to equip and condition ordinary people to serve the Lord. The anointing was not available apart from service. Today, the anointing is for all believers, for all are to serve: we are *"a royal priesthood."* Note carefully that anointing is not a kind of emotional pleasure, but it comes into activity when we serve. David did not feel anointed in any particular sense: but when he faced Goliath, his anointing became apparent. Samson became strong only when he went into action for God; then the Spirit of God came upon him. A strong man does not feel his strength when he is sitting down: only when he exerts himself. Look for every opportunity to "serve" the Lord today; and watch the anointing from God rise up big within you!

Warfare Gifts

The gifts of the Spirit are given to us freely: *"Now we have received, not the spirit of the world, but the Spirit who is from God, that we might know the things that have been freely given to us by God."* There are cheap imitations on the market: religious novelties, vibrations, spirit-powers, healing sunbeams, and sweetness and light from nowhere in particular: *"But know this, that in the last days perilous times will come … having a form of godliness but denying its power. And from such people turn away! … always learning and never able to come to the knowledge of the truth."*

In many countries, our work disturbs those who have their own claims to power, protection, and healing. I recall an especially powerful witch being brought over from America in order to cast a spell and destroy what I was preaching. She stood at the back of the crowd and went through her performance. I wore the whole armor of God as she attempted to launch a spiritual attack against me:

> "Therefore take up the whole armor of God, that you may be able to withstand in the evil day, and having done all, to stand."

Her attempt was futile against that armor!

The Holy Spirit waits at the cross, and those who kneel at that altar, and there alone, receive his limitless blessings. At Calvary, there are benefits far beyond the labored results of mantras, New Age processes and occultism. These are *"the weak and beggarly elements"* that Paul described.

> "Let no one deceive you with empty words, for because of these things the wrath of God comes upon the sons of disobedience. Therefore do not be partakers with them. For you were once darkness, but now you are light in the Lord. Walk as children of light (for the fruit of the Spirit is in all goodness, righteousness, and truth), finding out what is acceptable to the Lord. And have no fellowship with the unfruitful works of darkness, but rather expose them."

Walk as God's child in his light.

Today's Scripture
For you were once darkness, but now you are light in the Lord. Walk as children of light.
(Ephesians 5:8)

Daily Power!
I have cast off the works of darkness, and put on the armor of light.

Mark My Word
Romans 13:12
1 Corinthians 2:12
Galatians 4:8-11
Ephesians 5:6-11;
6:11-14
2 Timothy 3:3, 5, 7

The Bible In A Year

Morning
2 Kings 22
Hebrews 4

Evening
Joel 1
Psalms 140 and 141

10

Today's Scripture
Brethren, I do not count myself to have apprehended; but one thing I do, forgetting those things which are behind and reaching forward to those things which are ahead, I press toward the goal for the prize of the upward call of God in Christ Jesus. (Philippians 3:13-14)

Daily Power!
I shall not die, but live, and declare the works of the LORD.

Mark My Word
Psalm 118:17
James 1:22

The Bible In A Year

Morning

2 Kings 23
Hebrews 5

Evening
Joel 2
Psalm 142

Young And Old In The Last Hour

I am eternally grateful that I was a young man when Christ Jesus entered my heart and called me into his service. I knew that he had called me to be his servant; and I have never regretted a single moment, a single day of my life of service to him. The response to his gift of salvation and then the response to his call for service: these are important milestones in the lives of all believers, young or old. The awareness that we are living in *"the last hour"* is also pressing on our hearts, motivating us to be *"doers of the Word, and not hearers only, deceiving yourselves."*

Young people have a slightly different status in the same last hour, however. When an old person gets saved, a soul gets saved. When a young person gets saved, both a soul and a lifetime are saved. The young person has an hour that could be a lifetime, and what a glorious hour that can be! An hour full of love, joy, peace, purpose, and security, even if the last hour lasted an entire lifetime. The only way to live tomorrow is to live in faith and activity for Jesus today.

I once prayed for an old and dying man. Suddenly, a strange thought challenged me: "What would I pray if I were in his place?" A famous politician who expressed his last wish asked for, "One delicious pork pie!" It did not take long before I knew the answer for myself: I would ask the Lord to give me the strength and help to conduct one more gospel Crusade! I would like to hit the bull's-eye once more, and again lead one hundred thousand souls to the foot of the cross of Christ. There is nothing grander than that: nor is there a more glorious way to die, than fighting on that victorious battleground. I strongly encourage you to make that your goal!

Whirlwinds

In our great African gospel crusades, there are mighty victories over satanic powers and over sorcery. Gigantic piles of witchcraft materials are brought and burned. Their owners were delivered from satanic fears and oppressions when they received Jesus as their Lord and Savior. I often have pointed to the flames, saying: "That is like where the final home of the devil will be: in the Lake of Fire!" Satan is not in control of hell's fire; those flames are his judgment. When those *"works of the devil"* are reduced to ashes, we see the true Fire of the Lord fall on crowds "en masse."

The anti-anointing is a strange fire of destruction and death. But the flame from the presence of the Lord will devour it, just as it devoured the profane fire of Nadab and Abihu. After that, a sweet anointing of peace will flow over the church, all the way down to its feet and robe hems. Let us forget old fights among God's people over issues that do not lead to the salvation of men and women. Our enemy is not another denomination, or even denominationalism. Our enemy is the devil, and the many lies by which he deceives the world: the lie that God is dead; the lie that God is indifferent; the lie that we can do without Jesus. *"They overcame him by the blood of the Lamb."* Note that "him" is singular! We have one enemy – the devil. There is one power to oppose him – the Holy Spirit. When we walk in God's anointing: ready for service, filled with holy fire; then we are whirlwinds of destruction upon the enemy's stolen territory. We are unstoppable weapons of purpose and zeal, taking back what the enemy has stolen: the lives of men and women all around the world! Let that be your purpose today.

Today's Scripture

The thief does not come except to steal, and to kill, and to destroy. I have come that they may have life, and that they may have it more abundantly.
(John 10:10)

Daily Power!

When we walk in God's anointing, we are victorious.

Mark My Word

Leviticus 10:1-2
Isaiah 10:27
John 10:10
Revelation 12:11

The Bible In A Year

Morning

2 Kings 24
Hebrews 6

Evening

Joel 3
Psalm 143

The Word Brings Faith

Today's Scripture
Now to him who
is able to establish
you according to
my gospel and the
preaching of Jesus
Christ, according to
the revelation of the
mystery kept secret
since the world
began but now made
manifest ... to God,
alone wise, be glory
through Jesus Christ
forever. Amen.
(Romans 16:25-27)

Daily Power!
The entrance of your
words gives light. It
gives understanding
to the simple.

Mark My Word
Genesis 1:3; 2:12
Psalm 119:11, 97-98,
105; 130
Isaiah 50:11
Matthew 13:14
Romans 10:17;

The Bible In A Year

Morning

2 Kings 25
Hebrews 7

Evening
Amos 1
Psalm 144

The Creator, who cares enough to let this human race continue, obviously does not want to leave us in the dark about himself. He reveals himself. That is the only way we could know him. Our hard reasoning is like flint that only makes sparks, not light. *"Look, all you who kindle a fire, who encircle yourselves with sparks: walk in the light of your fire … [but] you shall lie down in torment."* Sparks, flashes of thought, do not illumine life's path very much. The philosophers are as lost as anybody, and yet they seek to guide us; the blind leading the blind. God said, *"Let there be light!"* He brought light to Abraham, Moses, David, the prophets, and finally through Jesus Christ.

"Oh, how I love Your law! It is my meditation all the day. You, through Your commandments, make me wiser than my enemies; For they are ever with me… Your word is a lamp to my feet and a light to my path." Too many ignore the Bible without realizing what damage they do. The Bible is dynamite. Scripture is unexplored territory to many, although *"the gold of that land is good."* To unfasten the clasps of the Bible and turn these healing leaves needs the fingers of faith. Yet *"faith comes by… the word of God."* God gives us faith to read it so we can gather faith: if we want it.

To get faith to read the Word, just read it. It is self-proving. Its chemistry explodes and brings us confidence about itself. *"Faith comes by hearing, and hearing by the word of God"* and *"Hearing, you will hear."* Abraham believed God when God spoke. The Creator fitted us with the power to recognize his voice, just as Abraham recognized it. That is what we will do now: let the Bible speak for itself to bring you faith!

Faith And The Promises

What is faith? It is not an extra brain lobe or a piece stuck on our soul. We choose to believe. Faith is an attitude. Faith is the only basis possible for any workable relationship. It seems to me that faith in God is not only good, but it is the only decent thing to do. It is ridiculous to expect dealings with God on any other terms. How else can an invisible God relate to us, now or during the unknown future? If we cannot go that far, what are we worth? If we cannot trust the Almighty of all beings, who do we think we are? It is the least God can expect: *"Without faith it is impossible to please him."* If anybody says, "I'm not a great believer" that is too bad, because God is not pleased with them! Would they – or anybody else – be pleased if somebody did not trust them?

Faith is not certainty; it is a personal issue. Somebody may have proved himself up to now: but the future holds only personal assurances. We trust them because we **know** them. If we thought that they would change, we would not trust them. We read in the Bible who God is. We may have proved him for ourselves up to this moment: but for the future, we can do no other but trust. No faith is needed to believe two plus two make four: but life is a degree more complicated. Circumstances change like the ocean. The vastness of things affects the future. Obviously, what God might do is affected; he does not cut across events as if they did not occur. He may work no magic, turn no pumpkins into golden coaches. But he is all-wise and all-powerful: so much so that we have to leave things to him to sort out; for we may understand no more of what he is doing, than we would understand the chaos of a shipyard building a fifty thousand-ton luxury liner. We look to him; and that is something God takes into account. He made the world that way. Prayer and faith will enable him to do what he could not otherwise do. No doubt it is true that God can do anything: but he does nothing without those who believe. That is his planned providence, his promise to you.

Today's Scripture
Without faith it is impossible to please him.
(Hebrews 11:6)

Daily Power!
God can do anything, but he does nothing without those who believe.

Mark My Word
Hebrews 11:6

The Bible In A Year

Morning
1 Chronicles 1 and 2
Hebrews 8

Evening
Amos 2
Psalm 145

Your Last Hour

Today's Scripture
So teach us to number our days, that we may gain a heart of wisdom.
(Psalm 90:12)

Daily Power!
Little children, this is the last second of the last hour!

Mark My Word
Psalm 90:12
Matthew 24:36
Romans 13:11
1 John 2:18

The Bible In A Year

Morning
1 Chronicles 3 and 4
Hebrews 9

Evening
Amos 3
Psalms 146 and 147

Suppose this was your last hour: what would you be doing? What a flurry of anxious preparations there would be! But let me tell you: *"Little children, it is the last hour."* I know that it seems that this "last hour" has lasted very long, as John wrote those words two thousand years ago, but do not let that confuse you. Of one thing we can be certain: if it was the last hour then, it most certainly is now! If John were writing today, he probably would write, "Little children, it is the last second of the last hour." When John wrote this verse, he was watching God's clock, not ours. Its hands have not stood still. How long will God's hour last, measured by earthly time-keeping methods? The one thing we know is that we do not know how near we are to the end: *"But of that day and hour no one knows,"* Jesus said. It is obvious, however, that we are much closer to the end every day. Paul saw it that way too: *"Knowing the time, that now it is high time to awake out of sleep; for now our salvation is nearer than when we first believed."*

If anybody thought that they had only sixty minutes left, they would certainly not spend the time on trivialities. With the microseconds running out like fine sand in an hourglass, they would see what was really important to them. They would not go shopping for the latest fashionable hat, or run an eye down the financial columns to see how their shares were doing. Focusing on the end would put all of life into its proper perspective. Somebody once said that most people live as if this life were a permanent arrangement. The Bible's message is that our days are *"numbered"* not, without number. There is actually only time for the important things. I am thinking about the church of Jesus Christ in particular. People often point out that life consists of a thousand details, but the minor must not outweigh the major. The church is to concern itself with one aim: the war with Satan and the campaign for souls. The great quality of Jesus is that he came when the Father sent him. And the great quality about us should be that we go when Jesus sends us. *"As the Father has sent me, I also send you."* The church should plan to neglect anything which interferes with going. Be mindful of the number of your days.

Last Hour Logic

When the Bible proclaims, *"It is the last hour,"* it truly is. For the message of the gospel, it is always the last hour. If you want to know how a single individual like Paul did so much, read his disclosure in Corinthians. He lived as if the end of all things was at hand:

> "But this I say, brethren, the time is short, so that from now on even those who have wives should be as though they had none, those who weep as though they did not weep, those who rejoice as though they did not rejoice, those who buy as though they did not possess, and those who use this world as not misusing it. For the form of this world is passing away."

The gospel is eternal: but we do not have eternity to preach it. One would think that we had, when we view the leisurely operations of the church. We have only as long as we live to reach those who live as long as we live. Today, over five billion souls are alive: alive in our present world, not in an indefinite future age which needs to be evangelized. *"It is the last hour."*

To make sure that the prodigal son was welcomed home properly, the father **ran**! I also have wanted to run since the Holy Spirit charged me with this: *"It is the last hour."* The world's airlines have found me to be a good customer! One of Paul's favorite Greek words was "spoude" – meaning "to stretch out the neck as a man running to get to the finish line." It is translated: "study, be diligent, be earnest, hasten, be zealous, be forward." Many churches are very active: doing what? To bring the gospel to a dying world is the true relevance! Giving all our thoughts to our personal spirituality when the fires of hell have broken out is like members of the fire brigade having a shave before answering a fire call. The command to evangelize is all that matters, snatching men from the flames of an eternal hell. That divine command was not given in a passing mood of the Lord. God himself is driven by the peril in which human beings stand without Christ. Calvary was his imperative! *"Other sheep I have which are not of this fold; them also I must bring, and they will hear my voice; and there will be one flock and one Shepherd."* **Run** to be a soul-winner!

Today's Scripture
Let us lay aside every weight and the sin which so easily ensnares us, and let us run with endurance the race that is set before us.
(Hebrews 12:1)

Daily Power!
The gospel is eternal: but we do not have eternity to preach it.

Mark My Word
Luke 15:11-31
John 4:3 5; 10:16
1 Corinthians 7:29-31
1 John 2:18

The Bible In A Year

Morning
1 Chronicles 5 and 6
Hebrews 10

Evening
Amos 4
Psalms 148 to 150

The Beauty From God

Today's Scripture
Let the beauty of
the Lord our God
be upon us, and
establish the work of
our hands for us.
(Psalm 90:17)

Daily Power!
God makes
everything beautiful in
its time.

Mark My Word
1 Chronicles 16:29;
Psalm 90:17;
Ecclesiastes 3:11;
10:1
Isaiah 64:6.

The Bible In A Year

Morning
1 Chronicles 7 and 8
Hebrews 11

Evening
Amos 6
Luke 1:1-38

Personal beauty is never condemned in scripture. Pride, lack of modesty, provocative dress, and brazen flirting certainly are. God makes people beautiful, and does not expect us to belong to the cult of ugliness and make the worst of ourselves. I do not believe God took pleasure in the saints of the early centuries who boasted of the population of lice in their hair and beards. Nor was he pleased with the nuns who boasted that water never touched their feet except when they crossed a river.

God does not give special honor to those who dress drably to win his favor. He creates beautiful things, from the glory of the dawn and majesty of the sunset, to the star-spangled velvet of the night sky. his dwelling is the light of the setting sun, multi-colored and glorious. Our ability to create beauty come from him. *"He has made everything beautiful in its time"* … *"Let the beauty of the Lord our God be upon us."* That is what the anointing is.

"The beauty of holiness" forbids pride. Pride is the *"dead flies [that] putrefy the perfumer's ointment, and cause it to give off a foul odor."* Our proud efforts at holiness are described as smelly and unclean: *"All our righteousnesses are like filthy rags."* That is because they produce a judgmental and condemnatory attitude,toward others we suppose to have lower standards. We put on spiritual airs with an unattractive correctness. A legalistic life has about as much chance of producing true fruit of the Spirit as arctic ice has of producing orchids. But when we: *"Give to the Lord the glory due his name; bring an offering and come before him"* then we invite the fragrance of God to permeate our lives. It may sound strange to hear this: but now you know what I mean when I say: "Smell like Christ today!"

Paid By The Hour

17

Years ago in northern Germany, I had the privilege of leading an elderly lady to the Lord. For most of her life she had been a church organist, but had never known Jesus as her own Savior. When she heard the gospel and opened her heart to the Lord, she was overwhelmed with the joy of the Holy Spirit. Three days later I met her again, but this time she was completely broken. Puzzled, I asked her why this was. With tears in her eyes, she told me: "I am already seventy years of age and have only just received Jesus as my Savior. I may live perhaps another five or ten years; but I have totally wasted seventy."

Of course, this touched me deeply. Then I said: "Yes, but I know what is going to happen. One day we shall stand before the Judgment Seat of Christ. But he will not be as concerned as much about how **long** we cut the furrow of our life for him, as how **deep**. Five or ten years, all-out for Jesus, are much more than having been a lukewarm Christian for fifty years."

Do you remember the laborers in the parable of Jesus? By the clock, some had worked only a single hour, but the farmer generously rewarded them, paying them the same as those who had labored throughout the day. Why? Because they had worked for as long as they had the chance. This is the principle of God. If anybody is worried about not having been at Jesus' side in the harvest when they could have been, the answer is to leave that with the Lord of the Harvest. Do not waste time on tears. Give God his due wholeheartedly, from this moment on! The apostle Paul's advice is this:

> "Brethren, I do not count myself to have apprehended; but one thing I do, forgetting those things which are behind and reaching forward to those things which are ahead, I press toward the goal for the prize of the upward call of God in Christ Jesus."

As long as you have breath within you, you are in time to be in on the last hour, the last day, the last month or the last year. You are not too late for that.

Today's Scripture
Forgetting those things which are behind and reaching forward to those things which are ahead, I press toward the goal for the prize of the upward call of God in Christ Jesus. (Philippians 3:13-14)

Daily Power!
I will be diligent to present myself approved to God, a worker who does not need to be ashamed, rightly dividing the word of truth.

Mark My Word
Matthew 20:1-16
2 Timothy 2:15
Philippians 3:13-14.

The Bible In A Year

Morning
1 Chronicles 9 and 10
Hebrews 12

Evening
Amos 6
Luke 1:39

18

Today's Scripture
Every good gift and every perfect gift is from above, and comes down from the Father of lights, with whom there is no variation or shadow of turning.
(James 1:17)

Daily Power!
I will walk in the Spirit, and shall not fulfill the lust of the flesh.

Mark My Word
Deuteronomy 8:18
Psalm 107:9
Matthew 6:19-21
Galatians 5:16
James 1:17; 4:2-4

The Bible In A Year

Morning
1 Chronicles 11 and 12
Hebrews 13

Evening
Amos 7
Luke 2

James was the half-brother of Jesus, and his Epistle carries us back to the typical teaching of Jesus as no other book does. *"Yet you do not have because you do not ask. You ask and do not receive, because you ask amiss, that you may spend it on your pleasures ... Whoever therefore wants to be a friend of the world makes himself an enemy of God."* This discussion concerns prayer for material goods. But if we pray as materialists of the world, we shall get no answer. To set our affection on possessions, affluence, and prestige is materialism and worldliness, and pushes God and his purposes aside.

> "Do not lay up for yourselves treasures on earth, where moth and rust destroy and where thieves break in and steal; but lay up for yourselves treasures in heaven, whether neither moth nor rust destroys and where thieves do not break in and steal For where your treasure is, there your heart will be also."

The number one prayer of many people is about number one: themselves. But when the kingdom of God is Number One, there is nothing wrong in asking God for his good things: *"Every good and every perfect gift is from above, and comes down from the Father of lights, with whom there is no variation or shadow of turning."* The material gifts around us are from God as gifts to his creatures. *"He satisfies the longing soul"* whatever its tastes. God gives us the power to get wealth, but nothing whatever was made only for materialists. Riches are not the primary object of faith. Faith has been given to lay hold of possessions. God did not display his vast wealth in our wonderful world just as a temptation to test Christians. Believers have as much claim on the good things of this life as anyone else. To concentrate our desires and prayers on them is a different thing, however. The motive for getting is giving: to relieve the hungry and distressed, and to make known the name of the Lord. Faith and prayer are a single subject, depending on one another. Keep them both active in your life, and watch them flow from you as one powerful force of blessing.

God's Wave

Marine scientists say that ocean waves travel thousands of miles, under the surface, across apparently calm stretches. Approaching land, they develop a majestic crescendo, hunch their mighty shoulders, and build up in rapid momentum and volume, to burst finally and magnificently upon the shore. A glorious swell of Holy Spirit power is gathering to a spontaneous crescendo today, world wide, as if hurrying to the shore. The lifting of the waves proves that the shore cannot be far. Jesus is coming soon! **It is the last hour!** The latter day Pentecostal outpouring of the Spirit began in 1901, and the truth of "the baptism in the Holy Spirit, with signs following" was recovered. The mightiest revival of all swept onward like a wave from heaven. It is the same tidal wave that started in Jerusalem nineteen hundred years before. A divine deluge of power – *"floods on the dry ground"* – had blessed the world for two or three hundred years. Then, through unbelief and worldliness, it seemed to ebb. The church even taught that such power was only for the apostles and the early disciples. The Holy Spirit became a mere Third Article of the Creed, locked up and relegated to the past.

With the outpouring of his Spirit, the Lord gave believers power to do the job: to evangelize and send out missionaries. John wrote: *"As you have heard that the Antichrist is coming, even now many antichrists have come, by which we know it is the last hour … But you have an anointing from the Holy One, and you know all things."* The church is being anointed for the last hour. The spirit of the age would be antichrist or anti-anointed. John's warnings concerning the last times have come home to us today, striking with an almost frightening truth about our times. The spirit of antichrist permeates human thinking and society, causing moral collapse. Hostile elements are raging worse and worse, like the early moments of a gathering storm. God's answer: his anointing for an anti-anointed latter day. He will never allow the devil to get the upper hand. The outpouring of the Spirit is his special provision for the last hour: *"And it shall come to pass afterward that I will pour out my Spirit on all flesh … before the coming of the great and awesome day of the Lord."* Christ's whole body on earth will be mobilized and armed for the last onslaught of the enemy.

Remember: Satan, the eternal loser, will lose again.

Today's Scripture
But you have an anointing from the Holy One.
(1 John 2:20).

Daily Power!
God's answer to the antichrist: his anointing.

Mark My Word
Isaiah 44:3
Joel 2:28, 31
1 John 2:18-27

The Bible In A Year

Morning
1 Chronicles 13 and 14
James 1

Evening
Amos 8
Luke 3

20

Today's Scripture

If you love me, keep my commandments. And I will pray the Father, and he will give you another Helper, that he may abide with you forever.
(John 14: 15-16)

Daily Power!

I am led by the Spirit of God, therefore I am a child of God.

Mark My Word

Isaiah 8:20
John 14:15-16
Romans 8:14

The Bible In A Year

Morning

1 Chronicles 15
James 2

Evening

Amos 9
Luke 4

After Jerusalem fell, many of the people wanted Jeremiah to inquire if they should leave the land. In their hearts, they wanted to go to Egypt and meant to do so; they only wanted Jeremiah to persuade God to approve their plans. Jeremiah inquired: and God did not approve at all. They went anyway, saying that Jeremiah had lied about what God had said, and they ran into great trouble as a result! God had not said anything about them leaving in the first place, because he had no new plan.

There is a safeguard for all "voices" and impulses, and that is the Word: *"If they do not speak according to this word, it is because there is no light in them."* It claims for itself the unique privilege of being the means through which God speaks. He has nothing to say except according to its precepts. his Word may come to us through ministry or prophecy – which often we need – but personal directives never come through a third party. He tells nobody else what you should do. There may be comfort, edification, and exhortation: but each of us is led of God if we are his children: *"For as many as are led by the Spirit of God, these are sons of God."*

None of the great men and women in Scripture who heard God's voice for themselves were asking and waiting for it. God wanted to speak and did so. People ask, "What is God saying to the church?" Why should God always be saying something to the church? Has he left us all in the dark about what he wants? There are spiritually superior persons who profess to know what nobody else knows, as if they were divine favorites who really stood before him as nobody else. The Spirit of the prophets is now the Spirit given to all believers. God reveals his secrets to his prophets, and we are all in that category today in Christ. When God speaks, it is a broadcast message, not a telephone call. You can hear his voice speaking clearly.

Many Callings

Evangelism happens to be my calling. There are other callings that will grip men and women: apostles, pastors, teachers, prophets, elders, musicians, organizers, intercessors, workers in a thousand different capacities. When God puts his Hand upon us, he does two things: first he gives us a ministry; then he opens a door to service. Each one of us has a unique and vital place in his kingdom. Every believer is individually chiseled, *"skillfully wrought in the lowest parts of the earth."* Some are far from being run-of-the-mill, yet they are hardly likely to be welcomed with a great cheer.

A new vision can be disturbing: not only to those who receive it, but to those who do not; especially if it puts a man in the limelight. There can be resentment, criticism, even jealousy. Sometimes a man's close friends and colleagues cannot believe God has put a call into his soul. But there is no accounting for God's choice, as Paul pointed out about Jacob. A call is entirely God's counsel, not man's. If God calls, the best proof is our patience when we are misjudged and criticized. The man who knows that God has sent him will rest content in God, and leave those who disapprove or misunderstand for the Lord to handle: *"Therefore humble yourselves under the mighty hand of God, that he may exalt you in due time."* We must be careful not to mishandle criticisms. Sometimes through the eyes of others, you see the back of your own head! What others say about us is important, be they foe or friend. I praise the Lord for those choice men and women to whom he has guided me, for their perception and insight. I would be a fool not to listen to them. Just like any other minister, evangelists need advice. The evangelist cannot be a law to himself. He is a member of the body of Christ. Find out where **you** fit in the body and allow yourself to be useful there!

Today's Scripture
May [we] grow up in all things into him who is the Head, Christ, from whom the whole body, joined and knit together by what every joint supplies, according to the effective working by which every part does its share, causes growth of the body for the edifying of itself in love.
(Ephesians 4:15-16)

Daily Power!
People who know their God shall be strong, and carry out great exploits.

Mark My Word
Psalm 139:15
Daniel 11:32
Ephesians 4:15-16
1 Peter 5:6

The Bible In A Year

Morning
1 Chronicles 16
James 3

Evening
Obadiah
Luke 5

22

Today's Scripture
Thus let all Your
enemies perish, O
Lord! But let those
who love him be
like the sun when it
comes out in
full strength.
(Judges 5:31)

Daily Power!
I will not be a
self-interested
Christian!

Mark My Word
Exodus 17:15
Judges 4:1-24; 5:1-31

The Bible In A Year

Morning
1 Chronicles 17
James 4

Evening
Jonah 1
Luke 6

Dan's Ship Shops

Israel had many troubles. They were often oppressed by invaders. God raised up leaders (judges) to unite and help them to defend themselves. One of these judges was Deborah, a prophetess. A Canaanite king, Jabin, had sent in his men under Sisera to plunder and kill Israel. The Spirit of God stirred Deborah to resist this attack; and by using her persuasive powers she inspired Israel to rally under the leadership of Barak. Each tribe received Deborah's call to unite, and do what they could not do alone – stand against Sisera. It is interesting to see how the various tribes reacted. In fact, this old story is like a mirror held up to the face of the church today. After their victory, Deborah asked one penetrating question about the tribe of Dan: *"And why did Dan remain on ships?"* (The Danites ran a mercantile marine service for Israel, bringing goods from far corners. Then, moored in a harbor, their ships became shops, selling directly to the public.) So here was Dan himself at the till of his shop, totaling receipts with satisfaction. Suddenly, a messenger arrives with a dispatch for Dan: "Dear Dan: Sisera is ravaging Israel. We are fighting with everything at our disposal, but the tribes must all unite to repel the enemy. Come and help – **now**. Your fellow Israelites are bleeding and dying. Please respond. Deborah (Judge of Israel)."

Dan, the businessman, was deeply moved. He looked inland where hostilities were in progress, possibly hearing the clash of arms and cries of his dying brothers. Just as suddenly came other thoughts: "If I go and fight, I will be risking my flourishing enterprise. The Canaanites are my customers, so I cannot upset them! I must remain neutral." He hurriedly stuffed a bundle of money into the messenger's pockets, saying, "Regretfully I cannot come myself, but here is my contribution. Tell Deborah that I am with her in spirit." So Dan went on counting his cash, while his brethren rallied round the standard of Deborah and Barak. Let others die for Israel, but Dan had a business to attend to. There was Dan in his ship of Self-Interest, Self-Love, and Greed. That sounds like our world today! Whatever you do, do not get on board that same kind of self-serving vessel or lifestyle. But rather, set a higher standard based on God's Word and his Will; and stay standing there next to Jehovah Nissi – The Lord is my Banner.

Immortal Work For Mortals

To be called by God costs nothing, as God does the calling: but to birth the call is another matter entirely! I was a hard-working missionary in Lesotho; but the vivid vision of a blood-washed Africa haunted me. Divine pressure always accompanies vision. An all-consuming desire drove me to make my first ventures towards mass-evangelism. Still I was hesitant: the members of my mission board disapproved. They were good, spiritual men, but they lacked vision. "Normal missionary work is the fruitful approach to the salvation of Africa, not mass evangelism. If this is God's way, why are other men not doing it?" While missionaries were content with the mission tradition, I was in turmoil. Divine pressure on my spirit grew stronger. Fellow evangelists shared a common experience of official discouragement. They had the burning fire of the Spirit within, the challenge of vast possibilities around: but criticism from without. I spent hours in prayer to keep my poise and peace. "How long would it take to bring about a blood-washed Africa without aggressive evangelistic crusades? We have only one generation to save a generation." I reached a crisis point, and locked myself in a hotel room, determined not to let go of God until I had a clear word from him. I boldly put before the Lord exactly how I felt: was this really his will for me, this constant impulse to campaign?

God made matters absolutely clear to me: "If you drop the vision that I have given you, I will look for another man who will accept it, and do what I want." I repented of my hesitations immediately, making my decision forever. God then began to smile upon me, sending divine encouragement. I have never looked back, learning how to handle critics and criticisms by letting God himself become my defender. Let them see that the Lord led me by the fruit of my ministry. I have trained myself to concentrate on what he wants me to do. The ministry and the results have grown, sometimes rather dramatically. Focus on God's will; and watch your life grow with increased blessings, purpose and fulfillment.

Today's Scripture
Unless the Lord builds the house, they labor in vain who build it.
(Psalm 127:1)

Daily Power!
We have only one generation to save a generation.

Mark My Word
Psalm 127:1

The Bible In A Year

Morning
1 Chronicles 18
James 5

Evening
Jonah 2
Luke 7

24

Leap Into The Light

Today's Scripture
Trust in the Lord
with all your heart,
and lean not on your
own understanding;
in all your ways
acknowledge him,
and he shall direct
your paths.
(Proverbs 3:5)

Daily Power!
Faith is a leap into the
light, not into
the dark.

Mark My Word
Proverbs 3:5
Matthew 6:25-30
Hebrews 11:1
Jude 1:24

The Bible In A Year

Morning
1 Chronicles 19 and
20
1 Peter 1

Evening
Jonah 3
Luke 8

Every day we exercise trust in countless things, often unfamiliar. People, food, chairs, gadgets, everything. It is natural. We do not stand and say, "Now, do I have enough faith to get on this bus?" or "Can I sit quietly trusting this driver?" We never think of it; we just go along trusting all the way. Examining your feelings to see if you have a bit of faith lurking around in some corner of your mind is quite absurd: *"Trust in the Lord with all your heart, and lean not on your own understanding; in all your ways acknowledge him and he shall direct your paths."* You do not really "feel" faith; at least faith and feelings do not always go together. You simply do what should be done when you know very well that you cannot succeed unless God helps you: *"Now faith is the substance of things hoped for, the evidence of things not seen."*

Faith is a leap into the light, not into the dark. It is out of the unknown into the known, out of not knowing Christ Jesus, into knowing him. Believing is like a child standing where it is not safe – but without any fear – because his father is waiting to catch him. He falls on purpose to be caught:

> "Now to him who is able to keep you from stumbling, and to present you faultless before the presence of his glory with exceeding joy; to God our Savior, who alone is wise, be glory and majesty, dominion and power, both now and forever. Amen!"

Each of us is important to God, more than all the stars of space. He wants us to trust him implicitly. He made us and will take pains with us. Faith allows him to see us through until we rest in him:

> "Therefore I say to you, do not worry about your life, what you will eat or what you will drink; nor about your body, what you will put on. Is not life more than food and the body more than clothing? … Now if God so clothes the grass of the field, which today is, and tomorrow is thrown into the oven, will he not much more clothe you, O you of little faith?"

Rest assured in God's loving provision for you today.

Greater Than Jesus?

A breathtaking view of the kingdom has been shown to us: *"He who believes in me, the works that I do he will do also; and greater works than these he will do, because I go to my Father."* The word for "greater" – "meizona" – does not specify what order of greatness, whether in number, quality, or magnitude. This has been a problem to many Bible students. Surely nothing could outclass the miracles of Jesus in intrinsic omnipotence, such as the raising of Lazarus! But there is a sense in which someone can do greater things than Christ.

First, there could be more numerous instances; and second, they could be spread over a wider area. Both took place as the disciples moved out in missionary travel.Obviously there are some works of his we could never do since he is the Son of God. He only is the redeemer. He alone could die for the sins of the whole world. The works that he referred to were works of mercy, deliverance, healing, and aid.

For centuries, since the invention of printing and modern technology, far more vast operations can bring results impossible even for Jesus when he was localized in this village, or that town. He was physically limited: but not limited in power! He needed more hands, more voices, more extensions of himself. That is why we are members of the body of Christ. We use our arms, our hands, our feet, our mouths to spread his gospel: but they are also his. This could only be possible through the power of the Spirit. Jesus repeated this emphatically:

> "Most assuredly, I say to you, he who believes in me, the works that I do he will do also; and greater works than these he will do, because I go to my Father... It is to your advantage (Greek: "sympherei" meaning expedient, advantageous) that I go away. For if I do not go away, the Helper will not come to you; but if I depart, I will send him to you."

This is our basis for the gifts of the Spirit. Allow the Holy Spirit to use you today.

Today's Scripture
He who believes in me, the works that I do he will do also; and greater works than these he will do, because I go to my Father.
(John 14:12)

Daily Power!
We use our arms, hands, feet, mouths to spread his gospel: but they are also his.

Mark My Word
John 14:12; 16:7
Romans 12:4-5
1 Corinthians 6:15;
12:12, 18, 27
Ephesians 5:30

The Bible In A Year

Morning
1 Chronicles 21
1 Peter 2

Evening
Jonah 4
Luke 9

26

Ancient Faith

Today's Scripture
Now faith is the substance of things hoped for, the evidence of things not seen. For by it the elders obtained a good testimony. (Hebrews 11:1-2)

Daily Power!
Faith is the life-blood of a child of God.

Mark My Word
Hebrews 11:1-40; 12:1-29

The Bible In A Year

Morning
1 Chronicles 22
1 Peter 3

Evening
Micah 1
Luke 10

We get what we live for, but do we live by what we get? Conditions are fantastic compared with the past. Are we fantastically more content and fulfilled? There have been fantastic people, relishing mortal existence like the finest wine, even when ignorance was profound: spiritual giants like Enoch, Abraham, and Samuel. They did not surf the Internet, skimming across world knowledge: but plummeted the depths of reality. A deep understanding burned in their eyes. If we met one of these tremendous characters, we would feel inferior in the presence of greatness.

Who are those in the "Honor Roll of Faith"? Abel, Enoch, Noah, Abraham, Sarah, Isaac, Jacob, Joseph, Moses, Joshua, Rahab, Gideon, Barak, Samson, Jephthah, David, Samuel; all the prophets. These were the ancients, people who knew God. They did not use the word "faith" as a state of mind. They thought only in practical terms; such as walking with God, serving, fearing, obeying, and cleaving to him. That is what faith is, and that is why the Bible must be our guide every inch of the way. Today, faith is thought of as a possession, stacked safely somewhere in our psychological cupboard. We bring it out, dust it off and exhibit it, as occasion requires.

> "Now faith is the substance of things hoped for, the evidence of things not seen. For by it the elders obtained a good testimony. By faith we understand that the worlds were framed by the word of God, so that the things which are seen were not made of things which are visible."

The ancients would no more go through the day without faith than without their clothes. It was the atmosphere they breathed, not just for the convenient moments. The world now thinks of religion as a subject or occasional practice. Sunday is given for religion. For these great men, their relationship with God was the essential quality of all their waking hours and unthinkable without him. You should have that kind of faith!

Faith Of A New Kind

The world of the ancients was a perilous place. The nations had no idea how to handle sickness, plagues, droughts, and famines. Enemies surrounded them. But Israel learned that God was "El Shaddai": their All-Sufficient One; their Protector, Deliverer, healer, Stronghold, "Shield and Buckler." Other nations looked to their gods: to the rain god if they wanted rains; to the god of fertility for their harvests. They offered a sacrifice at their shrine as a bribe when they wanted their help. That was all that the gods asked; otherwise, people forgot them. Pagans had no sustained sense of God's constant concern. Only Israel enjoyed that. In Israel, God sent the prophets to assure them of his faithfulness. He was their shepherd, and they were the sheep of his pasture. This was far beyond heathen thought. Even the greatest of the heathen, such as Socrates and Aristotle, had no such divine awareness. **The Israelites were the people of God.** But, for example, while the Ephesians gloried in "*Diana of the Ephesians*" (or Artemis, as in the Greek), they were not "the people of Diana"; they just patronized her.

In the New Testament, the trust communicated by the prophets of old continues; but it expands beyond a physical covenant, taking in more than even the prophets themselves understood. What Christ introduced embraced life here, and in the hereafter. Jesus showed us that physical dangers are not that all-important, neither is our material prosperity. The state of our real self, our soul, is the all-important and only issue. The body will die, but far worse is for the soul to perish:

> "And do not fear those who kill the body but cannot kill the soul. But rather fear him who is able to destroy both soul and body in hell."

Ezekiel wrote: "*The soul who sins shall die*"; but Jesus said that the soul that sins is dead already. He comes as the Resurrection and the Life!

Today's Scripture
I am the resurrection and the life. He who believes in me, though he may die, he shall live. And whoever lives and believes in me shall never die.
(John 11:25-26)

Daily Power!
In him I live and move and have my being.

Mark My Word
Ezekiel 18:4
Matthew 10:28
John 11:25
Acts 17:28
1 Peter 1:10-12

The Bible In A Year

Morning
1 Chronicles 23
1 Peter 4

Evening
Micah 2
Luke 11

28

Today's Scripture
For God so loved the world that he gave his only begotten Son, that whoever believes in him should not perish but have everlasting life. (John 3:16)

Daily Power!
The just shall live by faith.

Mark My Word
John 3:2 16; 11:17-27
Galatians 3:11
James 2:19

The Bible In A Year

Morning
1 Chronicles 24 and 25
1 Peter 5

Evening
Micah 3
Luke 12

There are various degrees of faith. We may begin with a limited vision of what to trust God for; or with only one prayer, "Oh God, help me!" I want to help you go up a kind of staircase, step by step, looking to God for an ever-wider area of your circumstances. Your faith may follow a process something like this:

First Step: Believing that something is true. James reminds those who believe in one God that the devils also believe the same thing, which is not too encouraging! Martha believed in the resurrection at the last day; but Christ wanted faith that leaped to resurrection there and then. Similarly, the Jews believed that their religion was true, although it did little for them in action - because it never was in action. This is still true today. Faith may be no more than agreement with a statement of truth, or an intellectual assent. Believing that there is a God is not a saving faith, any more than believing there is a planet called Pluto: but it is an essential start.

Second Step: Believing that a person is genuine. Nicodemus said: *"You are a Teacher come from God."* Jesus wanted a higher brand of faith than being regarded as a teacher. He talked to Nicodemus about believing in a new way; a way that Nicodemus had never conceived. Many believed in Jesus as Nicodemus did – as a good and genuine man. But, if he was good, then he was not a liar. Yet he claimed to be the Son of God. A good man would not claim such a thing, unless it was true, otherwise he would have been a blasphemer. Therefore, if he was a good man, He must have been what he said he was – Christ, the Savior of the world!

Step Three: Step Four

As we mature and progress in our lifelong walk of faith, we advance from childhood into adulthood:

> "And I, brethren, could not speak to you as to spiritual people but as to carnal, as to babes in Christ. I fed you with milk and not with solid food; for until now you were not able to receive it."

Let us see how our faith continues to grow:

Third Step: Believing in Jesus as an inspired person, like a prophet. The disciples told Christ that was how people thought of him, *"Some say (you are) John the Baptist, some Elijah, and others Jeremiah or one of the prophets."* He entered Jerusalem and, *"the multitudes said, 'This is Jesus, the prophet of Nazareth of Galilee.'"* They applauded him: but Jesus, like Jeremiah, wept. They had gone so far, but had not allowed him to take them under his wing and save them. We cannot say that he is a prophet, in the same way as saying Sir Christopher Wren was an architect. A prophet must be heard; and to **hear** Christ takes us a long, long way.

Fourth Step: Believing in God's power. In Jerusalem, everybody believed in his power. Many believed also in Christ's powers. They did not doubt what they saw: that he had healing power, that he was a miracle worker, and they even wanted to make him King. But Christ wanted a broader faith. They believed in his physical powers: but did not place him where he should be, as Lord and Savior. They asked him for miracles, but he had other ideas than to gratify their love of the sensational. Their faith was only in him as a healer, which is worth little more than faith in a man as a doctor, driver, or even a plumber. We trust a doctor as a doctor only, not as a daily help. Christ is to be trusted for all things, not a miracle or two.

Today's Scripture
Do not labor for the food which perishes, but for the food which endures to everlasting life, which the Son of Man will give you, because God the Father has set his seal on him.
(John 6:27)

Daily Power!
Christ is to be trusted for all things, not just a miracle or two.

Mark My Word
Matthew 16:14; 21:11
John 2:23-25; 6:36
1 Corinthians 3:1-2

The Bible In A Year

Morning
1 Chronicles 26 and 27
2 Peter 1

Evening
Micah 4
Luke 13

30

Today's Scripture
That Christ may dwell in your hearts through faith; that you, being rooted and grounded in love ... may be filled with all the fullness of God.
(Ephesians 3:17-19)

Daily Power!
I have been crucified with Christ; it is no longer I who live, but Christ lives in me; and the life which I now live in the flesh I live by faith in the Son of God, who loved me and gave himself for me.

Mark My Word
Psalm 27:10; 41:9
Galatians 2:20
Ephesians 4:14-15
1 Thessalonians 5:23

The Bible In A Year

Morning
1 Chronicles 28
2 Peter 2

Evening
Micah 5
Luke 14

The apostle Paul cared very much about maturing new Christians entrusted to his teaching: *"We should no longer be children, tossed to and fro and carried about with every wind of doctrine, by the trickery of men ... but speaking the truth in love, may grow up in all things into him who is the Head – Christ."* As you continue in your lifelong walk of faith, you will take these steps:

Step Five: Believing as trust. This turns faith into a personal relationship. We trust people, such as our parents. They know us; we feel that they will not fail us. That is the personal "faith" God wants us to place in him. Our lives are as open to him as if he sat in our living room. We may as well confess our sins; he knows them anyway. If we were trapped on a mountain ledge and an expert rescuer came, we would simply have to put our lives in his hands, no matter how brilliant, rich, strong, or stupid we were. That is saving faith, and Christ is our Rescuer.

Step Six: Believing in Christ. This is the real faith. We trust Christ in a way that we never trust even a close friend. Friends can let us down: *"Even my own familiar friend in whom I trusted, who ate my bread, has lifted up his heel against me."* Our own fathers may fail us. *"When my father and my mother forsake me, then the Lord will take care of me."* It means surrender, letting him take over, in every area of our lives. If he is going to keep your head above water, he has to get a grip on you completely.

That is how Paul wanted it to be for his converts: *"Now may the God of peace himself sanctify you completely; and may your whole spirit, soul, and body be preserved blameless at the coming of our Lord Jesus Christ."* Christ can only save what we give to him. Hand everything over to him: lock, stock and barrel; body, soul and spirit; into his total care, for all time. Then he can do something for us. He does not want to save us piecemeal. Satan is the only rival for that kind of possession of us, being hungry for us, wanting to "devour" us. But when you have "fullness of faith," you are God's own.

The blood of Jesus
has been around for 2000 years.
If it is so powerful, why are there still so
many sinful people in the world?
It is like working in a soap factory
Though you are surrounded by soap,
unless you apply the soap to your body
you are still dirty.

An unpreached gospel is no gospel at all.

Dignity is not a fruit of the Spirit
but joy is.

When Is Unbelief Forgivable?

Unbelief about God can be forgiven if people are ignorant about him. *"How shall they believe in him of whom they have not heard?"* But **ignorance** may need forgiving. In our Western society, not hearing the gospel is unpardonable bigotry. How can God forgive people who will not even listen after his Son died for their sins? *"Therefore we must give the more earnest heed to the things we have heard, lest we drift away … how shall we escape if we neglect so great salvation?"* If we have "truth" without the truth of Christ, we die without the truth of forgiveness.

A bishop went to a very talkative barber for a haircut. Having the churchman captive in his chair for fifteen minutes, he aggressively announced he was an unbeliever. The bishop asked the barber: "Do you read the Bible?" … "me, read the Bible? Of course not. I'm an unbeliever." … "Do you read religious Christian books?" … "You wouldn't catch me reading that rubbish. I'm an unbeliever, I told you." … "Do you ever go to church, or listen to TV or radio about God?" … "You bet I don't!" … "Have you any Christian friends who tell you about their religious experiences?" … "No, thank you!" … "What about anybody coming from a church to talk to you?" … "Those religion-pushers know me! They dare not even knock at my door twice!" The bishop waited, smiling. "You understand now?" asked the barber. "Perfectly!" answered the bishop. "I understand that you are not an unbeliever at all." The barber retorted, "I tell you, I believe nothing." The bishop answered: "You can't be an unbeliever. You don't even know what you are **not** believing. You can't disbelieve what you've never heard. I'll tell you what you are: you are a damned fool." The barber said: "Bishop, I'm surprised to hear you use language like that." The bishop replied: "I am not swearing. I'm quoting the Bible. It says: *The fool has said in his heart "There is no God"* **and** *'God will send them strong delusion … that they all may be condemned who did not believe the truth."* You are an ignoramus about God, and a fool for not wanting to know. So you are damned already!"

Know what you believe!

Today's Scripture
Therefore we must give the more earnest heed to the things we have heard, lest we drift away.
(Hebrews 2:1)

Daily Power!
If we have "truth" without the truth of Christ we die without the truth of forgiveness.

Mark My Word
Psalm 14:1
Romans 10:14
2 Thessalonians 2:11
Hebrews 2:1, 3

The Bible In A Year

Morning
1 Chronicles 29
2 Peter 3

Evening
Micah 6
Luke 15

2

God's Anointing – Man's Confirmation

Today's Scripture
Rejoicing to see your
good order and the
steadfastness of
your faith in Christ.
As you therefore
have received Christ
Jesus the Lord, so
walk in him, rooted
and built up in him
and established
in the faith, as you
have been taught,
abounding in it with
thanksgiving.
(Colossians 2:5-7)

Daily Power!
The anointing which
I have received from
him abides in me,
and I abide in him.

Mark My Word
Exodus 40:15
Leviticus 8:1-13
2 Samuel 1:21
Acts 10:38
Colossians 2:5-7
1 John 2:27

The Bible In A Year

Morning
2 Chronicles 1
1 John 1

Evening
Micah 7
Luke 16

God never anointed anybody twice. David was anointed of the Lord through Samuel: later, the elders of Israel anointed him a second time; thus confirming their acceptance of his kingly authority and divine anointing. Jesus was anointed by God: afterward, women poured ointment on him, which he said was for his burial; a very special part of his service to the Father and for mankind. *"How God anointed Jesus of Nazareth with the Holy Spirit and with power, who went about doing good and healing all who were oppressed by the devil, for God was with him."* Other than these examples, priests or kings only had an initial anointing at the beginning of their careers.

Some sing for a new anointing and pray for another Pentecost. But the whole concept of "another" or "new" anointing, as if the original had faded away, is strange to New Testament thought on the eternal Spirit. The anointing is self-renewing: it renews us, we do not renew it. He is the Spirit of newness. *"The anointing which you have received from him abides in you."* In the Book of Exodus, we read: *"You shall anoint them … that they may minister to me."* The second book of Samuel speaks of the *"shield of the mighty"* being anointed for battle, and the book of Leviticus tells us of the anointing for sanctified service and holiness.

We can lay our hands upon our friends, and pray to bring God's strength and blessing, but we must not suppose we can fill a person with the Spirit each time, assuming the filling has dried away. The Holy Spirit does not evaporate! If we are doing the work to which God has called us, the anointing rests upon us without ever diminishing. It is in the same pattern as "eternal life" – we receive it moment by moment, like a waterfall fed by a never-failing river. All that is necessary is that we release his energies by working in his name. Swim, fully immersing yourself in the river of God today.

The Gospel Of The Cross

The gospel that the disciples preached as they went out was the gospel of the kingdom of God: the Good News that the kingdom was close to them. But they preached it in terms not used by John the Baptist, and only occasionally used by Jesus himself. Their kingdom gospel was proclaimed in the language of Christ crucified. It was not a different gospel, but it contained a tremendous new fact – the **vital** fact about the kingdom of God: **the cross**. When Jesus had spoken of it earlier, Peter had even tried to rebuke him. What at first seemed outrageous to the disciples was (as they later realized) the all-important mystery of the kingdom: the self-sacrifice of the King for the kingdom. The kingdom is established by the titanic battle and victory of Christ. his blood marks its foundations. Calvary is the source of the redemptive dynamic of God, the nuclear power drive of the gospel, and of all the gifts of the Spirit.

Modern religionists are busy building Calvary bypasses. The gospel of the Bible is caricatured as a "gospel of gore" – as if in our world, anybody could be squeamish about blood! Roads that avoid Calvary prove to go nowhere. There are no roundabout routes. The kingdom of God has a checkpoint and border control, and it is at the cross. Without having been to Calvary, everybody lives a second-class existence as illegal immigrants. Passport and entry permits are repentance and faith in Christ Jesus. Then we may enter with the full privileges of citizens, no longer *"strangers and foreigners, but fellow citizens with the saints and members of God's household."* The *"covenants of promise"* are ours. We are not beggars asking the glorified saints to send us a few scraps of help. We do not need to collect their bones, hoping that some of their holiness or grace will brush off onto us, and stand to our credit. Believers are not bone-pickers. If we do what the apostles did, we shall get what the apostles got from the same Father, by the same Spirit, on the same terms of grace.

Today's Scripture
You are no longer strangers and foreigners, but fellow citizens with the saints and members of the household of God, having been built on the foundation of the apostles and prophets, Jesus Christ himself being the chief cornerstone. (Ephesians 2:19-20)

Daily Power!
If I do what the apostles did, I will get what the apostles got!

Mark My Word
Matthew 76:22
Ephesians 2:19

The Bible In A Year

Morning
2 Chronicles 2
1 John 2

Evening
Nahum 1
Luke 17

4

Fasting And Faith

Today's Scripture
So we fasted and entreated our God for this, and he answered our prayer.
(Ezra 8:23)

Daily Power!
When you fast, anoint your head and wash your face, so that you do not appear to men to be fasting, but to your Father who is in the secret place; and your Father who sees in secret will reward you openly.

Mark My Word
Ezra 8:23
Psalm 119:105
Matthew 6:171-18
Mark 9:25-29
Luke 4:18-19;
11:13; 24:49.

The Bible In A Year

Morning
2 Chronicles 3 and 4
1 John 3

Evening
Nahum 2
Luke 18

Some say they will fast, if necessary unto death, until God answers them. That is impressive: but does this affect God? Is it a sign of their patience that God will speak? Or are they trying to force the hand of God by a subtle spiritual threat? God does not yield to emotional pressures of any kind. It is an error to fast in order to twist God's arm. Fasting is just a manner of expressing our urgency, like calling on God loudly or persistently. The pagans thought that they could bring some kind of force to bear upon their gods by their exertions, bloodletting, and other efforts. But God is not like Zeus, Apollo, or Baal. It is God's pleasure to **hear** his children, and they do not need to make noise or demonstration. Prayer is effective when we are participating in the work of God, especially a particular work.

Jesus taught about fasting, emphasizing the necessity of fulfilling God's command. Since the disciples' mission was to *"preach the kingdom of God, and to heal the sick"* it was appropriate to explain that prayer and fasting were critical elements to ministry. *"(Jesus) rebuked the unclean spirit, saying to it: 'Deaf and dumb spirit, I command you, come out of him and enter him no more.' Then the spirit cried out, convulsed him greatly, and came out of him … (Then) his disciples asked him privately, 'Why could we not cast it out?' So he said to them, 'This kind can come out by nothing but prayer and fasting.'"* Again, the revealed will of God was being performed – and fasting contributed to their focus and ability to obey, not to persuading God.

To believe God when we ask, we must know that we are heard, and that we ask according to his Word and his revealed will. Jesus said: *"Your heavenly Father (will) give the Holy Spirit to those who ask him"*, and *"tarry … until you are endued with power from on high."* We should ask for healing; for spiritual gifts; for one another; for those in the assembly who sin; and for kings and governors. These are all subsidiary requests heading up the greatest purpose of God: the world's redemption. Pray the Word to make your prayers effective.

Not Conspicuous, Just Changed

The anointing is not to make us as conspicuous as Joseph in his coat of many colors. In a TV commercial, a young lady with a very bad cold has lost her sense of smell, and sprays herself with more and more perfume. When she opens the door to her admirer, her perfume overpowers him and knocks him down! It is human to want overwhelming power with an impact that everyone can feel. John the Baptist wore conspicuous rough clothing, and ate peculiar food; this indicated that he was a holy prophet. Jesus did neither: he dressed inconspicuously, and ate anything set before him. Many were awed in the presence of Jesus: but it was not by demonstrations of overwhelming power; it showed as concern and love for men and women. That is why they fell down and worshiped him.

The prophet Isaiah taught us about receiving God's anointing:

> "I said, 'Woe is me, for I am undone! Because I am a man of unclean lips, and I dwell in the midst of a people of unclean lips; for my eyes have seen the King, the Lord of hosts.' Then one of the seraphim flew to me, having in his hand a live coal which he had taken with the tongs from the altar. And he touched my mouth with it, and said, 'Behold, this has touched your lips; your iniquity is taken away and your sin purged.'"

The anointing of God changes us.

In ourselves, sinful and limited, we are completely unfit to become the temples of the Spirit: but we are made fit. We wonder and worship. When that mighty Spirit takes up his abode within us, then oil, hands, or anything else upon our outer flesh are only symbols of his indwelling greatness. Along with anointing, there are other symbols of the Spirit. The anointing cannot be learned as mere head knowledge, but it must enter the heart and be expressed in the life; it must "take root downward, and bear fruit upward." Allow the anointing of Christ Jesus to be a vital life-force in you!

Today's Scripture
And as we have borne the image of the man of dust, we shall also bear the image of the heavenly Man.
(1 Corinthians 15:49)

Daily Power!
The anointing of God changes us.

Mark My Word
Isaiah 6:5-7; 37:31
1 Corinthians 15:49

The Bible In A Year

Morning
2 Chronicles 5 to 6:11
1 John 4

Evening
Nahum 3
Luke 19

6

When Jesus met a blind man, he said: *"I must work the works of him who sent me while it is day."* By this he showed that the restoration of the blind was his Father's work. kingdom mercies continued as long as Jesus was in the world. Moreover, they eventually resumed after he had gone. Jesus said to his disciples: *"The night is coming when no one can work."* He meant that soon he would be crucified, night would fall, and there would be no blind receiving their sight. He said to the disciples, *"Without me, you can do nothing"* – and they did not for a long time. Then they received what Jesus had promised: *power* when the Holy Spirit came!

Now if the power of the kingdom is the Holy Spirit, then kingdom power was given to the church on the day of Pentecost. This is more than power and authority. In a saying of key importance, Christ announced to his followers: *"It is your Father's good pleasure to give you the kingdom."* Believers inherit the kingdom lock, stock and barrel. The kingdom power which rested on Christ Jesus was for working signs and wonders; the same Spirit is given to those within the kingdom of God for the same kingdom purposes. As John the Baptist revealed: *"Upon whom you see the Spirit descending and remaining on him, this is he who baptizes with the Holy Spirit."* The Spirit endowed Jesus, and his people, with the same power.

There is a difference between Christ and his followers; and it is rather noticeable! The difference is first who he is. Those who say: "The words of Christ on our lips are the same as on Christ's lips" must remember this: it is not the words which matter, but the person who speaks them. We may be adopted sons of God, but he is the eternal and only begotten. The second difference is that the Spirit comes from him. He is the Source. We are not sources, but channels; riverbeds through which the waters of his fullness flow. Open wide your channel-gate for him to freely access your life.

Today's Scripture
But if the Spirit of him who raised Jesus from the dead dwells in you, he who raised Christ from the dead will also give life to your mortal bodies through his Spirit who dwells in you. (Romans 8:11)

Daily Power!
The kingdom power which rested on Christ Jesus was for working signs and wonders; the same Spirit is given to those within the kingdom of God.

Mark My Word
Luke 12:32
John 1:33-34;
9:3-4; 15:5
Romans 8:11

The Bible In A Year

Morning
2 Chronicles 6:12
1 John 5

Evening
Habakkuk 1
Luke 20

Makers Of Money – Or History?

If we parallel Deborah's story in Judges with our world, who does the tribe of Dan represent? Dan is the Christian who belongs to God's family, knows what are God's claims upon him, hears God's call - but does not respond. He remains in his ship shop when God wants him to "*seek first the kingdom of God.*" The music of the tinkling till, applause of the unconverted, or opinion of family and friends deafen him to the call of the living God. Dan sings about "the sweet bye-and-bye on the beautiful shore", – but will his ship reach it, or just flounder in the Sea of Life? Can this be? Look at the wreckage of lives where people have chosen the wrong priorities. Some of the saddest people have been those who did not keep their eyes on God, and things went terribly wrong in the end. Success turned to ashes, popularity went sour. They chose the Danite opportunities of the ship shop: they let others follow Christ to his harvest field, or battlefield, or maybe mission field. In the end, they saw their joy and contentment turn to tragedy: "*The harvest is past, the summer is ended, and we are not saved!*"

The runner with Deborah's recruiting letter hoped for a better response as he reached the tribes of Zebulun and Naphtali. Two men were working in the fields, and looking forward to the end of the day and to the joy of their wives and children. They huddled around the dispatch runner to hear and consider Deborah's call to service. What should they do? There was only one choice: Go! "Praise the Lord," they shouted, "that God has anointed somebody to lead us. Let's make an end of this constant harassment from Jabin and his bandits. Thank God for Deborah! We'll back her to the hilt. Tell her we're on the way!" Zebulun and Naphtali exchanged their pruning hooks for spears. Children were hugged, weeping wives kissed, and the men marched away into the dust of battle. "*Zebulun is a people who jeopardized their lives to the point of death, Naphtali also, on the heights of the battlefield.*" That is high praise; the kind of praise that you want to hear from God.

Today's Scripture
When leaders lead in Israel, when the people willingly offer themselves, bless the Lord!
(Judges 5:2)

Daily Power!
He is Lord of lords and King of kings; and those who are with him are called, chosen, and faithful.

Mark My Word
Judges 4:1-24; 5:1-31
Jeremiah 8:20
Matthew 6:33
Revelation 17:14

The Bible In A Year

Morning
2 Chronicles 7
1 John 5

Evening
Habakkuk 2
Luke 21

Two Kinds Of People

8

Today's Scripture
Choose for yourselves this day whom you will serve. (Joshua 24:15)

Daily Power!
Blessed is the man who endures temptation; for when he has been approved, he will receive the crown of life which the Lord has promised to those who love him.

Mark My Word
Judges 4:1-24; 5:1-31
Matthew 10:39
James 1:12
Revelation 2:10

The Bible In A Year

Morning
2 Chronicles 8
3 John

Evening
Habakkuk 3
Luke 22

When the Israelite-Canaanite war was won, Deborah the Judge arrived at the quay-side to visit Dan, asking him one withering question: *"Why did Dan remain on ships?"* Dan sat still, fingers fumbling nervously with a coin. He could not lift his eyes to face this Holy Spirit-anointed woman of God. Her question haunted him the rest of his life; and that question will be heard again at the throne of God, when Dan and all the rest of us have to give account for our lives. Will Dan look at the Lord: or be too ashamed, not knowing what to answer, hanging his head in confusion? Zebulun and Naphtali did not have Dan's eye for business. Dan made money: but Zebulun and Naphtali made history that day, fighting to save Israel in a battle still talked about today. They risked everything, even life itself, fighting in the high places of the field. Dan staked nothing; he never took risks. When Dan died, he was the richest man in the country. Then, as his soul was leaving his body, perhaps Dan grabbed for his gold, wanting to take it with him. The Angel of Death could have swept him away with a laugh: "You've made your pile, now somebody else will spend it!"

The call of God is still heard by the Zebulun and Naphtali people today, but not by the Dan people. Churches are composed of one or the other kind. The Dan people are those who consider their businesses more important than God's work; their homes more precious than heaven for the lost; and saving money, more expedient than saving souls. Any pastor will tell you who are the Dan or the Zebulun and Naphtali characters in his congregation: "It's always the same people who respond, and give, and work. If it was not for them, this church would close." Some obey God's call at any cost, but others would not risk five cents for God. Zebulun and Naphtali died on the battleground for God's kingdom. Jesus said: *"He who loses his life for my sake will find it ... Be faithful until death, and I will give you the crown of life."* There is a nobility in that kind of dying, and even in one's readiness to give all, which we now recognize and honor on earth. But the Lord himself will recognize it when a glittering crown of life is placed upon one's head by the hand of Christ himself. Of the Dan folk, Jesus said: *"He who finds his life will lose it."* Make your choice today!

The Giver, Not The Gift

It is absolutely necessary to learn that the Holy Spirit is "he" not "it." The Spirit is not an impersonal force. The anointing of God is not just power or gifts: but the Holy Spirit himself. When people speaking with tongues first stepped into modern history, they were called "the tongues people" and similar names, by many who were opposed to the experience. In fact, the memory of those people is still among us. They carried an impressive godliness which was motivated by service, not sensation, seeking the Giver, not the gifts. They wanted to know Jesus better and be Christ-like. They did not seek power for the sake of power. Their daily desire was to: *"Let this mind be in (them) which was also in Christ Jesus, who ... made himself of no reputation, taking the form of a bondservant ... and became obedient."* Many laid down their lives for God.

When Jesus healed the sick, it was not just sheer electric power he wielded; it showed the power of his conquering love. He healed the sick by his stripes; that was the secret wonder of his anointing. He healed a withered arm, even though it provoked men to plot against his life. He risked everything and would go to any lengths, even the cross, for the sake of those who were suffering. Pain and the ministry of healing are strangely linked. If we are willing to know *"the fellowship of his sufferings"*, then we will feel the same anointing of love that Jesus had. If we have the same heartbreaking pity that forgets self; and will make any sacrifice for the afflicted, as Jesus did, then we will identify with those who suffer, sharing their suffering to ease their pain. If we *"took (their) infirmities"* as Jesus did, and realized what this means: *"If one member suffers, all the members suffer with it,"* then perhaps fewer people would go home unhealed. I know nothing more profane than healing the sick in Jesus' name to get rich or to make a name for oneself, or for the gratification of wielding power. The most precious thing we can ever possess is not the gift which God gives; but himself. Seek the giver today.

Today's Scripture

That I may know him and the power of his resurrection, and the fellowship of his sufferings, being conformed to his death, if, by any means, I may attain to the resurrection from the dead.
(Philippians 3:10-11)

Daily Power!

Jesus healed the sick by his stripes: the secret wonder of his anointing was compassion.

Mark My Word

Isaiah 53:5
1 Corinthians 12:26
Philippians 2:5-8; 3: 10-11
Hebrews 4:15

The Bible In A Year

Morning

2 Chronicles 9
Jude

Evening

Zephaniah 1
Luke 23

10

Today's Scripture
But you shall receive power when the Holy Spirit has come upon you; and you shall be witnesses to me in Jerusalem, and in all Judea and Samaria, and to the ends of the earth.
(Acts 1:8)

Daily Power!
The command is still the same: be witnesses to me!

Mark My Word
Daniel 12:3
Matthew 5:15
Mark 4:21; 16:15
Luke 11:33
Acts 1:8; 20:8
Philippians 2:15

The Bible In A Year

Morning
2 Chronicles 10
Revelation 1

Evening
Zephaniah 2
Luke 24

The Most Important Job

There was once a tribe that worshipped the moon. They explained why. The moon shines at night, they said, when it is dark and we need light; but the silly old sun shines during the day when there is plenty of light – what could be more pointless? Of course, there is light during the day because the sun shines, and there is light in America because the gospel light shines here. But there are many places in the world where it is very dark. I guess have been like the moon: trying to bring light to the dark places of the earth. When Paul preached in Troas all night and Eutychus fell asleep, the Bible says: *"There were many lamps in the upper room"* where he was talking. There are many shining lamps in America today. You are called *"in the midst of a crooked and perverse generation, among whom you shine as lights in the world,"* not as *"a lamp ...under a basket."*

Some people shine intellectually and talk brilliantly. I am just an evangelist. Any brightness on my part will have to come from the Holy Spirit and the Word of God. My hope is the promise: *"Those who turn many to righteousness (shall shine) like the stars forever and ever."* My natural environment is a platform in a field in Africa somewhere, not a university. But as far as I am concerned, an evangelist's job is the most important in the world.

People ask what God is saying to the church. He is saying what he has always said: *"Preach the gospel to every creature."* If Jesus himself were to take my place here in these last days before the final judgment, he would repeat his last words to the disciples: *"You shall receive power when the Holy Spirit has come upon you; and you shall be witnesses to me in Jerusalem, and in all Judea and Samaria and to the end of the earth."* Until we have done that, he has no further instructions for us. Listen well.

The Aim Of The Church

It has been suggested that there should be a moratorium on bringing in more converts until the church is fit and ready to receive them. But how can we ever hope to be fit if we stop obeying Christ? his great command is to bring in converts. Although training is vital, concentrating on our own holiness as a primary spiritual focus will never make us fit to reach others with the gospel. Sanctification does not take place in seclusion only: holiness looks outward to the spiritually lost. Nor is it just an academic subject to be studied with a view to passing examinations or writing a thesis: it is far more than that; the very work of God himself.

I know of no finer way to develop spirituality than to go all out to win others for Christ. When we try to reach people with the gospel, we know that we have to be real. When church boards omit evangelism, how can we keep the church from stagnation and sterility? If people do not see their overall purpose as winning people for Christ, they just become listeners, sermon tasters, choir critics, or leadership judges. The church is not a restaurant for spiritual gourmets, cultivating a discriminating palate for food from the pulpit: it is a canteen for workers. The primary aim of every church service, whether prayer meetings, Bible studies, young people's meetings, choir practice, or communion service should be evangelistic. Why should not every service be for outsiders? Especially at communion, when the emblems of bread and wine are taken, make sure the church is full of the godless! That cup of red wine is the greatest preacher in the world! It is the gospel in a cup; an opportunity to invite lost sinners to accept the sacrifice of the cross. Some churches do not trouble to include outsiders. What a lost opportunity! The precious blood of Jesus cleanses us from all sin. If a church has tried and failed in its attempts at evangelism, it is time for a serious evaluation of its efforts. Evangelism demands the most intensive thinking. The finance committee's job is soul-saving, not money-saving. Any surplus funds should go into the true business of the church: saving the world. Be a dedicated soul-winner.

Today's Scripture
he himself gave some to be apostles, some prophets, some evangelists, and some pastors and teachers, for the equipping of the saints for the work of the ministry, for the edifying of the body of Christ.
(Ephesians 4:11-12)

Daily Power!
If people do not see their overall purpose as winning people for Christ, they just become listeners, sermon-tasters, choir critics, or judges of those in leadership.

Mark My Word
Ephesians 4:11-16

The Bible In A Year

Morning
2 Chronicles 11 and 12
Revelation 2

Evening
Zephaniah 3
1 John 1

Simple, True Faith

Faith produces an interaction between Christ and me. Believing is a relationship: not like being related to your great-aunt whom you have never met; but alive, vibrant, affecting both Christ and yourself. We give ourselves to him; and he gives himself to us. We become *"partakers of the divine nature."* The Apostle Paul used a marvelous expression: *"Therefore, if anyone is in Christ, he is a new creation"* and *"There is therefore now no condemnation to those who are in Christ Jesus."* The simplest faith in Christ has this amazing effect. It is does not need algebra to find the value of X. The simplest person can believe and enjoy the same effect as the wisest.

The list of benefits of being *"in Christ"* is long! Faith in Christ brings: righteousness, peace, love, obedience, assurance, unity. It makes you a child of God, growing, justified, and alive; it can cause you to take risks, speak before great men, be famous throughout the world, and much more.

> "I also count all things loss for the excellence of the knowledge of Christ Jesus my Lord, for whom I have suffered the loss of all things and count them as rubbish, that I may gain Christ and be found in him ... that I may know him and the power of his resurrection."

Paul determined these benefits were worth everything!

Jesus heard all the religious jargon of the Scribes, which ordinary people did not appreciate. But the common people heard Jesus gladly. He talked about faith, but put it in other ways: *"Come to me"..."Love me"... "Abide in me"..."Follow me."* Faith is not one particular religious act. It is the transfer of responsibility for one's life to God completely, when our own resources are inadequate. It is spiritual fusion, making us one with Christ. It seems such a simple attitude, and it is. But there was no other way to acquire all that Christ accomplished on the cross for us. What could be greater? You are saved by faith!

Today's Scripture
That I may know him and the power of his resurrection, and the fellowship of his sufferings, being conformed to his death.
(Philippians 3:10)

Daily Power!
As true believers, we are all sons of God through faith in Christ Jesus.

Mark My Word
Romans 8:1
2 Corinthians 5:17
Galatians 3:26
Philippians 3:8-10
2 Peter 1:4

The Bible In A Year

Morning
2 Chronicles 13
Revelation 3

Evening
Haggai 1
John 2

Babel Reversed

Reading the Bible from the beginning, we find ourselves being told only about Israel: book after book, as if God were only the God of the Jews and had limited his interests to that tiny land and small nation. But as soon as we open the New Testament, the borders melt away, and the wide world comes into view. True, Jesus did say (of his own ministry): *"I was not sent except to the lost sheep of the house of Israel."* Yet he spoke in Nazareth concerning the foreign widow helped by Elijah. his statement against racial discrimination infuriated the congregation: but he went to Canaan later, where he healed a girl who did not belong to Israel. After Christ's resurrection, the disciples retained a Jewish outlook for a long time, thinking that their new faith belonged to Israel only. They even asked shortly before Christ ascended: *"Lord, will you at this time restore the kingdom to Israel?"* Jesus replied: *"It is not for you to know times or seasons which the Father has put in his own authority. But you shall receive power when the Holy Spirit has come upon you; and you shall be witnesses to me … to the ends of the earth."*

People had been trying to outwit God. He confused their language – so they would no longer be able to work together effectively – and scattered them over the face of the earth. *"Now the whole earth had one language and one speech."* The Lord confused the languages of all the earth: *"So the Lord scattered them abroad from there over the face of all the earth."*

On the day of Pentecost, he poured out his Spirit and reversed that curse: bringing knowledge of himself, and understanding of his goodness, to a great diversity of people. When the Holy Spirit fell, they spoke with the tongues of people from many different countries, displaying the ethnic interests of the Holy Spirit.

> "And they were all filled with the Holy Spirit and began to speak with other tongues, as the Spirit gave them utterance. And there were dwelling in Jerusalem Jews, devout men, from every nation under Heaven. And when this sound occurred, the multitude came together, and were confused, because everyone heard them speak in his own language."

And he speaks your language too!

Today's Scripture
We hear them speaking in our own tongues the wonderful works of God.
(Acts 2:11)

Daily Power!
I thank you, Father, Lord of heaven and earth, that you have hidden these things from the wise and prudent and have revealed them to babes.

Mark My Word
Genesis 11:1-9
1 Kings 17:8-24
Matthew 15:24
Luke 4:25-27
Acts 1:6-8; 2:4-6, 11

The Bible In A Year

Morning
2 Chronicles 14 and 15
Revelation 4

Evening
Haggai 2
John 3

Predestination And Evangelism

Today's Scripture
The people who sat
in darkness have
seen a great light;
and upon those who
sat in the region and
shadow of death,
Light has dawned.
(Matthew 4:16)

Daily Power!
The entrance of Your
words gives light; It
gives understanding
to the simple.

Mark My Word
Psalm 119:130
Matthew 4:16; 5:14

The Bible In A Year

Morning
2 Chronicles 16
Revelation 5

Evening
Zechariah 1
John 4

Predestination is an academic subject for high theological debate. My approach is not to get bogged down in theory: but to do the work of an evangelist. My response towards the controversy is to cut through the layers of theological concepts and step out in action. Whether people are among "the elect" or not, I want to make sure. I am not going to risk the eternal destiny of souls upon any doctrinal deductions or theories. There is nothing in the New Testament that says we should not preach the gospel, and nothing to say we should not do our best to persuade people into the kingdom. So that is what I do. We shall know the truth only when we get to heaven. If everybody I find there had been predestined – fine. I surely do not want to risk anyone in heaven saying to me: "Did you know for sure that I was elected? Why did you not preach the gospel to me? You gambled on your ideas being right and played dice with my soul. I could have been in hell instead of here."

Why should I, an evangelist, come to North America and "western culture"? Is there not light there already: more than in India, Egypt or Benin? Well, there is light there. The West has the gospel. In every town and city, on TV and radio, in the proliferation of Christian bookstores: there is light. Am I bringing light where there is already light? There is light in North America, but only because there are Christians here who shine. All the light comes from them. Jesus said: *"You are the light of the world."* So I am happy to shine with Westerners; we can always do with more light. Without Christians, night would fall on the West. The atheists, liberals, and agnostics would have it the way they wanted, but they would soon reap what they sowed. Without a guiding light, there would be anarchy. Let your light shine!

Evangelism Strengthens Nations

People say that they can live decent lives without Christianity: I wonder! We can all too easily forget that the very idea of decency comes from Christianity. We can briefly live without breathing; without food and water a bit longer; and without light for a while; but not forever. The Christian capital invested in the West by previous generations of believers will eventually be exhausted. We cannot live on the spiritual capital invested by past generations. We must be wealth creators: spiritual wealth, the riches of faith. It is Christ alone who can save, not Socrates or Plato. The condition for freedom is eternal vigilance: but vigilance alone will fail without faith in God. Freedom is a side-effect of godliness. You cannot have an effect without its cause; and you cannot have freedom without faith in God.

Many countries that I visit have no Christian tradition to shape their policies. It was Abraham who began a better order. He looked for a city whose builder and maker is God, which has foundations. A foundation reinforced with Bible faith is what distinguishes nations - and will extinguish them if abandoned. Something like it was done in my country, Germany. Centuries of liberal and rationalistic thought and biblical criticism diluted the Christian faith. Weak and unstable as water, it could not excel, as Jacob said about Reuben. In conditions like that, it was easy for a non-Christian regime to take over. The policies of Hitler and the Third Reich met with little moral resistance. In the 18th century, the experiment of a Christless state brought the Terror to France, with the slaughter of two million people. Britain was spared from it, mainly because of the impact of the Wesley-Whitefield revival movement. It will take at least a generation for Russia to recover from its seventy years of imposed atheism. Worse, perhaps, are the forms of Christianity, which are corrupted and mutilated beyond recognition. They devalue the gospel by unbelieving theories, or gross superstition and idolatry. They impart no freedom because they do not have it. This cries out for full-blooded gospel evangelism!

Today's Scripture
By faith Abraham obeyed when he was called to go out to the place which he would receive as an inheritance, and he went out, not knowing where he was going ... for he waited for the city which has foundations, whose builder and maker is God.
(Hebrews 11:8, 10)

Daily Power!
This is my comfort in my affliction, for your word has given me life.

Mark My Word
Genesis 49:3
Psalm 119:50
Hebrews 11:8, 10

The Bible In A Year

Morning
2 Chronicles 17
Revelation 6

Evening
Zechariah 2
John 5

16

Today's Scripture
Abraham believed
God, and it was
accounted to him
for righteousness.
(Romans 4:3)

Daily Power!
Christ has redeemed
us from the curse
of the law that the
blessing of Abraham
might come upon
us (the Gentiles) in
Christ Jesus, that
we might receive the
promise of the Spirit
through faith.

Mark My Word
Galatians 3:13-14
Romans 4:1-3

The Bible In A Year

Morning
2 Chronicles 18
Revelation 7

Evening
Zechariah 3
John 6

Abraham

Historians have listed the ten most world-changing battles: but it was rightly said that the greatest of them was fought in the heart of Abraham. If anyone thinks of Abraham as just a Bible character, they have not even begun to understand the world in which they live. The Bible names him 309 times: but because of his faith, his name is inscribed upon the whole of the Middle East, and upon world history to this day. He was the first man noted for the "obedience of faith." his life's career was consistent with his faith. *"Abraham believed God, and it was accounted to him as righteousness."* What is of faith, is forever.

Faith changes people, who change the world. Abraham was the man who began the civilizing process; fifteen hundred years before the Greeks and the Romans. The Pharaohs were in Egypt a thousand years before Abraham, and continued another two thousand years after him: but they affected the world less than he did. The Pharaohs left no moral mark, but only cluttered the desert sands with colossal monuments to their own egos. Abraham left not one single physical trace behind him for us to see: but all our lives today – religious or not – are different because of what he was.

Abraham was not "deeply religious." He was not "religious" at all in our modern sense. He had no creed, no hymns, no Bible, no images, and no theology. He probably did not really know much **about** God: but **he knew God**, personally, and very well. He walked with God. For this patriarch, God was not a go-to-church-once-a-week obligation, pushed into the spare corner of life; there was no church to attend. He did not believe God just to be faithful to tradition; there was no tradition. God was his way of life. God was to Abraham like money, sport, or sex is to most the world today. You and I should strive to have the great faith which Abraham owned!

Why Believe?

Abraham did not believe in order to save his own soul. his faith was neither a ticket for a joyride to heaven, nor an insurance policy to escape hell. We do not know what he thought about such a thing as the afterlife. He came from Ur of the Chaldees, and knew their pagan myths: but Abraham was starting on a new learning course. his tutor was the Lord. The nations had developed crude and cruel superstitions for themselves; Abraham threw himself upon God. To carry on without God was not in his ideas of living or of dying.

> "By faith Abraham obeyed when he was called to go out to the place which he would received as an inheritance. And he went out, not knowing where he was going. By faith he dwelt in the land of promise as in a foreign country, dwelling in tents with Isaac and Jacob, the heirs with him of the same promise, for he waited for the city which has foundations, whose builder and maker is God."

Abraham believed God for two reasons: first, he found that there was a living God; second, the only sensible thing to do was to carry out what He said. his faith changed the future, but that is not why he believed. He never dreamed of any such mission. In fact, he forsook the world and got as far away as he could from the world as it was. He changed it by leaving it. He believed God simply because God was there. That must still be the most rational thing anybody can ever do.

Astronaut Neil Armstrong stepped on the moon on July 20, 1969, and said that his one small step was a giant leap for mankind. Far bigger for mankind was the step that Abraham took when he left Ur of the Chaldees. He was the pioneer of walking by faith in God. Abraham began life in wealthy Ur of the Chaldees and then moved to Haran, still in the Fertile Crescent. After that, he sacrificed his fine dwelling for a black goat-skin tent in the wild moorland scrub of the Negeb Desert. He moved around only with his family, shepherds, and cattlemen, like a Bedouin sheikh. Secretly in his heart, he nourished the ideal of a new way of life. The God of Abraham is your living God today!

Today's Scripture
[Abraham] waited for the city which has foundations, whose builder and maker is God.
(Hebrews 11:10)

Daily Power!
Abraham believed God simply because he was there.

Mark My Word
Hebrews 11:8-10.

The Bible In A Year

Morning
2 Chronicles 19 and 20
Revelation 8

Evening
Zechariah 4
John 7

DECEMBER

18

Today's Scripture
But if I cast out demons with the finger of God, surely the kingdom of God has come upon you. (Luke 11:20)

Daily Power!
Spiritual gifts are not only for spiritual athletes.

Mark My Word
Luke 11:20
Acts 10:38
Philippians 4:2

The Bible In A Year

Morning
2 Chronicles 21
Revelation 9

Evening
Zechariah 5
John 8

Paul wrote to the Philippians about the beauty of Christ's humility; and then went on to mention two women who were at odds, Syntyche and Euodia. Then, with great tact, he thanked the Philippians for their recent kindness and described it as *"a sweet-smelling aroma"*, (in Greek, euodia), which was a gentle hint to Euodia herself. The inward Spirit is seen by outward effects – physical indications of an inward and spiritual source. To desire power merely to show off is corrupting and odious, not fragrant. The real power of God only comes with the Holy Spirit, who reveals the loveliness of the Christ life and his graciousness.

Receiving the Holy Spirit and his gifts has been marred by many innovative and novel approaches. Some realignment to the Word of God is needed in this area. The gifts are not tricks, techniques, or abilities we can pick up by watching others: God is pouring out his Spirit, and he does not need mere imitations of the gifts. It is not a matter of learning the correct approach, and then striving to obtain the gifts as prizes to be won. Gifts are not only for spiritual athletes. If they were prizes to be won, they would not be gifts. Gifts are for those in the kingdom of God: they belong there. Israel's blessings are covenanted to the commonwealth of Israel. Christ Jesus linked wonders to the new Christian commonwealth: *"If I cast out demons with the finger of God, surely the kingdom of God is come upon you."*

The "finger of God" is the Holy Spirit, as Peter tells us: *"God anointed Jesus of Nazareth with the Holy Spirit and with power, who went about doing good, and healing all who were oppressed by the devil."* There is no power greater than that of the Holy Spirit. That is kingdom power, and no other power matches it. By the Spirit, he distributes his ministries to whom he chooses. Allow his finger to point the way for you, to lead others.

Intellectualism

Abraham was not an intellectual, but *"the fear of the Lord is the beginning of wisdom."* Men of genius would burst upon the world scene in the distant future. They would cast their nets of thought far and wide, seeking knowledge and understanding. They would invent new ways to live, and new ways to rule cities. But they were destined never to know what Abraham knew. Their searching missed the ultimate discovery: *to know God.* Paul said: *"In the wisdom of God, the world through wisdom did not know God."* Their confession of failure was carved in stone upon an altar in Athens: *"To the unknown god."*

God would never wish to be unknown. Abraham had picked up a golden key marked "faith." By it, he opened heaven. Men of genius are as rare as icicles in summer. Abraham was not one of them. God is not the chairman of an exclusive club for intellectuals, but he keeps his front door open for anybody. He would never deprive himself of the love of the millions, in preference to the one-in-a-million prodigy.

> "And we know that the Son of God has come and has given us an understanding, that we may know him who is true, and we are in him who is true, in his Son Jesus Christ. This is the true God and eternal life."

The suggestion that we must not believe if men of intellect do not, is not a very intellectual notion. If we had to find him via a labyrinth of learning, He would have a very small company around him. To have the love of the vast mass of mankind, the means had to be different. He makes himself known to those who look up to him in childlike hope. You do not have to be some intellectual to know and love God: you simply love him by faith.

Today's Scripture
Whoever believes that Jesus is the Christ is born of God, and everyone who loves him who begot also loves him who is begotten of him.
(1 John 5:1)

Daily Power!
God makes himself known to those who look up to him, in childlike hope.

Mark My Word
Psalm 111:10
Acts 17:23
1 Corinthians 1:21
1 John 5:1-20

The Bible In A Year

Morning
2 Chronicles 22 and 23
Revelation 10

Evening
Zechariah 6
John 9

20

Today's Scripture
Therefore do not
be ashamed of the
testimony of our
Lord... who has saved
us and called us
with a holy calling,
not according to our
works, but according
to his own purpose
and grace which was
given to us in Christ
Jesus before
time began.
(2 Timothy 1:8-9)

Daily Power!
There is no real life
without the secret
of God.

Mark My Word
Genesis 17:1
John 3:36
Acts 17:30
Romans 1:22
2 Timothy 1:10
Hebrews 11:10

The Bible In A Year

Morning
2 Chronicles 24
Revelation 11

Evening
Zechariah 7
John 10

Abraham learned to trust God, and it revealed to him the paths of peace. In his day, cities existed by military might, founded on bloodshed. God gave Abraham a new vision: a city of peace, whose *"builder and maker is God."* his eyes scanned far horizons indeed. He was the first to discern the paths of righteousness, paths *"in the sea"* and ways in the wilderness. The paths of righteousness and peace have been found. They are marked and known. Used or not, they can now never be forgotten, but are there, freeways open for all. Many nations claim to follow them, but it is only feebly. If we traced them back, they would bring us to the tent door of Abraham, where God said to him, *"Walk before me and be blameless."*

The letter to the Hebrews sums up that for which Abraham lived: *"He waited for the city which has foundations, whose builder and maker is God."* In his day, nobody knew of any spiritual foundations. Rulers ruled only for their own benefit. Before Abraham, people's heads were vacant of any purpose or plan. Nobody knew why on earth he or she was on earth! Paul faced the agnostics and Stoics of Athens, saying: *"These times of ignorance God overlooked, but now commands all men everywhere to repent."* Therefore, he wrote to Timothy, *"Jesus Christ ... brought life and immortality to light through the gospel."* Paul also talks about those who *"professing to be wise, ... became fools."* We may live without knowing the distance to the nearest star, or the secrets of the atom: but there is no real life at all without the secret of God. We are lost before we start. Agnosticism is total disaster. We either live by faith – or we do not live. As Jesus said: *"He who believes in the Son has everlasting life, and he who does not believe the Son shall not see life."* Faithless life is lifeless life. Abraham knew very little about the world around him: but knew what life was all about. God made the first man, Adam, and the first civilized man, Abraham. Live in God.

Accomplishing Mission Impossible

John the Baptist, the divinely-sent forerunner who introduced Christ, proclaimed a new era: *"Repent, for the Kingdom of Heaven is at hand."* The central core of that proclamation was the Messiah who would baptize in the Holy Spirit. It was far greater than the restoration of Israel's greatness – it was nothing less than a cosmic change. John unfolded a map of the future, showing – not a river of water – but of fire! John used an earthly element – water – but Christ baptizes in a heavenly element – Divine Fire!

Jesus echoes the same words: *"John baptized with water, but in a few days you will be baptized with the Holy Spirit."* We should take note of the fact that Jesus did not baptize anybody with the Spirit while he was on earth but he painstakingly prepared his disciples for this vitally important event. Only if they were aflame could they set others on fire.

This was the only way that it was possible for the disciples of Jesus to evangelize the ancient World of their time in the short span of life they had at their disposal. For these ordinary fisherman and outsiders from Galilee to fulfill the Great Commission of Jesus Christ must have seemed like "mission impossible." But against all expectations it became "mission accomplished." How? They advanced with a new secret: God personally worked with them with signs and wonders.

More than that, he barbed their simple words with conviction and guided them to the hearts of hearers as unerringly and powerfully as David's stone to the head of Goliath. Without personal charisma, the *charisma* of the Spirit of God endued them. Their "secret?" The fire of the Holy Spirit!

Because the world hovers between spiritual life and death, the utmost consideration must be given to whatever can secure the destinies of precious people. A Fire-baptized church is the key!

Today's Scripture

But after me will come one who is more powerful than I ... He will baptize you with the Holy Spirit and with fire.
(Matthew 3:11b)

Daily Power!

Lord Jesus, I need your baptism with fire.

Mark My Word

Acts 1:5

The Bible In A Year

Morning
2 Chronicles 25
Revelation 12

Evening
Zechariah 8
John 11

22

Today's Scripture
For we do not have a high priest who cannot sympathize with our weaknesses, but was in all points tempted as we are, yet without sin. (Hebrews 4:15)

Daily Power!
Jesus Christ was born because he wanted to be born.

Mark My Word
Isaiah 9:6; 53:12
Hebrews 4:15

The Bible In A Year

Morning
2 Chronicles 26
Revelation 13

Evening
Zechariah 9
John 12

Family Planning

Christmas is really a birthday party, a celebration of Christ's nativity. We do not know the actual date of Jesus' birth, but it does not matter: the 25th of December is as good as any other day. If we can have national holidays for saints, battles, and victories, we certainly should rejoice about the birth of the greatest Person ever born! The great prophet Isaiah spoke seven hundred fifty years before Christ was born: *"For unto us a Child is born, unto us a Son is given; and the government will be upon his shoulder. And his name will be called Wonderful, Counselor, Mighty God, Everlasting Father, Prince of Peace."* All of which was fulfilled when Jesus came. Each Christmas, we can say: *"Unto us a son is given."* That is what Christmas is about.

And what a Son he turned out to be! Nobody else had a birth like his; and I am not just thinking of the virgin birth. Jesus Christ was born because **he wanted to be born**. Nobody else has ever chosen to be born, because people like us have never had that kind of choice! Jesus was not the result of family planning; he planned his birth himself with the Father in Heaven. But he planned the family of God, including its redemption by his own blood. The Son of God knew what life with us would be like: and yet he wanted to come to be with us. He came to a primitive home in a crude age, with basic food and hard work; and knew that he would be cruelly executed. Why on earth should he want to be on earth and endure and suffer such a life? The answer is that he wanted to be our redeemer. He was determined to join the human race at all costs. He called himself by only one title: *"the Son of Man"* identifying himself with the human race. Isaiah's words, *"Unto us a Child is born"* express solidarity with us. Even more, Jesus went for total involvement, being *"numbered with the transgressors."* Again and again, the Bible uses two words: *"for us."* He did not choose to be born for his own benefit, for anything he could get out of it for himself. Everything that he was and could do was only for his family. He drew his very breath *for us*, for the family. He is the greatest Gift that you have this Christmas!

What A Wonderful Son!

The gospel of Matthew begins by calling Christ the *"son of David"* and the *"son of Abraham."* Both David and Abraham had very special sons, but they were disappointments. The true son of Abraham was not Isaac, but Jesus; the true son of David was not Absalom, or Solomon, but Jesus. This is the son who is not a disappointment. Fathers failed, and their sons failed also, except this Son. He came to lift the family of man to a new level. Jesus never needed to go to a psychologist or a counselor; he was never at the end of his tether. Jesus was never fed-up, never had a nervous breakdown, never suffered a trauma, never had a burn-out. Jesus never had to apologize, never confessed any sin, or needed to repent. He met every situation with absolute poise and perfect reaction. What a Son to be proud of! We can hang on to him. He became a Son *"for us."* Because he lived like that, we can live! We do not just get by, scrape through, rowing hard, struggling all the way: but we voyage under a full sail. With a Son like that, we can face the music even when we do not like the tune. Jesus says: *"Because I live, you will live also."* Jesus is coming back *"for us."* Christ Jesus has never resigned from the human family; He is forever the Son of Man, born and bred here from infancy. He is due to come home anytime now – back to where he was born. What a homecoming! He loves this family of man, his own family. He wants to be with us, and wants to come back to where he belongs, to the world of men and women.

The family get-together at Christmas is a wonderful time, but it is only a picture of what is to come. When Jesus the Son comes home, what a reunion that will be! What feasting, what joy! Nobody who belongs there will be missing. Every born-again child of God will meet the Son of all sons, face to face. The celebrations will go on forever. So many have forgotten about all this. They know that the Son of Man came to earth: but think that he disappeared into the blue long ago. Christmas just keeps his memory alive. People read the Bible about Jesus and what he was like: but forget that he is coming back. He is coming for you!

Today's Scripture
Behold, I am coming quickly, and my reward is with me, to give to every one according to his work. I am the Alpha and the Omega, the Beginning and the End, the First and the Last.
(Revelation 22:12)

Daily Power!
When Jesus the Son comes home, what a reunion that will be!

Mark My Word
Matthew 1:1
John 14:19
Revelation 22:12

The Bible In A Year

Morning
2 Chronicles 27 and 28
Revelation 14

Evening
Zechariah 10
John 13

24

Read The Post-Script

Today's Scripture
Blessed are
those who do his
commandments,
that they may have
the right to the tree
of life, and may enter
through the gates
into the city.
(Revelation 22:14)

Daily Power!
We are two thousand
years nearer the
Second Coming now!

Mark My Word
Hebrews 9:28
Revelation 22:6-8;
12-14, 20

The Bible In A Year

Morning
2 Chronicles 29
Revelation 15

Evening
Zechariah 11
John 14

A family received a letter from their soldier-son on duty in a foreign land. They were all busy and it was a very long letter, so they read half a page or so. They intended to sit down after work and read it all. A little later someone knocked at the door and … there was their son, in person! They were astonished and said: "What are you doing here? We've just had your letter from where you were!" The son said: "Haven't you read it yet?" Well, they had not read as far as the postscript at the end, which said that he was coming home.

> "Then he said to me, 'These words are faithful and true.' And the Lord God of the holy prophets sent his angel to show his servants the things which must shortly take place. 'Behold, I am coming quickly! Blessed is he who keeps the words of the prophecy of this book.' Now I, John, saw and heard these things … 'And behold, I am coming quickly, and my reward is with me, to give to every one according to his work. I am the Alpha and the Omega, the Beginning and the End, the First and the Last.' Blessed are those who do his commandments, that they may have the right to the tree of life, and may enter through the gates into the city."

It is time to read God's post-script in the Bible. That great book closes with the words of Jesus: *"I am coming quickly!"* Jesus will come again. We have been waiting over two thousand years. People waited much longer than that the first time he came, but he did not forget to come. He will come the second time, and will not forget. As long as the family that he loves is here on earth, he will never rest. *"To those who eagerly wait for him, he will appear a second time."* We are two thousand years nearer the second coming now. If the first coming gave us the joys of Christmas, the second coming will bring the joys of heaven. *"Even so, come, Lord Jesus!"* Make that your song today!

Luke 2:1-20

"And it came to pass in those days that a decree went out from Caesar Augustus that all the world should be registered. This census first took place while Quirinius was governing Syria. So all went to be registered, everyone to his own city. Joseph also went up from Galilee, out of the city of Nazareth, into Judea, to the city of David, which is called Bethlehem, because he was of the house and lineage of David, to be registered with Mary, his betrothed wife, who was with child. So it was, that while they were there, the days were completed for her to be delivered. And she brought forth her firstborn son, and wrapped him in swaddling cloths, and laid him in a manger, because there was no room for them in the inn.

"Now there were in the same country shepherds living out in the fields, keeping watch over their flock by night. And behold, an angel of the Lord stood before them, and the glory of the Lord shone around them, and they were greatly afraid. Then the angel said to them, 'Do not be afraid, for behold, I bring you good tidings of great joy which will be to all people. For there is born to you this day in the city of David a Savior, who is Christ the Lord. And this will be the sign to you: You will find a babe wrapped in swaddling cloths, lying in a manger.' And suddenly there was with the angel a multitude of the heavenly host praising God and saying: 'glory to God in the highest, and on earth peace, goodwill toward men!'"

"So it was, when the angels had gone away from them into heaven, that the shepherds said to one another, 'Let us now go to Bethlehem and see this thing that has come to pass, which the Lord has made known to us.' And they came with haste and found Mary and Joseph, and the babe lying in a manger.

"Now when they had seen him, they made widely known the saying which was told them concerning this Child. And all those who heard it marveled at those things which were told them by the shepherds. But Mary kept all these things and pondered them in her heart. Then the shepherds returned, glorifying and praising God for all the things that they had heard and seen, as it was told them."

Today's Scripture
And she will bring forth a Son, and you shall call his name Jesus, for he will save his people from their sins.
(Matthew 1:21-23)

Daily Power!
Jesus was born so that we can have peace with God.

Mark My Word
Matthew 1:18-24; 2:1-18
Luke 2:1-20

The Bible In A Year

Morning
2 Chronicles 30
Revelation 16

Evening
Zechariah 12 to 13:1
John 16

"The Last Hour"

Today's Scripture
Turn the hearts of
the fathers to the
children, and the
disobedient to the
wisdom of the just, to
make ready a people
prepared for the Lord.
(Luke 1:17)

Daily Power!
I am not ashamed of
the gospel of Christ,
for it is the power of
God to salvation for
everyone
who believes.

Mark My Word
Luke 1:17
John 3:3, 7
1 John 2:18

The Bible In A Year

Morning
2 Chronicles 31
Revelation 17

Evening
Zechariah 13:2
John 16

The theme on my heart lately is a very simple verse: *"It is the last hour."* Some celebrate a year's end with frantic party-going, as if to make up for a whole year of dismal living. Others fall into deep depression, realizing that another year is passing; and feeling they have little to show for it. Some optimistic people take the end of a year to set themselves new goals and resolutions for the year to come. As for millennium awareness, international leaders spent millions trying to generate optimism that AD 2000 would be the start of a wonderful new age.

As in everything else, the Christian viewpoint is different. The end of each year, and the marking of the new millennium keeps me on the lookout, watching for Jesus' return. It was irrational to suggest that AD 2000 would automatically affect anything at all. Time has no power or magic to create a "golden age." For that to happen, a radical change in human nature would be needed. January 1, 2000 did not turn anybody into a saint; not even for a single day. New Year's resolutions always evaporate as quickly as they were made. Health authorities report that people are becoming overweight, warning of heart disease and other problems: so people start exercising in the New Year, but soon give up. Very few last even six months.

Only one power on Earth can bring a fundamental alteration in us, and that is the gospel. The kingdom of God will not come because God looks at a calendar. Nicodemus came to ask Jesus about Israel being restored to the kingdom glory of the times of Solomon, but Jesus answered: *"Unless one is born again he cannot see the kingdom of God."* Jesus meant Nicodemus **and** Israel. Getting rid of the Romans and creating political change, would do nothing to bring in a wonderful new order: but being born-again brings the kingdom of God near! You are in the kingdom of God!

Faith's Final Test

God planted Abraham in an unfriendly wilderness. God also planted the church in an unfriendly world, with the same purpose as that of Abraham. When Jesus sent out his disciples, he gave them a divine passport into every land on earth: *"Go into all the world and preach the gospel to every creature."* Christ was following the will of his Father expressed to Abraham: *"I will bless you … and you will be a blessing … and in you all the nations of the earth shall be blessed."* They could forget about saving themselves, he would look after that: their concern must be to save mankind. The Great Commission commits us to continue Christ's mission. Concerned only with itself, the church is purposeless in God's eyes; and harmless to hell. Faith only operates when linked with his purposes - and the first of them is to bless all families of the earth.

The strangest episode in Abraham's life was his call to sacrifice Isaac:

> "By faith Abraham, when he was tested, offered up Isaac, and he who had received the promises offered up his only begotten son, of whom it was said, 'In Isaac your seed shall be called,' concluding that God was able to raise him up, even from the dead, from which he also received him in a figurative sense."

It might shock us that Abraham would even contemplate human sacrifice: but four thousand years' distance makes it impossible for us to understand a man of his time. Human sacrifice was common, whereas today it is not so common (although it is still practiced). Abraham was the learner and beginner of faith in God. Spiritual lessons percolate very slowly into our human understanding.

God never meant Isaac to be sacrificed, but God tested Abraham on his own cultural level. Such a practice was then an expression of extreme religious devotion. Abraham learned, in fact, that God wanted no offering of human blood. God's purpose was to create a new culture in which bloodshed had no place. We are thankful that God taught Abraham a new covenant! And we are grateful that he allows us to walk in the fullness of the covenant today.

Today's Scripture
Christ has redeemed us from the curse of the law, having become a curse for us... that the blessing of Abraham might come upon the Gentiles in Christ Jesus, that we might receive the promise of the Spirit through faith.
(Galatians 3:13-14)

Daily Power!
The sacrifice on Calvary is the ultimate sacrifice.

Mark My Word
Mark 16:15
Hebrews 11:17-19

The Bible In A Year

Morning
2 Chronicles 32
Revelation 18

Evening
Zechariah 14
John 17

28

Today's Scripture
Repentance and
remission of sins
should be preached
in his name to all
nations ... and you are
witnesses of
these things.
(Luke 24:47-48)

Daily Power!
An evangelist's job
is to win people for
Christ, not preach to
sleeping Christians
and revive dead
churches!

Mark My Word
Matthew 28:19
Mark 16:15,20
Luke 24:47-48
John 17:18-21
Acts 1:8

The Bible In A Year

Morning
2 Chronicles 33
Revelation 19

Evening
Malachi 1
John 18

Evangelism Is For All Christians

No evangelist can go through life without referring to the Great Commission. That Commission, from the lips of Christ himself, is found in varying forms in the four Gospels and in Acts. Each time, the emphasis is on the nations: the unsaved masses all over the world. Matthew wrote: *"Go therefore and make disciples of all the nations."* Mark said: *"Go into all the world and preach the gospel to every creature"* – and what happened? – *"And they* (the disciples) *went out and preached everywhere."* Luke wrote: *"Repentance and remission of sins should be preached in his name to all nations."* John recorded Christ's most sacred moment when he spoke to his Father: *"As you sent me into the world, I also have sent them into the world ... that the world may believe that you sent me."* Jesus said: *"You shall be witnesses to me in Jerusalem, and in all Judea and Samaria, and to the end of the earth."*

Some people regard an evangelist as a revivalist: that is, someone who gives a church a good rousing shake-up about once a year. An evangelist's job is to win people for Christ, not to preach to sleeping Christians and revive dead churches! An evangelist's ministry is misdirected if it is aimed at the saints of God. The New Testament from Acts onwards makes evangelism the natural function of all those who follow Christ. In fact, evangelism is following Christ, for that is what he mainly did. Evangelism is part of Christianity; as light belongs to the sun. A believer has no option: he must be engaged in telling others about his faith; or in some way be involved in that business. Witnessing is the business of the Christian faith. The church is the "society for the propagation of the gospel." In its beginnings, people joined it expecting to be witnesses, although the risks were high. All religions have their sacred obligations: Sikhs must wear a turban, Hindus must avoid animal fats, Moslems repeat their sacred prayer. Christian sensitivities have their roots in the sacred obligation to witness to Christ. Witnessing is an essential part of our faith. Activate that in your life today.

Change Of Focus

Even before his conversion, Paul knew that witnessing is what a believer has to do. He got into so much trouble because he did what he was supposed to do. As an apostle, he displayed a very forgivable and natural pride that God had entrusted him with the gospel. He always speaks as if it was the most unexpected good fortune! The church is supposed to grow – that is implicit throughout the New Testament – yet it is also explicit: *"How shall they preach unless they are sent? As it is written: 'How beautiful are the feet of those who preach the gospel of peace, who bring glad tidings of good things.'"*

One striking difference between the Hebrew and Christian Scriptures is that the New Testament brings the world into focus. The Old Testament shuts us in to Israel's disappointing history. It narrowed and became introspective, its outlook only an "in-look." Its highest hopes were nationalistic. In the New Testament, the whole picture changes: there is bustle and excitement as men of Israel become world travelers, proclaiming the name of the Lord everywhere. That Jesus was the One who set them going is made clear: *"Other sheep I have which are not of this fold; them also I must bring."*

Jesus talked about shepherding and harvesting, but he also talked about fishing. One day, while taking a walk by the edge of the water, he watched fishermen at work. Simon and Andrew were casting a net. John and James were mending their nets. Some were little more than teenagers. He said: *"Follow me, and I will make you fishers of men."* Whether they are more like sheep or fish is not important: Christ wanted to gather people to himself. And that is still his great purpose, and should be ours too. Make that your purpose today!

Today's Scripture
For the Scripture says, "Whoever believes on him will not be put to shame." For there is no distinction between Jew and Greek, for the same Lord over all is rich to all who call upon him. For "whoever calls on the name of the LORD shall be saved." (Romans 10:11-13)

Daily Power!
Christ wants to gather people to himself; that is still his great purpose.

Mark My Word
Matthew 4:19
John 10:16
Romans 10:11-15

The Bible In A Year

Morning
2 Chronicles 34
Revelation 20

Evening
Malachi 2
John 19

30

Priorities Of The Kingdom

Today's Scripture
For the love of Christ compels us, because we judge thus: that if One died for all, then all died.
(2 Corinthians 5:14)

Daily Power!
The Christian purpose is still the same: to carry the light of the gospel into a murky world.

Mark My Word
Luke 19:13
John 9:4
1 Corinthians 7:29, 31
2 Corinthians 5:14

The Bible In A Year

Morning
2 Chronicles 35
Revelation 21

Evening
Malachi 3
John 20

For those who know Jesus, the passing of a year is a powerful reminder that *"the night is coming when no one can work."* Meanwhile, we follow the Lord's advice and go about our normal business *"until he comes."* Those who peruse the long story of the church of Jesus, will know one thing. Whenever dark clouds have rolled across the horizon, and the end has seemed imminent, it has incited men and women with faith in God to leave their firesides, and to carry the torch of gospel hope into the cold darkness.

The small figure of the apostle Paul mingled unnoticed with the crowds on the Roman roads, a thousand beliefs in their pagan heads. They never realized that he was swinging wide the gates of history in Europe. The whole might of the empire was not able to resist him. He made converts out of the licentious devotees of the gods, and said to them: *"The time is short, so that from now on, those who have wives should be as though they had none; those who use this world as not misusing it."* He meant that because of the time limits, our priorities must be those of the kingdom of God.

The Christian purpose is still the same: to carry the light of the gospel into a murky world: not driven by the pursuit of glory, nor in order to count our successes, or to fill pews. The church is not a business. Why was Paul so committed to spreading the gospel? Because he was convinced that if Christ died for all, then all could live, and because he was compelled by God's love. Paul – the number one evangelist – had one priority: the eternal destiny of men and women. It rose above all other interests. He gave all, and expected others to do the same. Yet for centuries, the church confined its interests to the Roman world, and not until the 8th century did notable churchmen turn their attention to "barbarians" beyond their borders, venturing with the gospel into regions where they knew they could be martyred. You can change your world with the gospel!

Your Primary Goal

31

Believers of the 19th century believed that the 20th century would bring Christ back, and they prayed for power to evangelize every tribe and nation on Earth. The prayers of those dedicated men and women were answered: the power of God is now exceeding everything ever known, as is evident as *Christ for all Nations* thrusts forward into the 10/40 window. One of our recent crusade seasons netted over seven million positive responses for Jesus Christ! It also brought miracles greater than anyone could imagine! I continued to target for a more powerful push in the third millennium, using new means, the best that a technological age has yet produced. This is one advantage that we have over earlier workers. The harvest is ready and ripe and the new millennium has catapulted this ministry onto a new level where we do not just see hundreds of thousands saved in one crusade, but, as was the case in Lagos, Nigeria, *one million souls* saved in one single service. God is speeding up the harvesting *"Behold, the days are coming, says the Lord, when the plowman shall overtake the reaper."*

And there is another advantage: affluence among Christians today was undreamed of a century ago. God has made wealth available; and to those who will give, he gives. Earthly conditions need earthly means and earthly currency. God's people can handle that: but only Jesus can provide the power, and that is there *"more abundantly."* Some may be waiting, resting on their laurels, looking for Christ's imminent return: but we dare not do that. We must be found working in the field when he comes to take us! In his day, Paul found that the whole world and the empire opposed him, yet he said: *"Behold, now is the accepted time; behold, now is the day of salvation."* If it was the *"day of salvation"* in those hostile conditions, what is it today, with a thousand open doors and millions of open arms and hearts, precious and lovely people, ready to embrace the message of the gospel?

Our resolve, until Jesus comes again, is not to miss any opportunity to take the gospel to the people who need it. As long as one person is found on earth without the knowledge of Christ, our Lord's command remains: *"Go into all the world and preach the gospel to every creature"* – to the last person and the very last moment. And this is what we will do. Make that your primary goal for the next year!

Today's Scripture

We then, as workers together with him, also plead with you not to receive the grace of God in vain. For he says, "In an acceptable time I have heard you, and in the day of salvation I have helped you." Behold, now is the accepted time; behold, now is the day of salvation.
(2 Corinthians 6:1-2)

Daily Power!

Our resolve is not to miss any opportunity to take the gospel to the people who need it.

Mark My Word

Amos 9:13
Mark 16:15
John 10:10
2 Corinthians 6:1-2

The Bible In A Year

Morning
2 Chronicles 36
Revelation 22

Evening
Malachi 4
John 21

Chronological Index

January

January 1	God First	New Year's Day, Priorities
January 2	Reason For Living	Evangelism, Priorities
January 3	Perfectly Certain	Christian Living, Salvation
January 4	Salvation Is Not Speculation	Christian Living, Salvation
January 5	Spiritual Need	Christian Living, Evangelism
January 6	The World's Need	Christian Living, Evangelism
January 7	Only Jesus!	Exalting Jesus Christ
January 8	Jesus Never Changes	Exalting Jesus Christ
January 9	The Faith Factor	Christian Power, Faith
January 10	The Faith Fuse	Christian Power, Faith
January 11	The Hands Of Jesus	Christian Power, The Blood Of Jesus
January 12	Jesus Is Real	Christian Living, Faith
January 13	God's Universal Health Plan	Healing, Faith
January 14	Streams In The Desert	Christian Power, Holy Spirit
January 15	Finding God	Christian Living, God The Father
January 16	God's Identity	God The Father, Evangelism
January 17	Revival Is Work	Christian Living, Revival
January 18	The Silent Planet	Christian Living, Prayer
January 19	Blood Different From All Others	Christian Power, The Blood Of Jesus
January 20	Divine Blood Type	Christian Power, The Blood Of Jesus
January 21	Proven Signs	Christ's Second Coming, Priorities
January 22	Miracle Territory	Christian Living, Miracles
January 23	Miracle Conditions	Christian Living, Miracles
January 24	Sickness Is Not God's Plan	Christian Living, Healing
January 25	Avoid Past Mistakes	Christian Knowledge, 2nd Coming
January 26	"Even So, Come, Lord Jesus!"	Christ's Second Coming, Salvation
January 27	The Golden Gift	Exalting Jesus Christ, Faith
January 28	A Present-tense Faith	Christian Living, Faith
January 29	Aspects Of The Holy Spirit	Christian Power, Holy Spirit
January 30	God's Infinite Blood	Christian Power, The Trinity
January 31	Knowing God	Christian Living, God The Father

February

February 1	The Principles Of Power	Christian Living, Power
February 2	The Divine Imperative	Evangelism, Priorities
February 3	Light Reflectors	Christian Living, Priorities
February 4	Unlocked Doors	Christian Living, Salvation
February 5	Terrible Truth	Christian Living, Redemption
February 6	Read The Bible	Christian Living, Prayer
February 7	The Heart-Interest Of God	God The Father, Evangelism
February 8	We Need A Deliverer!	Christian Living, Jesus Christ
February 9	Jesus The King	Jesus Christ, Kingdom Of God
February 10	Breakthrough Faith	Christian Living, Faith
February 11	Down-to-earth Faith	Christian Living, Faith
February 12	The Secret Of Revival	Christian Living, Revival
February 13	A Witness To The Light	Christian Living, Faith
February 14	Light Versus Darkness	Christian Living, Evangelism
February 15	Who Is The Holy Spirit?	Christian Living, Holy Spirit
February 16	Christ's Secret Weapon	Christian Power, Holy Spirit
February 17	Unusual Miracle Conditions	Christian Living, Power
February 18	We All Need Miracles	Christian Power, God The Father
February 19	Longing For God	Christian Living, God The Father
February 20	The King And His Kingdom	Christian Living, Kingdom Of God
February 21	Using Your Parachute	Christian Living, Faith
February 22	Riches Of Salvation	Christian Living, Salvation
February 23	The Power Comes With The Task	Christian Power, Evangelism
February 24	The Promise Of Power	Christian Power, Holy Spirit
February 25	The Acts Of The King	Kingdom Of God, Exalting Jesus
February 26	The Peak Of His Power	Exalting Jesus Christ, Power
February 27	The Banner Of God	Christian Living, God The Father
February 28	The True Banner	Exalting Jesus Christ, Evangelism
February 29	To Each Generation	Evangelism, Commission

March

March 1	Sin In The 21st Century	Christian Living, Jesus Christ
March 2	World-Wide Sin	Christian Living, Salvation
March 3	The World Depends On Us	Christian Living, Salvation
March 4	Ceaseless Light	Christian Living, Power
March 5	The Power Of The Blood	Christian Living, Salvation
March 6	Ringing Confidence	Christian Living, Salvation
March 7	The Forerunner	Exalting Jesus Christ, Faith
March 8	Strategic Weaponry	Christian Power, Prayer
March 9	The New And Living Way	Exalting Jesus Christ, Prayer
March 10	The Climax Of Time	Second Coming Jesus Christ
March 11	Bought Back	Christian Living, Salvation
March 12	The Mark Of The Blood	Christian Living, The Bloods
March 13	"Typical Revival"	Christian Teaching, Revival
March 14	All Prayer	Christian Living, Prayer
March 15	Equipped With Power	Christian Power, Salvation
March 16	Pentecost Gave Us Keys	Christian Power, Holy Spirit
March 17	God's Own Banner And Bow	Christian Power, God The Father
March 18	The Spirit Of God	Christian Living, Salvation
March 19	Christ Is The Light	Christian Power, Jesus Christ
March 20	Yesterday, Today, Forever	Christian Living, Jesus Christ
March 21	Allergic To God?	Christian Power, Salvation
March 22	Jesus' Imperative	Evangelism, Priorities
March 24	Our Highest And Noblest Task	Christian Living, Evangelism
March 25	John's Problem	Christian Living, Evangelism
March 26	Increasing Faith	Christian Living, Faith
March 27	The Secretary Of The Trinity	Christian Power, Holy Spirit
March 28	Understanding The Holy Spirit	Christian Teaching, Holy Spirit
March 29	Our Mission Is Compassion	Evangelism, Priorities
March 30	Under Attack!	Christian Power, Evangelism
March 31	"Classic Revival"	Christian Teaching, Revival

April

April 1	God's Counter-Attack	Christian Living, Power
April 2	How To Become A True Intercessor	Christian Living, Prayer
April 3	God's Property	Christian Living, Blood Of Jesus
April 4	Family Is A Divine Purpose	Christian Living, God The Father
April 5	The Objective Of Our Work	Christian Living, Evangelism
April 6	Searching In The Darkness	Christian Power, Priorities
April 7	Faith Is A Venture	Christian Living, Faith
April 8	Motivation	Christian Living, Faith
April 9	Daily Bread	Prayer, Christian Living
April 10	God Hears Prayer	Prayer, God The Father
April 11	The Spirit Yearns	Faith, Holy Spirit
April 12	Power!	Holy Spirit Baptism, Testimonial
April 13	Apply The Blood	Christian Power, The Blood Of Jesus
April 14	God's Unchanging Heart	Christian Living, God The Father
April 15	Samson And Christ	Christian Living, Salvation
April 16	"Kiss The Son"	Christian Living, Second Coming
April 17	History In Advance	Second Coming, Priorities
April 18	Made and Saved For God's Glory	Christian Teaching, Faith
April 19	The "Impossible" Jesus	Christian Living, Jesus Christ
April 20	Our God-given Rights	Christian Living, Second Coming
April 21	Intercession Results	Christian Power, Prayer
April 22	Moved By Feelings Of Concern	Christian Living, Prayer
April 23	Believers Who Didn't See Miracles	Christian Power, Faith
April 24	An Eccentric World	Christian Living, God The Father
April 25	God Made Families	Christian Living, Christian Power
April 26	Concentrated Care	Christian Power, God The Father
April 27	Jesus – God And Man	Jesus Christ, Prayer
April 28	Jesus In The Real World	Jesus Christ, Salvation
April 29	Saints In Lights	Christian Living, Salvation
April 30	Christ's Great Commission	Holy Spirit Baptism, Evangelism

May

May 1	God's Lively Stones	Christian Living, Christian Power
May 2	Hardly Supermen	Christian Power, Prayer
May 3	Jonah – The Reluctant Evangelist	Christian Teaching, Evangelism
May 4	Going Down	Christian Power, Evangelism
May 5	Seven Rules Of Prayer	Christian Power, Prayer
May 6	Perfect Wisdom	Christian Living, Prayer
May 7	Prepare Your Family	Christian Living, Salvation
May 8	First Generation	Christian Living, Salvation
May 9	The Logo Of God's Love	Jesus Christ, Salvation
May 10	Releasing God's Power	Christian Power, Jesus Christ
May 11	The Tingling Impulse	Holy Spirit Baptism, Testimonial
May 12	When The Spirit Comes	Christian Power, Spirit Baptism
May 13	Demystifying Faith	Christian Teaching, Faith
May 14	Character Test	Christian Living, Faith
May 15	Miracles And Skepticism	Christian Living, Faith
May 16	Revival Is Here!	Christian Living, Revival
May 17	Geared To God	Christian Power, Holy Spirit
May 18	Faith Pins Hope	Christian Living, Faith
May 19	The Eye To The Unseen	Christian Power, Faith
May 20	Transforming Power	Christian Living, Faith
May 21	The Voice Of Love	Christian Living, Jesus Christ
May 22	How Sin Happened	Christian Living, Faith
May 23	Godly Families	Christian Living, Prayer
May 24	From Zero To Ten	Christian Power, Jesus Christ
May 25	Witnesses, Not Lawyers	Christian Power, Faith
May 26	Two Gifts	Christian Living, Holy Spirit
May 27	When Jesus Comes	Christian Teaching, Faith
May 28	Becoming A Child Of God	Christian Teaching, Salvation
May 29	The New Way	Christian Living, Prayer
May 30	Why God Spoke	Christian Living, Faith
May 31	God At Work	Christian Power, Trinity

June 1	Reasons For Believing?	Christian Power, Faith
June 2	Faith Or Chaos?	Christian Power, Faith
June 3	Wonderful Knowledge	Christian Power, Evangelism
June 4	Truth, And The People Who Reflect It	Christian Power, Evangelism
June 5	"Our Father"	Christian Power, Prayer
June 6	God Is Unusual	Christian Power, Christian Teaching
June 7	The Continual Promise	Christian Living, God The Father
June 8	Overcomers	Christian Teaching, Faith
June 9	Faith Is A Decision	Faith, Salvation
June 10	The Size Of Faith	Christian Teaching, Faith
June 11	"Righteous Anger" & Right Priorities	Christian Living, Salvation
June 12	Christ "For Us"	Christian Living, Jesus Christ
June 13	Overcoming Love	Christian Power, Salvation
June 14	Power Demonstrated	Christian Living, Salvation
June 15	A World Vision	Evangelism, Priorities
June 16	Evangelism Is God's Initiative	Evangelism, Priorities
June 17	Low Resistance	Christian Power, Faith
June 18	Believing	Christian Power, Faith
June 19	One-Drink	Christian Power, Holy Spirit
June 20	Identified By Miracles	Christian Power, Healing
June 21	Acts Today	Christian Living, Power
June 22	God Raises The Dead	Christian Power, Evangelism
June 23	No Matter Where We Run	Christian Living, Evangelism
June 24	True Spirit Of Evangelism	Christian Power, Evangelism
June 25	Personal Presence	Christian Living, Power
June 26	Pulling The Revival Trigger	Christian Power, Evangelism
June 27	The God Who Creates	Christian Teaching, God The Father
June 28	The Good God	Christian Living, God The Father
June 29	Jonah's Problem	Christian Teaching, Evangelism
June 30	Our Ultimate Objective	Christian Living, Evangelism

July

July 1	Future Evangelism	Christian Priorities, Evangelism
July 2	A Modern Man	Christian Living, Power
July 3	Maxims Of Faith	Christian Living, Faith
July 4	Power Anywhere	Christian Power, Faith
July 5	In One Word – Compassion	Jesus Christ, Motivation
July 6	Christ The Giver	Christian Living, Jesus Christ
July 7	Resurrection – An Impossible Hoax?	Christian Living, Christian Power
July 8	Regeneration And Resurrection	Jesus Christ, Salvation
July 9	Join The Orchestra!	Christian Living, Christian Power
July 10	God Is Not Who Some Think He Is	Christian Living, Jesus Christ
July 11	Ammunition!	Christian Living, Holy Spirit
July 12	Reveling In Prayer	Christian Living, Prayer
July 13	Blood That Speaks	Christian Living, Evangelism
July 14	"To The Glory Of God The Father"	Christian Living, Salvation
July 15	Fish In The Sea Of Nations	Christian Power, Evangelism
July 16	The Lord Of The Sea Of Nations	Christian Power, Evangelism
July 17	Compelling Evidence	Christian Living, Salvation
July 18	The Eternal Mark	Salvation, Jesus Christ
July 19	From Faith To Faith	Christian Power, Faith
July 20	Completing Faith	Christian Living, Faith
July 21	Christ Is Our Home	Christian Living, Jesus Christ
July 22	The Glory Of The Lamb	Exalting Jesus Christ, Power
July 23	Rivers!	Christian Power, Holy Spirit
July 24	The Cross And Kingdom Miracles	Christian Power, Jesus Christ
July 25	Fear Not The Future	Christian Living, Christian Power
July 26	Get It Straight, Boys!	Christian Power, Evangelism
July 27	Jesus Corrects Us	Christian Living, Christian Power
July 28	We Cannot Escape	Jesus Christ, Salvation
July 29	Bondage Is Truth Corrupted	Christian Teaching, Christian Living
July 30	Leaps Of Faith	Christian Living, Faith
July 31	Faith Embrace	Christian Power, Faith

August

August 1	This Same Jesus	Exalting Jesus Christ, Living,
August 2	Time To Grow Up!	Christian Living, Christian Power
August 3	Dynamic Power Points	Christian Living, Power
August 4	"Proving" Salvation	Christian Living, Salvation
August 5	Critics Don't Get It	Christian Power, Holy Spirit
August 6	The Spirit's Difference	Christian Living, Holy Spirit
August 7	Ghostly Terrors	Christian Power, Second Coming
August 8	Sure Of Salvation	Christian Power, Salvation
August 9	Switch On The Light!	Christian Power, Holy Spirit
August 10	Life Blood	Christian Living, The Blood Of Jesus
August 11	The Precious Oil	Christian Living, Christian Power
August 12	Commitment	Christian Living, Holy Spirit
August 13	Only God Can Reveal God	Christian Power, God The Father
August 14	Divine Promises	Christian Living, Christian Power
August 15	The Golden Gift Of Faith	Christian Living, Faith
August 16	Faith In Three Tense	Christian Power, Faith
August 17	The Source Of Oil	Christian Power, Holy Spirit
August 18	Getting Somewhere	Christian Living, Christian Power
August 19	Flash Flood!	Christian Power, Evangelism
August 20	Miracles Characterize The Kingdom	Christian Power, Holy Spirit
August 21	His Greatest Work	Christian Living, Evangelism
August 22	No Imitations	Christian Living, Christian Power
August 23	Boast Only In Christ	Exalting Jesus Christ, Salvation
August 24	What A Servant!	Exalting Jesus Christ, Salvation
August 25	Power Conductors	Christian Living, Power
August 26	Plugged In	Christian Living, Power
August 27	The Secret Side Of Faith	Christian Living, Faith
August 28	Purely From The Word	Christian Teaching, Faith
August 29	Quickened By The Spirit	Christian Power, Spirit Baptism
August 30	Intercession	Christian Living, Prayer
August 31	Christ-like Compassion	Prayer, Motivation

September

September 1	Endurance	Christian Living, Christian Power
September 2	When Arson Is Not A Crime	Christian Power, Spirit Baptism
September 3	An Infectious Faith	Salvation, Evangelism
September 4	Household Salvation	Salvation, Christian Priorities
September 5	Working Out His Will	Christian Living, Christian Power
September 6	Action Words	Christian Living, Faith
September 7	The Proof Of Jesus	Exalting Jesus Christ, Power
September 8	A Conquest Of Christ	Christian Power, Evangelism
September 9	Miracle Challenge To Faith	Exalting Jesus Christ, Power
September 10	Faith Breakthrough	Christian Living, Faith
September 11	Laser Beams	Christian Power, Evangelism
September 12	The Distinction Of Intercession	Christian Living, Prayer
September 13	God And His Children	Christian Living, Prayer
September 14	Interdependency	Christian Power, Prayer
September 15	Fire-Starters	Christian Power, Holy Spirit
September 16	Two Courtroom Dramas	Christian Power, Salvation
September 17	"Made Innocent"	Christian Teaching, Salvation
September 18	Family Salvation	Christian Living, Salvation
September 19	No Alternative	Christian Living, Salvation
September 20	A Warning About Faith	Christian Power, Faith
September 21	Divine Principle Of Action	Christian Power, Faith
September 22	God Speaks Anytime, Anywhere	God The Father, Prayer
September 23	Three Pillars Of Wisdom	Christian Living, God The Father
September 24	Powers Of A New Order	Christian Living, Christian Power
September 25	A Million-Candlepower Light	Christian Living, Evangelism
September 26	Business In Great Water	Christian Living, Evangelism
September 27	Before-And-After Heroes	Christian Living, Faith
September 28	Eye-Opening Prayer	Christian Living, Prayer
September 29	The Fire Age	Exalting Jesus Christ, Power
September 30	Reunited	Exalting Jesus Christ, Power

October

October 1	Consumed By Fire	Christian Power, Spirit Baptism
October 2	Faith Breakthrough	Christian Living, Faith
October 3	Faith Giants	Christian Power, Faith
October 4	"Born Again"	Christian Living, Power
October 5	My First Missionary Efforts	Evangelism, Personal Testimonial
October 6	Invasion!	Christian Power, Evangelism
October 7	Natural And Spiritual Laws	Christian Living, Faith
October 8	What God Is Saying	Christian Living, Christian Power
October 9	Evoking Thoughts Of God	Christian Living, Power
October 10	Nobody Is A "Nobody"	Christian Living, God The Father
October 11	See And Believe!	Christian Living, Faith
October 12	The Axe And The Orchestra	Christian Living, Faith
October 13	Evangelists Sought!	Christian Living, Evangelism
October 14	Singleness Of Heart	Evangelism, Faith
October 15	A Gospel That Isn't	Christian Living, Evangelism
October 16	Marching Orders	Christian Living, Evangelism
October 17	The Authority Of Christ	Exalting Jesus Christ, Living
October 18	Fire Comes By Faith	Christian Power, Spirit Baptism
October 19	Biblical Anointing	Christian Power, Spirit Baptism
October 20	True Anointing	Christian Power, Christian Teaching
October 21	How Big Is Hell?	Salvation, Second Coming
October 22	Dummy Ammunition	Christian Power, Spirit Baptism
October 23	"Crazy Joy"	Christian Power, Spirit Baptism
October 24	Revelation In Revelation	Exalting Jesus Christ, Living
October 25	Read Carefully	Christian Living, Power
October 26	True Faith	Christian Living, Prayer
October 27	The Real Anointing	Christian Power, Spirit Baptism
October 28	George Jeffreys And Me	Christian Power, Personal Testimony
October 29	Satan's Chess Game	Christian Living, Power
October 30	God's Fire In Jesus	Exalting Jesus Christ, Living
October 31	Parakletos	Christian Living, Holy Spirit

November

November 1	Dead, Boring Christian	Christian Living, Christian Power
November 2	The Height Of Human Experience	Christian Priorities, Evangelism
November 3	Live Ammunition	Christian Living, Evangelism
November 4	Eternal Purposes	Christian Power, Evangelism
November 5	Worship And Praise	Christian Living, Prayer
November 6	Faith And Knowing	Christian Living, Faith
November 7	False Faiths	Christian Living, Christian Teaching
November 8	Anointing And Appointing	Christian Living, Christian Power
November 9	Warfare Gifts	Christian Living, Evangelism
November 10	Young And Old In The Last Hour	Christian Living, Motivation
November 11	Whirlwinds	Christian Power, Evangelism
November 12	The Word Brings Faith	Christian Living, Faith
November 13	Faith And The Promises	Christian Living, Faith
November 14	Your Last Hour	Christian Living, Motivation
November 15	Last Hour Logic	Christian Power, Evangelism
November 16	The Beauty From God	Exalting Jesus Christ, Power
November 17	Paid By The Hour	Christian Living, Evangelism
November 18	Faith Objectives	Christian Living, Faith
November 19	God's Wave	Christian Power, Spirit Baptism
November 20	God's True Voice	Christian Living, Christian Power
November 21	Many Callings	Christian Living, Christian Power
November 22	Dan And His Ship Shops	Priorities, Evangelism
November 23	Immortal Work For Mortals	Christian Living, Power
November 24	Leap Into The Light	Christian Living, Christian Power
November 25	Greater Than Jesus?	Christian Power, Spirit Baptism
November 26	Ancient Faith	Christian Living, Faith
November 27	Faith Of A New Kind	Christian Living, Faith
November 28	Step One: Step Two	Christian Teaching, Faith
November 29	Step Three: Step Four	Christian Teaching, Faith
November 30	Step Five: Step Six	Christian Teaching, Faith

December

December 1	When Is Unbelief Forgivable?	Christian Living, Salvation
December 2	God's Anointing – Man's Confirmation	Christian Power, Holy Spirit
December 3	The Gospel Of The Cross	Christian Living, Holy Spirit
December 4	Fasting And Faith	Christian Living, Prayer
December 5	Not Conspicuous, Just Changed	Christian Living, Holy Spirit
December 6	Kingdom Power	Christian Living, Christian Power
December 7	Makers Of Money – Or History?	Christian Living, Evangelism
December 8	Two Kinds Of Folks	Evangelism, Priorities
December 9	The Giver, Not The Gift	Christian Living, God The Father
December 10	The Most Important Job	Christian Living, Evangelism
December 11	The Aim Of The Church	Christian Living, Evangelism
December 12	Simple, True Faith	Christian Living, Faith
December 13	Babel Reversed	Christian Power, Spirit Baptism
December 14	Predestination And Evangelism	Christian Teaching, Evangelism
December 15	Evangelism Strengthens Nations	Christian Living, Evangelism
December 16	Abraham	Christian Living, Faith
December 17	Why Believe?	Christian Living, Faith
December 18	God's Finger	Christian Living, Christian Power
December 19	Intellectualism	Christian Living, Faith
December 20	Solid Ground	Christian Living, Faith
December 21	Accomplishing Mission Impossible	Evangelism, Faith
December 22	Family Planning	Christmas, Christian Living
December 23	What A Wonderful Son!	Christmas, Exalting Jesus Christ
December 24	Read The Post-script	Christmas, Christian Living
December 25	Luke 2:1-20	Christmas, Christian Teaching
December 26	"The Last Time"	Christian Living, Second Coming
December 27	Faith's Final Test	Christian Living, Faith
December 28	Evangelism Is For All Christians	Christian Living, Evangelism
December 29	Change Of Focus	Christian Living, Evangelism
December 30	Priorities Of The Kingdom	Christian Living, Evangelism
December 31	Your Primary Goal	Christian Living, Evangelism

Topical Index
by Main Theme

Principles Of Christian Living

January 5	Spiritual Need
January 6	The World's Need
January 12	Jesus Is Real
January 15	Finding God
January 17	Revival Is Work
January 22	Miracle Territory
January 23	Miracle Conditions
February 1	The Principles Of Power
February 3	Light Reflectors
February 4	Unlocked Doors
February 11	Down-to-earth Faith
February 13	A Witness To The Light
February 20	The King And His Kingdom
March 1	Sin In The 21st Century
March 3	The World Depends On Us
March 4	Ceaseless Light
March 22	How To Rout Doubt
March 25	John's Problem
April 3	God's Property
April 5	The Objective Of Our Work
April 7	Faith Is A Venture
April 23	An Eccentric World
April 24	God Made Families
May 1	God's Lively Stones
May 6	Perfect Wisdom
May 7	Prepare Your Family
May 15	Miracles And Skepticism
May 16	Revival Is Here
May 22	How Sin Happened
June 11	Righteous Anger And Right Priorities
July 7	Resurrection An Impossible Hoax?
July 9	Join The Orchestra
July 11	Ammunition!
July 25	Fear Not The Future
July 27	"Get It Straight, Boys!"
July 30	Leaps Of Faith
August 2	Time To Grow Up!
August 11	The Precious Oil
August 14	Divine Promises
August 18	Getting Somewhere

August 22	No Imitations
September 1	Endurance
September 5	Working Out His Will
September 24	Power Of A New Order
September 25	A Million-Candlepower Light
October 2	Faith Breakthrough
October 8	What God Is Saying
October 12	The Axe And The Orchestra
October 15	The Gospel That Isn't
November 1	Dead, Boring Christians
November 8	Anointing And Appointing
November 9	Warfare Gifts
November 14	The Last Hour
November 20	God's True Voice
November 21	Many Callings
November 24	Leap Into The Light
November 27	Faith Of A New Kind
December 1	Christian Living
December 3	The Gospel Of The Cross
December 4	Fasting And Faith
December 5	Not Conspicuous, Just Changed
December 6	Kingdom Power
December 17	Why Believe?
December 18	God's Finger
December 29	Change Of Focus
December 30	Priorities Of The Kingdom
December 31	Your Primary Goal

Evangelism And Revival

January 2	Reason For Living
February 2	The Divine Imperative
February 12	The Secret Of Revival
February 14	Light Versus Darkness
February 29	To Each Generation
March 13	"Typical Revival"
March 23	Jesus' Imperative
March 24	Our Highest And Noblest Task
March 29	Our Mission Is Compassion
March 31	"Classic Revival"
May 3	Jonah – The Reluctant Evangelist
May 4	Going Down

June 3	Wonderful Knowledge
June 4	Truth, And The People Who Reflect
June 16	Evangelism Is God's Initiative
June 23	No Matter Where We Run
June 24	True Spirit Of Evangelism
June 29	Jonah's Problem
June 30	Our Ultimate Objective
July 1	Future Evangelism
July 13	Blood That Speaks
July 15	Fish In The Sea Of Nations
July 16	The Lord Of The Sea Of Nations
August 19	Flash Flood!
Septembers 8	A Conquest Of Christ
September 11	Laser Beams
September 26	Business In Great Waters
October 5	My First Missionary Efforts
October 6	Invasion!
October 13	Evangelists Sought!
October 14	Singleness Of Heart
October 16	Marching Orders
November 2	The Height Of Human Experience
November 3	Live Ammunition
November 4	Eternal Purposes
November 15	Last Hour Logic
November 17	Paid By The Hour
December 7	Makers Of Money – Or History?
December 8	Two Kinds Of Folks
December 10	The Most Important Job
December 11	The Aim Of The Church
December 14	Predestination And Evangelism
December 15	Evangelism Strengthens Nations
December 21	Mission Impossible?
December 28	Evangelism Is For All Christians

God The Father

January 16	God's Identity
January 31	Knowing God
February 7	The Heart-interest Of God
February 19	Longing For God
February 27	The Banner Of God
March 17	God's Own Banner And Bow

April 4	Family Is A Divine Purpose
April 14	God's Unchanging Heart
April 26	Concentrated Care
June 7	The Continual Promise
June 28	The Good God
August 13	Only God Can Reveal God
September 22	God Does Not Pray
September 23	Three Pillars Of Wisdom
October 10	Nobody Is A "Nobody"
December 9	The Giver, Not The Gift

Jesus Christ

January 7	Only Jesus!
January 8	Jesus Never Changes
January 11	The Hands Of Jesus
January 19	Blood Different From All Others
January 20	Divine Blood Type
January 21	Proven Signs
January 26	"Even So, Come, Lord Jesus!"
January 27	The Golden Gift
February 8	We Need A Deliverer!
February 9	Jesus The King
February 25	The Acts Of The King
February 26	The Peak Of His Power
February 28	The True Banner
March 7	The Forerunner
March 9	The New And Living Way
March 10	The Climax Of Time
March 12	The Mark Of The Blood
March 19	Scripture Dynamite
March 20	Yesterday, Today, Forever
April 13	Apply The Blood
April 16	"Kiss The Son"
April 17	History In Advance
April 19	The "Impossible" Jesus
April 20	Our God-given Rights
April 27	Jesus – God And Man
April 28	Jesus In The Real World
May 9	The Logo Of God's Love
May 10	Releasing God's Power
May 21	The Voice Of Love

June 12	Christ "For Us"
July 5	In One Word – Compassion
July 6	Christ The Giver
July 8	Regeneration And Resurrection
July 10	God Is Not Who Some Think He Is
July 21	Christ Is Our Home
July 22	The Glory Of The Lamb
July 24	The Cross And Kingdom Miracles
July 28	We Cannot Escape
August 1	"This Same Jesus"
August 7	Ghostly Terrors
August 10	Life Blood
August 23	Boast Only In Christ
August 24	What A Servant!
September 7	The Proof Of Jesus
September 29	The Fire Age
September 30	Reunited
October 17	The Authority Of Christ
October 24	Revelation In Revelation
October 30	God's Fire In Jesus
November 16	The Beauty Of God
December 26	"The Last Time"

Holy Spirit

January 14	Streams In The Desert
January 29	Aspects Of The Holy Spirit
February 15	Who Is The Holy Spirit?
February 16	Christ's Secret Weapon
February 24	The Promise Of Power
March 16	Pentecost Gave Us Keys
March 27	The Secretary Of The Trinity
March 28	Introduction To The Holy Spirit
April 12	Holy Spirit Baptism
April 30	Christ's Great Commission
May 11	The Tingling Impulse
May 12	When The Spirit Comes
May 17	Geared To God
May 26	Two Gifts
June 19	One-Drink
July 23	Rivers!
August 5	Critics Do Not Get It

August 6	The Spirit's Difference
August 9	Switch On The Light!
August 12	Commitment
August 29	Intercession
September 2	When Arson Is Not A Crime
October 1	Consumed By Fire
October 18	Fire Comes By Faith
October 19	Origins Of The Anointing
October 23	"Crazy Joy"
October 27	The Real Anointing
October 31	Parakletos
November 19	Swelling Power
November 25	Greater Than Jesus?
December 13	Babel Reversed

The Gifts: Salvation, Healing

January 3	Perfectly Certain
January 4	Salvation Is Not Speculation
January 13	God's Universal Health Plan
January 24	Sickness Isn't God's Plan
February 5	Terrible Truth
February 22	Riches Of Salvation
March 2	World-Wide Sin
March 5	The Power Of The Blood
March 6	Ringing Confidence
March 11	Bought Back
March 15	Equipped With Power
March 18	The Spirit Of God
March 21	Allergic To God?
April 15	Samson And Christ
April 29	Saints In Lights
May 8	First Generation
May 28	Becoming A Child Of God
June 13	Overcoming Love
June 14	Power Demonstrated
July 14	Close Encounters With God
July 17	Compelling Evidence
July 18	The Eternal Mark
August 4	"Proving" Salvation
August 8	Sure Of Salvation
September 3	The Sinner's Prayer

September 4   Household Salvation
September 16   Two Courtroom Dramas
September 17   "Made Innocent"
September 18   Family Salvation
September 19   No Alternative
October 21   How Big Is Hell?

Faith And Prayer

January 9   The Faith Factor
January 10   The Faith Fuse
January 18   The Silent Planet
January 28   A Present-Tense Faith
February 6   Read The Bible
February 10   Breakthrough Faith
February 21   Using Your Parachute
March 8   Strategic Weaponry
March 26   Increasing Faith
April 8   Motivation
April 11   "The Spirit Yearns"
April 18   Not Me But We
April 23   Believers Who Did Not See Miracles
May 5   Seven Rules Of Prayer
May 13   Demystifying Faith
May 14   Character Test
May 18   Faith Pins Hope
May 19   The Eye To The Unseen
May 20   Transforming Power
May 23   Godly Families
May 25   Witnesses, Not Lawyers
May 27   When Jesus Comes
May 29   The New Way
May 30   Why God Spoke
June 1   Reasons For Believing?
June 2   Faith Or Chaos?
June 5   "Our Father"
June 8   Overcomers
June 9   Faith Is A Decision
June 10   The Size Of Faith
June 18   Believing
July 3   Maxims Of Faith
July 4   Power Anywhere

July 12	Reveling In Prayer
July 19	From Faith To Faith
July 20	Completing Faith
July 31	Faith Embrace
August 15	The Golden Gift Of Faith
August 16	Faith In Three Tenses
August 27	The Secret Side Of Faith
August 28	Purely From The Word
August 30	Intercession
August 31	Christ-like Compassion
September 6	Action Words
September 10	Faith Breakthrough
September 12	The Distinction Of Intercession
September 13	God And His Children
September 14	Interdependency
September 21	Divine Principle Of Action
September 27	Before-And-After Heroes
October 3	Faith Giants
October 7	Natural And Spiritual Laws
October 11	See And Believe!
October 26	True Faith
November 5	Worship And Praise
November 6	Faith And Knowing
November 12	The Word Brings Faith
November 13	Faith And The Promises
November 18	Faith Objectives
November 26	Ancient Faith
November 28	Step One: Step Two
November 29	Step Three: Step Four
November 30	Step Five: Step Six
December 12	Simple, True Faith
December 16	Abraham
December 19	Intellectualism
December 20	Solid Ground
December 27	Faith's Final Test

Christian Knowledge And Power

January 25	Avoid Past Mistakes
January 30	God's Infinite Blood
February 17	Unusual Miracles Conditions
February 18	We All Need Miracles

February 23   The Power Comes With The Task
March 30   Under Attack!
April 1   God's Counter-Attack
April 6   Searching In The Darkness
May 2   Hardly Supermen
May 24   From Zero To Ten
May 31   God At Work
June 6   God Is Unusual
June 17   Low Resistance
June 20   Identified By Miracles
June 25   Personal Presence
July 2   A Modern Man
July 26   "Get It Straight, Boys!"
August 3   Dynamic Power Points
August 17   The Source Of Oil
August 20   Miracles Characterize The Kingdom
August 25   Power Conductors
August 26   Plugged In
September 9   Miracle Challenge To Faith
September 15   Fire-Starters
September 20   A Warning About Faith
October 4   "Born-again "
October 9   Evoking Thoughts Of God
October 20   The Anointing
October 22   Dummy Ammunition
October 25   Read Carefully
October 28   George Jeffreys And Me
October 29   Satan's Chess Game
November 11   Whirlwinds
November 23   Immortals Work For Mortals
December 2   God's Anointing – Man's Confirmation
January 1   New Year's Day
December 22   Family Planning
December 23   What A Wonderful Son!

Seasonal

January 1   New Year's Day
December 22   Family Planning
December 23   What A Wonderful Son!
December 24   Read The Postscript
December 25   Luke 2:1-20

Scripture Index

The following Scripture References have been used throughout this devotional, and memorization of these verses is highly recommended!

Genesis 17:7

Exodus 3:13-14; 15:26

Numbers 23:19

Joshua 24:15

Judges 5:1, 31

1 Samuel 3:9

2 Chronicles 7:14

Ezra 8:22

Job 19:25

Psalms 19:7-10; 33:6-9; 37:4-5; 51:7-10; 68:19-20; 86:11; 90:12, 17; 100:5; 104:13-15; 107:21-24; 119:105; 124:8; 127:1; 132:9; 139:7-10

Proverbs 3:5; 4:14-15, 18; 6:30-31

Ecclesiastes 4:9-12

Song of Solomon 2:4; 6:1-3

Isaiah 9:6-7; 10:27; 11:10; 12:2; 40:24, 31; 43:1-3; 46:9-10; 48:16-17; 53:5; 55:6-7

Jeremiah 20:9; 29:11-13

Lamentations 3:22-23

Joel 2:28-29; 3:10

Jonah 2:9

Matthew 1:21-23; 3:11-12; 4:16, 19, 24-25; 5:13-14, 16, 45; 6:7-8, 10, 24, 33; 7:11-14; 10:8, 27-28, 38-39; 11:28-30; 16:18-19, 25; 17:20; 18:20; 19:26; 21:16; 24:13-14; 25:13; 28:18-20

Mark 1:15, 41; 6:34; 9:1, 23; 10:27; 11:23; 12:30; 14:67; 15:39; 16:15, 20; 28:18-20;

Luke 1:17; 4:18-19; 5:17; 6:35; 7:22-23; 9:1-2, 56; 10:20-21; 11:13, 20, 36; 15:7, 23-24; 18:1; 19:10; 21:27-28, 31: 24:47-48

John 1:1-4, 14, 29; 3:3, 6, 14-16; 4:14, 23, 34-35; 5:24, 39; 6:27, 35; 8:31-32, 36; 9:4, 31; 10:10-11, 14-18; 11:25-26, 40; 12:25-26, 32; 14:1-4, 6, 14-18, 27; 15:7-8, 14-16, 26-27; 16:7, 23-24; 17:3; 20:21-22, 29

Acts 1:7-8; 2:4, 8, 11, 38-39; 3:19; 4:13-14, 29-31; 8:16; 10:34-35, 38, 42-44; 16:31; 17:27-28; 26:18; 27:25; 28:31

Romans 1:16, 32; 3:22-23; 4:3, 12; 5:1-4, 8-9; 6:23; 8:1-2, 11, 14, 16, 26, 28; 10:1, 10-15; 12:1-2; 14:13; 16:25-27

1 Corinthians 1:18, 20-21, 23-25; 2:9; 3:1-2; 4:10; 6:20; 9:16; 12:4-7, 12, 27; 14:2, 15; 15:3, 20-22, 49

2 Corinthians 2:4; 3:12; 4:6; 5:14, 21; 6:1-2, 14

Galatians 2:5-7, 20; 3:13-14; 5:25; 6:14

Ephesians 1:3, 7, 17; 2:1, 8, 13, 19-20; 2:3; 3:17-19; 4:1-3, 11-13, 15-16, 32; 5:8, 18; 6:8

Philippians 1:6, 20; 2:9-11; 3:10-14

Colossians 1:19-20; 4:17

1 Thessalonians 1:2-5; 5:16-18

1 Timothy 1:12; 2:1

2 Timothy 1:8-9, 12

Hebrews 2:1, 4, 9; 4:15-16; 6:19-20; 7:25; 9:14, 27-28; 10:10; 11:1, 6; 12:1, 24, 28-29; 13:5, 8

James 1:7, 17; 4:10; 5:11

1 Peter 1:3, 7; 2:4-5, 9; 3:18; 4:6; 5:8-9

2 Peter 1:3; 3:9

1 John 1:3, 9; 2:1-3, 20; 3:14; 4:4; 5:1, 11-15

Jude 24-25

Revelation 1:5, 8; 3:20; 5:12-13; 12:11; 14:15; 22:12, 14, 17

NOTES

NOTES

Other books & booklets
by REINHARD BONNKE

The Holy Spirit Baptism

The greatest assurance of all flows from personal experience of the manifestation of God's power. Drawing from Scripture, this carefully explained and simple to understand booklet brings the believer to the place of faith where he or she can receive the Baptism of the Holy Spirit. Common misconceptions are answered and the reader is challenged to ask and receive!

• 32 pages
• ISBN 3-935057-12-1

How to have Assurance of Salvation

This booklet tackles the first and most vital crisis that every new believer faces. Before anything else, we must know we are saved! It is the crucial link between salvation and discipleship. Using graphic illustrations from Scripture, this message forms the basis of the booklet *Now that You are Saved*, given to new believers in every CfaN campaign.

• 28 pages
• ISBN 3-935057-11-3

First of all ... Intercession

"Evangelism without intercession is like an explosive without a detonator," says Reinhard Bonnke. Christians have a world to reclaim and regain for God. Prayer and intercession cast out the entrenched enemy, violate his borders and retake lost territory. This booklet explains the task of intercession clearly and concisely, and encourages Christians to use the weapon of prayer more consistently and effectively.

• 32 pages
• ISBN 3-935057-17-2

The Secret of the Power of the Blood of Jesus

The blood type of Jesus is unique. Since it was spiritually created it has spiritual power. As a young evangelist Reinhard Bonnke vowed that wherever he went he would preach on the blood of Jesus. This booklet contains that powerful gospel message in all its life-changing anointing.

• 24 pages
• ISBN 3-935057-10-5

The Coming One

Now that we are in the third millennium, millions of people are still looking for a great global leader. They even consult the stars looking for a new age under a super-personality to bring accord between the races, peace among the nations, and the rich caring for the poor. Christ declared that He would come back, and He will! This is the key hope of every Christian creed. The last prayer of the Bible is Amen! Come Lord Jesus!

- 28 pages
- ISBN 3-935057-84-9

New!

How to receive a Miracle from God

Perhaps the greatest single obstacle to accepting the reality of miracles is our inability to understand God's dynamics. The dynamics of the miraculous are the Word of God, Faith, and Obedience. When these three are in place, miracles happen. This booklet will unlock the doors of unbelieving hearts to expect a miracle from God.

- 24 pages
- ISBN 3-935057-13-X

The Lord Your Healer

God loves to heal. He still heals today. During CfaN campaigns, we see thousands receive healing and remain totally healed. This straight forward but profound booklet answers the critics and lifts our faith. We do not look to church leaders, special ministries or Reinhard Bonnke for healing, but to Jesus. He will answer.

- 24 pages
- ISBN 3-935057-14-8

The Romance of Redeeming Love

When God gave his Son Jesus to die for us, it cost Him everything. The gift of Redemption is the ultimate expression of God's love. This booklet reveals through Scripture, God's unique and perfect Redemption plan. Creation was easy, but for our Redemption, God gave Himself.

- 32 pages
- ISBN 3-935057-15-6

Evangelism By Fire
Igniting your passion for the lost

"This book is not only mighty, but it is meaty! It will rekindle the corners of your soul and turn its center to a white-hot focus on what matters most to God - the salvation and deliverance of eternal souls. Bonnke's words have a way of bringing you to that altar anew - to be baptized with Jesus' fire once again." Jack W. Hayford, D. Litt.

- 320 pages
- 16 page color photo section
- ISBN 3-935057-19-9

- Supporting Workbook & Study Guide available
- ISBN 3-935057-28-8

Mighty Manifestations
The Gifts and Power of the Holy Spirit

A book to challenge the believer to step out and use the 'power tools of God', the gifts of the Holy Spirit. All the gifts are covered in detail. Reinhard Bonnke shows how we can be effective in using the gifts we have been given.

- 248 pages
- 16 page color photo section
- ISBN 3-935057-00-8

- Supporting Workbook & Study Guide available
- ISBN 3-935057-27-X

Faith ...
the Link with God's Power

Reinhard Bonnke draws from his years of personal study and ministry to millions to reveal that Faith is the fertile ground in which God moves and it is not the size of your faith, but the size of your God you believe in that determines the results. Faith is like a wiring system that carries power into our lives. Faith itself is not the power, but it links us to the power source. There is no link to God's power without faith.

- 346 pages
- 16 page color photo section
- ISBN 3-935057-29-6

- Supporting Workbook &
  Study Guide available
- ISBN 3-935057-26-1

Time is Running Out

With his passionate desire to see souls won for Christ, Reinhard expounds the biblical principles of successful evangelism. Proven and effective techniques for reaching the lost are skillfully, yet simply, described, in order to teach, inspire, and encourage others to take up the challenge to reach out to their neighbors, friends, and the world.

In just three years, after preaching face to face to over 31 million people, over 20 million of them made a positive decision for Jesus Christ, and have been added to the Kingdom of God and to the local churches.

- 288 pages
- 16 page color photo section
- ISBN 3-935057-60-1

- Supporting Workbook &
  Study Guide available
- ISBN 3-935057-85-7

CfaN CHRIST
FOR ALL NATIONS

For further information about the ministry of Reinhard Bonnke or Christ for all Nations, please visit our web site on the internet or contact the office nearest to you;

Christ for all Nations
Postfach 60 05 74
60335 Frankfurt am Main
Germany

Christ for all Nations
P.O. Box 51121
Nairobi, Kenya
East Africa

Christ for all Nations
P.O. 590588
Orlando
FL 32859-0588, USA

Christ for all Nations
P.O. Box 25057
London, Ontario
N6C 6A8. Canada

Christ for all Nations
250 Coombs Road
Halesowen
West Midlands
B62 8AA. UK

Christ for all Nations
P.O. Box 13010
Witfield, 1467
South Africa

Christ for all Nations
P.O. Box 10899
Ikeja, Lagos
Nigeria
West Africa

Christ for all Nations
Singapore Post Centre Post Office
P.O. Box 418
Singapore 228461

www.cfan.org

Full Flame

For information about the purchase of other books and booklets by Reinhard Bonnke contact;

Full Flame, LLC
P.O. Box 593647
Orlando, FL 32859
USA

Full Flame, GmbH
Postfach 60 05 95
60335 Frankfurt am Main
Germany

Full Flame, Pte
11 Mount Sophia
Block B, B1-04
Singapore 228461

info@fullflameonline.com
www.fullflameonline.com

info@fullflame.com
www.fullflame.com

sea@fullflame.com
www.fullflame.com